Introduction to
POLITICS

THIRD EDITION

Vernon Van Dyke
The University of Iowa

THE NELSON-HALL SERIES IN POLITICAL SCIENCE
Consulting Editor
Samuel C. Patterson
The Ohio State University

Nelson-Hall Publishers/Chicago

Chapter Opening Cartoon Credits

p. 3. © Paul Conrad

p. 11. © Bruce Shanks

p. 25. © Luddas Matyi

p. 37. Library of Congress

p. 57. © Cecil Jensen

p. 69. © Bob Saylor

p. 85. Library of Congress

p. 109. © Bill Mauldin

p. 133. © Herbert Block

p. 145. © *Rius In Siemprel* (Mexico City)

p. 161. © *The Times of India* (Bombay)

p. 181. © Herbert Block

p. 195. © Herbert Block

p. 209. © Gonzalo Angarita

p. 233. © Don Wright

p. 255. © Henry Payne

p. 277. © L.D. Warren

p. 299. Library of Congress

p. 315. © Etta Hulme

p. 337. © Brian Duffy

p. 350. © William Gropper

p. 351. © Tom Little

p. 373. Library of Congress

p. 389. © Bob Schochet

p. 401. © Don Wright

p. 415. © Fitzpatrick

p. 429. © Jack H. Ficklen

p. 437. © Herbert Block

Senior Editor: Libby Rubenstein
Typesetter: Alexander Graphics
Printer: The Maple-Vail Book Manufacturing Group
Cover Painting: Peg Sindelar, "Village with Sun"

Library of Congress Cataloging-in-Publication Data

Van Dyke, Vernon, 1912-
    Introduction to politics / Vernon Van Dyke. -- 3rd ed.
      p. cm.
    Includes bibliographical references (p. 459) and index.
    ISBN 0-8304-1437-1
    1. Comparative government. 2. Political science. I. Title.
JF51.V36 1996
320--dc20

95-22999
CIP

Manufactured in the United States of America

10 9 8 7 6 5 4 3 2 1

 ™ The paper used in this book meets the
minimum requirements of American
National Standard for Information
Sciences—Permanence of Paper for
Printed Library Materials, ANSI
Z39.48-1984.

Contents

■ **PART V: EPILOGUE**

INTRODUCTION

Introduction

To ignore values would be to ignore an important aspect of politics.

Among the values not to be ignored are those of the Bill of Rights. Here, cartoonist Paul Conrad warns that people denied their first amendment rights, including freedom of speech, are like people behind bars.

This book concerns politics, both domestic and international. It focuses on institutional arrangements for handling public issues, on the rules and processes for handling them, and on related ideologies, principles, policies, and arguments. It pays special attention to the kinds of values that are significant to political action, such as those prescribed for governments in the American Constitution, the Charter of the United Nations, and the covenants on human rights.

■ Structure and Topics

The book is divided into three parts, focusing on domestic and international politics and on political ideologies.

Part I on domestic politics focuses almost entirely on democracy, both because we live in a democracy and because, at least in the realm of thought and argument, democracy reigns almost unchallenged. People who call themselves Communists rule in China, but they have abandoned important features of Communist ideology. Scarcely anyone upholds Fascism and National Socialism, identified with Mussolini and Hitler. Military dictators and other authoritarians rule in some countries, but none of them make an intellectual case for their dictatorship. Instead they tend implicitly to apologize for what they do, putting up a democratic facade or claiming that they are saving their countries from some kind of crisis and that they will restore or establish democracy at some point in the future. In a few countries, with Indonesia and Singapore as the main examples, political leaders seek to justify authoritarian controls on the ground that discipline is needed. But this book's emphasis on democracy reflects the prevailing reality.

Democracy exists to the degree to which government is responsive and accountable to the people. This definition suggests most of the problems the chapters on democracy address. Who count among the people? Why make government responsive and accountable to them? How and how well are responsiveness and accountability achieved? What rights must people have if they are to formulate and express a will and if they are to hold government accountable? What duties and responsibilities do they have, and what are the reciprocal duties and responsibilities of governments? More generally, what rules and practices relating to parties, interest groups, voting, and elections go with democracy, and how is government organized so that it operates in accordance with the will of the people? What issues arise, and what arguments are advanced relating to them?

In the background and penumbra of these questions are others: Why does democracy develop? Why in one time or country and not in another? And what makes for its success or failure? What roles do violence and revolution, or threats thereof, play?

International institutions have not yet crystallized into government, so the first question for Part II is why; and the second question is how we conduct international affairs without government.

The international system is based on the sovereignty of states and is shaped and influenced by nationalism, imperialism, and demands for the self-determination of "nations" or "peoples." What do these terms mean? What are the criteria for deciding whether sovereignty is being maintained or lost? Who comprise a nation or people, how and how often may a nation or people exercise its right of self-determination, and what may they determine? By what standards do you decide whether a person is a nationalist and whether a government is imperialist? What is the counterpart at the international level of the refrain that we want a government of laws and not of persons? How much good, and what kind of good, is it realistic to expect from the United Nations? What acts by one country count as intervention in the affairs of another, and what issues arise over intervention? Why do governments choose to go to war? Can war be just? Why are some countries rich and others poor?

If nations or peoples have a right of self-determination at the international level, how about distinctive ethnic groups at the domestic level? If the residents of New York City were to proclaim that they constitute a people with a right of self-determination, meaning that they claim a right to secede, what would your argument be in response?

People interested in politics develop ideologies, and these are the focus of Part III. The central ideological issue of our time concerns the role of government. What should government do, and what should be left in private hands? Nobody really wants "big government" as a good in itself, but some want government to do so much that it becomes big. Others want to restrict or reduce the functions of government to the point that it becomes "minimal" or even disappears.

Your stand on such matters indicates the ideology that you endorse. Theoretically, you could be a Communist, putting unlimited political and economic control in the hands of one party and one central government with a view to remaking people and society. At the other extreme you could be a libertarian anarchocapitalist, attaching supreme value to the liberty of the individual and wanting to do away with the state and its coercive powers.

You will presumably want to place yourself somewhere between these extremes. If you say that you are a liberal, you need to go further and say whether your liberalism is classical, progressive, or neo-. If you say that you are a conservative, you also need to go further, saying what kind of a conservative you are. I am going to classify conservatives as conservative, economic, social, progressive, and neo-. Yes, I will call some conservatives conservative and others progressive.

I am not making these terms up, although I do not claim that they are everywhere accepted as the proper labels for ideological positions. We are in a time of ideological confusion, with people endorsing a mix of attitudes that do not come with agreed-upon labels. To make the problem more difficult, a person can adopt one attitude that belongs, say, in the progressive liberal category and another that belongs in the progressive conservative category, making it possible, perhaps, to classify the attitudes but not the person. In any event, intellectual problems exist about ideologies—problems that need to be sorted out and clarified.

I deal with both domestic and international politics in the belief that the problems arising at the two levels have much in common and that an understanding of politics at each level enhances understanding at the other. I do it also in the belief that politics at each level is vitally important. The reasons for that belief are so obvious that I will not try to spell them out.

■ A Perspective on Values

I take it for granted that a book of this sort must pay great attention to "the facts"—that is, to empirical knowledge. The importance of such knowledge would be difficult to exaggerate. But I also think that a book of this sort should pay great attention to values—to conceptions of the desirable. That values of all sorts (moral values included) play a significant role in politics is among the facts.

Jefferson began the Declaration of Independence with assertions about values, holding that we are all created equal and endowed by the Creator with certain rights. The Constitution requires the upholding of values: Congress shall make no law abridging freedom of speech. The Charter of the United Nations asserts values: All members shall settle their international disputes without endangering peace, security, or justice. The Charter also requires members to promote human rights, and more than half the states of the world have ratified the covenants on human rights, which reflect values. To ignore values would be to ignore an important aspect of politics.

I am of course aware of the argument that values are subjective, not open to objective validation; and I agree. I do not propose to try to validate them. I simply point to the fact that the values with which I will be dealing are enshrined in major political documents that have wide acceptance, imposing obligations and conferring rights on governments and on individuals.

The problem is that language expressing values is generally vague. What is the meaning of the statement that all men are created equal? What counts as free speech, and what counts as a violation of free speech? What counts as a free election? What counts as aggression?

Such questions are endless, and most of them give rise to argument. I think wryly of the fact that the UN Charter simply requires UN members to "promote" human rights, which might conceivably permit a dictator to meet his obligation by giving human rights three cheers.

Nevertheless, much has been done to clarify the vague language in which values are expressed, and even where the meaning has not become clear the issues have in most cases been identified. In dealing with values, I expect to acknowledge the difficulties. My major aim, in this connection and in others, is to put you in a better position to take a stand on questions that arise and to argue convincingly that you are right.

■ Reading

Almond, Gabriel A. (1990) *A Discipline Divided: Schools and Sects in Political-Science*. Newbury Park, Calif.: Sage.

Penton, Geoffrey, and Peter Gill (1993) *Introduction to Politics*. 3d ed. Cambridge, Mass.: Blackwell.

Ricci, David M. (1984) *The Tragedy of Political Science: Politics, Scholarship,and Democracy*. New Haven: Yale University Press.

Van Dyke, Vernon, and Lane Davis (1977) "Values and Evaluation in Teaching Political Science," in Vernon Van Dyke, ed. *Teaching Political Science: The Professor and the Polity*. Atlantic Highlands, N.J.: Humanities Press.

DEMOCRACY

The principal questions taken up in the chapters of Part II are the following: What is democracy, and what is its rationale? Who participates in politics, and why? What are the characteristics of presidential and parliamentary systems? What functions does each branch and each level of government serve? How does democracy relate to the idea of majority rule? What are the characteristics of "unitary" and "federal" systems? What rights and liberties go with democracy? How and how well can they be justified? What duties and responsibilities do people have in democracies? What conditions make for the development of democracy and for its success or failure? What roles do violence and revolution play in domestic government and politics?

Democracy

This chapter focuses on democracy. What is it? Why favor it? What criticisms are appropriate?

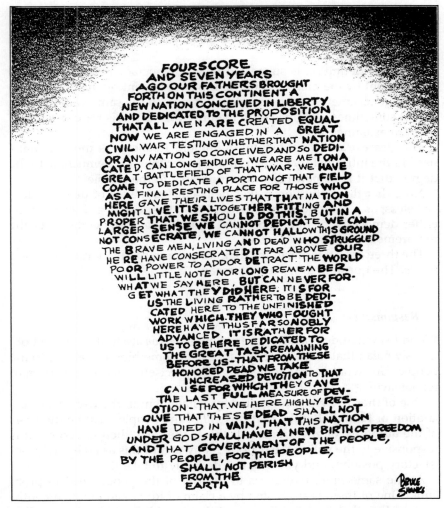

FOURSCORE AND SEVEN YEARS AGO OUR FATHERS BROUGHT FORTH ON THIS CONTINENT A NEW NATION CONCEIVED IN LIBERTY AND DEDICATED TO THE PROPOSITION THAT ALL MEN ARE CREATED EQUAL NOW WE ARE ENGAGED IN A GREAT CIVIL WAR TESTING WHETHER THAT NATION OR ANY NATION SO CONCEIVED AND SO DEDICATED, CAN LONG ENDURE. WE ARE MET ON A GREAT BATTLEFIELD OF THAT WAR. WE HAVE COME TO DEDICATE A PORTION OF THAT FIELD AS A FINAL RESTING PLACE FOR THOSE WHO HERE GAVE THEIR LIVES THAT THAT NATION MIGHT LIVE. IT IS ALTOGETHER FITTING AND PROPER THAT WE SHOULD DO THIS. BUT IN A LARGER SENSE WE CANNOT DEDICATE, WE CANNOT CONSECRATE, WE CANNOT HALLOW THIS GROUND THE BRAVE MEN, LIVING AND DEAD WHO STRUGGLED HERE HAVE CONSECRATED IT FAR ABOVE OUR POOR POWER TO ADD OR DETRACT. THE WORLD WILL LITTLE NOTE NOR LONG REMEMBER WHAT WE SAY HERE, BUT CAN NEVER FORGET WHAT THEY DID HERE. IT IS FOR US THE LIVING RATHER TO BE DEDICATED HERE TO THE UNFINISHED WORK WHICH THEY WHO FOUGHT HERE HAVE THUS FAR SO NOBLY ADVANCED. IT IS RATHER FOR US TO BE HERE DEDICATED TO THE GREAT TASK REMAINING BEFORE US—THAT FROM THESE HONORED DEAD WE TAKE INCREASED DEVOTION TO THAT CAUSE FOR WHICH THEY GAVE THE LAST FULL MEASURE OF DEVOTION—THAT WE HERE HIGHLY RESOLVE THAT THESE DEAD SHALL NOT HAVE DIED IN VAIN, THAT THIS NATION UNDER GOD SHALL HAVE A NEW BIRTH OF FREEDOM AND THAT GOVERNMENT OF THE PEOPLE, BY THE PEOPLE, FOR THE PEOPLE, SHALL NOT PERISH FROM THE EARTH

BRUCE SHANKS

In this 1954 cartoon, Bruce Shanks reminded Americans of the democratic values that Lincoln endorsed in the Gettysburg Address. Shanks evidently thought that Senator Joe McCarthy and his followers were undermining those values by the "witch hunt" they used in their search for communists in government.

■ The Meaning of Democracy _____

In a much-quoted statement, Abraham Lincoln described democracy as government of the people, by the people, and for the people. The statement is good, though it is not as sharp as it might be in distinguishing democracy from other forms of government. All governments are "of the people" in the sense that they rule over people; all governments have people as their subjects. Most or all governments claim to be "for the people" in the sense that they serve the interests of the people or promote their good. Lincoln's central phrase is thus the key one: democratic government is government *by the people*. Democracy provides for self-government.

A similar definition is suggested when democracy is identified with government by the many as opposed to government by the few (oligarchy) or government by the one (dictatorship). In the same vein, democracy is sometimes identified with majority rule, but this raises problems that are examined later.

The clearest and most helpful definition, I believe, is the one that I used in the introductory chapter: that a government is democratic to the degree that it is responsive and accountable to the people.

Note that this definition makes democracy a matter of degree. Nevertheless, as a matter of convenience, I tend to speak of governments as either democratic or not. Those that I think of as democratic meet the requirements in varying degrees.

The three crucial terms in the definition are *responsive, accountable*, and *people*. The question is what they mean.

Responsive

When I say that democratic government is *responsive* to the people I obviously mean that it acts in accordance with something pertaining to the people. But what is that something? To precisely what is government responsive?

One of the answers is suggested by a statement in the Universal Declaration of Human Rights, that the *will* of the people shall be the basis of the authority of government. If this is the case, then government is responsive to the will of the people. Many regard this as an entirely satisfactory position, and you will not do badly to take it.

At the same time, references to the *will* of the people lead to problems. One of them is suggested by a claim of Rousseau (an eighteenth-century French political philosopher) that in addition to having a will of which they are conscious (their apparent will), people also have a "real" will—the "real" will being the one they would develop if they were fully informed and fully rational. This line of thought permits anyone to attribute to people a "real" will of which they are entirely unaware and then claim that government responsive to that real will is democratic.

This danger is eliminated if the requirement is that government be responsive to the *preferences* of the people, or responsive to their *wishes* or *desires*. This seems to me the best position to take—that the responsiveness of a democratic government should be to the preferences or the wishes of the people insofar as possible.

I say "insofar as possible" for good reason. Sometimes government must act when no one can tell what the preference or wish of the people is. Perhaps the people are uninformed or indifferent about the matter; in fact, it is really out of the question for people to be sufficiently informed about all the problems of government to make intelligent judgments about them. And sometimes those who are informed and concerned are so divided that no one preference or wish can be said to prevail. Further, even when it is clear that people want action on a given matter (for example, "welfare reform"), their agreement may not extend much beyond the generality, leaving government with a wide range of choice concerning the specifics. Elections may not do much to clarify these questions, for voters make their choices on the basis of a wide variety of considerations. Thus, it may be impossible to tell what, if any, the collective preference of the people is on any given issue. In such circumstances, what can be said concerning responsiveness?

One of the possibilities is that government (through either elected or appointed officials) acts on the basis of anticipations. The office or agency involved makes a judgment about what the people would prefer or wish if they became aware of the problem and informed about it. Another possibility is that in the absence of any known and agreed-upon popular preference or wish, government acts so as to meet the *needs* of the people or to promote or protect their *interests*. The assumption is that action along these lines will meet with the approval of the people if the issue is ever raised. A considerable portion of the actions of democratic governments are clearly taken on one or the other of these bases.

These considerations suggest that those serving in a democratic government may play either of two roles. On the one hand, they may serve as agents, doing the bidding of their principal. The principal may be an appointing official or an electoral constituency. On the other hand, they may serve as trustees, using their own best judgment in deciding what to do. In practice, political leaders are likely to shift back and forth between these two roles. In the one role they are responsive to the manifest preferences or desires of the people, and in the other role they are responsive to anticipated preferences or desires. And judgments about anticipated preferences or desires are surely approximately the same as judgments about the needs or interests of the people.

Accountable

What is required for a government to be accountable?

First, it must keep people informed concerning its activities. This requirement does not preclude a few secrets, but they must be justified as an exception to the rule. The rule is that the people have a right to know what government is doing. The main problem connected with this principle arises when governments claim that certain matters must be kept secret lest the national security, or some other interest pertaining to foreign affairs, be jeopardized.

Second, public officials must be prepared to justify their behavior, giving reasons for what they do or fail to do. They are not free simply to act or refuse to act and then to keep silent. They must open up their reasoning processes and their decisions to public scrutiny and debate.

Third, procedures must exist by which the people or their representatives determine who will hold public office. A high proportion of the offices at the top level must be elective. Terms of office must be limited, and if elected officials want to serve an additional term, they must run in another election. The people must have the opportunity to refuse to re-elect. Further, the people must be free to form political parties and to put forward candidates; and they must be free to vote out of office all the candidates of a party they oppose and install all the candidates of a party they favor.

Those who serve in nonelective offices must be subject to removal, perhaps by the official who appointed them or perhaps through impeachment proceedings.

It goes without saying that government officials who are responsive and accountable are subject to law like everyone else. No one is above the law.

The above makes the problem of accountability look simpler than it in fact is, for in practice the complexity and the sheer number of issues make it difficult for people to hold even their own representatives accountable, let alone government as a whole. Given a complex issue, the tendency is to rely on experts and to hope that they make the right decisions. Given a multiplicity of issues, voters are likely to divide in a number of different ways, making it possible for representatives to get support from different sets of people on different issues and thus leaving it unclear as to precisely whom they are accountable. Of course, if a representative comes up for re-election, voters can make an overall judgment, which means that the representative is accountable for her general record although perhaps not for the separate items in that record.

The People

It has come to be accepted that accountability to *the people* means accountability to adult citizens. Universal adult suffrage is the rule. For a country to be democratic, virtually all adult citizens must have the vote, and votes must be weighted equally. The common statement is that the majority rules, although as I will show later this does not really hold true. Stated succinctly, the democratic requirement is: one person one vote, one vote one value, and "majority rule."

■ Arguments for Democracy

I am classifying governments as either *democratic* or *authoritarian*, recognizing that at the margins it may be uncertain where a particular government belongs. I use *authoritarian* as an umbrella term to cover all non-democratic governments. They are otherwise called autocracies, oligarchies, tyrannies, despotisms, and dictatorships.

Perhaps I should describe and analyze authoritarian governments before asking about the case for democracy. But the very names *autocracy, oligarchy, tyranny, despotism*, and *dictatorship* suggest the nature of the governments in question. And I assume that you will find the study of democracy more interesting if you know why so many endorse it. You may want to keep asking yourself whether the case for democracy is good. I devote a later chapter—chapter 10—to the question why democracy develops and succeeds or fails.

In stating arguments for democracy, I am not assuming that democracy is suitable for every possible set of people. That will become clear below. But given a population that makes a suitable unit for government, what are the arguments for democracy rather than for some kind of authoritarian rule?

Robert A. Dahl makes a case for democracy in his *Democracy and Its Critics* (1989), and what follows is a sketch of his argument. The starting point is a belief in the equality of all human beings. Jefferson's statement in the Declaration of Independence is that all men are created equal. The more elaborate statement of the international Covenant on Civil and Political Rights is that:

> All persons are equal before the law and are entitled without any discrimination to the equal protection of the law. In this respect, the law shall prohibit any discrimination and guarantee to all persons equal and effective protection against discrimination on any ground such as race, colour, sex, language, religion, political or other opinion, national or social origin, property, birth or other status.

Numerous other articles of the international covenants further spell out the idea. The rights recognized are for "everyone," for "all persons," and prohibited actions are to be directed against "no one."

This right to equality or equal treatment goes to people simply because they are human beings. It goes to them automatically, without any requirement that they do something to earn it.

In a way, the claim that we are born equal looks like nonsense. People are obviously unequal in many ways: in talent, wealth, and health, in their zeal to improve themselves and get ahead, and so on; and they differ in the circumstances that they confront. Jefferson knew all this, and so do those who subscribe to the international covenants on human rights. No sensible person could deny the differences or argue that they should not be acknowledged. It would be preposterous to hold that everyone should be treated alike. This means that the principle that we are created equal calls for interpretation so as to avoid the absurd.

The interpretation usually accepted is that our right to equality is a right to the equal consideration of our interests. Your interests are to get equal consideration with mine, and vice versa.

This kind of statement helps give meaning to the idea of equality, but the idea still looks suspicious. Suppose that I have an interest in getting a particular job. What does it mean that this interest is to be considered equally with the interests of others who also want the job? After all, we cannot all get it.

The solution to this problem lies in the idea of reasonableness. People may be treated differently when it is reasonable to do so; that is, when there are good grounds for doing so. What is to be avoided is differential treatment that is arbitrary rather than reasonable. The employer gives equal consideration to the interests of the various applicants if he is fair in weighing their qualifications, if he has good grounds for the choice that he makes.

What is reasonable and what is arbitrary is of course not always obvious. The provision of the Covenant on Civil and Political Rights, quoted above, lists a number of grounds for differentiation that were once regarded as reasonable but are now prohibited. For example, it was once generally considered reasonable to give the vote only to men, but now differentiation based on sex is generally considered preposterous. And ideas about what is reasonable are likely to change in the future as they have in the past.

Now, if my interests are to get equal consideration with yours, what reasonable basis is there for differences in our rights of political participation? If anyone has free speech, why should you not have it, too? If anyone has the right to vote, why should you not have it, too? Why should any person or group of persons have a right to rule over the others without the consent of the others? Is not any kind of autocratic rule automatically incompatible with the idea of equality? Why should one person or set of persons be entitled to enact and administer the law if others are denied any role in the process?

It is always possible, of course, that a person or group will claim to know the interests of the people better than the people do themselves and that, given autocratic power, they will promote those interests more fully or effectively than would be possible in a democracy. We generally accept this principle where children are involved, conceding autocratic powers to parents, but in a sense this indicates the main point: that adults are not to be treated like children. The assumption is that government should not put people down. On the contrary, it should contribute to their development—to their sense of self-respect and to their dignity and maturity. And this means that it should treat them as rational beings who are more likely than anyone else to know what their interests are, who are more motivated than anyone else to protect and promote those interests, and who are capable of deciding for themselves what course of action is best. This does not mean that individuals are never to seek or take advice from others or never to permit delegates or representatives to act on their behalf, but if they do, it should be of their own volition, and they should have good reasons for what they do. They are to be treated as responsible, morally autonomous persons, not as incompetents who need to be under paternalistic authority.

Further, any claim by authoritarian rulers that they know and will serve the interests of the people better than the people could themselves is automatically suspect. The claim is discredited by experience. Rulers everywhere and at all times tend to look out primarily for their own interests and, perhaps, for the interests of a segment of the population on which their rule especially depends. And they tend to ignore or neglect the interests of those barred from political participation. As John Stuart Mill put it, "The interest of the excluded is always in danger of being overlooked." The vote is a weapon that people may use to induce government to defend and promote their rights and interests. Further, the vote makes it somewhat surer that the voters' own conception of their interests is the one that counts rather than a conception that some paternalistic benefactor entertains.

The principles described above, mainly the principles of equality and moral autonomy, combine to require democracy. They rule out other forms of government. Every other form of government denies either equality or moral autonomy or both.

The critic can say, of course, that the above is a prescription for utopia, or perhaps that it is a prescription for social paralysis, for equality and moral autonomy might be taken to call for a unanimity rule. But a unanimity rule would be unreasonable. It is to be expected that when considerable numbers of people are involved, their interests will differ. So choices have to be made. And the reasonable view, as Tocqueville put it long ago, is that the interests of the many are to be preferred to the interests of the few.

Giovanni Sartori makes a somewhat different case for democracy in *Democratic Theory* (1965). Sartori starts by making a comparative appraisal. He does not argue that the people are always right, but points out that rule by them implies "a long process of adjustment and compromise" with innumerable checks on the wisdom of the actions proposed and taken. In contrast, he looks at the rule of an autocrat as potentially arbitrary and menacing. As compared to democracy, "autocracy is a much more dangerous and frightening prospect" (Sartori 1965, 168). He grants that the democratic method of selecting political leaders has drawbacks, but asks why, if we have the choice, we should accept a ruler who is self-appointed or who is selected by a small group that is itself self-appointed. Such a ruler might neglect our rights and interests, and do it with impunity.

Sartori points out, too, that a democratic system is more open to change than an authoritarian system. A democratic system includes legal and peaceful procedures for replacing one set of rulers with another. In contrast, an authoritarian system implies that one person or one small set of persons is in control indefinitely, with the probability that a system of privilege will develop and that government will serve the privileged.

Further, Sartori assumes certain values, and he argues that democracy best reflects and promotes them. He assumes that "individual freedom, personal security, and respect for human life are 'good' and rank among the highest values." He says that "from the very beginning of time . . . once men have begun to enjoy the values of respect for human life and for the dignity of the individual person, their reaction has always been the same, namely, to prize these values" (Sartori 1965, 170–72). And to him it follows naturally that those who prize such values should prefer democracy to authoritarianism.

Earlier in this chapter I quoted the provision of the international Covenant on Civil and Political Rights concerning equality. That Covenant includes another article saying that every citizen has the right

a. to take part in the conduct of public affairs, directly or through freely chosen representatives;

b. to vote and to be elected at genuine periodic elections which shall be by universal and equal suffrage and shall be held by secret ballot, guaranteeing the free expression of the will of the electors.

This provision is not entirely unambiguous, but its thrust is clearly in support of democracy, intimating that democracy ought to exist as a matter of right.

■ Limitations on Democracy and Arguments Against It _____

As I indicated in chapter 1, democracy reigns in the world without serious intellectual challenge. Communism is dead and along with it all advocacy of a dictatorship of the proletariat. National Socialism and Fascism disappeared with Hitler and Mussolini, though revival is always a possibility. Many states have been and are under dictatorships, but none of the dictators champions a theory or ideology that seeks to justify his rule on an enduring basis. Of course, anyone can dream of an all-wise and benevolent dictator who will rule a country better than any democracy could, but no one has found a reliable way to select such a dictator or to make sure that he or she continues to be all-wise and benevolent through a long term of office.

Nevertheless, democracy has its limitations and problems. One of them concerns the population unit, or the universe, for which it is suitable. No one has yet come up with a generally satisfactory rule for handling the problem. Humankind divides not simply into individual persons who can be treated equally and accepted as morally autonomous. It divides into groups distinguished by racial, ethnic, and other characteristics. People form into families, clans, tribes, and nations, develop different languages and religions, and come to share different values and traditions. Their cultures and civilizations differ. Some have been conquered or otherwise despoiled by others, which means that current relationships are burdened by historic attitudes of superiority, resentment, and enmity. In most cases, people have a passionate, even fanatical, devotion to the collectivity (the ethnic group, the tribe or nation) to which they belong, their collective identity being more important than their individual identities. Nationalism and national patriotism are among the most powerful emotions. People want to be proud of the nation with which they identify and find national subordination, or any kind of national humiliation, intolerable. They are willing to fight if need be, risking and sacrificing their lives and killing others, so that their nation can have a suitable place in the sun. Their usual demand is for self-determination, if they do not already enjoy it. Insofar as possible, they want to be able to control their own affairs and their own fate and do not want to share that control with a different people.

Now think of putting two or more such groups under one government. It has happened, and democracy has been attempted in such circumstances. In some instances it works out satisfactorily, Switzerland being a major illustration. The demand for self-determination may be satisfied with a considerable measure of decentralization and local autonomy, complete independence not being necessarily imperative.

But differences are sometimes too great to be bridged. It is possible that no government, even a democratic government, is equal to the task. In a minor way, the point is made by asking whether the Pilgrim Fathers, arriving at Plymouth Rock, should have suggested that the local Indians join them in establishing a common, democratic government. Or, the point is made by asking whether it would today be sensible to erase all boundary lines and put the whole world under one democratic government. Surely the people of the United States would reject any such proposal, and the people of every other country would probably do so as well.

To approach the same problem from a different direction, think of the Soviet Union and Yugoslavia, both of which were multinational and multiethnic. In both countries, a communist party, exercising dictatorial control, managed for many years to keep frictions from leading to open conflict, but when the grip of the party loosened, both countries broke up. And then some of the peoples involved, especially in what had been Yugoslavia, began fighting over the location of boundary lines between them and, in many areas, began requiring people to move (insisting on "ethnic cleansing") so that national or ethnic purity could be achieved. It would be naive to think that democracy would have solved the problems of either the Soviet Union or Yugoslavia.

Similar problems exist in many other countries in greater or less degree. The United States itself was once threatened with breakup over the slavery issue and fought a civil war. Democracy did not avert the war. Even after the war, democracy was left incomplete, partly because the blacks were so weak that they could not effectively insist on their rights. Sometimes it happens that government "for the people," even ostensibly democratic government, is really government for one segment of the people.

Democracy functions reasonably well when the differences are mainly between separate individuals who can organize themselves in different ways and when the composition of the majority group is thus open to change. Democracy is endangered, just as any sort of government is endangered, if the people involved are deeply and permanently divided (perhaps by race, language, religion, or sense of nationality), with one element always on top and another always oppressed.

The existence of deep divisions in a society may lead to a problem of a slightly different sort. Suppose, for example, as was the case in Algeria in the early 1990s, that an Islamic fundamentalist party seems likely to win a democratic election. No one can be entirely sure what the party will do if it gets control of the government, but the likelihood is that it will impose strict, traditional Islamic law, which, among other things, will deprive women of the suffrage and deny their equality in other ways. Should a majority be free to vote the destruction of democracy? In other words, should the present majority be allowed to deny future majorities the right to rule themselves? In times past, communist parties have in effect raised this question, although as it turned out none of them ever got enough popular support to get control of government in a democratic way.

Problems arise relating to democracy even where divisions are not so deep. Among other things, the principle of one person, one vote and one vote, one value is mocked by the fact that equality in voting power does not assure equality of influence. A number of differences make it inevitable that, as George Orwell said, some are more equal than others. Those who are wealthy are likely to have more influence than those who are poor; those who are educated and informed are likely to have more influence than those who are uneducated and ignorant; and those who organize, combining their efforts, are likely to have more influence than those who are inactive and apathetic. What, then, happens to democracy and to the willingness of people to support it if equal voting strength is simply a formalistic rule, a facade covering the fact of control by a few?

An additional problem, even if a less serious one, arises from the fact that people whose votes have equal weight may differ greatly in the intensity of their feelings about the issue voted on. And if those whose feelings are intense are in a minority, they may resent a situation in which outcomes are controlled by those who don't much care.

Democratic responses to such problems are not always satisfactory. They take several forms, focusing on moral and legal rights, on institutional arrangements, and on social and political attitudes. I will deal with the responses mainly in later chapters and will only suggest their nature here.

The focus on moral and legal rights led to the addition of the Bill of Rights to the Constitution of the United States, limiting the powers of Congress and (by subsequent interpretation) of the states. And in more recent times it has led to the emphasis on human rights throughout the world—rights that government is bound to respect and promote regardless of majority attitudes. Rights are a means of safeguarding certain cherished interests against the desires even of a majority. Rights give scant comfort to believers in democracy, however, if it is plain that, say, an Islamic fundamentalist party will repeal or deny those rights once it gets control of government.

The focus on institutional arrangements, where it exists, appears in constitutions. The Constitution of the United States, for example, contains safeguards against what some of the Founding Fathers described as a tyranny of the majority. In the main, the safeguards take the form of the separation of powers and checks and balances. That is, the powers of government are divided among the different branches and agencies and offices of government, reducing the chance that any one person or party or set of interests can gain complete control and making action by any one agency or office subject to check by another.

Some countries go much farther than the United States in their efforts to protect minorities, especially minorities identified by language, race, religion, or tribal or national affiliation; they guarantee such minorities a specified role in government or give them a veto over certain kinds of change. The practice leads Arend Lijphart to speak of "consociational democracies"—democracies in which certain kinds of minorities ("societies") are guaranteed a role as collective entities.

Perhaps the most widespread criticism of democracy is one on which I have not touched so far. It is advanced most notably by libertarians, to be described in chapter 22, and by students of "public choice." The problem stems from the fact that government can confer benefits. Moreover, it can concentrate the benefits enough to win the support of those benefited and spread the costs thinly enough that those burdened are not moved to resist. Approximately the same problem takes a slightly different form when 51 percent of the people vote benefits for themselves and compel the other 49 percent to pay part of the costs.

Given this kind of possibility, according to the libertarian critics, political parties and candidates can scarcely resist the temptation to promise benefits in order to win votes, and the consequence is that government gets bigger and bigger, taking a larger and larger share of the gross national product (GNP) in taxes, thus (according to "supply-side economics") tending to stifle economic growth.

This line of thought does not necessarily suggest a repudiation of democracy, although it did lead Friedrich Hayek, a leading libertarian theorist, to recommend constitutional arrangements designed to provide safeguards. What it leads to more generally is an adamant demand that the role of government be cut back, or at least that it be strictly limited. More on this in Part IV on ideologies.

■ Review

This chapter focuses on the meaning of democracy and the pro and con arguments.

A government is democratic to the degree that it is responsive and accountable to the people. Responsiveness should be to the will or, better, to the preferences—or perhaps to the interests—of the people. Accountability implies that the people have a right to know what the government is or is not doing and why; and it implies that the people can vote individual officeholders and a whole political party out of office. For the purposes of this definition of democracy, the people are the adult citizens. One person, one vote; one vote, one value; and "majority rule" are the guiding principles. The majority, however, is not to infringe on constitutionally protected rights.

Why favor democracy? Dahl bases the case mainly on a belief in equality, or a belief that the interests of all persons are entitled to equal consideration, and on a belief in the moral autonomy of persons; that is, on the belief that they know their own interests better, and are more likely to pursue them effectively, than anyone else. Sartori argues that the processes of decisionmaking are more trustworthy in a democratic than in an authoritarian regime, that democracy is more open to change, and that democracy is more compatible with certain cherished values. The Covenant on Civil and Political Rights gives a basis for the argument that democracy is a human right.

Democracy has limitations and problems. Diversities among persons and groups are so great that neither democracy nor any other kind of government is suitable for some combinations of them. Even the United States fought a civil war. Majority rule may mean a tyranny of the majority and oppression of minorities. It may lead to majority votes undermining or destroying democracy. It may lead to bigger and bigger government as people vote themselves benefits. The will of the people, if any, is not always clear. How such problems are managed is an issue mainly for subsequent chapters.

■ Reading _____

Birch, Anthony H. (1993) *The Concepts and Theories of Modern Democracy*. New York: Routledge.

Copp, David, Jean Hampton, and John E. Roemer, eds. (1993) *The Idea of Democracy*. New York: Cambridge University Press.

Dahl, Robert A. (1989) *Democracy and Its Critics*. New Haven: Yale University Press.

Held, David (1993) *Prospects for Democracy. North, South, East, West*. Stanford, Calif.: Stanford University Press.

Huntington, Samuel P. (1991) *The Third Wave: Democratization in the Late Twentieth Century*. Norman: University of Oklahoma Press.

Pangle, Thomas L. (1992) *The Ennobling of Democracy. The Challenge of the Postmodern Era*. Baltimore: The Johns Hopkins University Press.

Sartori, Giovanni (1987) *Theory of Democracy Revisited*. Chatham, N.J.: Chatham House.

Sorensen, Georg (1993) *Democracy and Democratization. Processes and Prospects in a Changing World*. Boulder: Westview Press.

Parties and Interest Groups

A government should be classified as democratic only if it permits more than one party to compete in elections.

A Hungarian cartoonist is asking, in effect, whether the United States really has two different major parties.

At the core of democracy is the idea that the people rule. But how is this arranged? When people number in the millions, as they do in most countries, they cannot rule as so many individuals. In isolation, each person is likely to feel, and actually to be, helpless. What happens is that people organize, and they seek to affect the course of events through the organizations to which they belong.

Political parties are among the organizations that they form, so we must give attention to them. What is a political party? What kinds of functions do parties perform, or what kinds of roles do they play? What are their policies concerning membership? How many parties get formed, and why? How do they select their candidates for public office? Are there ways of determining the extent to which the policies of a government vary depending on which party is in power?

People also form associations other than political parties, and some of them get involved in politics. When they do they are likely to be called pressure groups or interest groups. What kinds of roles do such groups play? How do their activities fit the democratic ideal of government "by the people"? Do other features of the political process raise the question of whether government is really "by the people"?

These are the questions to which this chapter is addressed.

■ Political Parties _____

Political parties are the major organizations (other than the government itself) through which people combine for collective political action. The essential and defining feature of a political party is that it provides the label under which candidates seek election to governmental office (Epstein 1975, 230), but most parties do much more than this bare-bones definition suggests.

Harry Eckstein lists the usual functions of parties as follows (Eckstein 1968, 437–38). They perform an aggregative function. That is, they draw people together to support or oppose something. It might be a candidate or slate of candidates, a legislative proposal, or some action, policy, or institution. Parties aggregate people—draw them together—in various ways. Mainly they formulate platforms and take stands on issues. And they publicize what they do, calling attention to their causes in whatever ways they can. They publish newspapers and journals, hold meetings, put commercials on TV, and so on. They induce citizens to register and to vote.

Instead of saying that parties aggregate people, some say that they aggregate *interests*. The two statements have approximately the same meaning, for an interest is a group of people who all have a stake in what happens concerning a given matter.

Parties help keep government responsive and accountable by providing a two-way channel of communication between government and the people. They inform government of the people's wishes, perhaps through members who hold office. And they convey information in the other direction, too—from government to the people. They make criticisms to which government leaders find it necessary to respond.

Parties may help either to divide or to unify a country. This function is especially significant in *plural societies*, in which the people divide into different nations or tribes or into different racial, linguistic, or religious communities. Such societies are said to be divided ethnically, divided along communal lines. If political parties form along those lines, they may accentuate the divisions and threaten to break up the state. But political parties may play the opposite role, emphasizing the importance of attitudes and policies that integrate the country or keep it integrated.

Parties perform a recruiting function. Mainly they recruit political leaders, attracting them to political service and giving them experience and visibility that may help their careers.

The most prominent function of political parties is to nominate candidates and mount campaigns to get them elected. In performing this function they necessarily perform another—an educational function: they enlighten people on the issues, teach members how to campaign, and nurture political skills. They may operate for such educational reasons even when they have no chance of winning.

In addition, parties may serve what seem to be nonpolitical functions. Eckstein speaks of them as providing "frameworks for their members' social life." They do this mainly in some non-Western countries where drastic changes cut people loose from traditional ties and expectations and leave them in need of various kinds of encouragement and support. And everywhere political leaders and parties may offer help and favors to people in the hope of winning votes.

It is interesting to compare Eckstein's conception of parties with observations by Samuel Eldersveld (Eldersveld 1982, 8–11). Eldersveld speaks of three "images" of a party. The first image pictures a party as "a group seeking power by winning elections." This view of parties focuses on all of the activities associated with efforts to get candidates into public office. The second image pictures a party as "a group that processes interest-group demands." This view focuses on the clash of interests and on the role of the party as a broker or mediator that works out compromises and bargains. The party manages conflict. It may itself be a coalition of contending interests or factions; or one party may make compromises or bargains with another party. The third image pictures the party as "an ideological competitor." It champions principles and policies, hoping thereby to win in competition with other parties that champion different principles and policies.

Membership in a political party, as a rule, is open. Parties welcome all those who want to join. They may or may not have any arrangement for expelling members and may or may not require that members pay dues. Those who want to work for the party on an unpaid basis do so. Members who show up for meetings at the local level have a vote in party affairs. At each level leaders are selected who operate at that level and who represent the party at the next higher level, right up to the central organs of the party. In the upper reaches of the hierarchy, officials of the party may be paid.

Communist parties have in various ways provided an exception to the above characterization. I will deal with them later.

The policies of different countries vary with respect to the formation of political parties. At one extreme only one party may be permitted to operate. At the other, anyone who wants to form a party is free to do so. In between are countries that, though generally granting freedom to form political parties, outlaw a particular party or a particular kind of party—presumably an extremist party. One of the possible justifying theories is that a commitment to democracy is not a suicide pact—that even a democratic society need not grant the full set of political rights to a party that would destroy freedom and deny human rights if it came to power.

The view I am taking—and it is a common view—is that a government should be classified as democratic only if it permits more than one party to operate. The people should be free to organize and support a party that opposes the government, provided the party is committed to the promotion of human rights. And if people form an opposition party they should be free to vote it into office and thus to oust the governing party. This is an essential condition of accountability.

It is theoretically possible to have a one-party system in practice even if the law leaves people free to form additional parties; they may not take advantage of the opportunity, or they may give so little support to a second or third party that it remains inconsequential.

Where the law leaves people free to form parties, the number actually formed varies considerably. Scholars and others speak of one-party, two-party, and multiparty systems, and they advance various theories to explain why the different systems develop.

One theory is that the number of political parties is strongly influenced, if not determined, by the electoral system itself. The theory focuses on arrangements for electing multimember bodies, such as legislatures. The theory is that if the system permits a party to win some seats even if it gets only a small proportion of the votes, then a multiparty system is likely to develop. Political leaders can form a splinter group or a new party, confident that they won't be thrown into oblivion. With 10 percent of the votes, say, they can get 10 percent of the seats. This may happen in a system of proportional representation, as in Israel.

In contrast, if the system gives seats only to parties that get a plurality or a majority of the votes, then political leaders have to stick together—probably on the basis of compromises and bargains—in order that collectively they can win enough votes to get some seats. Given such circumstances, the theory is, a two-party system is likely to develop. (A party that gets less than half the votes cast but more than any competing party has a *plurality*.)

The theory that the electoral system influences or determines the number of parties looks logical and thus plausible. The only trouble is that it does not always hold true. India, for example, requires winners to get a plurality or a majority of the votes, but during most of its history since independence it has not had a two-party system. It has had one party that has usually been dominant, plus a number of smaller ones, some of which have on occasion joined in coalitions.

Another theory is that political parties tend to form around the major *interests* to which people attach importance. If a country is deeply divided —for example, along tribal, religious, or linguistic lines—the theory is that each community is likely to have its own party. Thus, the greater the number and depth of the divisions, the greater the number of parties. The corresponding theory is that if a country is ethnically homogeneous, the only serious division is along class lines, so a two-party system is likely. One party represents the working class, and the other represents the owners and managers (the bourgeoisie).

Still another theory is that party systems "are largely creatures of their own histories" (Eckstein 1968, 450). Once a system gets going, for whatever reason, it tends to keep going. Parties don't like to die any more than people do, and people find it more advantageous to work within established parties than to start new ones. This theory is advanced especially with respect to former colonies in which one dominant party developed in connection with the struggle for independence. The tendency after independence is for people to continue to work within that party, which means that it continues to dominate.

As you might guess, those who advance these theories can all cite cases supporting their views. Each theory seems to hold good somewhere. But unhappily for those who seek simple explanations, none of the theories holds good everywhere. The world is complex.

Parties select their candidates in a number of ways. Most spectacular are the party conventions held in the United States every four years to nominate candidates for president and vice president. They are large, with more than 6,000 delegates and alternates attending recent Democratic conventions. Seats (and thus votes) in each convention are allocated to the fifty states on the basis of a complicated formula, and the party in each state selects the delegates and alternates to send. At the convention, aspiring candidates are placed in nomination, and voting then occurs until someone wins a majority, thus becoming the party's candidate. Similar conventions are held in many of the states to nominate party candidates for governor and other state offices, and conventions may be held in cities, counties, or any other political unit in which public officials are elected.

In the United States, the principal alternative to the party convention as a means of selecting candidates is the party primary. This is an election held according to state laws. Voters participate in the primary of only one party. Some states require prospective voters to register in advance as members of that party; others have open primaries, permitting voters simply to request the ballot of the party of their choice. The usual rule in primary elections, as in the later regular elections, is that whoever wins the most votes is the candidate, even if the number of votes is less than a majority; that is, a plurality vote is enough.

Government makes the rules for primaries and elections and administers them. Among the rules are the requirements that a political party must meet in order to have its candidates named on the ballot, the crucial requirement for a new party usually being a certain number of signatures of eligible voters on a petition. Some countries require parties to post a specified amount of money, which they forfeit to the government if their candidates fail to win a certain percentage of the votes cast in an election.

Theoretically, the voters' choice of the party to support should be based on the extent to which they share the views expressed in the platforms and the extent to which they find the candidates of the party appealing. Actually, of course, many people adhere to a given political party on the basis of less rational considerations. Perhaps they simply do what their parents did.

Responsiveness and accountability are not easy to achieve. Even within the same party, especially if it is large, the members are likely to have somewhat different wishes or preferences. A party that reflects a voter's wish in one respect may fail to do so in another. Moreover, just as "the people" are not one coherent unit with one set of wishes, so "government" is not one coherent entity. Elective offices may be filled by persons belonging to different parties, and these persons then presumably seek to satisfy different sets of wishes. Many offices and agencies in the bureaucracy are filled by people who are appointed rather than elected, and though they are theoretically and legally accountable to an elective official or agency, many of them operate independently and are called to account only if they go against the wishes of a supervising official or agency in an especially offensive way.

The influences on government are so complex and varied that it is difficult to demonstrate clear correlations between the support given to political parties and the policies that the government decides to pursue. G. Bingham Powell, however, offers enlightenment on some aspects of this question. He focuses on sixteen industrialized democracies and points out that, in these countries, parties on the left and parties on the right tend to take contrasting positions on a series of issues: on the emphasis to be placed on a progressive income tax, on the expansion of governmental welfare services, and on efforts to reduce the spread between the incomes of the rich and the poor.

Powell finds the kind of correlations you would expect. Increased voting along class lines and greater strength for leftist parties correlate with (a) a greater reliance on progressive income taxes, (b) a greater proportion of the gross domestic product (GDP) taken in taxes and spent by the government, and (c) a greater proportion of the total income of the country going to the poorest 80 percent of the people. "The contrast between countries having weak class voting and no leftist victories and countries having strong class voting and clear leftist majorities is quite stark. The latter collected income taxes that were twice as great as the former in proportion to GDP" (Powell 1982, 187– 91).

No one can say how many other kinds of policies correlate with election returns.

■ Nonparty Associations _____

In addition to organizing themselves into political parties, people also form other kinds of associations. In the United States we tend to do this somewhat more than people in other countries, but it happens universally. The American Medical Association illustrates the kind of association I have in mind, and so do trade unions, the Farm Bureau, the National Association of Manufacturers, Common Cause, the National Organization for Women (NOW), and so on. In addition to reasonably well-known associations, there are hundreds of others whose central concerns are narrow and specialized. Manufacturers of buttons, for example, may have their own association.

Such associations may or may not involve themselves in politics. If they do, they are likely to be called *pressure groups* or *interest groups.*

Pressure groups or interest groups pursue varied objectives. They may seek to influence the shaping of party platforms and the outcome of elections. They may seek to influence the selection of persons for appointive offices. They may engage in lobbying, seeking to influence the action of a legislative body or of an administrative agency. They may seek to influence public opinion, hoping through the public to put pressure on government.

Pressure groups may work through political parties. Parties and candidates always need money; and they always need help in appealing to the voters for support, registering voters, and getting the voters out on election day. Given concern about governmental action, pressure groups stand ready to give support to sympathetic parties and candidates. Conversely, their main motive may be to bring about the defeat of a candidate known to be unsympathetic; they may have "hit lists."

In the United States, members of Congress risk their political careers if they incur the hostility of organized labor, organized medicine, Jewish organizations demanding support for Israel, or any of a considerable variety of other interest groups. When help is given, bargains may be made, but both sides are more likely to proceed on the basis of tacit expectations.

Individuals representing pressure groups in lobbying activities generally have substantial expertise about matters with which they are concerned and may know more about them than the legislator who has to vote or the administrator who has to act. This knowledge can give them power.

The political implications of the activities of pressure groups go in different directions. On the one hand, such activities may well be desirable features of a democratic process. Democratic government is expected to be responsive to the wishes of the people, and pressure groups are among the instruments that the people may use to make their wishes known. In truth, pressure groups and political parties perform some of the very same functions. As Almond and Verba (1963, 4) say,

> Voluntary associations are the prime means by which the function of mediating between the individual and the state is performed. Through them the individual is able to relate himself effectively and meaningfully to the political system. These associations help him avoid the dilemma of being either a parochial, cut off from political influence, or an isolated and powerless individual, manipulated and mobilized by the mass institutions of politics and government.

Almond and Verba further note, "If there is a political revolution going on throughout the world, it is what might be called the participation explosion. In all the new nations of the world the belief that the ordinary man is politically relevant—that he ought to be an involved participant in the political system—is widespread" (300).

Political parties facilitate participation, and so do voluntary associations. Such associations—pressure groups—may induce government to be more responsive than it would otherwise be, and support for democracy may increase as people get concrete evidence that government responds to their desires.

Some are so impressed by the importance of interest groups in social and political life that they want to make them the basis for representation in government. Instead of giving representation to people according to the district in which they live, they want to accept the clustering of people around this or that interest and grant representation to the interest. They speak of the "corporate state" and of "corporatism." (I will not devote space to an appraisal of the idea. You might want to see what you can say for and against it.)

In contrast to the above, some implications of the activities of pressure groups go in a more troubling direction. Responsiveness to the special wishes of a set of interest groups does not necessarily add up to responsiveness to the wishes or needs or interests of the people as a whole. To be sure, most or all of those acting for private associations or interest groups no doubt think of themselves as acting also for the common good. A well-known indication of this is the often-cited statement allegedly made some years ago by a spokesman for General Motors that what's good for General Motors is good for the country.

Now, in many cases what is good for General Motors may be good for the country, but surely not always. It may be good for General Motors to have tariff protection against Japanese competition, but that would not necessarily be good for the country. And it may be good for those who grow tobacco to have the government safeguard their profits, but that is not necessarily good for the country either.

I should acknowledge that what is good for the country—or what responds to the wishes or needs or interests of the people—is often a matter of controversy; and people who are qualified to judge may judge differently. My point is simply that conflicts are to be expected, at times, between the interests of an association or pressure group and the interests of the country and that this creates a problem.

An interest group is particularly likely to have its way if no other interest group has a directly conflicting stake in the matter. Those who are apathetic present no obstacle, and those who think that the special interest conflicts with the public good may or may not have the means or the motivation to put up much of a battle. The theoretically possible result is that each of a series of interest groups will control public policy in its area of special concern.

Joseph A. Califano, who served as secretary of Health, Education, and Welfare under President Carter, was so impressed by the problem posed by interest groups in the United States that he abandoned his championship of the idea of a national health service. He explained his reasoning as follows:

> So long as the congressional system is as vulnerable to special-interest groups as it now is, I doubt that we have the political independence and integrity in the Congress to enact a sound national health plan. The doctors, specialists, hospitals, nurses, unions, medical equipment suppliers, pharmaceutical industry, insurance and computer companies, medical schools, and others will all demand and get significant concessions as part of any national health program. By the time they do, the resulting legislation is likely to carve in the marble of U.S. statutes many of the least effective and most costly and wasteful elements of the present system. Without substantial changes in the structure and process of Congress, I believe that we are incapable of enacting a health plan that will serve the national interest (Califano 1981, 210).

This view is especially interesting in light of the failure of the Clinton administration to secure the adoption of a national system of health care in 1994.

Interest-group pressures are not peculiar to the United States or to democracies. They occur in authoritarian systems, too. But they have a special significance in democracies in that they raise the question of whether government is still "by the people."

■ The Ulterior Interests of Political Leaders

A fairly obvious potential conflict exists between the idea of government by the people and the fact that political leaders sometimes pursue ulterior interests of their own. Perhaps the ulterior interest is in getting rich. Perhaps it is simply in getting elected and re-elected.

In different degrees in different countries, government (even democratic government) is associated with corruption, and one of the important motives of many political leaders is to enrich themselves. Thus, writing about India, the London *Economist* says that most of the people there "regard all politicians as crooks and gangsters and elections as a choice between predators." In Italy during most of the period since World War II, the Christian Democratic party has been the dominant party; but in 1993 it lost most of its leaders because they were revealed to be corrupt, and it decided to change its name.

Re-election comes close to being a universal goal of elected political leaders, which means that cultivating support among their constituents is imperative. In the United States, some members of Congress are notorious for finding ways to direct federal largesse into their own electoral districts and maintaining the flow once it is established. Thus, a governmental agency may be located in one place rather than another because an influential senator or representative wants to serve the interests of his constituents.

Members of Congress tend to engage in logrolling—trading votes for their mutual advantage—perhaps in order to get pork-barrel legislation adopted: I'll vote for that pet project for your constituents if you'll vote for this project for mine. Re-election may depend on it. Paradoxes develop, such as the agricultural one in which the United States is now involved: while helping farmers expand production by providing cheap water that subsidizes irrigation, it pays farmers to restrict their crops.

■ Foreign Participation

Government by the people is government by those living within the country. Nevertheless, "outside money"—foreign money—sometimes comes in. Any agency in a given country (a trade union, a corporation, a political party, or the government itself) may believe that it has a stake in the outcome of an election in another country. Or it may believe that it has a stake in a decision that a foreign government is about to make. It may therefore use money and other means in an effort to get what it wants.

For example, the Central Intelligence Agency of the United States is reported to have devoted large sums of money to efforts to influence elections in El Salvador in 1984, just as a dozen years earlier it attempted to influence events in Chile, and just as still earlier it (or its predecessor agency) sought to influence elections in Italy. When such efforts succeed, they raise the question of whether the government of the other country is really a government "by the people."

In the United States, so much money is spent in connection with elections and so many factors affect their outcomes that participation from abroad is unlikely to have much influence. In any event, the law of the United States requires that agents of foreign governments identify themselves publicly and that candidates in federal elections file public reports concerning funds received and spent. Administrative efficiency in the United States is at a high enough level that the law presumably is obeyed. But in a country like El Salvador, money provided secretly by a foreign power has more chance of shaping the attitudes of the voters and thus of determining the outcome of the election. And of course, money used to buy votes or bribe officials may well get precisely what is bought. When practices like these occur on any scale, it may not be appropriate to speak of government "by the people."

■ Review

This chapter focuses on political parties and nonparty associations.

As a rule, democracies, being responsive to the will of the people, permit people to organize parties as they please. Two-party and multiparty systems are the rule, although in some circumstances a single party dominates. Different theories are advanced to explain the development of differing numbers of parties. Most parties are open to anyone who wants to join.

Parties perform a number of functions. Formally, their main function is to nominate candidates for governmental office and to get them elected. To some extent, at least, the policies of a government reflect the distribution of popular support for the different parties.

Nonparty associations that participate in politics are often called "pressure groups" or "interest groups." They do not nominate candidates, but they may seek to influence voters; and they try to influence the actions of government. Their activities sometimes raise the question of whether the government is responding to the will of the people or to the will of one small portion of the people.

Political leaders sometimes pursue purposes having little or nothing to do with the will of the people. They may, for example, seek self-enrichment. Also, foreign money, and thus the will of foreigners, sometimes influences the outcome of elections and the policies of governments.

■ Reading

Beck, Paul Allen (1992) *Party Politics in America*. 7th ed. New York: Harper Collins.

Berry, Jeffrey M. (1984) *The Interest Group Society*. Boston: Little, Brown.

Crotty, William (1985) *The Party Game*. New York: St. Martin's.

Epstein, Leon D. (1986) *Political Parties in the American Mold*. Madison: University of Wisconsin Press.

Maisel, L. Sandy, ed. (1994) *The Parties Respond: Changes in American Parties and Campaigns*. 2d ed. Boulder: Westview Press.

Olson, Mancur (1965) *Logic of Collective Action: Public Goods and the Theory of Groups*. Cambridge: Harvard University Press.

Pomper, Gerald M. (1992) *Passions and Interests: Political Party Concepts of American Democracy*. Lawrence, Kan.: University of Kansas Press.

Schlesinger, Joseph A. (1991) *Political Parties and the Winning of Office*. Ann Arbor: University of Michigan Press.

Voting and Elections

Questions of fairness arise in connection with the drawing of the boundary lines of electoral districts.

In 1812 Governor Gerry of Massachusetts drew the boundary lines of electoral districts so as to maximize the electoral strength of his party. Among the districts was one that reminded cartoonist Elkanah Tisdale of the mythical salamander. The word gerrymander was the result. Charges of gerrymandering are common when the boundaries of electoral districts are drawn.

Like political parties and interest groups, elections are at the core of democracy. Some of the rules concerning them are obviously necessary, while others are the focus of controversy. Who votes, and what kinds of voting systems are employed? What is a plurality system, and what is proportional representation? What are the arguments for and against them? What does it mean to speak of elections in single- or multimember districts, and what does it mean if voting is "at large"? What is malapportionment? Are the different voting systems equally suitable for all possible constituencies, whether homogeneous or deeply divided? Under what circumstances, if any, should constituencies be communal instead of territorial? If you were a political leader and if a political opponent of yours was fixing the rules and arrangements for elections, in what ways might he rig them to your disadvantage? Why do people vote, other than to elect government officials? How much basis is there for the view that government by the people has become government by the rich? These questions are addressed below.

■ Voting

Government by the people is presumably government by *all* the people. The basic assumption is that, insofar as possible, people should have the right to participate, directly or through representatives, in the decisions of the government that rules over them. The assumption is that they may thus be able to protect themselves against oppression and obtain consideration of their interests. And the further assumption is that unnecessary subjection denies people equal treatment and moral autonomy, impeding their development.

The right to participate, including the right to vote, is not absolute. Exceptions are necessary. Few if any would say, for example, that a five-year-old should have the right to vote. So the question is what the qualifications for voting should be.

The answer to this question is dictated largely by the right to equal treatment described in chapter 2. The rule is that people are to be treated the same in the absence of good grounds for treating them differently. Thus, the presumption is that if anyone has a right to vote, everyone should have it. But this presumption is rebuttable: the vote may be denied, provided the denial is reasonable and not arbitrary. So, assuming that one person may vote, the question is what reasonable grounds exist, if any, for denying the vote to anyone else. Or, to put the same question differently, what qualifications for voting are compatible with the rule of equal treatment?

Most of the historical qualifications once considered reasonable have now been rejected. I will mention them in a moment. The only remaining qualifications of any great significance relate to *citizenship, age,* and *residence.*

The Covenant on Civil and Political Rights itself accepts *citizenship* as a qualification. It says that "every citizen" shall have the right to take part in public affairs and to vote, implying that aliens have no comparable claim. And a citizenship requirement is in fact imposed all over the world.

Whether it should be is debatable. Presumably everyone would agree that it is reasonable to deny the vote to aliens who are in a country on a short-term basis, but how about aliens who are long-term residents and who are therefore affected by government as much as citizens? The question takes on different dimensions, depending on the number and character of the aliens involved, becoming most serious when large-scale immigration occurs during a period of foreign occupation.

The Baltic countries provide the sharpest current illustration. The Soviet Union conquered and annexed them in 1940, after which it deported large numbers of the indigenous people to Stalin's slave-labor camps, and large numbers of Russians came in as immigrants. And the immigrants had children. In Estonia, taking it as an example, Russians came to comprise approximately a third of the population, and most of them wanted to remain in the country after it regained its independence in 1991. What to do? From the point of view of the indigenous Estonians, the Russians were adulterating their culture, and if the Russians remained and were allowed rights of political participation they would diminish the control that Estonians had over their own country. Many of the Russians did not even bother to learn Estonian. But many of the "Russians" were native-born (that is, born of parents who had immigrated from Russia) and on this basis had as good a claim to citizenship as those born of Estonian parents. And if the government tried to expel the Russians, it would incur the wrath of Moscow. What it has so far done is to allow the Russians to continue to live in the country but to deny them the vote. It restricts the suffrage to citizens of pre-1940 Estonia and their descendants. Surely this "solution" to the problem will not last.

Cyprus, Fiji, Malaysia, and a number of other countries have faced comparable problems. Turks came into Cyprus in large numbers when it was part of the Ottoman Empire and stayed there after Britain took over. Indians came into Fiji and Chinese into the Malay Peninsula when they were parts of the British Empire. Britain conferred citizenship on the immigrants in all three of these countries, and thus they became entitled to vote. But animosities between the Greeks and Turks on Cyprus were so great that the country has split in two. The Turks, being a minority, are particularly insistent on the view that the population of Cyprus does not constitute one community in which the majority should rule. They hold that, instead, the population divides into two communities and that the interests of these communities, considered as collective entities, must be safeguarded in any arrangement for government.

In other words, they deny that the population of Cyprus consists of a single set of people who should be in a single democracy on a one-person-one-vote basis. Similar tensions and problems exist in Fiji and Malaysia, making government difficult. Elections (democracy) cannot be counted on to bridge gaps in deeply divided societies. It may even be impractical to hold elections in which members of the different communities participate.

The question of the requirements for voting comes up in connection with small-scale as well as large-scale immigration. Sweden, for example, does not make citizenship an absolute requirement. It permits noncitizens who are long-term residents to vote in local elections.

A minimum *age* requirement for voting is universal and is usually between eighteen and twenty-one. Any higher age would surely appear to be unreasonable and therefore a denial of equal treatment.

A *residence* requirement is also common—that is, a requirement that those voting in a given electoral district shall have lived in it (or in the larger jurisdiction of which it is a part) for a specified period. People do not want outsiders coming in on election day and perhaps controlling the outcome.

Other qualifications imposed in times past have been generally eliminated on the ground that they are discriminatory—that they differentiate without good reason and thus deny equal treatment. Discrimination based on *sex* was once universal, but the United States amended its Constitution in 1920 to bring such discrimination to an end, and during and since World War II the movement to enfranchise women has swept the world. The dominant belief now is that the sex of a person has no relevance to the right to vote.

Property, income, tax, and *literacy* qualifications were also once common, but these qualifications, too, are now almost entirely gone. They were discriminatory, serving mainly to minimize the political power of the poorer classes. For the most part, the language qualification has disappeared along with the literacy qualification, but in a few instances it is still a problem. Those applying for citizenship in Estonia, for example, must meet a stringent language qualification.

The fifteenth amendment to the Constitution forbids the denial of the right to vote on account of *race*, but for a number of decades some states accomplished the denial by indirect means. For example, some administered a literacy qualification in such a way that whites always passed and blacks always failed. South Africa was long explicit about denying the vote on the basis of race, abandoning such discrimination in 1994 as one aspect of the general repudiation of policies of apartheid.

In a curious way Western Samoa is an exception to the rule of universal adult suffrage. The population of that country divides between the indigenous Samoans and others; the others are mainly of European extraction. The tradition among the indigenous Samoans is to emphasize family groupings, each group naming one of its members as a *matai*. When Western Samoa became independent the constitution provided for two kinds of electoral constituencies—territorial constituencies for the Samoans and communal constituencies for the Europeans. In the territorial constituencies only the *matai* vote; and among the Samoans, only *matai* are eligible for election to public office.

In the present context the term *constituency* refers to a body of people set apart for purposes of elections and representation. A territorial constituency consists of the residents of a given geographical district. A communal constituency consists of members of a given community, identified primarily by ancestry or by such characteristics as race, language, and religion.

Given a set of voters, *one person, one vote* is the rule; this is an aspect of equal treatment. Until 1949 Britain had some university constituencies in addition to its territorial constituencies, which meant that many of those associated with the universities could vote twice. At the end of the period of British control in Kenya, too, the electoral system permitted voters to cast from one to three votes, depending on how many qualifications they met.

Although the one-person-one-vote rule flows from the right of people to equal treatment, in another way it defies common sense. When people vote, they are not simply making choices affecting themselves, they are also prescribing for society as a whole; and it goes against all reason to suppose that all are equally well equipped to do this. At the same time, no one has yet come up with good criteria for identifying those who are especially well equipped to prescribe or for determining how many votes each should have. So in the absence of good ground, differentiation does not occur.

The secret ballot is now also the rule in democratic elections (though not necessarily in party caucuses or conventions). Secrecy is designed to make it as sure as can be that each vote reflects the preference of the voter and nothing else. The secret ballot frees the voter from intimidation and control by others, giving no basis for retribution. And it makes it impossible for the voter to prove that he deserves a payoff for having voted in a particular way.

Along with the rule of one person, one vote and the secret ballot go rules concerning the registration of voters, the location of polling places, the hours during which the polls are open, the presence at the polling places of various persons who watch over the proceedings, the counting of ballots, and so on. The object (at least the legitimate object) is to assure that those legally qualified have an adequate opportunity to vote, that only such persons in fact vote, that they vote only once in a given election, and that the votes are counted and credited as intended.

■ Plurality and Majority Voting versus Proportional Representation _____

Probably the most widely debated issue relating to elections concerns the rules for deciding who wins. The alternatives fall roughly into two categories: those focusing on a plurality or majority vote and those focusing on proportional representation (PR). I used these terms, and defined them briefly, in the preceding chapter.

In a plurality system (also called a first-past-the-post system), the candidate who gets the most votes wins. In a majority system, the winning candidate must have more than half of the votes.

In a PR system, each party gets representation in proportion to its electoral strength. Ideally, for example, a party that gets 10 percent of the votes gets 10 percent of the seats. This system is obviously not possible when only one office is to be filled. It is possible, however, when a number of persons are being elected—for example, to a parliament.

The argument over the two systems turns largely on a theory mentioned in the preceding chapter—the theory that plurality and majority systems tend to make for two-party systems and that PR tends to multiply the number of parties.

Competing values are basic to the argument. Some say that the prime purpose of elections is to produce a government that can govern and that this outcome is most likely with a two-party system. The assumption is that one of the two parties will get control and be able to govern in a stable and effective way until the next election.

In contrast, others say that the prime purpose of elections is to choose representatives who accurately reflect the wishes of the voters. And the greater the number of parties, the more likely it is that this value can be served. The need for accurate representation, it is claimed, is especially great in deeply divided societies where ethnic communities are historically hostile to each other. If one community is allowed to dominate government, it may use its power to oppress or even destroy the other.

Those on each side of the argument have criticisms of the other side. The criticism of PR gets a bit complicated, for it relates mainly to the *parliamentary* system as opposed to the *presidential* system. I describe these systems in the next chapter. Briefly, in a parliamentary system the person becomes prime minister who can get majority support in parliament. If her own party is not a majority party, she must form a coalition, getting the support of one or more other parties in addition to her own.

Critics point out that the very process of forming the coalition may be slow. And once the coalition is formed, it may be unstable, for any party in it may withdraw. If a withdrawal occurs that deprives the prime minister of majority support in parliament, she and her cabinet must either resign or call a new election. So for an indefinite period the country may be in a transition from one government to the next. This means, according to the argument, that the more accurately the outcome of the elections mirrors the wishes of the people, the more unstable the central government is likely to be.

The main criticism of both plurality and majority systems is that they leave so many people unrepresented; that is, they leave those who vote for losing candidates unrepresented. A minority party may not win any seats. Further, these systems waste votes, for once a candidate has a plurality or majority, all additional votes cast for that candidate have no effect.

One implication of the above is that a legislative body elected under a plurality or majority system may not be very accurate in reflecting the distribution of the vote. For example, in 1983 in Britain an alliance of two parties got 26 percent of the vote but won only 3.5 percent of the seats in the House of Commons. Another party got a lower percentage of the votes in 1983 than it had in 1979, but substantially increased its percentage of the seats in the House (Lijphart and Grofman 1984, 165). In a plurality system it is possible that a majority is left unrepresented.

The assumptions and arguments stated above are all controversial in one way or another. The claim is either that they do not always hold true or that they do not have much significance. First, as indicated in the preceding chapter, plurality voting does not always lead to a two-party system, and PR does not always lead to a multiparty system. What we have here is a tendency, not a scientific law.

Second, although the plurality system may leave minority *parties* unrepresented, it does not necessarily leave minority *groups* unrepresented. Depending somewhat on circumstances, minority groups may be able to join one or another of the major parties, extracting concessions in return for their support. When this is possible, what amount to coalitions are formed before the election instead of after.

With respect to minority groups a quite different argument is also possible: that if it is really vital to assure them representation, they can be given a certain quota of seats in parliament and then, in effect, be permitted to have an election within their own ranks to determine who will fill the seats. New Zealand does this, permitting Maoris to register on a separate electoral roll and then to elect their own members of parliament. The Maoris are the indigenous people, analogous to the American Indians.

Third, two-party systems may or may not be more effective and stable than multiparty systems. The two-party system involves the possibility that different parties may control different offices or branches of government. In the United States, for example, one party may control the presidency and the other may control Congress; or one party may control the House and the other the Senate. This necessarily causes difficulties and may lead to gridlock. The troubles of coalition government under systems of PR are rarely severe. Between elections, if a cabinet loses majority support and has to be reconstituted, most of its members are likely to show up again in the new cabinet, perhaps under the same prime minister. This is not unusual, for example, in either France or Italy. And while a cabinet is being constituted or reconstituted the permanent civil service keeps functioning.

Fourth, although it is logical to expect that PR would provide a more accurate representation of the voters, it does not always do so. In a plurality or majority system, those left unrepresented by the outcome in one district may in a sense get representation indirectly as a result of the victory of their party in other districts. Moreover, plurality systems vary among themselves, and so do PR systems.

Richard Rose has analyzed the results produced by seven plurality systems and seventeen PR systems, assigning each system a score depending on how closely the distribution of legislative seats among the parties corresponded to the distribution of the votes. His conclusion is that "the most representative plurality system, the United States House of Representatives, is at least as proportional as seven of the seventeen PR systems. The least proportional PR system, Spain, is more disproportional than five of the seven non-PR systems" (Lijphart and Grofman 1984, 74).

Rose's view is that "the case for or against a given electoral system will depend more upon many national contextual factors than upon arguments derived from abstract principles, for the way in which a system actually works depends upon the interaction of election law and social and political conditions" (Lijphart and Grofman 1984, 81).

Majority systems work in different ways, and different methods are employed to obtain proportional representation. For example, one of the methods of assuring majority support for the successful candidate is known as the *alternative vote system*. It invites voters to rank the candidates in order of preference. A candidate who gets a majority of first-choice votes wins; but if no candidate gets a majority, the one with the fewest first-choice votes is eliminated, and his or her ballots are redistributed according to the voters' second choice, the process being continued until some candidate has a majority.

Some jurisdictions in the United States and elsewhere use a *cumulative* voting system. Suppose, for example, that a city council of five persons is to be elected at large; that is, the city is one big electoral district, and each voter has five votes. The cumulative voting system allows voters to allocate their votes as they see fit, giving one vote to each of five candidates or all five votes to one candidate or making some other allocation. The big advantage of the cumulative system is that it allows minorities to concentrate their votes on one or a few candidates and thus gain representation that they would be unable to get under the usual kind of plurality or majority system. So people may favor or oppose a cumulative voting system, depending on whether they favor or oppose giving a minority a good shot at gaining representation.

The two main types of PR are the list system and a system based on the single transferable vote. The list system is simplest and most easily illustrated. Israel uses it. For parliamentary elections the whole country is one big constituency, and each party submits a list of candidates to the voters. Voters cast their ballots for the list of their choice. Any party that gets more than one percent of the votes then gets seats in proportion to the votes received. If votes entitle a party to, say, five seats, then the first five candidates on the party list are declared elected.

Actually, the list system is more complex than this because of the problem of fractions. What happens if a party is entitled to, say, 4½ seats? The problem arouses controversy, which is handled in various ways too complex to describe here.

The other main type of proportional representation is based on the *single transferable vote*. This vote is like the alternative vote, mentioned above, except that the object is to assure proportional representation rather than to assure that the candidate elected has majority support.

Let us assume that five seats are to be filled and that 6,000 votes are cast. Each voter votes for five candidates, ranking them in order of preference. To be elected, a candidate must receive a certain quota of votes. The usual rule for figuring the quota is to divide the number of votes cast by the number of seats to be filled plus one and to fix the quota at the next highest whole number. In this case 6,000 is divided by six, leading to a quota of 1,001. The quota is the smallest number that five candidates can receive but six cannot.

On the first count, ballots are distributed according to first choices, and any candidates who have the support of at least 1,001 voters are declared elected. Candidates ranked first by more than 1,001 voters have surplus votes. The ballots counted as surplus are selected to reflect the proportion of second choices going to each candidate and are distributed to the other candidates accordingly; and this process continues until all surplus votes are distributed.

If five candidates fail to reach the quota in this way, the candidate with the fewest votes is eliminated, and his ballots are distributed to the other candidates according to the voters' next effective choices, the process continuing until five candidates are elected.

New Zealand combines plurality voting and PR. To elect the parliament (a unicameral body with 120 members) each voter casts two votes, one for a candidate in a single-member district and one for a party list. In sixty districts, "general" electorates choose candidates by plurality vote. Maori electorates choose a variable number (five in 1993), also in single-member districts. The remainder are elected from party lists. To be entitled to seats, a party must get at least 5 percent of the total vote or win in at least one district. If it meets this test, list seats are added to its district seats as necessary to give it proportional representation.

■ Single- or Multimember Districts? _____

Some voting systems (for example, PR and cumulative voting) can be employed only in districts. Others permit a choice between single- and multimember districts, and various pros and cons are relevant. Let us assume that a city council is being elected. Jones argues for single-member districts. She wants to divide the city into wards and to elect one member of the council from each ward. She assumes that the council member elected in each ward will be a resident of that ward. Her argument is that this is the best way to assure that the people and the interests of each section of the city get due consideration.

In opposition to Jones, Smith argues for multimember districts and at-large elections. She wants the whole city to be one big constituency, with voters all over the city voting for all members of the council. Her public argument is that all members ought to represent the people and interests of the whole city rather than the people and the narrower interests of one section of the city. Moreover, she thinks of the possibility that more than one good candidate may live in the same neighborhood, and she does not want an electoral system that deprives the city of their services.

In addition to these public arguments, Smith may have other considerations in mind. Let us assume that she is a member of the Conservative party and that she is a Wasp (white Anglo-Saxon Protestant). She knows that in the city as a whole the Conservatives outnumber the Progressives, though the reverse is the case in a couple of sections of the city. If the city is divided into wards, the Progressives will elect council members from the wards where they are most numerous. In contrast, if elections occur at large, the Conservatives can swamp the Progressives and elect the entire council. Thus, the reasons that Smith gives in public for supporting at-large elections may be reinforced by considerations that she thinks it politic to keep private.

If the division of chief importance to Smith is between whites and blacks, or between Anglos and Hispanics, or between Protestants and Catholics, her reasoning can be the same. At-large elections may permit the whites to swamp the blacks, or the Anglos to swamp the Hispanics, or the Wasps to swamp the Catholics.

Smith is not attacking anyone's right to vote. Progressives, blacks, Hispanics, and Catholics can all vote and have their votes counted. But privately Smith wants to select the electoral system that will give the greatest possible advantage to the ethnic community with which she identifies.

If the choice between single- and multimember districts turns on the arguments I have described as public arguments, people are likely to make different judgments. The arguments on both sides are respectable and good.

The more private considerations, in contrast, are not compatible with the requirement of equal treatment. Nor are they compatible with the elementary rules of fairness. Especially when the purpose or effect of at-large voting is to strengthen whites at the expense of blacks, the courts of the United States have been condemning it as unconstitutional—as denying equal protection of the laws.

■ Boundary Lines and Apportionment

When the choice is to divide a large area into single-member districts (for example, when the choice is to divide a city into wards, with one council member elected from each ward), additional choices have to be made about drawing the boundary lines. A general presumption exists in favor of respecting lines already established for other purposes, but the presumption is rebuttable.

Some countries specify that those drawing the lines must take "community of interest" into account. One of the objects in Kenya, for example, is to put members of the same tribe into the same electoral district. Finnish law requires that the boundary lines of electoral districts follow linguistic boundary lines insofar as possible—the purpose being to group members of the Swedish-speaking minority together to make it more likely that they can gain representation.

Gerrymandering is often a problem in connection with the drawing of the boundary lines of electoral districts. The word comes out of US history. Long ago a political leader named Gerry (later to become vice president) had a hand in delimiting electoral districts. He did it so as to give his own party a plurality in as many districts as possible, which meant that he ended up with oddly shaped districts, one of them looking like a salamander. So "Gerry" and "salamander" were combined to get "gerrymander."

Given the precedent, districts with all sorts of shapes showed up in subsequent years, sometimes even consisting of areas not contiguous to each other. The technique was to draw lines either to *disperse* the vote of the other party, leaving that party unable to win anywhere, or to *concentrate* the vote of the other party in as few districts as possible, giving it surplus votes in them and no chance elsewhere.

There is no sure way to prevent gerrymandering. The practice is reduced by the rule that districts are to be compact and are to consist of contiguous territory, but this is not a constitutional requirement. And it is reduced by the prospect of outcries and the possibility of later retribution if lines are drawn in a manifestly unfair way.

Gerrymandering also occurs for racial purposes. Most generally, whites drawing the boundary lines have done it so as to maximize the strength of the white community and minimize the strength of the black community. To combat this, the Voting Rights Act of 1965 includes a preventive of sorts. The act lays down a rule for identifying jurisdictions with a record of racial discrimination and requires that they get the approval of the US attorney general if they want to change arrangements for elections. The attorney general is to approve only if she is satisfied that the change does not have the purpose and will not have the effect of denying or abridging the right to vote on account of race or color. And deliberate racial gerrymandering, plainly designed to maximize the strength of the white community and minimize the strength of the black community, is construed to abridge the right to vote.

An attorney general who finds that a plan to redraw boundaries constitutes a gerrymander may order changes. For example, North Carolina redrew boundary lines when the 1990 census showed that it was entitled to increase the number of its congressional districts from eleven to twelve. Blacks constituted 20 percent of the population of the state, which suggested that they might reasonably hope to win two of the twelve seats, but the changes that North Carolina proposed made it probable that they would be able to win in no more than one. This led the attorney general to require a re-drawing of the lines so as to create a second district in which blacks were predominant, whereupon North Carolina proposed to create a narrow shoestring district running for 160 miles along the I-85 interstate highway. The attorney general did not object, but some white voters in North Carolina did, and they went to court claiming that the deliberate segregation of voters into separate districts on the basis of race is unconstitutional, violating a right to a color-blind electoral process. Lower federal courts rejected the claim, but by a five-to-four vote the Supreme Court called for additional consideration of the issue. It granted the possibility that race-based districting might reflect a compelling governmental interest, but held that such districting calls for "close judicial scrutiny" to make sure that it has "sufficient justification." The ruling has led to a flood of cases in which whites are challenging boundary lines drawn so as to give blacks a chance to gain representation more nearly proportionate to their numbers. In 1994 the Supreme Court handed down a judgment indicating that, once boundary lines are drawn so as to make it possible for minorities to achieve representation in rough proportion to their number, it is not necessary to go farther; boundaries need not be drawn to assure minorities the maximum possible representation.

Another problem associated with the drawing of the boundary lines of electoral districts is *the problem of equal representation*. The problem has arisen in country after country. Currently it is an issue in Japan. People there have moved from the countryside into the cities, but electoral boundary lines have not been changed accordingly. Some of the electoral districts into which the country is divided for electing members of the Diet (the parliament) have 4½ times the population of others. This means that in terms of potential impact on the work of the Diet, each vote in the larger districts has considerably less weight, value, or efficacy than votes in the less-populous districts.

Such over- and underrepresentation is called *malapportionment*. Japanese courts are following the example set in the United States, holding that malapportionment, giving some votes more value than others, is a denial of equal treatment, and they are insisting on *reapportionment*. In the United States the courts have insisted that electoral districts be as nearly equal in population as practicable; this is the *equal population principle*. Japan is not so strict; its requirement is that the largest district shall not include more than three times as many people as the smallest.

It goes without saying that if the equal population principle is to be observed on a continuing basis, periodic reapportionment is necessary. In the United States, reapportionment of seats in the House of Representatives occurs every ten years—that is, after each census.

■ Democracy and "Majority Rule"

Democracy has come to be associated with *majority rule*, and majority rule has thus come to share the high value often attached to democracy. But the tendency to define democracy in terms of majority rule leads to problems.

The association between democracy and majority rule obviously has some basis, for many decisions are made by majority vote. The general rule is that a majority of those present and voting in a legislative body control its actions. It takes a majority vote in the electoral college to elect the president of the United States. The British prime minister has to have majority support in the House of Commons. Some electoral systems are designed to make it more likely, or to guarantee, that a majority of the voters support whomever is elected.

But the limitations on majority rule, and exceptions to it, are extensive, ranging from some that are relatively trivial to others that are of fundamental importance. The relatively trivial limitations are perhaps the most obvious, notably that all over the world elections occur more commonly on a plurality basis than on a majority basis, and that, though a candidate must have the support of a majority in the electoral college to be elected president of the United States, she does not necessarily have to get a majority of the popular vote.

Of somewhat greater importance are the limitations on what "the majority" can do. No country has *majoritarianism*, if that is interpreted to mean that the majority can democratically do whatever it pleases. Democracy is to be identified at least as much with limitations on the majority as with its powers. This will become clearer in the chapter on the rights that go with democracy, but we can stress the fact here that in a democracy the individual has rights that are, or are supposed to be, beyond the reach of the majority; for example, the right to freedom of expression and freedom of religion, to equal treatment, and to due process.

In the United States the separation of powers and the system of checks and balances constitute, in effect, limitations on majoritarianism. A party that sweeps the country in an election may nevertheless be prevented from working its will by those in the Senate who are holdovers from earlier elections or by the courts. Judges in the federal courts, incidentally, as well as members of the civil service, are appointed, not elected. Moreover, most of them are appointed for life, and thus do not necessarily reflect the wishes of the majority at any specific time.

More fundamentally, we can recall a question already dealt with in chapter 2: whether democracy or "majority rule" is suitable for societies that are deeply divided as well as for societies whose members accept each other as members of the same community. Both civil and international wars over demands for self-determination indicate that the answer to this question must be no. For majority rule to have a chance, the people involved must share a constitutional consensus. They must believe that they are members of the same community, sharing the same future. The people of Yugoslavia, it turns out, did not accept this belief, so the country has broken up and fighting occurs over the boundaries of the new political units. The people of the United States and China do not share the belief either, indicating that it would make no sense to put them together in the same country and tell them to operate by majority rule. The people of each country must have their own law-making and law-enforcing authority so that they can manage their own affairs. And this proposition applies very widely. Although the peoples of western Europe are working their way cautiously toward greater unity, and conceivably toward majority rule, the stronger trend in the world has recently been toward the abandonment of any effort to apply majority rule to multinational units.

How about the United States itself? Do the American people make up a universe that is suitable for majority rule? Even here, the fact is that we have considerable decentralization. The country is divided into fifty states, which in turn are subdivided. The majority in the United States as a whole does little. Majorities (or rather pluralities) in the states, counties, and cities do much more.

Further, in evaluating majority rule, it is helpful to contemplate the fate of American blacks during most of the century following their emancipation. Majority (plurality) rule led to gross discrimination against them, and (as noted earlier) this has commonly been the pattern in plural societies—that is, in societies that are deeply divided by nation, tribe, race, or ethnicity. In such societies, majority rule permits one community (perhaps a racial community) to get control over government and then to use government to advance its own interests and to oppress and exploit (in truth, sometimes even to exterminate) minorities.

Thus, it is not desirable to identify democracy with majority rule. Especially if majority rule is taken to connote majoritarianism, with a majority free to work its will, it is highly suspect. References to the "tyranny of the majority" are sometimes justified.

Demands for "majority rule" may have little or nothing to do with elections and democracy. When Southern Rhodesia was a British colony, the blacks of the country (95 percent of the population) adopted "majority rule" as their slogan. But it turned out that their demand was not primarily for democracy but for rule by a member of the majority race.

■ Individualism versus Communalism in Electoral Arrangements

Some pages earlier I mentioned Western Samoa, pointing out that the indigenous Samoans are grouped into territorial constituencies, whereas the Europeans are grouped into communal constituencies. This kind of distinction is made in enough other countries that it deserves attention. It provides a possible response to the problem of diversity.

In the fifty states of the United States, we have territorial constituencies only. Even when race influences the drawing of boundary lines, the constituencies are territorial. In elections (as opposed to primaries) all those in a given electoral district are on the same electoral roll and choose among the same set of candidates. Offices are not earmarked in advance for members of one or another racial or ethnic community. Rules governing elections fit with the idea of "one nation, indivisible" and with the idea of the melting pot. A substantially homogeneous society is assumed whether as the fact or as the goal.

Significantly enough, however, the United States deviates from the principle underlying territorial constituencies in some respects. Racial considerations intrude, even though racial groups as such are not given representation. A political party may seek a "balanced" ticket—one that gives recognition to different groups in the community. And in making appointments the president may seek "balance," too; in recent years he has been under great pressure to give greater recognition to blacks and to women.

Some countries have *plural societies*. Their population divides into distinct national, racial, ethnic, or tribal communities that cherish and want to preserve their distinct identities, the divisions being sharp and deep. In addition to being different, the communities may be traditional enemies.

In such a situation, if one community is sufficiently numerous, as the whites were in the United States after the Civil War, its members can enjoy the luxury of dividing into two or more parties according to their ideological bent; but if members of every community feel surrounded and beleaguered, they are likely to put up a common front against their adversaries or enemies, joining together in one party.

When each community forms its own political party, party struggles become communal struggles, and if one community has enough votes to win, government becomes its instrument in carrying on the struggle with other groups. Perhaps the governing communal party will treat opposing communities benignly, but even benign treatment is likely to be paternalistic and therefore offensive. And the record shows that a governing communal party is more likely to be oppressive and may even be genocidal. The victims have no reason to be loyal to such a government. Democracy is likely to be limited in this kind of situation, and it may be impossible.

One of the ways of seeking to make democracy work in a plural society is to assure every significant group of quota representation in legislative bodies and to invite every significant group to accept a role in other decision-making bodies of government as well. To do this, it is obviously necessary to abandon purely individualistic policies, by which all persons get equal treatment regardless of differences, and to adopt communal policies instead.

A communal system may take different forms. One form of communalism involves registering voters on communal rolls and reserving certain offices for persons communally elected. Thus, the seats in a legislative body are sometimes allocated on a quota basis to the different communities, and each community elects the persons to fill the allocated seats.

This kind of arrangement is working in New Zealand, as indicated earlier. There the indigenous Maoris may register on a separate electoral roll, and those who do so are entitled to a certain number of seats in parliament. A comparable arrangement worked for a number of years in Fiji, which had three electoral rolls—one for the indigenous Fijians, one for citizens whose ancestors immigrated from India, and one for Europeans and others. All three groups were assured seats in both houses of parliament and (in practice) in the cabinet as well. In 1987, however, a Fijian military leader seized power rather than permit Indians to have a greater voice in the cabinet, and the future of Fiji's system is uncertain.

Communal representation has been tried in both Cyprus and Lebanon but has failed in both cases. Democracy is obviously at risk, no matter what the electoral system, when ethnic or racial divisions are deep and when mutual trust and tolerance are in short supply.

■ Referenda

Popular voting occurs for purposes other than the election of officeholders. Sometimes the question is whether to *recall* an office holder—that is, to get him out ahead of schedule. More frequently the question is whether to adopt a specific measure of some kind—for example, to approve the borrowing of money to build a new school. California and Switzerland are notable for their use of *referenda,* considering and sometimes enacting major pieces of legislation in this way.

It is easy to argue that if government is to be "by the people," referenda are the best method. But legislation considered in referenda may or may not get the careful scrutiny it presumably gets in the more normal legislative process, and participation in a referendum may not be extensive enough to justify the view that "the people" have spoken. Rule by those interested enough to turn out to vote in a referendum may be rule by a minority.

At various times debate has occurred in the United States over the wisdom of a constitutional amendment that would take the power to declare war away from Congress and give it to the people in referendum. The proposal has never won out, critics describing referenda as too slow and cumbersome for use in crises and asserting that the requirement of a referendum is likely to weaken the voice of the president in his or her conduct of foreign affairs.

Majority rule usually prevails in referenda, except that when approval for borrowing money is sought, a special majority is common—perhaps 60 percent.

■ Who Is Really Represented?

So far in this chapter the assumption has been that elections give representation to voters, but this assumption needs to be questioned.

To be sure, the assumption is correct in a sense, for election and re-election depend on votes. But election and re-election also depend, ordinarily, on money; and those elected may also want money for other reasons. It is theoretically possible that money might be of more fundamental importance than votes. Moreover, money and votes are likely to come from different sets of people, and candidates and officeholders may turn out to be more responsive to those who give them money than to those who give them votes.

This suggests the possibility that government by the people may be just a charade, concealing the fact of government by the rich. At the crudest level, the rich might rule through outright bribery, with money given for explicit quid pro quos; and candidates or officeholders might solicit money through blackmail, threatening noxious action or costly inaction unless the rich pay up. At subtler levels, bargains might be tacit, with each side quietly accepting the view that those who give money, especially large amounts of money, can expect some kind of favor in return.

Election and re-election also depend on communication, and the days are gone when communication occurred mainly in relatively inexpensive local meetings. Candidates tend to hire media consultants and to mount campaigns including costly TV ads; and of course they need to attract and facilitate whatever free coverage the media will provide. Outcomes may depend not so much on reasoned voting as on success in playing upon the ignorance and prejudices of the voters.

Elections may be stolen. Laws concerning the secrecy of the ballot and honesty in counting votes are not always observed, which leaves open the question as to whom the successful candidate really represents (Caro 1982, 718–23, 736–37).

I know of no general comment on these possibilities that would always hold true. In varying degrees at different times and places, government is corrupt. What is nominally government by the people may in fact be government by the rich, or perhaps by the unscrupulous. It depends on the laws and on the effectiveness of the government in enforcing the laws.

The United States attacks these problems in several ways. It of course makes various actions, including bribery, criminal offenses. It maintains freedom of the press in the hope that threats of exposure will deter candidates and officeholders from engaging in practices inconsistent with democracy. In federal elections it limits the contributions a person or an agency can make to a candidate's campaign, seeking to keep them below the level at which they might serve as the equivalent of bribes. It offers to fund the campaigns of the presidential candidates of the major parties, provided the candidates agree not to incur expenses above the amount given to them or to accept private contributions.

Reactions to these practices differ. Some voters are alienated and others are influenced by appeals to ignorance and prejudice. The most common judgment is that, with relatively rare exceptions, those elected to office are honest. Philip M. Stern registered a dissent from this view in using a quip by Will Rogers as the title of a book that he published in 1988: *The Best Congress Money Can Buy.* In contrast, in *Money in American Elections* (1988), Frank J. Sorauf grants that legislators often vote in ways that please their contributors, but he is not at all sure that they do it because of the contributions. Similarly, Larry J. Sabato is inclined to reject the charge that members of Congress are unduly influenced by those who contribute money to support their campaigns (Sabato 1989, 13).

■ Review

This chapter concerns voting and elections. The most significant qualifications for voting are citizenship, age, and residence, and issues arise about them, especially the first two. Almost all countries have eliminated other traditional qualifications on the ground that they are incompatible with the requirement of equal and nondiscriminatory treatment.

One person, one vote and the secret ballot are both the rule. To determine winners, the choice is between plurality and majority systems and proportional representation. Cumulative voting may be employed in plurality or majority systems, offering the possibility of proportional representation. When multimember bodies are to be elected, the choice is between single- and multimember districts.

Different principles are followed in drawing the boundary lines of electoral districts. Some countries draw the lines without paying any attention to ethnic, racial, and cultural differences, whereas others respect these differences and draw lines accordingly. The territory included in a district should ideally be compact and contiguous, but gerrymandering —both partisan and racial—occurs regardless of this ideal. Boundaries should be drawn so that districts having an equal number of representatives will also have equal populations, but malapportionment sometimes occurs. Representation may be on a communal rather than a territorial basis.

Some countries or jurisdictions employ referenda, perhaps on the question of recalling an official before the expiration of her or his term but more frequently on the question of adopting some kind of legislation.

Questions arise whether money and the media play political roles that subvert the idea of government by the people.

■ Reading

Bogdanor, Vernon, and David Butler (1983) *Democracy and Elections: Electoral Systems and Their Political Consequences.* New York: Cambridge University Press.

Clawson, Dan, Alan Neustadtl, and Denise Scott (1992) *Money Talks. Corporate PACs and Political Influence.* New York: Basic Books.

Dummett, Michael (1985) *Voting Procedures.* Oxford: Oxford University Press.

Ferguson, Thomas (1995) *Golden Rule.* Chicago: University of Chicago Press.

Franklin, Mark N., Thomas T. Mackie, Henry Valen et al. (1992) *Electoral Change.* New York: Cambridge University Press.

Grofman, Bernard, ed. (1990) *Political Gerrymandering and the Courts.* New York: Agathon Press.

Grofman, Bernard, and Chandler Davidson, eds. (1992) *Controversies in Minority Voting. The Voting Rights Act in Perspective.* Washington, D.C.: Brookings.

Grofman, Bernard, Lisa Handley, and Richard G. Neimi, eds. (1992) *Minority Representation and the Quest for Voting Equality.* New York: Cambridge University Press.

Guinier, Lani (1994) *The Tyranny of the Majority: Fundamental Fairness in Representative Democracy.* New York: Free Press.

Jackson, Brooks (1988) *Honest Graft: Big Money and the American Political Process.* New York: Random House.

Lewis-Beck, Michael S. (1988) *Economics and Elections: The Major Western Democracies.* Ann Arbor: University of Michigan Press.

Lijphart, Arend (1994) *Electoral Systems and Party Systems: A Study of Twenty-seven Democracies, 1945–1990.* New York: Oxford University Press.

Lijphart, Arend, and Bernard Grofman, eds. (1984) *Choosing an Electoral System. Issues and Alternatives.* New York: Praeger.

Sabato, Larry J. (1989) *Paying for Elections: The Campaign Finance Thicket.* New York: Priority Press.

Sorauf, Frank J. (1988) *Money in American Elections.* Glenview, Ill.: Scott, Foresman.

The Branches of Government

The separation of powers, providing for checks and balances, makes hasty action difficult, but increases the danger of gridlock.

The President and Congress, depicted in this Cecil Jensen cartoon, are each trying to get control of the balance of power. The implied outcome is political/gridiron gridlock.

The preceding several chapters focus on the meaning of democracy and on participation in democratic government. This chapter concerns the branches of government: legislative, executive, and judicial. But first we must distinguish between presidential and parliamentary systems.

■ Presidential and Parliamentary Systems

Democracies operate on the basis of either a *presidential* or a *parliamentary* system. The United States has a presidential and Britain a parliamentary system, and I use them for purposes of illustration. Other democratic countries in general follow one scheme or the other, although with numerous variations.

In the United States the voters elect the members of the House of Representatives for two-year terms, the members of the Senate for six-year terms, and the president for a four-year term. So far as the Constitution is concerned, the House, the Senate, and the presidency might be controlled by three different political parties. Cooperation among them is not assured. Congress and the president may be at loggerheads on issues of either domestic or foreign policy, and so, for that matter, may the two houses of Congress. The scales are weighted against action, or at least action is difficult unless a substantial consensus exists. This was, in fact, what the Founding Fathers intended. Their memory of King George III was still fresh. And, as suggested in chapter 2, some of them wanted to adopt safeguards against a tyranny of the majority.

The *presidential* system can be described in terms of the separation of powers and checks and balances. Both houses of Congress and the president have their separate powers. Where agreement between the Congress and the president is necessary to action, each can check the other; and in many respects so can the two houses of Congress check each other. Thus, the possibility of ill-considered action is reduced, and so is the possibility that one faction or one segment of the population will gain complete control. At the same time, the possibility of paralysis within government is increased.

In a presidential system, the president has a cabinet, which he or she selects. Its members are heads of the various departments of government—for example, the Department of State, the Department of Defense, the Department of Justice, and so on. In the United States, those appointed to these posts are not members of Congress, though the appointments must be approved by the Senate.

In Britain's *parliamentary* system, the voters elect the members of the House of Commons—the lower house of parliament. They do not elect anyone to the executive branch of the government. Nominally, executive powers are in the hands of the queen (or king), but actually they are in the hands of a prime minister, for the queen acts on his or her advice.

The queen names the prime minister, selecting a person who can command majority support in the House of Commons. This ordinarily means that the prime minister is a member of the House and the leader of its majority party. In the absence of a majority party, the prime minister is a person who can form a majority coalition. The prime minister selects others who serve in the cabinet, administering the various departments of government. They are ordinarily drawn from the House of Commons, though a few regularly come from the House of Lords.

The House of Lords is the upper house of parliament. Its members get their positions by heredity or through appointment by the queen. The powers of the House of Lords are limited.

The prime minister does not have a fixed term of office. She must resign (and the cabinet with her) whenever she loses a vote of confidence in the House; and in no event is she to serve for more than five years without resigning and calling for a new election.

In 1990 Margaret Thatcher lost the support of so many members of her own party in the House that she chose to resign both as party leader and as prime minister, but her party remained the majority party in the House, so the queen simply requested the new party leader to become prime minister and form a new cabinet. No general election occurred. Transfers of power without new elections are more common in other parliamentary systems in which the cabinets tend to be based on multiparty coalitions.

Despite Thatcher's experience in 1990, the British prime minister tends to get more stable support from the House than the president gets from Congress, even when his own party is in control. This is so for several reasons. In the United States the parties are loosely organized and concern themselves with local and state affairs as well as with national affairs. National organs of the party and the president himself rarely have much influence over the selection of the party's candidates for election to the Senate and House. Once the candidates have been selected, national organs have a choice about contributing to their campaigns, and the president has a choice about the nature and extent of the support that he gives, but few of those elected are so dependent on national or presidential support for re-election that they must toe a party line. Mavericks—those who are persistently independent—may suffer a few penalties, but defiance of the president or other national leaders does not necessarily impair their careers to any serious extent.

In Britain the situation is different. The parties are more tightly organized, and the people are oriented more toward national affairs. In selecting candidates for the House of Commons, the local branches are more inclined than their counterparts in the United States to limit themselves to persons whose loyalty to the national party leadership is unquestioned.

Further, members of the majority party in the House have a special reason to be loyal to the prime minister, for if they deprive her of majority support, they put their own tenure of office in potential jeopardy, for she may ask the queen to dissolve the House and call for new elections. And at the extreme a prime minister in good standing with her party can see to it that a defiant party member is not renominated when the next election occurs. Any member of the party who refuses to toe the party line may be expelled (Birch 1982, 133–38).

In addition to all this, the prime minister controls patronage that she can use to encourage loyalty. She appoints not only members of the cabinet but also numerous junior ministers and others. Over 100 of Margaret Thatcher's parliamentary supporters, for example, depended on her for their paid posts (Rose 1989, 73).

Nevertheless, as Thatcher's experience suggests, it would be wrong to think that the prime minister is secure in her tenure and that the House is simply a rubber stamp. The two main parties—the ones that have formed all the cabinets in recent decades—both face a certain amount of dissidence within their own ranks. In Thatcher's case the dissidents specifically challenged her leadership, and ultimately she faced the threat of a vote of no confidence. In other cases members have tended increasingly to take an independent line on specific issues without meaning to pose any general challenge (Schwarz 1980), and prime ministers have tended to put up with the dissidence rather than use the weapons at their disposal to enforce conformity. They have simply accepted defeat without resigning. And the opposition party, remaining a minority, has had no good basis for complaint. The dissidents rarely transfer their loyalty to the other party.

■ Legislatures and Their Functions

Virtually all states, even those that are authoritarian, have a legislative assembly of some kind.

When an assembly has two chambers, it is said to be *bicameral*. Countries set up bicameral assemblies for a variety of reasons. One chamber is always thought of as representing the people in general. Second chambers permit the recognition and representation of some kind of subdivision of the people. Perhaps the subdivisions are the states in a federal system—which is the case in the United States. Perhaps the subdivisions are distinct national, tribal, or ethnic communities. Perhaps the subdivision is a social class, as in Britain.

Much more often than not, one of the two chambers becomes dominant. This is the case in Britain. The United States is an exception to the rule.

Legislatures perform a number of functions. As the name suggests, the *legislative* function—the enactment, amendment, and repeal of laws

—is nominally the central function. In performing this function, the House and Senate in the United States proceed in parallel, duplicating each other's efforts to a considerable extent. Any member of either house may introduce a bill, of which she may or may not be the author. Most members of Congress are willing to introduce any bill a constituent wants introduced; or they may introduce a bill sponsored by a lobbyist, by some governmental agency, or by the president.

Once introduced, a bill goes to a committee, which may take no action at all or which may give it varying degrees of consideration. The holding of public hearings is the most prominent type of consideration, as people from inside and outside government testify for or against whatever is proposed. If the committee then chooses to proceed, it reports the bill to the House or the Senate, as the case may be, either in its original form or revised, and recommends for or against adoption. Then the House or Senate decides whether and when to consider the bill.

If both houses adopt a bill in precisely the same form, it goes to the president for his signature. He may sign it, in which case it becomes law. Or he may veto it, in which case it does not become law unless Congress overrides the veto by a two-thirds vote in each house. Or he may do nothing, in which case the bill becomes law anyway, provided Congress remains in session for more than ten days after submitting it to him; if he fails to sign, and if Congress adjourns in less than ten days, a *pocket veto* is said to occur.

In the British parliamentary system, a high proportion of the bills considered are sponsored by the cabinet, and since the cabinet represents a majority in the House of Commons, it can ordinarily get its bills adopted, though they may be subjected to searching criticism, especially by members of the opposition. Members sometimes introduce bills of their own, but the cabinet can ordinarily block them if it chooses to do so.

Legislatures in other advanced democracies play comparable roles. In countries that are minimally democratic if not authoritarian, the legislative function is likely to be weaker and more marginal than in Britain. In such countries the executive branch proposes the legislation in the confident expectation that it will be endorsed. The most that the legislature is likely to be able to do is to influence the executive by means that do not involve an open confrontation.

In the United States, Congress has an important *oversight* function. That is, it watches over the administration of the law. Members may speak out in Congress as they please without fear of punishment, criticizing as they will. Either house may hold hearings on virtually any subject or on any aspect of the work of any governmental agency. Officials in the executive branch can be obliged to testify at these hearings and to answer questions that members of Congress pose. Through hearings, Congress can put the spotlight of publicity on any kind of governmental action or inaction, and either house may initiate new legislation on the basis of what its hearings reveal. Congress can create and abolish executive agencies, and it controls appropriations for each agency.

The General Accounting Office may play a role in the oversight function. It serves Congress and for the benefit of Congress can make special studies of the performance of executive and other governmental agencies.

In Britain, the House of Commons does not exercise the oversight function to the same extent as Congress, but it schedules sessions (question periods) during which members of the House may pose questions to cabinet ministers. And the conventions of the British government require the minister questioned to respond in serious fashion, even if the response involves an acknowledgment of some kind of governmental shortcoming.

It goes without saying that in performing the above functions, legislatures share in managing conflict. And depending on circumstances, their decisions may promote loyalty to the system or make for national disunity and perhaps disintegration.

In some countries legislatures perform *judicial* or *quasi-judicial* functions. In Britain the House of Lords is the highest court of appeal, its judicial functions being performed by members known as "law lords." In the United States the House may impeach federal officials, in which case the Senate serves as the trial body. If the Senate convicts, the impeached person is removed from office.

Legislators everywhere perform a *communication* function. It is their job to inform governmental agencies about attitudes back home. And it is their job to explain governmental policies to their constituents and to provide critical appraisals.

One of the incidental functions of a legislature is to serve as *a forum in which political leaders can gain experience, build up a network of contacts and friends, and become visible,* thus preparing themselves and making themselves available for higher office. Of course, this function is shared with other agencies. In the United States activities in various realms—for example, in a political party, or in the business world, or in connection with state government (notably in the governorship)—may give a person the standing that takes her into the cabinet or even into the presidency. Nevertheless, a considerable number of those who go into the highest levels of government have had previous experience in Congress. In parliamentary systems, as indicated, the performance of members in the legislature is likely to be crucial to their selection for service in the cabinet and in the prime ministry.

Legislatures perform a *symbolic* function. They symbolize participation by representatives of the people in the processes of government. They thus help promote the belief that the government is legitimate—

that it is worthy of support. Especially in some marginally democratic countries, the government needs this symbol, weak as it may be.

■ The Executive Branch

The executive plays a powerful role in both the presidential and the parliamentary systems. The executive includes not only the president and prime minister but also their staffs and the whole civil and military service of the government.

The president and prime minister perform a number of functions. They are *party leaders*. Candidates for the presidency and the prime ministry lead in the election campaign and, if they are successful, tend to carry others into office on their coattails. Whether or not that happens, the political fortunes of many others are in some degree dependent on the political fortunes of the president or prime minister. It is in their interest that he should do well. The situation thus strengthens his role.

Further, the executive takes the lead in *formulating the policies* of the government in both domestic and foreign affairs. In the United States the president proposes the budget—the general plan for raising and spending money. She proposes particular pieces of legislation and has the opportunity to veto bills adopted against her will. She makes decisions on which the security and peace of the country depend—the most fateful decisions that anyone can make. In Britain the prime minister plays a comparable role.

The president and prime minister have *recruiting* functions. In addition to the members of their cabinets, they must appoint a great many other persons to governmental and party positions. Their appointments are crucial to the quality of their administrations—and also to the political careers of those involved.

Generally, presidents and prime ministers are *opinion leaders*. They have fuller and more ready access to the media than do members of the legislature. This puts them in a unique position to influence the public and thus to put indirect pressure on members of the legislature to support their program.

A qualifier needs to be added, with the United States as an illustration. The power of the president varies with his personality and skills and with the assertiveness of Congress. Especially since a president led the United States into the Vietnam War, and since Nixon was forced out of office because of Watergate, the US Congress has played a relatively more powerful role with respect to both domestic and foreign affairs than had earlier been the case. And that role is all the more powerful now that the elections of 1994 have implicitly repudiated the leadership of the president and put his adversaries in control of both houses of Congress. Similar variations in the power of the two branches of government are to be expected in other countries, though the parliamentary system does more to assure the dominance of the executive.

The president and prime minister have *ceremonial functions*. In Britain the queen and the royal family perform a large portion of these functions, and in the United States the president can delegate some of them to the vice president and other members of the administration. But some of the ceremonial functions must inescapably be performed by the president and prime minister themselves.

With the presidency and the prime ministry go considerable staffs, and the president and prime minister are heads of the whole administrative branch of the government. They not only appoint people to many positions, as noted above, but also direct their subordinates in work and are responsible for what their subordinates do. Nominally their control over the whole executive branch is complete, and people speak of "the administration" of a president or prime minister.

Again, however, as in the case of power relations between the executive and the legislature, the situation is mixed. Neither the top elective officials in government nor their political appointees can attend to everything. Especially in the larger countries, the activities of government are too extensive to be controlled in any direct way by those who temporarily occupy this or that political position.

Every long-established government has a permanent *civil service*, and it, too, is likely to be powerful. Its members are for the most part experienced and knowledgeable, commanding more expertise than the political leaders who rotate in and out of the top offices. They are likely to be in close touch with the interest groups affected by what they do, and are thus able to negotiate some degree of consensus among those most intimately concerned with a given problem. In the absence of any special issue, they can simply follow standard operating procedures in implementing established policies. The president or prime minister, or the members of the cabinet, or even the legislature, can reach into the civil service here and there for special purposes and work their will, but by and large the civil service goes on functioning regardless of comings and goings in the top executive offices and in the legislative branch of government.

Roughly the same kinds of propositions hold true with respect to the *military*. In democratic countries (and, for that matter, in some nondemocratic countries as well) the military is subordinate to the civilian government; in the United States the president is the commander in chief. But at the same time, the career military leaders are presumably competent and knowledgeable and have a set of more or less stable expectations concerning the government's policies and their own role. Political leaders generally find it wiser to try to keep the military happy than to intrude in ordinary operations. They necessarily play an important role in fixing the budget for the armed forces, which implicitly gives them considerable power; but apart from that, they tend to give the military a relatively loose rein. Military leaders, however, are subject to the law like everyone else.

■ The Judiciary

Democratic government, like all government, includes courts, whose function is to interpret the law and to determine whether and how it applies in particular cases. The cases may concern a variety of matters— among them the legitimacy (the legality) of a governmental action, disputes between private parties concerning their respective rights, and questions of the violation of criminal law.

With respect to the *legitimacy of a governmental action*, we start with the proposition that those who administer the law necessarily interpret it, saying that the law permits or requires them to take or not to take some action. In most cases everyone agrees, and no problem arises; but it is always possible that someone who is affected by the decision may disagree.

In the United States, where the *doctrine of judicial review* is accepted, the person who disagrees may say that the law is somehow contrary to the Constitution, that it is therefore not valid law, and that the executive must therefore be barred from enforcing it. Or the dissenter may accept the law as valid but claim that the executive is giving it a wrong interpretation. In either case, the issue is argued before a court, which renders a judgment. The judgment of a lower court may be appealed, of course, but the appeal is to a higher court, ultimately the Supreme Court, and not to any agency in another branch of government.

In Britain and in some other democracies, the doctrine of judicial review is not accepted. In Britain's case, the easy explanation is that it lacks a written constitution, and therefore any measure enacted into law through proper procedures is valid. But the rejection of judicial review does not necessarily depend on the absence of a written constitution. Whenever any legislature adopts a bill and whenever any executive signs it into law, they are both saying implicitly that they have a right to do what they are doing. They find that the constitution permits it, whether the constitution is written or unwritten. And it is arguable that their finding should bind the courts.

Disputes among private parties concerning their respective legal rights may be settled by courts in civil suits. One party submits a claim to the court, and the other party must respond. Representatives of each side present their arguments, whether to a jury or to a judge, and a judgment is then rendered. If enforcement action is required, the executive branch of government becomes involved, but otherwise the matter is one for the courts alone.

Public prosecutors take the initiative in criminal actions, the theory being that the public has an interest in acting against crime. Democracies generally accept the assumption that an accused person is innocent until proven guilty. *Due process* must be afforded—which substantially means (in this context) that the judicial proceedings must be fair. A jury may or may not be involved. In the case of those found guilty, the court imposes the kind of penalty for which the law provides; and it is the duty of the executive branch to enforce the penalty. An international consensus on most of these matters is registered in the Covenant on Civil and Political Rights.

Courts are arranged in hierarchies, from lower to higher. The general rule is that cases come into the court system at one of the lower levels, and the judgment of the court at the lower level may be accepted by the parties as final. At the same time, the law always grants the possibility of appeal (on questions about the law, not necessarily about findings of fact). If an appeal occurs, the case goes to a higher court, and it must decide what to do. If it sees fit, it may hear relevant arguments and then either affirm or reverse the judgment of the lower court. Potentially, depending on circumstances, appeals may go up to the highest court of the land—in the United States, the Supreme Court.

■ Review

This chapter concerns the institutions of democratic government— presidential and parliamentary. The United States and Britain provide illustrations. The presidential system of the United States is based on the separation of powers and on checks and balances. The president is elected for a fixed term and may or may not have majority support in either house of Congress; the cabinet members, whom the president appoints, are not members of Congress.

The parliamentary system of Britain is based on the fusion of powers. The voters elect the members of the House of Commons, and the queen then invites to become prime minister the person who has the support of a majority in the Commons. The prime minister appoints a cabinet from among fellow members of parliament—mainly from the House of Commons. Theoretically, the Commons can force the resignation of the prime minister by withdrawing support, but in practice the prime minister ordinarily has the upper hand.

Legislatures in democratic countries serve a number of functions. They enact laws. They oversee the activities of other branches of government. They may perform quasi-judicial functions. They serve as a two-way channel of communication between the executive and the people. They provide a forum in which political leaders can gain experience and achieve prominence. And they symbolize popular participation in government.

The executive likewise serves a number of functions. The president and prime minister are party leaders. They take the lead in formulating policy, preparing a budget, and proposing legislation. They are responsible for the administration of the laws, appointing many government officials. They supervise the civil and military services and conduct foreign affairs. They perform ceremonial functions.

The judiciary consists of courts that decide whether the law has been violated in specific cases. American courts have the right of judicial review; British courts do not.

■ Reading

Birch, Anthony H. (1993) *The British System of Government*. 9th ed. New York: Routledge.

Copeland, Gary W., and Samuel C. Patterson (1994) *Parliaments in the Modern World: Changing Institutions*. Ann Arbor: University of Michigan Press.

Jones, Charles O. (1994) *The Presidency in a Separated System*. Washington, D.C.: Brookings.

Lijphart, Arend (1984) *Democracies. Patterns of Majoritarian and Consensus Government in Twenty-One Countries*. New Haven: Yale University Press.

Rose, Richard (1989) *Politics in England*. 5th ed. Basingstoke, Hampshire: Macmillan.

Sundquist, James L. (1992) *Constitutional Reform and Effective Government*. Washington, D.C.: Brookings.

The Levels of Government

The main reason for the centralization of power is the belief that certain values, programs, and policies are in the interest of the whole country and that they should be pursued in an assured and coherent way.

'Wake up . . . It's your vehicle'

The apathy of voters is one of the problems of democracy at every level. A great many people are willing to leave decisions to others. The cartoon, by Bob Saylor of the *Houston Post*, concerns the apathy of the citizens of Texas when the constitution was being revised.

Government operates at different levels. In the United States the levels are usually referred to as federal, state, and local. Comparable terms apply in other countries.

The existence of different levels implies that decisions must be made about the allocation of functions and powers—in other words, about centralization and decentralization—and this suggests three questions. What are the reasons for centralizing? What are the reasons for decentralizing and what methods are employed? Given the fact that some governments are *unitary* and others *federal*, what do these terms mean, and what is the relationship between centralization and decentralization, on the one hand, and unitary or federal, on the other?

■ Why Centralize?

To Promote Fundamental and General Interests

Centralization exists to the degree that governmental agencies in or near the national capital exercise the powers of government. States go in the direction of centralization for a variety of reasons. The most general of them is the conviction that a given value, program, or policy is of fundamental and general interest to the whole country and that it must therefore be pursued in an assured and coherent way.

Not surprisingly, *central governments take the view that their own survival is of fundamental and general interest* to the whole country. They therefore allocate to themselves the necessary powers. Moreover, they want to survive in a secure way and not precariously; they want to be in control, to dominate, to maintain law and order.

What does it mean to say that governments want to survive? As far as domestic challenges are concerned, the statement needs to be construed somewhat differently with respect to democratic and authoritarian regimes. To say that a democratic regime wants to survive is to say that the persons who constitute the government want to serve out their legitimate terms in office, perhaps to run for re-election, and to preserve the constitutional system. To say that an authoritarian regime wants to survive is to say that the set of persons in office wants to stay there or at least to control the succession. The desire to survive also includes a desire to be able to deter or defeat any attempt at illegal secession.

As far as foreign challenges are concerned, survival relates to sovereignty and territorial integrity. A country is *sovereign* when it is independent—when it is not subordinate to a foreign power. Within the limits of international law, it is free to shape its domestic law as it sees fit. Governments of sovereign states almost always want to preserve their sovereignty rather than accept foreign dictation. If they are to be subordinated to an international organization or a foreign government in any way, they want it to be by their own consent. And, with rare exceptions, they want to keep their territorial integrity intact. They seek the security of the state against external enemies.

If central governments are to survive, they must have *powers* and *power;* that is, they must have some kinds of legal authority, and they must command coercive force. They must command enough force to support their legal authority, including their authority over governments at lower levels. Ideally, they should be able to overwhelm any possible challenger. Criminals are always defying governments, and political dissidents may seek to undermine and overthrow them. Central governments may even be challenged by governments at lower levels.

The *powers* (legal authority) of central governments must enable them to maintain and use the *power* (force) necessary to their survival. Among other things, they must be able to regulate or prohibit the possession of arms by private persons. They must be able to forbid the raising of private armies. If they have reason to doubt the loyalty of military personnel, they must be able to take whatever measures are necessary to keep the military in check.

If a government fails in any of these respects, it may or may not continue to exist. Failures repeatedly occur, as the many military coups suggest. Loyalties cannot always be known or counted on. But if a government commands overwhelming power, it can ordinarily assure its own survival.

Governments (central governments) likewise need whatever power it takes to deter or defeat any attempt at illegal secession. The United States failed in this respect in 1860, and a number of other countries have failed before and since. As the American Civil War attests, the penalty may be severe. Most central governments are so determined to avert rebellion and secession that they do their best to keep political subdivisions militarily helpless, even nationalizing control of the police.

The United States does not do this. In the United States control of the police is lodged with state and local governments, and the governors may use the National Guard for certain purposes. But the National Guard is also at the disposal of the president, and he may remove it from the governor's control if he wishes. While Eisenhower was president, for example, the governor of Arkansas refused to take the measures required by a Supreme Court judgment to bring about the racial integration of the schools of Little Rock. Faced with this defiance, Eisenhower took the necessary action himself. Among other things, he assumed control of the Arkansas National Guard and ordered it to protect blacks attending schools that previously had been for whites only. Behind the Arkansas National Guard stood all the power of the US armed forces.

Governments also need whatever power is necessary to provide *security against foreign enemies.* Costa Rica gets along without armed forces, and a number of other states are only lightly armed; but history shows that states that are too weak to defend themselves, or that lack a Big Brother to do it for them, are living dangerously. It goes without saying that responsibility for national defense must be lodged with the central government.

The history of the American Indians provides eloquent testimony to the fact that national defense on a decentralized basis does not work. When the Europeans arrived in the Western Hemisphere, the Indians were politically divided. Under their system, or lack of it, responsibility for defense lay on the shoulders of the tribe that happened to be on the front line. The European intruders could thus defeat the tribes one by one.

It would be difficult to exaggerate the importance of the above points. When a country becomes involved in war, civil or international, its very existence may be at stake. For most countries, including the United States, no other activity of government is more important than national defense, and everywhere national defense is regarded as a function of the central government.

Just as national defense must be the responsibility of the central government, so must the *conduct of foreign relations* in general. It would be potentially incompatible with the continued unity of the state, and dangerous to its continued existence, if subdivisions were allowed to act independently in relations with foreign countries.

Central governments must also have the authority to *regulate commerce*, both foreign and domestic. Authority to regulate foreign commerce goes with the authority to conduct foreign relations, and authority to regulate domestic commerce is essential lest governments at lower levels impose tariff and other barriers to trade that deny the country the advantages of specialization and the division of labor.

To say that the central government must have the power to regulate commerce within the country is to leave many questions unanswered, for it is not always obvious what constitutes commerce; and when the power is to regulate commerce "among the several states," as it is in the United States, the problem of distinguishing between interstate and intrastate commerce also arises. Even if all sovereign states started with the same general rule, the actual powers of the central governments would vary.

Not only is the regulation of commerce thought to be a fundamental and general interest, but so is the *promotion of public welfare and economic prosperity*. Thus, additional powers go to central governments. They must have the authority to *issue and regulate the currency*. It would be incompatible with the whole idea of a unified country if subdivisions could have currencies of their own. Further, central governments always have, and must have, the power to *tax, borrow, and spend*—unlike the United Nations, which cannot impose taxes but must depend on the voluntary contributions of member states.

The power to tax, borrow, and spend is like the power to regulate interstate commerce, in that it can be interpreted flexibly. The United States illustrates the point. The government in Washington has used these powers to vastly expand its functions and to bring about a greater and greater degree of centralization. It tells the states, for example, that it will provide a certain portion of the cost (a grant-in-aid) if they will adopt a certain kind of program, meeting the specifications fixed. The grant-in-aid may cover anything up to 100 percent of the cost. The money that the federal government offers comes, sooner or later, from taxpayers in every state. If a state cooperates, it shares in the benefits; if it refuses to cooperate, its citizens pay in taxes but get nothing in return. Thus, the pressure to cooperate is strong. In effect, the federal government is using the states as its instrument to secure the adoption and administration of various programs.

For example, the construction and maintenance of roads and highways is assumed to be a function of state and local governments, not of the federal government. But years ago the federal government decided that an interstate highway system should be built. It therefore drew up the specifications and offered financial support to states willing to build and maintain the highways. Of course, it found them willing to cooperate.

The principle that central governments take on functions deemed to be of fundamental and general interest operates in other areas, too. It explains, or at least it helps explain, why central governments become involved in promoting education, science, and the arts. In the United States it explains why the federal government takes the lead in legislation designed to protect civil rights and the environment. And it explains why many central governments assume responsibility for projects too expensive or too risky for private enterprise: it ought to be done, and neither local governments nor private entrepreneurs can be counted on to do it; therefore the central government acts. The support given by the federal government to research relating, for example, to health illustrates the point.

Some central governments take the view, too, that they must keep powers centralized in order to assure and promote the *unity of the country*. They fear that if regional subdivisions are allowed to play a significant role, demands for secession may develop. This fear operates primarily in multinational or multiethnic states. The question is whether the centralization of power in such states may not be counterproductive, accentuating the very danger it is designed to avert. As will be noted shortly, an opposite policy is possible—one designed to win or hold the loyalty of national or ethnic minorities by a policy of decentralization.

Central governments sometimes expand their roles in order to *minimize dependence on foreign capital*. They want a project undertaken, but not by foreign business concerns. They therefore undertake the project themselves, seeing this as the only alternative.

Concern for national prestige and pride may also lead to an expansion of the role of central governments. Thus, some countries operate a national airline ,at a loss, or build buildings or monuments that they cannot afford. The equivalent for the United States has been the space program. The Soviets were first to put an object into orbit around the earth. They did this in 1957, and it was a spectacular achievement. It led many to conclude or to fear that the Soviet Union had become the world's leader in science and technology. In response, the United States immediately expanded its space program, and President Kennedy called for a program to land Americans on the moon. Concern for national pride and prestige was a major motivation.

To Assure Adherence to Common Standards

A concern for fairness usually supplements a concern for matters of fundamental and general interest. The underlying assumption is that people in similar circumstances should get similar treatment. More specifically, the assumption is that when government provides benefits or opportunities to anyone, it ought to provide them equally to everyone who is similarly situated.

Canada illustrates this point. It acts quite deliberately to provide for equalization. In general, Canada has one of the most decentralized governmental systems in the world, the powers of the provinces being jealously protected and preserved. Yet it has adopted the principle that citizens are to have "equal access to opportunities provided by or influenced by public action." Canada considers it unfair if discrimination occurs among people in different provinces with respect to certain governmental services or benefits. This attitude prevails, for example, with respect to Medicare, hospital insurance, social assistance, and provisions for higher education. The principle is that in such matters national standards ought to be maintained and that people in the poorer areas should not have to pay at a higher rate to enjoy the benefits of the national standards. To assure this the central government makes equalization payments to the provinces so that "an individual will receive the same level of public services and incur the same tax burden wherever he [lives] in the country" (Smiley 1972, 56, 122).

The United States attacks the problem in a similar way. As noted above, it is the federal government that has led the way in civil rights legislation, experience having demonstrated that states varied considerably in their zeal for assuring equal treatment regardless of race. And it is the federal government that leads the way in legislation designed to protect the environment, lest states try through their laxity to compete with each other in attracting industry. Welfare and unemployment insurance programs are nominally within the sphere of action of the states, but the federal government offers the states grants-in-aid, with conditions attached. The conditions are designed, first, to induce the states to adopt the necessary legislation, if they have not already done so, and second, to make sure that the various states follow more or less common standards. On the basis of the power of the purse, but because of a belief in the need for equalization, a nominally decentralized system is thus coordinated if not centralized.

In some cases decisions about centralization and decentralization are influenced by the *availability or scarcity of personnel with suitable training and skills.* The point is illustrated by the fact that some of the African colonies that gained independence in the 1960s had no more than a handful of people with college degrees. Some of these countries had to hire foreigners—usually people from the former imperial country—to staff offices in the central government. Decentralization was impractical.

Beer on Centralization in Washington

Samuel H. Beer's article "The Modernization of American Federalism" includes an interesting analysis of the reasons for the expansion of the powers of the government in Washington. He speaks of four kinds of coalitions in Congress or in the federal bureaucracy: pork-barrel, spillover, class, and technocratic coalitions.

A *pork-barrel coalition* comes into existence when members of Congress exchange votes so as to provide benefits for their respective constituencies; in effect they conspire against the federal treasury for the advantage of people back home. One wants a new canal built. Another wants a new airport located in his district. Another wants a space center located in her state. Another wants to block the closing of a military installation. Another wants a new weapon financed, knowing that the contract to produce it will go to a concern in his state. And so on. If each project were considered separately, they might all be rejected, but if they are considered as a package deal, the members of Congress can scratch each other's backs. They thus expand the role of the central government and bring about a greater centralization of power.

A *spillover coalition* comes into existence when the benefits of a function performed by the states extend across state lines. Members of Congress and others from the states providing the benefits tend to form a coalition to induce the federal government to pay the costs or to take over the activity. If they succeed, greater centralization is the result.

A *class coalition* is concerned with the distribution or redistribution of values among social classes. In Beer's analysis, the outstanding case of a class coalition in US history is associated with the New Deal that Franklin D. Roosevelt championed after his inauguration as president in 1933. New Deal legislation included, for example, a labor relations act, protecting the right of workers to organize into trade unions and requiring employers to engage in collective bargaining with the unions. Enforcement of the legislation, of course, became a federal function. The New Deal also included the introduction of an old age and survivors insurance program—a social security program—that greatly expanded the role of the federal government. And the New Deal included other measures regulating the behavior of one class for the benefit of another or taxing one class for the benefit of another. In most cases the change expanded the role of the federal government relative to that of the states.

Beer's fourth kind of coalition is a *technocratic coalition*, reflecting "the great and growing power in government of technically and professionally trained persons." Centralization breeds more centralization as members of the bureaucracy see the possibility of serving additional needs through the action of the central government, and so make proposals that lead to action by the Congress or the president expanding the sphere of federal activity (Beer 1973, 58–80). Further, given a certain degree of centralization, those who are launching new programs are likely to take the view that the necessary administrative skills are more fully available at the national level than at lower levels and that it will be easier and quicker to set up the new program on a centralized rather than a decentralized basis.

■ Methods of Decentralizing

Given a highly centralized government, those who want to decentralize have three lines of action open to them: *deconcentration, delegation*, and *devolution*. The reference here is to political decentralization. If a government has socialized economic life, bringing commercial activities under its own ownership and management, it has an additional option in this realm: it can *privatize*. I get these four categories from Rondinelli, Nellis, and Cheema (1983), and my discussion is based on their work.

Deconcentration occurs when ministries or agencies of the central government set up field units. They shift authority and some of the workload to offices located at suitable points around the country. They provide guidelines within which the local and regional offices must work, leaving these offices varying degrees of leeway in taking initiatives and implementing their programs. Examples within the United States are provided by the Social Security Administration and the Internal Revenue Service; in addition to their headquarters in or near Washington, both have field offices around the country.

Delegation occurs when the central government transfers functions to an organization that is not a part of the governmental structure. The organization may be quasi-governmental or private. It may be a public corporation, charged with certain responsibilities and allowed to act pretty much as a private corporation. It may be a mixed enterprise, with government owning some of the stock and private investors owning the rest. It may literally be a private corporation or organization with which the government contracts to perform a function that government itself might otherwise have to perform.

In the United States both Amtrak and the Tennessee Valley Authority (TVA) are examples of delegation. Amtrak runs state-owned railways, and the TVA operates dams and produces and sells hydroelectric power. In Mexico, Pemex is an example in the oil business; among other things, it operates filling stations around the country.

Devolution occurs when the central government transfers powers to governmental units at lower levels. Thus, the states of the United States devolve powers to counties and cities. France divides itself into departments (analogous to provinces), each department exercising a specified set of governmental powers. Nigeria devolves a wide range of functions to local government—for example, the construction and maintenance of public roads and bridges.

In a number of the states of the United States, the question arises of whether devolution is in effect a strategy for denying the equal protection of the laws. Thus, devolution has become an issue in the field of education in that some school districts have a richer tax base than others and are thus able to provide higher-quality education. And it may well become an issue in metropolitan areas because of the disparity in the services that the richer suburbs and the poorer inner cities are able to provide. In the case of the schools, the courts have been ordering state governments to make new arrangements, perhaps assuming greater responsibility themselves, so as to assure equal treatment.

Devolution assumes a centralized system, but some states are more or less decentralized from the beginning. Thus, the United States was born decentralized, in the sense that the thirteen separate states already existed. The Founding Fathers had no practical choice but to incorporate them as units in a federal system and to permit them to retain many of the powers they already enjoyed. Switzerland was born decentralized, too, consisting of cantons that had previously been independent.

Privatization concerns relationships between government and the economy. The subject is covered in a later chapter.

■ Why Decentralize?

The arguments for decentralization differ, depending on whether the focus is on deconcentration, delegation, or devolution.

Deconcentration may produce several sorts of gains. It is convenient for people to deal with a local or regional office rather than with a central office in the national capital. It makes people more aware of government and its activities if they see government offices and government personnel in their midst. If field offices are free to adapt to special circumstances, local and regional needs and desires are likely to be better served; and field offices provide the central government agency with sources of information about local and regional needs and desires. The hope behind deconcentration is usually that work will be handled more efficiently than if it were all concentrated in the national capital.

Delegation may also produce several sorts of gains. The practices of NASA, responsible for the American space program, offer illustrations. To a considerable extent, NASA contracts with private concerns both to get research done and to have equipment produced. It thus avoids building up the governmental bureaucracy as much as would otherwise be necessary. It presumably strengthens the free-enterprise system. For good or ill it escapes various civil service regulations, because the contractors can hire and fire in accordance with their own rules. It probably gets results faster than it would if it tried to build governmental agencies and enterprises to do all its work. And it achieves some of the same gains associated with deconcentration, in that government work is contracted out to firms in different parts of the country.

The *principal arguments for devolution* cluster around the ideas of home rule and access to or participation in government.

The idea of *home rule* is that political issues of primarily local interest should be handled at the local level. The idea can be expressed in a more general way: political issues of particular interest to regions or localities should be handled by governments at the regional and local levels.

The idea is reasonable. After all, as compared with those in the central government, local officials are likely to be better informed about local issues and to handle them on the basis of a concern for local interests. They have seen the issue develop; they know whom it affects and in what degree; they are more likely to see possible alternative solutions; and they are somewhat more apt to care about the solution adopted, for it affects their own lives. If outsiders make decisions about local issues, it is always possible that they would act in relative ignorance or on the basis of considerations that local people would regard as irrelevant.

Believers in democracy add that *participation in government* is good in itself and governmental arrangements should facilitate it. In every reasonable way people should be made responsible for their own fortune and fate. One way of acting on these principles is to emphasize local and regional self-government.

The question of home rule takes on special importance if national, ethnic, or racial differences are involved. *Minorities that are geographically concentrated generally want some degree of autonomy.* Insofar as possible they want to be ruled by their own kind. They want their community to have a status that contributes to their pride. Moreover, they usually believe that they will be better than outsiders at managing their own affairs. Just as people in colonies come to resent external imperialism, so may minorities within a country come to resent what to them is internal imperialism—rule by people from a different communal group. Given a degree of self-government or autonomy, they may accept membership in a wider system; denied it, they may become rebellious and swing toward secession and full independence.

Canada has been mentioned above as one of the most decentralized states. The principal reason for the emphasis on decentralization in Canada is that the people of the province of Quebec, French-speaking and Catholic, are determined to maintain their cultural identity. And they think that their cultural identity would be threatened by a centralized system—which would surely be dominated by the more numerous English-speaking Protestants. Those sharing the French Catholic culture do not want to blend with others in a melting pot. Instead they want to maintain a considerable degree of provincial autonomy, if not to gain complete independence. They are sufficiently determined about this that the very unity of Canada is threatened.

An argument can be made that recognition of distinctive communities within the state is dangerous—that its net effect will be to strengthen divisive forces and encourage demands for secession. "Give them an inch and they'll take a mile." In fact, this line of thought prevails within the United States. The US system is based on individuals, not on communal groups. When people are set apart for purposes of government, it is done on territorial, not communal, lines. The stress is on civil rights and equal treatment for individuals, not on status for minority communities as political entities. In societies that are more deeply divided, however, *the formal recognition of communal differences* may be unavoidable.

Still another reason for devolution is that it may make it easier to impose the *costs* of a given project exclusively on those who derive its benefits. For example, if farm land can be made more productive by developing a drainage system, a drainage district can be created. The drainage district then manages the enterprise and imposes the necessary taxes on those who derive the benefits and not on all of the taxpayers in the county or the state. Where "spillover" leads to centralization, its opposite may lead to devolution.

I noted above that devolution may in effect be a strategy for denying the equal protection of the laws. No one is likely to argue for it explicitly on this basis. The argument is more likely to be that devolution is desirable in order to enable different communities to make different choices concerning the quality of the schooling to aim at and the nature of the services that government should provide.

In Western Europe, the counterpart of the movement toward unification is an insistence on the principle of *subsidiarity*. According to this principle, policy decisions should be made, and administrative authority should be lodged, at the lowest practicable level. The reasons cited above for supporting deconcentration, delegation, and devolution also serve to recommend subsidiarity. An additional reason might be cited, too: Application of the principle of subsidiarity permits what amounts to experimentation in different jurisdictions. What works best can be discovered more quickly than otherwise, and the consequences of mistakes are more limited.

■ Partisan and Political Considerations

Every decision about centralization and decentralization necessarily has political implications. Political parties and political leaders are bound to be affected differently. Some gain and others lose. They gain or lose in terms of what usually counts in politics: their control over offices and budgets, their ability to deliver the goods to party followers and constituencies, their opportunities for personal gratification of some sort, and so on. The considerations mentioned earlier, therefore, may or may not be decisive. The controlling consideration may well be the implications of a decision for the fortunes of a political party or of a particular political leader.

■ Unitary and Federal Systems

Eighteen countries are *federal,* covering more than half the land mass of the world (Riker 1964, 1). The rest (more than 140) are *unitary.* What do these terms mean, and how does the idea of federal and unitary systems relate to the idea of centralization and decentralization?

The general practice is to distinguish unitary and federal governments in a legalistic way, even though this is a bit misleading and requires clarification.

A *unitary* government may centralize all powers in its own hands or may create governments at lower levels. If it creates governments at lower levels, it bestows powers on them, and they have only the powers they are given. The central government, having created them and endowed them with power, can abolish them or change their powers at will. At least that is the theory.

A *federal* system necessarily includes two or more levels. Considering only the two main levels, government exists at each level independently of the will of government at the other level; neither is free to destroy the other. And the formal distribution of legislative powers to the two levels cannot be altered or amended at the unilateral discretion of either one (Smiley 1972, 3–4).

Within a federal system, governments at the lower level may be unitary. Thus, the United States is federal, according to the definition given above, but the individual states are unitary, creating subordinate governments (counties, cities, and so on) and endowing them with powers.

In the United States the federal government has only those powers assigned to it in the Constitution; all other powers—residual powers—

belong to the states. Legislation adopted by the federal government within the limits of its constitutional authority supersedes any conflicting state legislation; but if the federal government adopts legislation not based on its enumerated constitutional powers, that legislation cannot constitutionally be enforced. Conflicting state legislation prevails.

Canada's rules are the opposite: the powers of the provinces are enumerated, with residual powers left to the central government; but again government at each level is denied the authority to take away any powers assigned to the other level.

Actually, the division of powers is not necessarily so sharp, for (as already indicated) *the crucial words of constitutions rarely have one and only one precise meaning*. They are open to interpretation, and political leaders and courts have choices. In the United States the struggle was between the "strict" and the "loose" constructionists, and the loose constructionists won.

The struggle is illustrated by the constitutional provisions authorizing Congress to regulate interstate commerce and stipulating that no state shall deny to any person the equal protection of the laws. These and other provisions of the Constitution can be interpreted in a number of different ways and have been interpreted so as to make the powers of the federal government much more extensive than they would otherwise be. As already noted, Congress and the courts have interpreted the interstate commerce clause to permit federal regulation of almost any activity that has an impact, or that might have an impact, across state lines. And the federal courts have interpreted the equal protection clause and various other provisions in an equally far-reaching way; among other things, federal courts have required some states to change fundamental policies—for example, policies with respect to segregation in education.

As a result of the "loose" construction of a number of provisions of the Constitution, the US system is much more centralized than anyone could reasonably have predicted a century and a half ago. In contrast, the equivalent of strict construction won out in Canada, with the result that Canada remains markedly decentralized.

Further, *central governments can take advantage of their power to tax, to borrow, and to spend*. They can offer money to governments at lower levels, provided those governments meet conditions that the central government fixes. I have already noted that the government in Washington offers grants-in-aid to the states and to cities and other governmental units within the states. It also offers block grants, which help finance any of a variety of possible programs within a designated area of activity; like grants-in-aid, block grants are given with strings attached.

Both types of grants are likely to affect the choices that states make—inducing them to undertake programs that they would not otherwise have undertaken at all, or inducing them to shape and administer programs differently than if they had proceeded on their own. The constitutional requirement is technically respected; that is, the federal government is acting only within its enumerated powers and is not depriving the states of any constitutional power left in their hands. But this formal situation is deceiving. Whatever the legal or technical situation may be, the powers of the federal government are enlarged, and those of the states and their subdivisions are reduced.

To be sure, governments at the lower levels could refuse to accept federal money and thus remain free of federal conditions, but such a refusal would be difficult. People within the state would be paying taxes to the federal government without getting full benefit in return. In fact, governments at lower levels are generally eager enough to get the money offered that they accept the conditions attached, which means that they accept a centralization of power. What has come to be called "cooperative federalism" results.

In Canada the central government also makes conditional grants to the provinces, but it is much more restrained about it than is the government in Washington.

One of the minor mysteries is why developments in the United States and Canada proceeded so differently. In the first instance, of course, the explanation is that political leaders and courts made differing judgments, but how should this fact be explained? The answer, no doubt, is in part that, since the US Civil War, Canada has faced a greater danger of breakup. Its principal minority community—the French-speaking and Catholic community—has become increasingly self-conscious and nationalistic, threatening secession. Moreover, the people of Canada are spread out sparsely over great distances, and they have never felt so threatened by a foreign enemy that they thought it imperative to extend the powers of the central government. The result is that the political parties of Canada are more decentralized than those of the United States, and they have seen to it that substantial powers are left with the provinces.

The differences between the United States and Canada suggest why the focus in this chapter is on *centralization and decentralization* and not on *unitary and federal* forms of government. The reason is that unitary and federal forms do not seem to make much difference. Unitary governments are free to create subdivisions and delegate powers to them, and often do. They can set up a governmental structure and allocate powers so as to create a system that is virtually indistinguishable from a federal system.

Formally, the unitary government that creates subdivisions can destroy them or take away powers that it has given, but that possibility is usually more theoretical than real. The government presumably created the subdivisions and granted them powers for good and enduring reasons, and it is unlikely to want to undo what it has done. Moreover, vested interests develop around any arrangement, producing resistance to change. It is difficult to imagine that the state of Illinois would abolish the municipal government of Chicago or that the government of France would abolish the municipal government of Paris.

Comparable statements apply to federal systems. Though a federal government cannot take powers from constituent units, it can in many areas reduce those units pretty much to its control. It can do this with offers of money that the units will get only if they agree to follow specified policies.

The main difference that federalism necessarily makes is that the central government cannot abolish the constituent units. An implication is that the constituent units elect their own officials, which gives them a better basis than they would otherwise have for defending and promoting regional and local interests.

■ Review

This chapter concerns the allocation of powers to the different levels of government within countries.

Centralization exists to the degree that powers are allocated to and exercised by the government in the national capital. Decentralization occurs through deconcentration (with work turned over to field offices), delegation (with work transferred to organizations outside the governmental structure), or devolution (with powers transferred to governmental units at lower levels). Decentralization, delegation, and devolution reflect the principle of subsidiarity.

Why centralize? One argument is that centralization facilitates a coherent and integrated effort to promote the fundamental and general interests of the country; and further that it promotes fairness by making it more likely that common standards will be maintained. Beer gives a different sort of analysis of the reasons for the expansion of the powers of the government in Washington. He speaks of the influence of porkbarrel, spillover, class, and technocratic coalitions.

Why decentralize? The answer varies, depending on whether the focus is on deconcentration, delegation, or devolution.

Those favoring centralization or decentralization for the reasons usually offered may also have ulterior partisan or political motives.

In a unitary system all power resides in the central government, except insofar as it chooses to create governments at lower levels and confer powers on them. A federal system necessarily includes two or more levels, with governments at each level existing independently of the will of government at any other level. In practice, the difference is rarely, if ever, as sharp as these statements suggest.

■ Reading

Anton, Thomas J. (1989) *American Federalism and Public Policy. How the System Works*. New York: McGraw-Hill.

Conlan, Timothy (1988) *New Federalism. Intergovernmental Reform from Nixon to Reagan*. Washington, D.C.: Brookings.

Dye, Thomas R. (1990) *American Federalism: Competition Among Governments*. Lexington, Mass.: Lexington Books.

Riker, William H. (1975) "Federalism," in Fred I. Greenstein and Nelson W. Polsby, eds. *The Handbook of Political Science*. Vol. 5, *Governmental Institutions and Processes*. Reading, Mass.: Addison-Wesley.

Sharpe, L. J., ed. (1979) *Decentralist Trends in Western Democracies*. Beverly Hills, Calif.: Sage.

Smith, B. C. (1985) *Decentralization. The Territorial Dimension of the State*. Boston: Allen & Unwin.

Tushnet, Mark, ed. (1990) *Comparative Constitutional Federalism: Europe and America*. New York: Greenwood.

Zimmerman, Joseph F. (1992) *Contemporary American Federalism: The Growth of National Power*. New York: Praeger.

Rights: Civil, Economic, Social, and Cultural

A right is a justified claim, a claim that must be honored if justice is to be done.

THE CHINESE QUESTION. —
COLUMBIA. — "HANDS OFF, GENTLEMEN!
AMERICA MEANS FAIR PLAY FOR ALL MEN."

For cartoonist Thomas Nast, the so-called Chinese Question was
based on claims of racial superiority. Does Nast consider this
claim justifiable?

Earlier chapters deal with rights of political participation. This one focuses on civil rights and on economic, social, and cultural rights, which are spelled out in the international covenants on human rights. Civil rights include the right to freedom of expression and religion, to personal security and due process of law, and to freedom of movement and residence. Economic, social, and cultural rights include the rights to education, to work, to health care, and to social security. Neither covenant mentions a right to property, but the question of whether such a right exists is unavoidable.

In chapter 2 I note the danger that democracy may lead to a "tyranny of the majority," and I say that safeguards against this possibility are sought in three ways: through institutional arrangements such as the separation of powers and checks and balances; through a system of rights that government is bound to respect and promote; and through the development of appropriate social and political attitudes. Here the focus is on the second of these ways of buttressing democracy and keeping it within desirable limits.

Before discussing any particular rights, we should focus on the idea of rights itself. What do we mean by a *right*, and where do rights come from? Are rights to be regarded as absolute? That is, must each right be respected fully and unconditionally, regardless of circumstances?

■ The Meaning and Origin of Rights

The reference here is to *moral* rights, not to rights established by law. And it is to rights of a general sort—to rights that are shared by all—and not to the special rights of particular persons.

The term *right* refers to an entitlement, a justified claim, a claim that must be honored if justice is to be done. It is "a power which a creature ought to possess, either because its exercise by him is itself good or else because it is a means to what is good, and in the exercise of which all rational beings ought to protect him" (Plamenatz 1938, 82).

The most widely accepted theory about the origin of rights is that they are in some sense "natural." John Locke (d. 1704) was the chief early expositor of this view. People are born, he said, "with a title to perfect freedom, and an uncontrolled enjoyment of all the rights and privileges of the law of nature" (Locke [1690] 1956, ch. 7, para. 87). People have natural liberties. Some passages in Locke's writing give the impression that natural law and natural rights or liberties stem from the *state of nature*—that is, from the circumstances that existed prior to the formation of governmental and other institutions. Other passages give the impression that he identified natural law and natural rights with human nature.

Given the first of these views, the idea is that people retain all those natural rights or liberties that they have not foresworn in a social contract—an agreement to create government. Given the second, people have those rights that their own biological and psychological nature makes necessary. This can easily be construed to mean that they have those rights that are necessary to the full development of their talents—to full self-actualization or self-realization. Thus, if work is necessary to self-realization, people have a right to work.

Locke had to acknowledge, of course, that no book of nature exists in which natural rights are recorded. To determine what they are, he said, one needs to consult reason and think in terms of common equity. He did not give clear guidance on the question of what to do if the reasoning of different people leads to different conclusions.

The idea of natural rights may be oriented to the future. Thus, according to David G. Ritchie the "would-be reformer" decides what rights an ideal society ought to recognize and then calls them natural rights (Ritchie 1916, 80–81).

Thomas Jefferson was influenced by conceptions of natural rights in writing the Declaration of Independence. In it he said that it is "self-evident" that all "men" (Jefferson's term) are created equal. In other words, it is self-evident that all men have a right to equal treatment. Reason presumably tells us what is self-evident. Jefferson also implicitly endorsed another theory when he said that men are "endowed by their Creator" with certain rights, for he thus attributed rights to a divine source.

The idea that reason reveals rights can be expressed in a different and modified form. The basic proposition is that moral rights have an entirely human source, existing because human beings decide that they ought to exist. They rest on *interests*—on the stake that people have in conditions, rules, and practices relating to *values*. Some interests are never anything other than interests, but others are separated out and are classified as rights. A moral right can be conceived as an interest that has a strong presumption in its favor—that ought to be respected in the absence of compelling argument to the contrary.

The process of selecting the interests that are to be classified as rights necessarily involves choice and judgment, and so the outcome is uncertain. But those doing it have tended to accept four guiding rules: that to be eligible for classification as a right, the interest should be of such a nature as to give rise to a moral claim; that it should be universal (shared by everyone); that it should be fundamentally important; and that it should be open to effective promotion or achievement. Put conversely, an interest should not be classified as a right—at least not as a human right—if it does not provide a basis for a moral claim, if it relates only to one person or set of persons, if it is trivial, or if it is impossible to promote effectively or to achieve in a future for which it is reasonable to hope.

According to this theory, any person or any decision-making agency can decide that an interest should be a human right. If only one or a few persons or agencies make such a judgment, it is not of much moment, but the judgment takes on more importance the more widely it is endorsed. And a surprising amount of consensus exists around the world as to what should count as a human right. That consensus is indicated, among other ways, by the fact that in 1948 the General Assembly of the United Nations adopted a Universal Declaration of Human Rights and by the fact that in 1966 it expanded on them and put them into the two covenants mentioned above. More than half of the states of the world have ratified the covenants.

Those who believe (with me) that rights have an entirely human source, in the way just described, tend to dismiss claims about the natural or divine source of rights as efforts to get undeserved authority for what in fact are personal judgments.

Issues arise not only over the question of what moral rights people should be said to have but also over the question of which of them should be incorporated in the law and thus made legal or juridical or constitutional rights. The United States led the way in including civil rights in its Constitution through the first ten amendments, called the Bill of Rights. Other countries have led the way in developing the idea of economic, social, and cultural rights and incorporating them into law. And a so-called third generation of rights is developing, including, for example, rights relating to the environment.

■ Are Rights Absolute?

According to one view, nothing should be called a "right" unless it can be honored here and now, unconditionally. The argument is that a distinction between *rights* and *ideals* needs to be maintained, lest the notion of rights be debased.

The very statement of the argument suggests that it has merit. But in fact most people do not find it persuasive, and for fairly obvious reasons.

In the first place, conflicts between rights are always arising, making it impossible to honor all of them simultaneously. The right of one person to freedom of expression, for example, may conflict with the right of another person to freedom from slander. The right of one person to swing his fist may conflict with the right of another to keep her nose intact. When rights conflict, they cannot be equally and fully honored. One overrides the other, or some kind of an adjustment is made. In protecting the rights of one person, government must give due consideration to the rights of others who may be affected.

US courts tend to couch this point in different language, asking whether a significant or compelling public interest justifies the abatement of a right. But, like as not, the significant or compelling interest is an interest in protecting people in the exercise of a conflicting right. More on this below.

In the second place, some declarations of rights have about them the aura of manifestos naming goals that governments and peoples should seek to achieve. Even the right to a fair trial is not one that all governments are in a position to assure here and now. Respect for the right may depend on training lawyers and judges and developing appropriate institutions and traditions. This is all the more true of some of the rights in the economic, social, and cultural category—the right to education, for example. Such rights are sometimes called "program rights," rights whose implementation depends on a program of action conducted over a number of years.

The Covenant on Economic, Social, and Cultural Rights recognizes this problem in specifying that the obligation of the ratifying governments is to "take steps . . . with a view to achieving progressively the full realization" of the rights named. It would no doubt be unwise to name something as a right if there were no conceivable way of achieving it in a future for which it is reasonable to hope, but political leaders and others have not hesitated to call something a "right" if they think they know a program of action that might well lead to its realization. Appeals and demands for action are likely to be strengthened if the value in question is called not simply an "interest" but a "right."

■ Freedom of Expression

The Arguments for It

Freedom of expression is among the most important of the civil rights. The statement in the first amendment of the US Constitution is that "Congress shall make no law . . . abridging the freedom of speech or of the press." The corresponding statement in the Covenant on Civil and Political Rights is that:

> Everyone shall have the right to freedom of expression; this right shall include freedom to seek, receive, and impart information and ideas of all kinds, regardless of frontiers, either orally, in writing or in print, in the form of art, or through any other media of his choice.

At first look, it is not at all clear why any government should grant the right to freedom of expression. Somebody is bound to use her freedom in an effort to thwart the government's intentions, and somebody is bound to use it, deliberately or not, to propagate error and to lead people in what government regards as an undesirable and perhaps antisocial direction. The temptation is necessarily strong for those in public office to restrict freedom of expression, whether for the crass purpose of avoiding criticism and holding on to power or for the more noble purpose of defending and upholding what they regard as the good and the right.

Nevertheless, freedom of expression is always included among the human rights and among the central principles of the democratic creed. Really, anyone who believes in democracy must believe in freedom of expression. The case is axiomatic. If government is to be based on the desires or preferences of the people, then the people must be free to develop and shape them. A marketplace of ideas must be kept open so that arguments and criticisms can be exchanged. It would be a mockery to say that government should be "by the people" and then to allow government to control communications in an effort to induce people to think only what it approves.

On this basis, people are said to have a "right to know." Government has no right to keep its activities and decisions secret. The proposition is that in connection with all matters that are legitimately of public concern, people must have access to relevant information and argument and must be free to advance and defend whatever point of view they wish.

These propositions lead to difficult questions. Freedom of expression may sometimes do harm, forcing a choice between accepting the harm or limiting the freedom. Later I will discuss the prevailing view that in some circumstances some limitations are justifiable. Here, however, I want to emphasize the rule and not the exceptions to it; and the rule—as stated by the Supreme Court of the United States—is that debate on public matters should be uninhibited, robust, and wide open.

Note that the above argument is of the if/then variety: if you believe in government "by the people," you should believe in freedom of expression. Other arguments of the same type can be advanced—arguments that if you believe in certain values, you should also believe in freedom of expression.

One such value is that it is important to know the truth. The statement would be that if you believe that it is important to know the truth, you should believe in freedom of expression. Of course, some believe that they already know the truth, and such persons may decide that, since the truth is already known, further debate should not be permitted. This is the position that authoritarians usually take. The thought is presented in a classic way by a former justice of the Supreme Court, Oliver Wendell Holmes:

> Persecution for the expression of opinion seems to me perfectly logical. If you have no doubt of your premises or your power and want a certain result with all your heart, you naturally express your wishes in law and sweep away all opposition. . . .
>
> But when men have realized that time has upset many fighting faiths, they may come to believe even more than they believe the very foundations of their own conduct that the ultimate good desired is better reached by free

trade in ideas—that the best test of the truth is the power of the thought to get itself accepted in the competition of the market . . . That at any rate is the theory of our constitution *(Abrams* v. *U.S. 1919.* 250 U.S. 616).

There is no guarantee, of course, that freedom of expression will in fact lead to the truth. What later is thought of as error sometimes prevails for a surprisingly long time, despite freedom of expression. Think, for example, of the long period when people all over the world thought it justifiable to deny women the vote or when the dominant view in some US states was that white supremacy should be maintained. But though freedom of expression offers no guarantees, the chance that truth will prevail is surely greater with freedom of expression than without it.

Justice is another value on which the argument for free speech may rest: if you believe in justice you ought to believe in free speech. After all, people disagree both about what constitutes justice and about how best to promote it. If speech is limited, the implication is that efforts to develop a better conception of justice or to find the best way to promote it are limited. Moreover, government is more likely to get away with the unjust treatment of particular persons or groups if they and their friends are denied the freedom to shout out their complaints. Those who are politically weak are especially likely to suffer.

The liberal ideal of the autonomous, rational person is another value that calls for freedom of expression. Autonomous, rational persons must be free to seek ideas and knowledge from every possible source. They are not to be protected from false beliefs or even from influences that might lead them to commit harmful acts, for such protection is incompatible with autonomy. There is to be no paternalism—no condescending claim that "father (government) knows best." Freedom to make good and justifiable choices must include freedom to make mistakes. And if people are to be free to seek knowledge and ideas from every possible source, they must also be free to serve as a source for others—free to disseminate knowledge, information, and argument without restraint.

Finally, anyone who accepts equal treatment as a value should believe in freedom of expression. At least, if any person has such freedom, the rule of equal treatment requires that all should have it in the absence of good reason to the contrary. The burden of the argument is placed on those who, though granting free speech to some, would deny it to others.

This last point suggests a negative argument for freedom of expression: that no valid and reliable way exists for selecting a censor. Too much danger exists of getting someone (or some set of persons) who will decide on the basis of unacceptable criteria or pursue ulterior motives. And if no prospective censor is trustworthy, then freedom of expression for all is the obvious residual choice.

Accepted Restrictions on Free Expression

As noted earlier, rights are not absolute. That is, they are not entitled to unconditional respect in all circumstances. Rather, a right is an interest that has a strong presumption in its favor—that ought to be respected in the absence of compelling argument to the contrary. To agree that an interest is a right is to put the burden of the argument on anyone who thinks that the right should be overridden or abated. He must demonstrate that the right in question conflicts with some other right or interest and that the other right or interest is more urgent.

The above holds with respect to the right to freedom of expression. It is not absolute. In a variety of ways an exercise of the right to freedom of expression by one person may infringe the rights of other persons, or may be incompatible with obligations that go with one's position, or may be contrary to some compelling public interest. Thus, by general consent certain restrictions are accepted as necessary and as compatible with democracy. The need for restrictions may stem either from related circumstances or from the nature of the message.

Problems arising from related circumstances are easily illustrated. Suppose that a stranger claims the right to enter your living room and exercise his right to free speech there. Suppose that a group tries to parade down the main street of a city during the rush hour to publicize its program. Suppose that a general in the armed forces, acting in his official capacity and wearing his uniform, makes a speech over TV attacking policies being pursued by the president. Suppose that before a mob, when passions are running high, an agitator makes a speech that incites a riot.

It is not to be assumed that the right to freedom of expression covers such actions. Your right to privacy in your home obviously takes precedence over the right of the stranger to free speech; he can exercise his right elsewhere. The group wanting to hold a parade is of course justified in claiming that the parade is a form of expression, which ought to be free. But the holding of a parade on a busy street interferes with others who also have a right to use the street. So a permit is required, and those authorized to give the permit must be sensitive to rights and interests that will be adversely affected. They may judge it more important to maintain the normal flow of traffic than to permit a parade on that particular street at the particular time desired.

The principle at stake here is also at stake in connection with pro-life demonstrations at abortion clinics, which the demonstrators regard as an exercise of free speech. But in exercising the right, should demonstrators be free to congregate around the doors of an abortion clinic in such a way as to block access to it? Should they be free to harass those who work in the building when they try to enter or leave? Should they be free to harass clients? Should they be free to use bull horns and make noise in other ways that disturb the normal operation of the clinic? Those facing these kinds of questions can differ some in their responses, but the general stand of the Supreme Court is that the government has a significant interest in protecting people in the exercise of their legitimate rights, including the right to operate an abortion clinic and the right to enter and leave the premises of the clinic. In a 1994 case, for example, the court approved an injunction issued by a lower court requiring demonstrators to stay outside of a thirty-six foot buffer zone around the entrances to a building where abortions were performed. To demonstrators, this violated their rights of free speech.

The second illustration mentioned above relates to a general who wants to criticize his commander in chief, the president. If he wants to do this, he should do it as a civilian, not in his official capacity as a general; and he probably should take a leave from active duty or retire. The obligation of the president to uphold the right of freedom of speech does not extend to the toleration of efforts by his subordinates to influence public opinion against him.

The agitator poses a difficult problem. On the one hand, he has the right to speak, and democratic government should protect the right if at all possible, perhaps adding to the number of police in the area to deter the threatened riot. On the other hand, if government has no reasonable means of deterring the riot, most observers would say that its obligation to protect life and property takes precedence, justifying it in preventing the agitator from making his speech.

Britain has long had a rule that when a matter is before the courts, freedom of expression concerning that matter should be limited, lest public discussion prejudice judicial proceedings and lead to injustice. Thus, newspapers were restricted in what they could report. But when a case involving this rule was appealed to the European Court of Human Rights, it held that the danger that injustice would be caused was not great enough to justify the restriction.

Problems arising from the nature of the message are also easily illustrated. Suppose that a newspaper publishes an article saying that Jones is a liar and a thief. Suppose that in time of war a radio station broadcasts military secrets to the enemy. Suppose that an agitator wants to prevent a black family from moving into his neighborhood and distributes leaflets saying that blacks are subhuman and degenerate. Suppose that a candidate for public office invokes racial or religious prejudice in his appeal for votes.

Again, it is not to be assumed that the right to freedom of expression protects such actions. In the case of the accusation that Jones is a liar and a thief, much depends on the circumstances. As the courts have interpreted the right to freedom of speech, the media have wide latitude in making statements about public figures—for example, about those holding public office or running for election. Deliberate and malicious lies presumably give basis for a libel suit, but the media are not required to make sure that everything they report about a public figure is true. They must, however, be much more solicitous of the reputations of private persons. With respect to them the right to freedom of expression does not extend to the use of "fighting words"—words that threaten to provoke a breach of the peace.

In time of war a government has a right to prohibit actions that aid the enemy. Circumstances combine with the nature of the message to lead to this conclusion. The public interest in the successful prosecution of the war is more urgent than the private right to disseminate information freely.

Whether the agitator should be prevented from distributing his racist leaflets is a question on which believers in freedom of expression disagree. The dominant view in the United States is that, deplorable as the distribution of such leaflets is, it ought to be permitted—that the remedy is to try to counteract the harm by somehow disseminating a different and a sounder message.

But an argument can be made that government should prevent the distribution of the leaflets. The most general form of the argument is that it is permissible to restrict freedom of expression to avert serious threat to a compelling public interest. More specifically, the argument goes, it is a compelling public interest to combat racism. And the argument is stronger if the distribution of the leaflets threatens to lead to a breach of the peace. Furthermore, distribution of the leaflets tends to undermine the right of persons to choose their place of residence.

Similarly, reasonable persons disagree on rules pertaining to elections. Should candidates be left free to appeal to racial or religious prejudice? In the United States, no law prevents it, but a number of other democratic countries make such appeals illegal.

Arguments justifying restrictions on freedom of expression prevail to a limited extent at the international level. Thus, the Covenant on Civil and Political Rights calls for the prohibition of "propaganda for war" and of "any advocacy of national, racial, or religious hatred that constitutes incitement to discrimination, hostility, or violence."

Suppose that a university schedules a speech by a scholar who is not an agitator and who does not advocate racism or deliberately appeal to prejudice. But his research suggests inferiority on the part of blacks, and it is known that he will report on that research. Antiracists let it be known that they are against holding the meeting at all, and when it begins, they seek to disrupt it.

The dominant view in the United States about the issue they raise has already been indicated: to permit a "heckler's veto" denies freedom of expression. Government should exercise its police power, arresting hecklers if need be. Let the hecklers hold a meeting of their own where they can say what they please.

One of the most difficult questions concerning freedom of expression is whether it should be extended to its own enemies. This is an aspect of the question, raised in chapter 2, of whether democracy should be permitted to vote its own destruction. Some say yes. Their view with respect to freedom of expression is that it is inconsistent to deny freedom in order to preserve it and that if it needs defending, the defense should be based on education and open argument, not on repression. Further, their view is that the chance of combating the enemies of freedom effectively is greater if what they are saying is publicly known.

Others, however, put paramount emphasis on keeping the future open and thus on preventing those who think they command some final Truth from fastening their grip on society. They may concede freedom to its enemies as long as the threat is remote, but would resort to repression, if need be, rather than allow enemies of freedom to get control over government. They argue that the preservation of human rights in the long run justifies some restriction of them in the short run. Those who take this second position obviously face a problem in assessing the situation so as not to deny freedom prematurely or unnecessarily.

The international Covenant on Civil and Political Rights permits the adoption of the second position. It says that nothing in it shall be interpreted to imply a right to engage in activities aimed at the destruction of any of the rights and freedoms set forth. The Covenant also permits the suspension of various rights, including the right to freedom of expression, "in time of public emergency which threatens the life of the nation." Each government makes the initial judgment whether the suspension of the right to freedom of expression (and perhaps of other rights) is justified, but in principle its judgment is then subject to international review.

When Is Expression Free?

The prevailing view is that freedom is what exists in the absence of legal restraint. We enjoy the right to freedom of expression, therefore, when government does not impose censorship or any other kind of restriction. This view rests on the assumption that, in the absence of governmental control, control will be dispersed—that it will be divided among a number of persons. If the absence of governmental control meant that control came to rest in the hands of one private person, or in the hands of a few, those persons would enjoy freedom, but the freedom of others would be in question.

Some deride this view, claiming that, even if control is dispersed, it is silly to contend that a penniless, unemployed person and the owner of a newspaper both enjoy the right to freedom of expression, and that it is also silly to say that an illiterate person enjoys the right along with those who have college educations. They say that, realistically, freedom can be said to exist only when there is a capacity and an opportunity to exercise it—only when choice of some kind is possible.

Approximately the same argument can take a different form: that we should be concerned not simply with freedom but with its worth to individuals; and that if freedom is defined simply as the absence of legal restraint, it will be worth a great deal to some (for example, the owner of a newspaper) and practically nothing to others (for example, the illiterate and the poor).

The argument that freedom calls for something more than simply the absence of external restraint is made stronger by trends toward the centralization of control in the hands of fewer and fewer persons. So far as newspapers are concerned, at least, it is clear that (in the United States) their number has tended to decrease, and those that remain have tended to be joined in chains under common ownership. Anyone can thus argue that freedom of expression is an illusion even in the absence of governmental censorship—that what passes as freedom of expression is freedom for the few, with no significance for the many.

Several points are possible in rebuttal. One is that, regardless of how many persons control the media, the real question is how responsible they are—that is, how responsive they are to the needs of people in a democratic society, how fair, and how objective. Another is that, even if the press is in relatively few hands, their control over the flow of information is incomplete, for radio and TV stations also operate, and cable TV is making an increasing number of channels available.

Further, knowledge and information are disseminated in a number of additional ways, permitting anyone who knows how to go about it to learn almost anything that anyone else knows. Even a penniless person may manage to write a book and get it published, and even an illiterate person may gain knowledge by listening to the radio and watching TV. In some eyes the problem is not that information and knowledge are too scarce but rather that they are too abundant, creating problems of selection for everyone.

Some of the smaller countries of the Third World have special problems with respect to the dispersal of control. The number of newspapers and radio and TV stations that it is economically feasible for these countries to have is not large, and professional standards are not always high. It is then not surprising if governmental leaders say that, since more or less concentrated control is inevitable, it had better be in their own hands. Of course, ulterior motives may influence such views, for when the media are in the hands of the government, the government has the opportunity to spare itself from criticism and to reinforce its hold on power.

Freedom of Expression across International Boundary Lines?

As noted earlier, the Covenant on Civil and Political Rights provides for freedom "to seek, receive, and impart information and ideas of all kinds, regardless of frontiers." In other words, it provides for what has come to be called "free flow" across international boundaries.

But especially from the point of view of the leaders of many of the smaller and poorer countries, including most Third World countries, *free flow* brings problems. The argument is that free flow gives undue control to the richer countries, for they are technologically advanced and have most of the skilled personnel. They send out the foreign correspondents and manage the major news agencies. They provide movies and TV programs. Their magazines outsell those published elsewhere unless differences of language intervene. Thus, the complaint is that the richer countries select what the world learns about the poorer countries and what the poorer countries learn about the world and about each other.

Further, richer countries are in an especially good position to take advantage of the satellites that can broadcast programs directly into Third World homes without any use of ground distribution networks and thus without giving the local governments an easy means of controlling what their people receive.

It goes without saying that an unbalanced flow has cultural consequences. What the richer countries select and provide reflects their values and the style of life associated with them and tends to undermine the traditional cultures of the countries served. These latter countries speak of being "Coca-Colonized."

If they choose, governments in the more advanced and richer countries can accentuate tendencies that would exist in any event. They can make radio broadcasts across international boundaries and disseminate TV programs from satellites for the deliberate purpose of undermining the government of a foreign country or otherwise influencing the course of events there. And, as both the United States and the former Soviet Union have done in a number of countries, they can use money both legally and illegally to influence and control what is published or broadcast through the local media.

The upshot is a demand for a "new world information order," advanced mainly by Third World countries (supported through the 1980s by the communist countries). Along with this demand comes a claim that a "right to communicate" exists. The idea of a right to communicate is vague, but it focuses on the question of "balance." What is sought is a two-way flow.

Actually, of course, no one has been preventing the dissatisfied countries from initiating a flow and creating balance, any more than anyone prevents poor and uneducated persons within advanced countries from speaking out. The lack of balance results not from a deliberate decision but from the historical circumstance that educational and technological development has taken place more fully in some countries than in others.

Third World countries have found it easier to interfere with communications emanating from the advanced countries than to develop their own capacities. And they interfere despite the requirements of the Covenant on Civil and Political Rights. Some of them impose censorship on foreign correspondents, and a number refuse to receive such correspondents at all. A few seek to jam radio and TV broadcasts directed to their people. A few exclude foreign periodicals or censor them.

No simple solution exists to the problem of differential access to the mass media and channels of communication. According to the view that prevails in the democratic West, it is important to maintain and, if possible, to increase *diversity*—that is, to keep control over the collection and dissemination of news and information divided among as many people as possible and thus to keep the market open and free. The corollary is that those involved must be responsible—that is, responsive to such values as truth and fairness.

In the longer run, solutions can be sought through education and training—especially the education and training of those who hope to be involved in activities having to do with communications; and special assistance can be given to Third World countries not only to educate and train people but also to develop their technical capacities.

But differential access is bound to endure. It does not take much calculating to show that, where masses of people are involved, it is totally impracticable to assure them equal space in newspapers or equal time on radio or TV. And one has the sneaking suspicion that not many have much to say that is new and different, anyway.

In the above, I focus on Third World attitudes toward freedom of communication across international boundary lines. I should acknowledge, however, that the problem is more widespread. For example, some countries (including Canada and France) impose restrictions on their own TV stations, requiring that a specified proportion of the programs be domestic in origin. They do not want to be the victims of what they regard as the cultural imperialism of the United States.

■ Freedom of Religion

Democracies routinely grant freedom of religion, and most nondemocratic states do as well. The relevant statement in the US Constitution is that "Congress shall make no law respecting an establishment of religion, or prohibiting the free exercise thereof." The statement in the Covenant on Civil and Political Rights is:

> Everyone shall have the right to freedom of thought, conscience and religion. This right shall include freedom to have or to adopt a religion or belief of his choice, and freedom, either individually or in community with others and in public or private, to manifest his religion or belief in worship, observance, practice and teaching.

These statements suggest two kinds of issues—those relating to the *establishment* of a religion and those relating to the *free exercise* of religion. Precisely what the ban on *establishment* means is itself a question, but surely it prohibits naming one religion as the official state religion, and surely it prohibits singling out any one church and financing it with tax funds.

The Covenant on Civil and Political Rights does not explicitly repeat the Constitution's ban on the establishment of religion, but it is arguable that both the Covenant and the United Nations Charter itself impose the ban implicitly. The argument is that in providing for freedom of belief the Covenant is providing for freedom from taxes that go to support a state religion, and that in prohibiting distinction as to religion the Charter is prohibiting the rule that only those who share the official religion are eligible to be head of the state or to hold certain other offices.

The fact is, however, that scarcely anyone takes the words of the Covenant and Charter to mean what they seem to say. Many countries, both democratic and other, maintain established religions. Britain and the Scandinavian countries do. So do many Catholic countries and almost all of the countries that are predominantly Muslim. The arrangement sometimes becomes an issue, but choice in the matter tends to be regarded as free, not controlled by international agreements relating to human rights.

As to the *free exercise* of religion, the problems differ in different countries and regions. In the United States they fall into several categories. First are cases arising when a person claims that the performance of some obligation to the state is incompatible with her religion. Conscientious objectors provide the most notable illustration, and the law is adjusted for them, providing for exemption from compulsory military service on grounds of "religion or belief." No one is entitled to pick and choose among the wars in which he might serve, but those whose religion or belief bars participation in any war are permitted to perform some other public service instead of being compelled to serve in the armed forces. Similarly, those whose religion bars service on a jury or saluting the flag are excused.

Second are cases of a conflict between religion and eligibility for some legal right or benefit. Thus, a person cannot be barred from public office because she is unwilling to take an oath that expresses a belief in God, nor can a person be barred from receiving unemployment insurance benefits because his religion prevents him from working on Saturdays.

Third are cases where the right of the person to freedom of religion conflicts with the right of the state to protect and promote public health, safety, and morals. The states of the United States ban polygamy, regardless of any claim that it is an aspect of the free exercise of religion. A court may order that a child be vaccinated or receive a blood transfusion despite the claim of parents that this conflicts with the religion in which the child is being reared. After all, the child too has rights.

Fourth are various cases relating to education. Parents are free, for religious or other reasons, to send their children to private schools, provided these schools maintain standards prescribed by law. And the Old Order Amish of Wisconsin won the right to take their children out of school entirely once they graduate from the eighth grade, regardless of a state law requiring attendance until the sixteenth birthday. In another notable case a private school claimed that the free exercise of religion entitled it to follow a whites-only admissions policy without losing tax-exempt status, but the courts said that the interest of the state in promoting racial integration was compelling enough to justify the withdrawal of tax exemption from any private school engaging in discrimination.

Issues have been arising, too, concerning "secular humanism"—an outlook deriving moral and other values from human rather than from divine sources. Secular humanists are likely to hold, for example, that human reason and choice are the sources of moral values. One argument in response is that secular humanism should itself count as a religion, and that in teaching it in the public schools the state is establishing a religion. The opposite argument is that if the schools adjust their teaching to the religion of the students (or their parents), it is establishing *their* religion. A related argument makes no use of the concept "secular humanism" but holds that the teaching of certain ideas undermines religious beliefs that parents want upheld and therefore violates their right to the "free exercise" of religion.

Perhaps the most notable feature of freedom of religion in the countries of western Europe concerns "parents' rights"—the right of parents to bring their children up in accordance with their own faith or philosophy. Parents have insisted on the right mainly in connection with the schools, with the result that a number of the European countries (and also the provinces of Canada) operate two or more school systems. In each sizable community, parents have the choice of sending their children to a Catholic, a Protestant, or a neutral public school; and the general practice is to give tax support to these schools in proportion to their enrollment.

Some of the governments of Western Europe (that of Germany, for example) officially recognize certain churches, permit these churches to fix the rate at which their members are to contribute support, and then collect the money on behalf of the church. Government may also treat the clergy in recognized churches as if they were civil servants, paying the cost of their training and putting them on the public payroll.

In some countries the people are so overwhelmingly of one religion that it alone is taught in the schools. This is true in some Catholic countries. The concordat between Colombia and the Vatican, for example, stipulates that "the education provided in public educational institutions at all levels shall be organized and directed in conformity with the Catholic religion." Church authorities may designate the texts to be used in religious instruction and may force the removal of teachers who fail to conform to Catholic doctrine. A similar arrangement exists between Spain and the Vatican. Whether such arrangements are compatible with the idea of the freedom of religion is questionable.

Similar arrangements exist in most of the Islamic countries. One of the rules of Islam is that there is no right of apostasy: once a Muslim, always a Muslim. Most of the Islamic countries require that the head of the state shall be a Muslim, and usually they also specify the sect to which he must belong—Sunni or Shia. And a number of them have a comparable requirement for members of the cabinet and perhaps for members of the parliament. The theocracy that rules Iran has gone much farther, persecuting those adhering to minority religions, especially the Baha'is. It has executed and imprisoned large numbers of Baha'is and so maltreated others that they have been rendered homeless or fled the country.

There was a time in Europe when questions about freedom of religion dominated the domestic and international politics of the day, but after centuries of struggle the temporal authorities emerged clearly victorious, and religion is no longer the burning issue it once was. The principle of freedom of religion is rarely challenged. Issues arise, but they concern the specific meaning or application of the principle and not the acceptability of the principle itself. In recent times, questions about the place of religion in public life have been in the foreground mainly in a few Islamic countries—Iran, Pakistan, and Algeria, for example.

■ Security of the Person and Due Process _____

"Every human being," according to the international Covenant on Civil and Political Rights, "has the inherent *right to life*. This right shall be protected by law. No one shall be arbitrarily deprived of his life."

Great controversy attends this rule, but it is not over the general principle asserted. The controversy concerns abortion and focuses on the question of when life begins. This formulation prejudices the issue, for in the case of a living cell, life has obviously begun. The neutral way to put the question is to ask whether, or at what point, a zygote, embryo, or fetus becomes a human being, a person.

The statement that no one is to be *arbitrarily* deprived of life means that no one is to be deprived of it without good reason. The rule does not necessarily exclude capital punishment, which many consider reasonable, nor does it prevent the killing of enemy soldiers in war.

The Covenant goes on to set forth a number of other rights having to do with the security and integrity of the person. No one is to be arrested or detained arbitrarily. Those arrested are entitled to be informed of the reasons and are entitled to a fair trial within a reasonable time. Torture and inhuman or degrading treatment are prohibited. So is slavery. No ex post facto laws are to be passed—that is, no action is to be made a crime retroactively. Nor is anyone to be punished on the basis of a bill of attainder—that is, an action of a legislature that declares a specific person guilty of a crime. Government is to extend equal and nondiscriminatory treatment to everyone.

The Constitution of the United States prohibits *unreasonable searches and seizures*. The corresponding provision of the Covenant is that individuals are not to be subjected to arbitrary or unlawful interference with their *privacy, family, home, or correspondence*. As this provision attests, the idea of a right to privacy has been developing in recent decades, with disputes still occurring over what it includes.

Democracy calls for the *rule of law*. No one is above the law. Everyone is expected to act in accordance with the law, and public officials have a duty not only to obey the law themselves but to enforce it on others. Allegations about President Clinton's behavior before he became president raise the question of whether the courts should hear a civil suit against him during his term of office, but no one claims that he is above the law. And quite apart from possible proceedings in a civil or criminal court, many government officials, including the president, are liable to removal from office through impeachment proceedings.

■ Rights of Movement and Residence

The Covenant on Civil and Political Rights declares that everyone lawfully within the territory of a state has *freedom of movement* and *freedom to choose his or her residence*. South Africa's policies of apartheid violated these requirements, but the legislation involved has been repealed. The Covenant also declares that all persons have the *right to leave any country*, including their own.

Although providing for freedom of movement and residence, the Covenant says nothing about a *right to own property*. I will deal with this question more in a moment but note here that restrictions on the right may have implications for the choice of a place of residence. Finland, for example, is under a treaty obligation to concede to the inhabitants of the Aaland Islands the right to prevent outsiders from coming in and buying property there. The inhabitants are Swedish speaking, and the object is to safeguard them from the dangers to their language and culture that an influx of Finnish-speaking people would entail. For a similar reason the United States limits the right of non-Samoans to purchase land in American Samoa. In neither case is there an explicit and direct restriction on rights of residence, but the restrictions on the right to buy property are intended to deter people from moving in. You can argue the question of whether such restrictions are justified. Which right or interest should have priority—that of the Swedish-speaking Finns and the Samoans to preserve their language and culture or that of outsiders to come in and buy property?

Democratic governments generally respect the right of persons to leave the country. Communist countries have been the principal violators of the right. The Berlin Wall symbolized their stand, and the tearing down of the wall in 1989 symbolized the termination of their policy. The Soviet Union, which long either barred the emigration of Jews or made it difficult, reversed the policy prior to its breakup. However, along with a few other countries, it continued to restrict the right of its citizens to take up residence in a few of its cities—most notably, Moscow. The scarcity of housing was the principal alleged justification. The general question is whether the right of people to choose their place of residence should prevail over the governmental interest in reducing the problems that follow from overcrowding in urban areas.

Whether democratic or authoritarian, governments generally allow citizens who have left the country to reenter. Governments are, however, free to bar aliens. No one has a right to immigrate.

■ Economic, Social, and Cultural Rights _____

Economic, social, and cultural rights include the rights to education, to work, to health care, to an adequate standard of living, and to social security.

Rights in this category differ from civil and political rights. For the most part, civil and political rights are rights of a negative sort. They indicate what government shall not do. It shall not deny free speech. It shall not deny adult citizens the right to vote. It shall not kill or imprison arbitrarily, and so on. Theoretically, such rights can be enforced by a court order: an aggrieved person can go into court and get an order requiring the government not to do, or to cease doing, whatever is prohibited.

Economic, social, and cultural rights are positive. Far from telling government what it shall not do, they call for action by the government. Government shall provide for education. It shall honor the right to work. It shall in some way assure health care to all, promote adequate standards of living, and set up a social security system. Rights in this category may or may not be susceptible to enforcement by a court order. As noted earlier, they may well call for a program of action on the part of government—a program that may take a number of years to implement.

Most rights are vague, calling for interpretation, and this is especially true of economic, social, and cultural rights. Does the right to education, for example, begin with nursery school and end with the conferral of a Ph.D.? The Covenant gives some guidance concerning the answer but leaves governments with considerable leeway. Primary education (its duration unspecified) is to be compulsory and free. Secondary education is to be "generally available," and higher education is to be "equally accessible to all." Education at the two upper levels is to be made progressively free, a requirement that is causing problems in a period of inflation when tuition rates need to be raised. Needless to say, it also causes problems in developing countries that are short of everything an educational system calls for.

Where a right to work is recognized, what must government do to honor it? The Covenant specifies that the measures taken must include technical and vocational guidance and training programs and policies aimed at full employment. It does not explicitly impose on governments an obligation to provide jobs to those who would otherwise be unemployed.

Along with the right to work go related rights: to just and favorable conditions of work and to form and join trade unions.

The right to health care is also vague. The specific statement in the Covenant is that everyone has the right "to the enjoyment of the highest attainable standard of physical and mental health." And the Covenant goes on to say that government shall take steps necessary for the reduction of infant mortality, improvement in environmental and industrial hygiene, the prevention and control of disease, and the creation of conditions assuring medical services for the sick. How resources are to be mobilized for these purposes is not specified, nor is there clear guidance on the limits of the responsibility of the state.

This is one of the most difficult issues that governments face. On the one hand, widespread support exists in most democratic countries for the principle that government should somehow see to it that everyone has access to health care. On the other hand, the potential costs of assuring to everyone the highest attainable standard of health care are high. Britain and a number of other countries maintain national health services that offer care to everyone. The United States is more selective, restricting its offer of health care at government expense mainly to the elderly and the indigent. In 1994 Congress considered, but failed to adopt, a proposal by President Clinton for universal health care.

The statement in the Covenant concerning an adequate standard of living refers to food, clothing, and housing. Everyone is said to have a "fundamental right" to be free from hunger. The Covenant does not say, however, that government must provide food. Rather, its obligation is to take measures aimed at improving methods of production, conservation, and distribution.

As to social security, the Covenant simply asserts, without any elaboration, that everyone has the right to it, "including social insurance."

The United States has not ratified the international Covenant on Economic, Social, and Cultural Rights, and such rights are not included in the Bill of Rights. Of course, governments in the United States are active in these fields at either the state or the federal level, or both, establishing a variety of legal rights (for example, to education and to social security), but the prevailing attitude is that this is done as a matter of policy and not in recognition of a human right. Some of those pressing for the adoption of a national system for health care seek to strengthen their argument by claiming that such care is a right, and in most other advanced countries this view is accepted; but skeptics and critics take the view that the issue is one of discretionary policy.

The Universal Declaration of Human Rights recognizes a right to property, but the covenants do not. The Universal Declaration says that "everyone has the right to own property alone as well as in association with others. No one shall be arbitrarily deprived of his property."

The provision of the Universal Declaration reflects a strong tradition, suggested by the statement in the French Declaration of the Rights of Man and of Citizens (1789) that "the end of all political associations is the preservation of the natural and imprescriptible rights of man; and that these rights are liberty, property, security, and resistance to oppression."

Actually, all governments recognize the right to property. The Constitution of the United States simply assumes it, specifying that individuals shall not be deprived of their property without due process of law and that private property shall not be taken for public use without just compensation. Even communist governments recognize the right. Legal and moral injunctions against theft imply a right to property.

The right is obviously important. No modern society could function without it. At the same time it is by no means absolute. Rather, it is hedged about by limitations.

Perhaps the most obvious limitation is the right of the government to take property in the form of taxes. And government also claims the right of eminent domain, that is, the right to take property for public use, paying just compensation.

Further, government claims the right to regulate the use and exchange of property—to regulate trade and commerce. It regulates in the name of protecting people from harm, as in the prohibition of the sale of certain drugs without a prescription. It regulates in the name of the general welfare, as in zoning ordinances and in measures aimed at protecting the environment. The right of government to take property for public use is rarely challenged, but disputes are arising increasingly over what constitutes "taking" and thus over when compensation is required. Does government "take" property when it adopts a zoning ordinance that restricts its use or when it forbids logging in order to preserve the spotted owl?

Government itself has a right to own property, and some of the ways in which it exercises the right put implicit limits on the opportunities open to individuals, if not on their rights. By going into a business itself, it may deter the prudent from offering competition. And it may establish a legal state monopoly.

Moreover, the proposition that a right to property exists does not necessarily mean that the right extends to every possible kind of property and every possible form of ownership in every kind of circumstance. Should it be considered morally necessary to permit anyone with enough money to own an oil well or a coal mine or a bridge that is strategically located? Should the right to own property include the right to establish a monopoly and manage it without regard for the public welfare?

Questions thus arise about the right to property. What is most desirable is more a question of policy than a question of moral right. The policies adopted range from those that emphasize private ownership and the play of the market to those that emphasize social ownership and central controls. These policies will be described and appraised in later chapters.

■ The Question of Priorities Among Rights _____

Considerable discussion has occurred of the question of the relative importance of civil and political as against economic, social, and cultural rights.

The Western tradition gives priority to civil and political rights, and if the question is what rights are most essential to democracy, this tradition is justified. By its very definition, democracy calls for such rights as the right to vote and to enjoy freedom of expression; and it is possible to have democracy while leaving standards of living, health care, and so on to the operations of a free market.

Some assume other standards of judgment about the relative importance of different rights. One argument is that basic needs must take priority—that the need for food, clothing, and shelter, for example, takes priority over everything else—that the starving person has little interest in or need for a right to freedom of expression or political participation.

In a sense, that argument looks irrefutable, and many governments take advantage of it in seeking to justify their dictatorial ways. Their argument is that free elections and freedom of speech are luxuries that poor countries can ill afford—that the whole country must maintain a united front in the face of daunting economic problems.

The argument is not nearly as compelling as it looks at first sight, for it assumes that government knows how to attack economic problems and is efficient in doing so. The truth is, however, that many of the political leaders who seek to safeguard themselves against a free electorate and against freedom of speech are so wrongheaded or inefficient or corrupt that they are a major part of the problem. Authoritarian and totalitarian governments, including those of Eastern Europe and the Soviet Union, have managed their economies so disastrously in so many cases that one is justified in looking with great suspicion on the claim that the denial of political rights is justified so that economic rights can be enjoyed.

■ Review _____

Civil and political rights are an essential feature of democracy, and many hold that economic, social, and cultural rights must be recognized as well. Rights are justified claims, claims that must be honored if justice is to be done. They may be justified morally, legally, or both. People differ in their conceptions of how moral rights come into existence, and they differ in deciding about priorities when rights conflict.

Civil and political rights include rights to participate in politics and government, discussed in earlier chapters, and the right to equal treatment, to be discussed in the next chapter. Here the focus has been on freedom of expression, freedom of religion, rights relating to the security of the person and due process, and rights of movement and residence.

Issues arise in relation to all rights. Why should there be freedom of expression? When is expression to be regarded as free? Are restrictions justifiable in any circumstance? Should "free flow" across international boundaries be the rule?

Freedom of religion is surely called into question when one religion is made the religion of the state. The Constitution of the United States, far from naming a state religion, prohibits the "establishment" of religion, which raises problems of its own. All over the world issues arise about the "free exercise" of religion—for example, issues concerning religion and the schools.

Issues arise, too, concerning security of the person, due process, movement, and residence. What meaning should be given to the right to life? When is search and seizure unreasonable? What does the right to privacy cover? Given a right to choose one's residence, what limitations, if any, are acceptable? Is there a right to leave one country and enter another?

Economic, social, and cultural rights bring up other problems. The first is whether they should be regarded as rights. Others concern their meaning and the policies that should be followed in honoring them. The international covenants do not assert a right to property.

■ Reading

Berlin, Isaiah (1970) *Four Essays on Liberty*. New York: Oxford University Press.

Claude, Richard P., and Burns Weston, eds. (1992) *Human Rights in the World Community: Issues and Action*. Philadelphia: University of Pennsylvania Press.

Crawford, James, ed. (1988) *The Rights of Peoples*. Oxford: Oxford University Press.

Donnelly, Jack (1989) *Universal Human Rights in Theory and Practice*. Ithaca, N.Y.: Cornell University Press.

Forsythe, David P. (1989) *Human Rights and World Politics*. 2d ed. Lincoln: University of Nebraska Press.

Goldman, Alan H. (1979) *Justice and Reverse Discrimination*. Princeton: Princeton University Press.

Mill, John Stuart (1975) *On Liberty*. New York: Norton.

Robertson, A. H. (1989) *Human Rights in the World: An Introduction to the Study of the International Protection of Human Rights*. 3d ed. New York: St. Martin's.

Robertson, A. H., and J. G. Merrills (1993) *Human Rights in Europe. A Study of the European Convention on Human Rights*. 3d ed. New York: Manchester University Press.

Sunstein, Cass R. (1993) *Democracy and the Problem of Free Speech*. New York: Free Press.

Justice and Equal Treatment

Arbitrary differentiation is discriminatory. Reasonable differentiation is compatible with the rule of equal treatment.

"HANG ON, KIDS — WE'RE DECELERATING."

To require racial segragation in the schools is to engage in arbitrary differentiation, violating the equal protection clause. But the integration of schools has been a slow process.

109

Justice is one of the universal values, endorsed by virtually everyone throughout the world. That individuals would announce themselves to be champions of injustice is scarcely credible. But those who agree on the proposition that justice is good may or may not agree on the distinctions between the just and the unjust and how justice can best be promoted or achieved. Issues concerning justice are among the most prominent in the world, the basis for political struggles waged by both peaceful and violent means.

Equal treatment (nondiscriminatory treatment) at the hands of government is also a universal value. Jefferson endorsed it in the Declaration of Independence, holding it to be self-evident that "all men are created equal." Virtually every constitution in the world includes a provision—sometimes more than one provision—requiring government to uphold the rule of equal treatment and to avoid discrimination. In the Constitution of the United States, the provision is in the Fourteenth Amendment, stipulating that no state shall deny to any person the equal protection of the laws; and by implication the rule extends to the federal government as well as to the states. The Charter of the United Nations obliges members to promote human rights "without distinction as to race, sex, language, or religion," which means that it obliges them to observe the rule of equal and nondiscriminatory treatment. The idea of equality of opportunity is also everywhere endorsed. Scarcely anyone explicitly endorses regimes of special privilege.

But again, as in the case of endorsements of justice, agreement on the principle of equal and nondiscriminatory treatment does not necessarily extend to agreement in answering questions to which the principle leads. People differ both about the meaning of equal and nondiscriminatory treatment and about the best means of promoting and achieving it. Claims of discrimination and agitation for equal treatment lead to political struggles all over the world.

My object in this chapter is to clarify the idea of justice and the idea of equal and nondiscriminatory treatment; and I identify issues concerning them. In the first section I focus on conceptions of justice. This leads in the second section to a focus on the idea of equal treatment and on related rules. In the third section I take up the question of when differentiation should count as discrimination, and I focus on the following possible bases for differentiation: property or income, birth or other status, language, religion, sex, race, age, and handicap. In the fourth section I ask when equality of opportunity can be said to exist, and in the fifth I state the cases for and against preferential treatment.

■ What Is Justice?

A number of writers offer conceptions of justice, but they disagree among themselves. No one conception is generally endorsed. I will identify some of the issues and then focus on the common denominator that several of the theories share.

A basic issue is whether to take a utilitarian point of view, which has as its central feature the rule that what should be sought is the greatest happiness (or the greatest good) of the greatest number. Utilitarianism is associated with Jeremy Bentham, a British writer who died in 1832.

The fundamental problem with Bentham's view is suggested by the possibility that the greatest aggregate amount of happiness might be achieved if 5 or 10 percent of the people were enslaved for the benefit of the rest. Utilitarians squirm in the face of this possibility, knowing that their central rule would permit it to happen (Miller 1976, 39–40).

Those rejecting the utilitarian approach generally support the proposition that justice is done when all persons get their due or that justice is done when benefits and burdens are allocated fairly. This is elementary and obvious, but it gives no guidance on how to decide what is due to each person or what the criteria of fairness are.

Three solutions are advanced, summarized in three supplementary propositions. One of them focuses on rights (morally justified claims) and holds that justice is done when everyone's rights are respected. The second supplementary proposition focuses on deserts and holds that justice is done when all persons get what they deserve. The third focuses on needs and holds that justice is done when all persons get what they (legitimately) need (Miller 1976, 27).

Sometimes the three supplementary propositions work harmoniously together and suggest the same allocation of benefits and burdens, but sometimes they conflict with each other. A person may have a right to either more or less than she deserves or needs; and she may deserve or need either more or less than she has a right to get.

No general agreement has developed on how to solve this problem, and I will not attempt to solve it here. A fact that I have repeatedly noted, however, is relevant again: that the members of the United Nations have agreed on a Universal Declaration of Human Rights and that more than half of them have ratified the Covenants on Human Rights. And they have adopted and ratified a number of other treaties and conventions concerning human rights, including one on racial discrimination. Clearly, one of the main purposes of these treaties is to promote the development of just societies; and vague as the treaties are, they nevertheless offer substantial guidance. Even if the concern for rights sometimes needs to be supplemented or qualified because of a concern for deserts or needs, the various international agreements give a head start and special leverage to those who seek justice through a stress on rights. In this chapter, though not claiming that "to each according to his rights" fully assures justice, I will put special stress on rights.

The rights that people have are both particular and general. A right that is special to one person is a particular right. A right to which all are entitled is a general right. Let us focus on general rights. Collectively, these have been referred to over many centuries as natural rights. Since World War II natural rights have been redefined and extended to make up the body of human rights—that is, the rights to which people are entitled simply by virtue of the fact that they are human beings. It is these rights that I will stress.

An additional consideration supports a stress on rights. Several of the theories mentioned above have a common denominator, one that is so important and so basic that it is sometimes advanced as the central feature of justice. The common denominator is that justice is related to equal and nondiscriminatory treatment. In fact, some marry the two ideas, holding that they necessarily go together and that justice is substantially achieved when equal and nondiscriminatory treatment is afforded (Ginsberg 1965, 56–57). Whatever the rule (to each according to his rights? to each according to her deserts? to each according to his needs?), it is to be applied impartially to all.

It happens, too, that one of the basic human rights is the right to equal and nondiscriminatory treatment, which is further reason for a stress on rights in relation to justice.

■ Equal Treatment

Aristotle led the way long ago in linking the idea of justice and the idea of equal treatment. His much-quoted statement is that "injustice arises when equals are treated unequally, and also when unequals are treated equally."

Note that Aristotle implicitly rejected the idea that equal treatment is necessarily the same treatment. On the contrary, he said in effect that justice requires that people be classified, with those in the same category ("equals") getting like treatment and those in different categories ("unequals") getting different treatment.

The application of these principles would be difficult enough if we considered only the activities of government, but they need to be applied also to businesses that offer goods and services to the public—hotels, stores, restaurants, theaters, building contractors, and so on. Such businesses are said to be "affected by a public interest" sufficiently that they must abide by the same rules that apply to government.

Focus first on government. Aristotle's principle suggests a danger. If government could classify and differentiate at will, it could nullify the rule of equal treatment, so a safeguard is necessary. In US practice, the safeguard lies in a formal presumption that people are to get the same treatment but that *differentiation is permissible when it is reasonable*; and to qualify as reasonable, it must meet both negative and positive requirements.

The negative requirement is that the classification must not differentiate among persons in an arbitrary or capricious way. It must not be based simply on bias or prejudice. And the positive requirement is that it must be for the public good or in the public interest. Where it is based on certain highly suspect grounds, such as race, it must serve a compelling or overriding public interest. And it must be based on general rules or principles that are impartially applied.

A contrasting formal presumption applies in the private realm: that the right to liberty includes a right to differentiate. But the further presumption, as indicated above, is that some private activities are sufficiently affected by a public interest that the rules against discrimination apply.

Questions arise at almost every turn over the application of these principles. What seems reasonable to one person may seem unreasonable to another, and people differ in their judgments of what the public good requires or what the public interest justifies. In the private realm questions arise over whether a public interest is sufficiently involved to override the right that we all have to liberty—that is, to behave as we please.

The international Convention on Racial Discrimination endorses a somewhat different criterion than the one employed in the United States for deciding whether classification and differentiation are acceptable. The Convention says in effect that when differentiation has the purpose or effect of promoting the equal enjoyment of human rights it is to be accepted, and when it has the opposite purpose or effect it is to be condemned.

■ Bases for Differentiation Most Questioned or Condemned

That government must differentiate in many ways is everywhere accepted. It differentiates when it hires some but not others for work in the civil service. It differentiates in the wages and salaries paid to civil servants. It differentiates when it conscripts some but not others into the armed forces. It differentiates when it requires some but not others to go to school. It differentiates when it puts some but not others in prison.

No one questions the need to differentiate, but some of the bases for differentiation have been so much abused (used so unreasonably) that their use is generally questioned or condemned. Thus, the provision of the United Nations Charter, quoted already, names race, sex, language, and religion as characteristics that are not to be the basis for "distinction." The comparable provision of the Covenant on Civil and Political Rights is more elaborate. It calls for the promotion of human rights without distinction "on any ground," and then it illustrates: "on any ground such as race, color, sex, language, religion, political or other opinion, national or social origin, property, birth, or other status."

The vital point to note is that the grounds for differentiation listed are not unconditionally ruled out. Rather, they are automatically made suspect, a presumption being established against their use. If any governmental agency wants to differentiate on one of the grounds named, it may perhaps do so, but it must accept the burden of demonstrating that what it does is justifiable. And it can meet this burden, as indicated above, by showing that it is acting reasonably in the public interest or by showing that its action will promote the equal enjoyment of human rights.

In what follows, I examine these grounds for differentiation and add two more that the Covenant does not mention—age and handicap. The object is to see to what extent, if at all, differentiation based on the various grounds occurs and is justifiable and what the issues are.

■ Property

Alexander Hamilton proposed that the rich and the wellborn should have a special share in government. He thought that they would check the unsteadiness of the mass of the people, who were turbulent and changing, seldom able to judge things rightly. The rich and wellborn would maintain good government. Regarding the rich, various other reasons are cited for assuring them a special role. They are said to have more at stake in government than the poor; their very wealth is taken to prove their responsibility and competence. They are viewed as entrepreneurs, as people who are creative and inventive, able to manage affairs at least for their own benefit and perhaps for the benefit of all.

Further, the idea that government should be in the hands of the rich has been reinforced by fear that the poor, if they had the chance, would despoil the rich—doing injustice to them and, in effect, killing the goose that lays the golden eggs.

In accordance with this line of thought, property and income qualifications for voting were once common, and it followed that only persons of property could hold office.

Most of this line of thought is now repudiated. To be sure, wealth counts in politics. Those who have it exercise more political influence than those who do not. But it is the wealth itself that leads to the disproportionate power, and not any law that confers privilege. The law may serve the advantage of the rich, but it does not confer rights on them that are denied to others. Formally, the egalitarian argument prevails that the interests of the poor are just as deserving of consideration as the interests of the rich. And the democratic view is that the way to get consideration for the interests of the poor is to allow them to participate in politics—to have a vote and to be eligible to hold public office.

Further, no political system now accepts the idea that the rich necessarily have a special capacity to rule. The rich person may have inherited wealth or may have gained it at the expense of others rather than in ways that contributed to their well-being. It is possible to motivate and reward the innovators, the entrepreneurs, the managers in other ways than through political privilege.

■ Birth or Other Status

The statement by Alexander Hamilton, cited above, referred not only to the rich but also to the wellborn. Differentiation by birth was in fact common in medieval and early modern Europe. People were born into a particular station in life—into a class or caste that had its own distinctive rights and obligations.

Thomas Jefferson and other Founding Fathers disagreed with Hamilton. The Declaration of Independence proclaims that all men are created equal—not that the wellborn should have special political power. The French Declaration of the Rights and Duties of Man, adopted in connection with the French Revolution of 1789, likewise rejected Hamilton's view. It endorsed the idea that the careers of individuals should depend on their own industry and talents, not on the status of their parents. And it is these ideas of equality that have prevailed. Hereditary monarchies remain, of course—either in violation of the rule against differentiation based on birth or as an exception to the rule.

■ Language

If consensus has been achieved that government should not impose differentiations based on property or birth, the same can scarcely be true of differentiation based on language, for such differentiation is inevitable wherever more than one language is spoken.

The policies of the United Nations itself suggest a few of the issues. Delegates come to the meetings of the General Assembly from all over the world, speaking many different languages, but the United Nations accepts only a few of them as "working" or "official" languages. This means that it provides for the translation of speeches only when they are made in one of a few selected languages, and it prints its documents only in those few languages. The delegates who happen to know one or more of these languages are thus advantaged over the others, raising the question whether the differentiation is reasonable.

The justification is based on the fact that when two or more rights conflict, they cannot all be honored, at least not fully; and correspondingly, when two or more obligations conflict, they cannot all be met. The right of delegates to equal treatment as to language conflicts with the right of the General Assembly, and of the United Nations in general, to get its work done with reasonable efficiency. And the obligation to promote human rights without distinction as to language conflicts with the obligation of the United Nations to perform the various functions and duties assigned to it. If it gave delegates free choice of the language to use, and if it then provided equal services regardless of the language chosen, the costs would be extremely high. Thus, it is held to be reasonable to differentiate among the languages.

The principle involved is relevant elsewhere: that when rights or obligations conflict with each other, some kind of choice or compromise is unavoidable. This implies a principle already noted: that rights are not to be regarded as absolute; that is, they cannot always be unconditionally and fully honored. To say that a right to equal treatment exists is to say that a strong presumption exists in favor of equal treatment, but it does not repeal the rule of reasonableness.

The United Nations differentiates as to language not only in selecting official and working languages but also when it selects people to work in the Secretariat, for it must take their command of language into account. To hire people who are unable to communicate easily with others in the organization would be incompatible with the achievement of its mission. The principle involved is again one that is widely relevant—that differentiation is permissible when it is based on a bona fide occupational qualification. The principle is accepted so generally that it is expressed in an acronym: bfoq.

Like the United Nations and other international organizations, most of the countries of the world face problems about distinctions based on language. Belgium and Canada have almost been torn apart because of them. Cyprus has in fact been torn apart, with differences of language among the reasons. Malaysia is insisting that its Chinese and Indian population (almost half the total population) learn Malay; consequently, school is taught in Malay only. Nigeria has so many languages that it is thought impracticable and undesirable either to use all of them as media of instruction or to make any one of them the sole language of instruction, so school is taught in English. Pupils are thus treated equally in that all are taught in a language other than their own, and all emerge with knowledge of a common language. In some of the countries of Africa, differences of language, and the choice of the language(s) in which parliamentary debates are conducted, have the effect of restricting membership in parliament to a small portion of the population. Switzerland is notable for the accommodation it has achieved among its language communities: German, French, Italian, and even Romansh. Many other countries might be mentioned as well.

To illustrate the problem of differentiation as to language more fully, I will focus on India. Its largest language community speaks Hindi, but the Hindi community includes only 28 percent of the population. The eleven next largest language communities range in size from 45 million (8 percent) down to 14 million (3 percent). Eighty-five percent of the population speak one of the twelve leading languages, and the remaining 15 percent speak a minimum of 269 more. Ninety-three percent of the population know only one language. Of the 7 percent who know a second language, most know English, though almost as many know Hindi (India 1971).

In the light of such a situation, how can either the central government of India or the various states avoid "distinction" as to language? To be able to function, they must make choices, just as the United Nations must, and no matter what choice they make, they favor some citizens and leave others at a disadvantage.

No good solution to the problem exists, but the rule of equal treatment does not require the impossible. Given the emphasis on reasonableness, what it requires is that unfairness be kept at a minimum. India's choice is to make Hindi the official language for the central government and also to permit the free use of English. And to avoid giving an undue advantage to those speaking Hindi, the rule is that any state may insist that communications between it and the central government be in English.

The United States is also among the countries with problems concerning language. According to a 1979 survey, persons in the United States fourteen years old and over divide as follows with respect to mother tongue: English, 77 percent; Spanish, 4 percent; German, 3 percent; all other languages, 12 percent. This means that at least 19 percent of those fourteen or over have a mother tongue other than English. (The mother tongue of 4 percent was not reported.)

Among the problems resulting from the linguistic mixture in the United States are those relating to elections and to education. In 1975, finding that "voting discrimination against citizens of language minorities is pervasive and national in scope," Congress required bilingual elections in districts where more than 5 percent of the citizens of voting age are members of a single language minority.

The problem with respect to education is more difficult. Suppose, for example, that in San Francisco a sizable group of children shows up at school knowing only Chinese. Suppose that another group shows up knowing only Spanish. And suppose that most of the children know only English. The Chinese and Hispanic students are likely to be disadvantaged regardless of the policy followed. They are obviously disadvantaged if they are taught in English, a language that they do not understand. Similarly, they face a special burden if they are required to learn English while those who already know it face no comparable requirement, and they will face a different special burden later if they are allowed to leave school without knowing English.

The rule followed in the United States is that if the government requires pupils who do not know English to attend school, it must help them learn it. And where the non-English-speaking group is sizable, a number of the states (with federal assistance) provide bilingual instruction.

You may think that I have devoted too much space here to language. I give it considerable attention first because I believe that the subject is much more important than most English-speaking Americans think. In many countries, language policy is a major issue. And the issue is likely to become increasingly important in the United States as the size of the Spanish-speaking population grows. In any case, I have used the language issue to illustrate several general points concerning equal and non-discriminatory treatment.

Religion

Most of the issues that arise concerning equal treatment as to religion relate to the whole religious community as one entity, a subject that belongs in chapter 17. Whatever affects the community as an entity also affects individual persons, and that aspect of the subject might be treated here, but in the interest of coherence I will postpone treatment of it until later.

Sex

When is it reasonable to classify and differentiate on the basis of sex? Consensus has been achieved on some of the answers to this question, but by no means on all.

In 1979 the General Assembly of the United Nations adopted a Convention on the Elimination of All Forms of Discrimination Against Women. Its provisions identify areas within which discrimination occurs; they relate to political and public life, nationality (citizenship), education, employment, health care and social welfare, legal capacity, and marital and family relationships. The subject is too big to be fully treated here. Illustrations will have to suffice.

With respect to political and public life (as noted in chapter 4), the view has come to prevail that no reasonable basis exists for denying women the vote or excluding them from public office. Historical attitudes still work strongly against women, which means that what is called passive discrimination continues, but legally mandated differentiation with respect to voting and office holding is substantially gone. (Discrimination is passive when arbitrary differentiation is accepted on all sides, perhaps as a matter of tradition, with no one taking arbitrary action. For example, passive discrimination occurs when a woman fails to prepare for a certain career, or to apply for a certain job, simply because it has traditionally been reserved for men.)

Perhaps the principal issue with regard to discrimination against women in public life relates to the armed forces. Should women be drafted on the same basis as men? Should they be permitted to volunteer? If they find themselves in the armed forces, whether as conscripts or as volunteers, should they be trained, given opportunities, and assigned to duty on the same basis as men? Most specifically, should they be trained for combat and sent into combat? What policies should the armed forces follow with respect to women who become pregnant? Should married women be treated differently in any way than single women? Should women with babies or young children be treated differently than other women? Should women have dependency allowances on the same basis as men? Do rights of privacy exist, and if so, how should the armed forces give respect to them in the treatment of men and women?

The reference to nationality in the international convention on discrimination against women reflects the fact that discrimination based on it was once common. If a woman married a foreigner, she was likely to lose her citizenship forthwith, and might or might not be accepted as a citizen in her husband's country. His citizenship was not affected. And sex discrimination relating to nationality still occurs. For example, Kuwait's law provides that a male citizen married to a foreigner passes citizenship on to his children, whereas a female citizen married to a foreigner does not.

In the field of education, discrimination against women has been common, much of it of the passive sort. A papal encyclical of 1929 took the view that there was not in nature anything to suggest equality in the training of the two sexes, and a similar attitude has characterized the Islamic, Hindu, and Judaic faiths. For that matter, many have manifested it irrespective of religion. Such attitudes have been changing, but it might be noted that even UNESCO's Convention Against Discrimination in Education permits legally mandatory separation by sex, provided the separate schools are equal.

In general, save perhaps in some Islamic countries, the issues that now arise relating to education concern not so much discrimination by government as what government should do to combat discrimination by others. In the United States, federal law prohibits discrimination on the basis of sex in any educational program receiving federal aid. You might play the part of a judge and try to decide how this prohibition should be applied in the realm of sports (see Van Dyke 1990, 85–87).

Issues arise all over the world concerning differentiation by sex in the field of employment—issues relating to recruitment, promotion, pay, sexual harassment, sick leave, pregnancy and childbirth, pensions, and other matters. Over most of the world, men long ago managed to stack the deck in their own favor, following practices that were so obviously discriminatory that anyone committed to the idea of equal treatment would have no choice but to denounce them.

Some of the issues that arise, however, are extremely difficult. For example, given the fact that women tend to live longer than men, is it reasonable to differentiate between men and women in retirement plans?

More specifically, is it reasonable either to require working women to pay more money than men into the retirement fund or to give them lower monthly payments once they retire? Does a failure to differentiate indicate discrimination against men? Whatever the judgment might be on grounds of reasonableness, the Supreme Court says that the law prohibits the differentiation.

A different and very troublesome issue is still pending: given the fact that, for a variety of reasons, the "equal pay for equal work" formula leaves women disadvantaged, should the "comparable pay for comparable work" formula be adopted? If so, precisely what meaning should be given to the formula, and how can it be sensibly applied and enforced?

Problems concerning discrimination in marital and family relationships are suggested by the Muslim law that a husband may divorce his wife by saying "I divorce you" three times, whereas the wife has no comparable right. And under the laws of some countries, title to a woman's property shifts to her husband immediately on marriage; and if and when they divorce, the property is his.

In recent years issues have come to the fore concerning equal treatment for homosexual persons. The issues rarely if ever concern eligibility for elective or appointive office; rather they concern such questions as whether the law should prohibit homosexual conduct and whether a homosexual person is fit to be a teacher or to serve in a police department or the armed services. For example, it was for many years the policy of the armed services of the United States to discharge any member found to be homosexual. President Clinton took a stand against this rule, with the upshot that a compromise was made based on the rule "Don't ask, don't tell." That is, the armed services do not ask recruits about their sexual orientation, and neither recruits nor persons in the service need to say what their sexual orientation is. But the armed forces remain free to discharge anyone for homosexual conduct. People differ on the question of whether this is reasonable or arbitrary.

Race

Discrimination as to race has a long history and continues yet today. European peoples practiced racial discrimination by engaging in the slave trade, and the United States practiced it first by maintaining slavery and later by following Jim Crow rules. European and US imperialism were also associated with racial discrimination, for the imperialists were white and the subject peoples were of other colors. Tragic injustices occurred, and powerful resentments developed along with widespread feelings of guilt.

In recent decades issues relating to racial discrimination have arisen mainly in the United States and South Africa. In the United States blacks were slaves (with some exceptions) until Lincoln emancipated them during the Civil War. After that war, several constitutional amendments were adopted to assure blacks equal treatment, and Congress adopted some legislation for the same purpose, but the amendments and the laws were given interpretations that permitted discrimination to continue on a grand scale. Moreover, laws that seemed to be racially impartial were sometimes administered in discriminatory ways. Blacks came to be excluded from participation in political life, and they suffered discrimination in many connections, at the hands of both government and private parties.

Among other things, states with sizable black populations provided for the separate treatment or segregation of blacks in the schools, in public transportation, and in other settings. In *Plessy* v. *Ferguson* (1896) the Supreme Court approved the practice, stipulating blandly that the separate treatment must be equal. "Separate but equal" thus became the approved principle, but the "but equal" part of the principle was widely ignored. In addition to itself discriminating, government permitted private parties to do the same—for example, in employment practices and in places of public accommodation. During most of the century following the Civil War, whites maintained a system of privilege and preference for themselves by discriminating against blacks. The discriminatory laws and customs go by the name Jim Crow.

The first successful line of attack on Jim Crow centered in the courts, with one case after another leading to a judgment that a challenged kind of differentiation based on race was arbitrary and invidious (unreasonable), denying the equal protection of the laws. The most notable case was *Brown* v. *Board of Education of Topeka, Kansas* (1954) concerning segregation in the schools. In it the court reversed the *Plessy* decision. It held that even if the school facilities and teachers for blacks were as good as those for whites, segregation as such was a denial of equal treatment and therefore unconstitutional.

Not only did the court thus rule out segregated schooling, it also took the view that the various units of government are obliged not simply to drop their unconstitutional practices but to adopt affirmative measures with a view to undoing, insofar as possible, the damage done. They were to do what they could to prevent the effects of illegal discrimination from being carried into the future. Most notably, in the field of education it was not enough to permit "freedom of choice"—that is, to permit students to attend the schools of their choice; nor was it acceptable to require students attending public schools to attend the ones nearest their homes. The courts held that such hands-off policies would be insufficient to undo the damage and that affirmative measures (for example, busing) had to be taken to bring about integration.

The second successful line of attack on Jim Crow was political. The civil rights campaign of the early 1960s was its primary feature. The campaign began with black students sitting at a lunch counter hitherto reserved for whites and requesting service, and it included dramatic boy-cotts, demonstrations, and marches. Some rioting also occurred. Two of the results were the Civil Rights Act of 1964 and the Voting Rights Act of 1965, landmark federal measures in the history of racial discrimina-tion.

As the title of the second measure indicates, assuring blacks the right to vote was an important objective, but a number of other objectives were also served. For example, the Civil Rights Act put severe limits on racial discrimination by state and local governments by prohibiting it in any program or activity that the federal government helped finance; and the act, reaching into the private realm, endorsed the principle of equal economic opportunity: it prohibited discrimination in any industry af-fecting interstate commerce and employing twenty-five persons or more.

Both passive and active discrimination continue, but they are much reduced. Scarcely anyone explicitly defends racial discrimination any-more. Virtually everyone presumes that in public affairs, differentiation by race is illegal and wrong; those who want to differentiate thus have the burden of justifying what they do. The most serious remaining prob-lems of principle concern affirmative action and preferential treatment, to be discussed shortly.

What conditions made possible the changes in the racial policies of the United States? The answer varies, depending on whether an individu-alistic or a communal perspective is adopted. Most Americans uncriti-cally assume an individualistic perspective that calls for an emphasis on reason, with racial differences ignored. People are to be looked upon not as blacks and whites but as human beings, all of whom go equally into the melting pot. The thought is frequently advanced that government should be color-blind.

The view is more tenable than it otherwise might be because of the fact that almost all American blacks have been born within the country, just like whites, and a high proportion are culturally indistinguishable from whites. Though some blacks speak of black nationalism, most are either in the mainstream or want to join it.

Those who dwell on these conditions can go on to assume that in re-cent decades many whites have had a change of heart about racial dis-crimination. It is, after all, incompatible with the Constitution and with an individualistic creed.

The communal view contrasts with the individualistic view. The com-munal view assumes continued race consciousness, whites identifying themselves primarily with whites and blacks with blacks. The related ex-pectation is that whites and blacks will each tend to give their votes and their political support to their own kind. Thus, whites will tend to op-pose developments that shift political power to blacks, and vice versa. Not that either the whites or the blacks necessarily claim superiority, but they think in terms of distinct communities that are conscious of their separate identity, and they want political offices to be held by members of their own community.

If a communal view is assumed, then why would American whites have conceded so much to American blacks? The answer presumably has several parts. One part of the answer is that the whites who took or tolerated racist or racialist views were trapped by their own rhetoric. They had talked the language of reasonableness and the language of equality for so long that they had no intellectual defense when the blacks and their white allies began demanding what the language said was their due. And the blacks did start demanding it, not only with words but also with sit-ins, marches, demonstrations, and riots, with latent threats of more drastic action.

In this situation, according to the communal view, many whites— intuitively or deliberately—began calculating their prospective gains and losses, and in these calculations relative numbers played a crucial role. Whites far outnumber blacks. They outnumber them by something like nine to one. They could thus fully incorporate blacks in a democratic polity and still keep substantial control, and it might be less costly to do precisely that than to maintain the system of exclusion and discrimination. Regardless of the extent to which the whites gave conscious consideration to this distribution of voting power, it surely played a significant role.

The same kind of consideration long worked the other way in South Africa. There the whites comprise only about 16 percent of the population. The rest of the population is black African (72 percent), "colored" (9 percent), and Asian (3 percent). The coloreds are mainly mulattoes, and the Asians are mainly of Indian ancestry. The black Africans cover a considerable range in the degree to which they have taken up the culture of the whites. Some are culturally indistinguishable from the whites, but most, especially the rural blacks, retain enough of their traditional tribal cultures to present a constant reminder that they come from a different world.

Early relationships between the white settlers and the blacks in South Africa were not far different from early relationships between the whites and the Indians in the United States. And when the need arose, the South African whites established their political hegemony over the blacks, just as the American whites established their political hegemony over the Indians.

The parallels between the two countries, however, do not go very far. The whites of South Africa have always been in a small minority, fearful that they would be engulfed and subordinated. They could not switch to individualistic principles without inviting black domination and risking the loss of what they call their identity. They therefore maintained a communal system, insisting on a political monopoly for themselves and denying the blacks any share in political control.

After World War II, when the rest of the world was beginning to emphasize human rights, and when the United States was swinging toward the dismantlement of the Jim Crow system, South Africa swung the other way. The National party won majority support among the whites and began formalizing an apartheid system, a system of legally enforced racial separation. But this system turned out to be unsustainable. Official spokesmen of the National party did not claim racial superiority. By the 1980s they were agreeing with others that their system of racial domination was indefensible as a matter of principle, but they faced a fundamentally different problem from the one faced by the white people of the United States. If the whites of South Africa enfranchised the blacks, the consequence might well be simply the transfer of domination from one racial group to the other.

In 1984 the National party led in the adoption of a new constitution that gave a minor share of political power to the coloreds and the Asians but still excluded the blacks. In 1990 the white government released from prison the outstanding black leader Nelson Mandela and began negotiations that culminated in an agreement on a transitional constitutional arrangement. Far from seeking revenge, and far from seeking simply to turn the tables and substitute black domination for white domination, Mandela and the African National Congress sought conciliation and interracial cooperation in the hope of assuring stable progress. Under the agreement the blacks, of course, have the vote along with members of other racial groups, and in 1994 they elected Mandela president. But the transitional agreement assures the various parties seats in parliament on the basis of proportional representation, and it assures the various racial groups a role in the executive branch of government. What the final constitution will provide remains to be seen.

I will return to South Africa's problems and policies in chapter 17 in connection with the question of special arrangements for minorities.

Racial discrimination also occurs, of course, against people other than blacks and in countries other than the United States and South Africa. For example, Russia is noted for its anti-Semitism, and anti-Semitism exists elsewhere, too, though on a minor scale as compared with the practices of Hitler's Germany. In the early 1970s Uganda expelled its Indian (Asian Indian) population, and Indians suffer discrimination elsewhere in East Africa; the Chinese in Indonesia and Vietnam have also been the targets of racial hatred.

Age

Differentiation by age is common and in some connections is accepted without question—for example, in connection with voting. It is reasonable to deny the vote to persons below a certain age (though what the minimum age should be is a matter of dispute). In a number of other connections, differentiation by age is controversial. Is it reasonable to make retirement mandatory solely because of age? Is it equally reasonable in all occupations and positions? If the principle of mandatory retirement by age is accepted, what should the age be? Should it be different at different times and in different countries, depending on health conditions and life expectancy?

Similar questions come up in connection with recruitment policies. Is it reasonable for employers to give weight to age in choosing among applicants? Is it reasonable for them to give decisive weight to age? Are the answers the same regardless of the nature of the job? How about the regulation or prohibition of child labor? Should minimum wage laws apply regardless of age?

The Handicapped

Suppose that people without handicaps have ready access to a government building or office while those with handicaps do not. Should this be considered a denial of equal treatment? Or should the view be that where government is not responsible for the handicap, it has no responsibility for the consequent burdens? Since the 1960s more and more people have come to the view that both government itself and enterprises affected by a public interest have an obligation to take all reasonable measures to assure equal treatment to the handicapped. And in the United States the law has been adjusted accordingly. Congress adopted the Americans with Disabilities Act in 1991.

Other Bases for Differentiation

Questions sometimes arise about differentiation on grounds other than those mentioned above. How about weight and height requirements for service on a police force when these screen out women more than men? How about various kinds of tests that screen out blacks more than whites? Does discrimination occur only when there is a discriminatory intent, or may it also be inferred from the impact or effect of a given practice?

The general principle, to repeat, is that differentiation, when it occurs, must be reasonable and not arbitrary; the grounds for it must be substantially relevant to the purpose being pursued, and the purpose itself must be to serve the public good through rules that are impartially applied.

■ Equality of Opportunity

Just as almost everyone endorses equal treatment, so does almost everyone endorse equality of opportunity

But again the generality is one thing and the particulars are another. When can it reasonably be said that equality of opportunity exists?

Any of several interpretations is possible (Goldman 1979, 170–88). One is that equality of opportunity is what exists in the absence of discrimination, that is, in the absence of arbitrary and unreasonable differentiation either by government or by enterprises affected by a public interest. So the problem is what kinds of differentiation to count as arbitrary and unreasonable. Given this meaning, it follows that the way to assure equality of opportunity is to eliminate discrimination.

A second possible interpretation of equality of opportunity is broader—that equality of opportunity is what exists not only in the absence of discrimination but also in the absence of any kind of disadvantage or handicap for which government (or "society") is responsible. The first problem here, of course, is to decide what government is responsible for. Surely it is responsible for the discriminatory laws and discriminatory governmental practices of the past. And it presumably is also responsible for its past failure to act against discrimination in enterprises affected by a public interest. But does the responsibility extend only to the direct, identifiable victims of past discrimination? Must they be able to prove that they were victims? What about responsibility for passive discrimination, and how could its victims prove their case? What about the disadvantages and scars that many decades of discrimination have inflicted on the children and grandchildren of those who suffered it directly?

And to what kinds of action should the acceptance of responsibility lead? To undo the effects of the unconstitutional and illegal policies of the past, should government now take affirmative action and require private enterprises to do the same? Should affirmative action include preferential treatment? Are those who have benefited from the illegal discrimination to be allowed to retain their advantage indefinitely, or are they roughly in the position of those who have received stolen goods?

The third interpretation of equality of opportunity is still broader, specifying that it is what exists not only in the absence of discrimination and socially caused disadvantages but also in the absence of natural and accidental handicaps. This meaning is clearly more extreme than the second. Where the second focuses on disadvantages for which society is responsible, the third focuses on those for which the individual is not responsible.

John Rawls proposes a variation of this definition. He speaks of the undeserved inequalities that flow from the "natural lottery" and says that "in order to treat all persons equally, to provide genuine equality of opportunity, society must give more attention to those with fewer native assets and to those born into the less favorable social positions." And he advances the principle that those who have been favored by nature should be permitted to gain from their good fortune only on terms that improve the situation of those to whom nature has been unkind (Rawls 1971, 100–101). Inequality is justified, he argues, only when it is to the benefit of the least advantaged (302). It may at the same time, of course, be to the benefit of others. His general recommendation is that "those who are at the same level of talent and ability, and have the same willingness to use them, should have the same prospects of success regardless of their initial place in the social system, that is, irrespective of the income class into which they are born" (73).

How far the government should go in responding to the third meaning of equality of opportunity is a good question for debate. Governments in most or all of the advanced countries accept the third meaning in some degree. For example, they generally provide health care for children in poverty and special educational programs in addition to free public education through the primary and secondary levels. In higher education, however, equality of opportunity in the third meaning does not exist.

Consideration of these questions leads to another: whether the pursuit of equality of opportunity, so broadly defined, is entirely compatible with the promotion and protection of other values that are also important. Perhaps it is important, for example, to encourage parents to give their children the best possible start in life even though this means providing them with more opportunities than other children enjoy. And perhaps it is important to give maximum encouragement to individual liberty and maximum rewards to free enterprise. This view calls for keeping taxes low and minimizing the role of government. Those who incline in this direction may say, "Yes, we support equality of opportunity, and we want to go a long way toward assuring it, but we also support conflicting values, and so must accept some kind of adjustment or compromise."

■ Preferential Treatment

The reference here is to preferential treatment for those disadvantaged by earlier discrimination, mainly the blacks. In using the term in this way, I go along with the common practice but must nevertheless note that the practice is at best questionable. What I have been calling discrimination up to now was also preferential treatment: the counterpart of discrimination against blacks, for example, was preferential treatment for whites. Every act of discrimination against a black implied preferential treatment for a white; and passive discrimination against blacks likewise had as its counterpart the passive preferential treatment of whites. The coin has two sides. Preferential treatment goes right along with discrimination in the American tradition. This fact, however, tends to be forgotten now that preferential treatment is more commonly for the benefit of those who have hitherto been the victims of discrimination.

Two kinds of arguments are made for preferential treatment, one backward looking and the other forward looking (Goldman 1979, chaps. 3 and 4). The backward-looking argument focuses on injustices of the past and seeks to undo them or at least to reduce their persisting effects. The forward-looking argument focuses on conceptions of a future good and calls for action to promote it. I will relate these arguments to the problem in the United States, though the principles are applicable everywhere.

First consider the backward-looking argument. In the above discussion of discrimination based on race, I spoke of different outlooks, one focusing on individuals and the other focusing on communities. Those outlooks are relevant here again, for the backward-looking argument may be based on either an individualistic or a communal outlook.

Given an individualistic outlook, the problem is minimal if a black, say, gets preferential treatment at the expense of a white person who has discriminated against him or who has benefited from that discrimination. The injured party then gets redress at the expense of the guilty party or at the expense of a person who has gained unfairly.

But suppose preferential treatment goes to a black who may or may not have suffered any specific act of discrimination; and suppose it is at the expense of a white who is personally guilty of no relevant wrong. The black gets the preferred treatment because other blacks have suffered discrimination in times past, and the white is injured because of the behavior of other whites long ago. Here the possibility is obvious that the undeserving may benefit at the expense of the innocent.

In one view, this is what happens when US courts order ratio hiring. In ordering such hiring, the courts take into account the composition of the relevant labor pool. If blacks comprise 25 percent of those in the relevant labor pool, the presumption is that in the absence of discrimination they would have 25 percent of most sorts of jobs in a given manufacturing plant; and if they do not, the court may order that every other person hired be black (provided qualified black applicants are available) until the 25 percent figure is reached. Even with the proviso, it may work out that a more qualified white is passed over so that a less qualified black can be hired. In issuing their orders, the courts do not require that the blacks who are favored prove that they personally suffered discrimination, nor do they require that the white persons passed over be shown to be personally guilty of some wrong.

The basis for criticism is obvious. But if the remedy limits preferential treatment to cases in which blacks are preferred only at the expense of individual whites found guilty of discriminating against them, a high proportion of the cases of discrimination would go unredressed. What kind of proceedings would be necessary to prove the white guilty? Given the pervasiveness of discrimination in the past, is it practical to try to decide on a case-by-case basis who is entitled to remedial action? Who would bear the costs? What of cases of discrimination that occurred long enough ago that relevant evidence and testimony are no longer available? What of passive discrimination, where by definition no one guilty party is identifiable?

A communal view provides a possible alternative. According to this view, there is no need to prove that an individual black person has suffered discrimination at the hands of a specific white person. Instead, the focus is on the two communities considered as units or entities—as collective wholes. For many decades, acting as a community in part through law, whites maintained a system of preference and privilege for themselves and of discrimination and oppression for blacks. In a great many connections, individual characteristics and merit did not matter. Rather, it was membership in the community that was decisive. To lynch one black was to warn them all, and to educate one black was to encourage them all.

The whites, the argument goes, went so far in a communal direction when it was to their advantage that they are not now in a good position to plead individualism. The blacks and the friends of the blacks are now justified in insisting on a continuation of a communal outlook; just as the whites in the past maintained their community of privilege by the arbitrary mistreatment of individual blacks, so now they can provide redress to the black community by extending preferential treatment to some of its members. A collective societal responsibility exists that needs to be discharged.

Those who champion this argument must admit that it calls for injustice to whites who have not been personally involved in racial discrimination, but to reject the argument is to leave injustice to many blacks unredressed. Everyone concerned thus faces a dilemma. Some propose to resolve the dilemma by saying that the right of the black community to redress takes priority over the right of individual whites to equal consideration. And others propose to resolve it by endorsing the proposition that two wrongs do not make a right.

Following the practice of the courts, I speak above of ratio hiring as a remedial measure. In the political forum the debate has come to focus more on "quotas" and their relationship to merit and equality of opportunity. You might ask yourself to what extent the whites who oppose quotas in the name of merit and equality of opportunity are wanting simply to deny remedies to blacks and to preserve the privileged position that they enjoy partly because of several centuries of preferential treatment.

The rhetoric of the American tradition is so fully individualistic that the communal line of argument may not commend itself. Those unhappy with it may shift from a backward- to a forward-looking view and ask what kind of society they want for the future and how to go about attempting to achieve it. If the answer is that they want a society in which equality of opportunity prevails, then they must ask what needs to be done to make equality of opportunity a reality. The job is made easiest by accepting the first of the definitions advanced in the preceding section, calling simply for the termination of discrimination. But if handicaps and disadvantages for which society is responsible need to be reduced or eliminated before equality of opportunity can be said to exist, then special measures of various sorts, including preferential treatment in some connections, are essential.

Further, those taking a forward-looking view can plausibly hold that it is important to reduce the gaps between the levels of advancement and well-being of the different racial communities and that some sorts of preferential treatment are justified to bring this about. Preferential treatment might be granted, for example, in the selection of workers for special training programs and in connection with admissions to educational institutions and the granting of scholarships.

An argument for ratio hiring is also possible that ignores the question of individualism versus communalism. The argument is based on the premise that it is vital to bring the whole discriminatory system to an end and that this goal is unlikely to be achieved as long as those inclined toward discrimination are left with free choices: they will always think that a white is more highly qualified than a black. In such circumstances, court-ordered ratio hiring may be the only practicable road to take.

■ The Framework for Comparisons

A point implicit in the above should be made explicit: the comparisons providing a basis for judgments about equal treatment or equality of opportunity are made within the national framework. Ideally, the framework should no doubt be universal. Ideally, persons living in Colombia, France, India, and Zambia should have equal treatment and equality of opportunity when compared with each other. But it would be utopian (though perhaps sobering) to make comparisons on this basis. When we talk about equal treatment and equality of opportunity, we are talking about what happens within the boundaries of a given state or jurisdiction.

■ Review

Virtually everyone favors justice, equal and nondiscriminatory treatment, and equality of opportunity, but arguments nevertheless arise. People disagree about the meaning of each of these values and about the policies that will promote them most effectively.

Justice is sometimes said to be done when everyone gets his or her due or when burdens and benefits are allocated fairly. Supplementary propositions are advanced to help in the interpretation of these basic rules; they concern rights, deserts, and needs.

Equal treatment is not necessarily the same treatment. It permits classification and differentiation if what is done is reasonable and not arbitrary. This rule has been violated and abused so much that certain bases for differentiation have become suspect, meaning that people who want to base differentiation on them have the burden of justifying what they do. Among the suspect bases for differentiation are property and income, birth or other status, language, religion, sex, race, age, and handicap.

Equality of opportunity is defined in several ways. The basic proposition is that equality of opportunity is what exists in the absence of discrimination. Some endorse a broader definition: that equal opportunity is denied if anything for which society is responsible puts one person under greater disadvantage than another. And a few go still farther, holding that equal opportunity is denied if anything for which the individual is not responsible puts him or her under greater disadvantage than another.

Discrimination against one person is preferential treatment for another, so one is as much a part of the American tradition as the other. But whereas preferential treatment once occurred mainly for the benefit of whites, now it occurs more for the benefit of blacks. Arguments concerning preferential treatment may be either backward- or forward-looking. So far as the backward-looking argument is concerned, the main issue arises when remedial measures appear to benefit the undeserving at the expense of the innocent. And the question then arises of whether the issue should be considered purely in terms of individuals or whether whole communities are involved. With respect to the forward-looking argument, the obvious question concerns the kind of society desired for the future and the kinds of methods that are acceptable in promoting its achievement. Preferential treatment, and more especially ratio hiring, may be justifiable simply as the most effective attack on the discriminatory system.

The comparisons that are made in judging questions of equal treatment are made within the national framework.

■ Reading

Berlin, Isaiah (1955–56) "Equality," *Proceedings of the Aristotelian Society*, 56:301–26.

Dorn, Edwin (1979) *Rules and Racial Equality*. New Haven: Yale University Press.

Ginsberg, Morris (1965) *On Justice in Society*. Ithaca, N.Y.: Cornell University-Press.

Glazer, Nathan (1975) *Affirmative Discrimination: Ethnic Inequality and Public Policy*. New York: Basic Books.

Goldman, Alan H. (1979) *Justice and Reverse Discrimination*. Princeton: Princeton University Press.

Miller, David (1976) *Social Justice*. Oxford: Oxford University Press.

Sen, Amartya Kumar (1992) *Inequality Reexamined*. Cambridge: Harvard University Press.

Van Dyke, Vernon (1990) *Equality and Public Policy*. Chicago: Nelson-Hall.

Duties and Responsibilities

A responsible person is responsive to appropriate values.

Herbert Block's (Herblock's) view is that the world leaders are not responsible to appropriate values and are as responsible as the Serbs for the tragedy in Bosnia.

133

The first two editions of this book did not contain a chapter on duties and responsibilities. The emphasis was on rights rather than obligations, and that emphasis reflected the approach that has been dominant in teaching about politics and government and in public debate on political matters. But different varieties of conservatism have been coming to the fore in life in the United States, and one of the themes of the conservative movement is that in addition to emphasizing rights we should also emphasize duties and responsibilities. The point is obviously sound and deserving of endorsement not only by conservatives but also by others. Thus the present chapter.

Of course, all of the preceding chapters provide knowledge important to the exercise of duties and responsibilities. A knowledge of rights implies knowledge of the duties and responsibilities that are their counterpart: if one person has a right, others have a duty to respect that right. And the presumption is that knowledge contributes to responsible behavior: those with knowledge of democracy are more likely than others to act as good democrats, and those with knowledge about voting and elections are more likely than others to manage them fairly.

Further, subjects yet to come relate somehow to duties and responsibilities, especially the chapters in Part IV on political ideologies.

Nevertheless, the subject of duties and responsibilities deserves explicit, separate treatment. A difficulty appears at the outset, however, in that although rights are spelled out in the Bill of Rights and in various documents such as international treaties on human rights, no corresponding enumeration of duties and responsibilities exists. What the subject properly includes is therefore open to argument.

We will begin here with a discussion of the source of duties and responsibilities and meanings of the crucial terms. Although the idea of doing one's duty seems clear and uncomplicated, even it calls for explication, and the idea of acting *responsibly* calls for even more. Given a treatment of the meaning of these terms, we will proceed with discussions of duties and responsibilities relating to (1) good government, especially democratic government, (2) self-support and self-fulfillment, and (3) international affairs.

■ Duty and Responsibility

Just as observers differ on the source of moral rights, so they differ on the source of moral duties and responsibilities. In fact the same theories are advanced, which is to be expected because, for the most part, rights and duties go together: if I concede that you have a certain right, the logical implication is that I have a duty to respect it. Since duties are in large part corollaries of rights, they can be traced to the same theoretical sources. Thus, those who believe in natural rights can go on to identify natural duties: for every right a corresponding duty. Similarly, those who say that we are endowed by our Creator with rights can cite Him as a source of duties and responsibilities; more concretely, they can point to the Ten Commandments and other such injunctions.

A secular view is also possible. It is that every person is a source of moral judgment about duties and responsibilities, just as every person is a source of moral judgment about rights, and that no moral judgment is objectively valid. As in the case of rights, it does not matter much if one or a few persons take a particular view, but the greater the number of people who take that view, the greater significance it has; and if a general consensus develops, as it does on many matters, the implications for daily life are profound. Social pressures then reinforce personal judgments concerning duties and responsibilities, and the performance of certain duties or the acceptance of certain responsibilities may be made a matter of law.

The secular view lends itself readily to change. People who agree at one time that rule X reflects a duty or responsibility can later agree that it has become obsolete, perhaps superseded by rule Y.

The terms *duty* and *responsibility* both connote obligation. People do their duty and behave responsibly when they meet their obligations. Although an obligation may be legal, it is surely moral: people *ought* to do their duty and *ought* to behave responsibly. To fail to do so is to be morally delinquent.

The central obligation is to be concerned for the consequences of our choices for ourselves and others. If people act without giving a thought to the consequences, they are irresponsible, perhaps failing to do good that they might have done or perhaps harming themselves or others. Insofar as reasonably possible, they need to anticipate consequences and adjust their behavior accordingly. This is not always easy. Intuition and common sense provide a basis for anticipations in many situations, but in many others some kind of special knowledge is required. And where special knowledge is relevant and available, it is vital to take it into account. To fail to do so is to act irresponsibly.

I say above that once a right is conceded, an obligation to respect it is a logical implication. The more difficult question is whether, once a right is conceded, other obligations also follow. Is there an obligation to protect or help others in the exercise of their rights? This itself is, in the first instance, a question of moral judgment on which people may reasonably differ. It is also a question of practicality: you have no duty to do the impossible. An obligation to help others has more force with respect to your next-door neighbor than with respect to an unknown person in China. The consensus is, nevertheless, that obligations exist, though precisely what they are is a matter of never-ending dispute.

Criminal and civil law reflects the consensus. In connection with criminal law, we say that the social obligation to protect the rights of individuals is so great that government itself should assume the responsibility: it should take the initiative by providing police protection and by prosecuting offenders. In connection with civil law, we say that the social obligation is simply to define rights in law and then make it possible for injured persons to file suits in court against alleged offenders. The theory with respect to criminal law is not only that others are entitled to protection but also that if you fail to give protection you risk becoming a target of crime yourself; it is important to your own ultimate safety to give protection to the other fellow who is the target now. Although almost everyone accepts these principles, disagreements obviously arise over the question of which rights to protect and exactly how to do it.

The consensus also is that a social obligation exists to help people in the exercise of rights. It is accepted, for example, that a person accused of crime but unable to pay a lawyer is entitled to a public defender. It is accepted that young people are entitled to a certain amount of education at public expense. It is accepted that certain categories of people are entitled to health care. The extent of the obligation to help others is a matter of dispute, but the principle is accepted. This means a duty and responsibility not only to respect the rights of others but also in some connections to help vindicate those rights where it is practicable to do so.

Further, not only the government but also private persons have an obligation to protect and help others in the exercise of their rights. Private persons must help others in some circumstances if they can do it without serious cost or risk to themselves. That statement is admittedly vague. What kinds of harm and what kinds of need trigger the obligation? How much risk is it reasonable to expect people to accept, or how much cost is it reasonable to expect them to bear, for the benefit of others? It is much easier to state the principle than to decide on its detailed meaning in specific circumstances. But, to give an illustration, a bystander clearly has a duty to wade into a shallow pool if need be to save the life of a drowning child. And a bystander has a duty to summon the police if she sees a bank robbery in progress and is free to act. To deny any responsibility for the rights and well-being of others would be irresponsible.

A concern for consequences implies a concern for values. Responsible behavior is responsive to values. The assumption is that what happens matters—that the desirable and the good are to be promoted, and the undesirable and the bad are to be minimized or avoided. The consequences that concern us here, and therefore the values, are those relating to the three areas identified above relating to good government, the treatment of individuals, and international affairs.

■ Good Government

Good government requires responsible behavior by both private citizens and public servants.

Duties and responsibilities attend law making, law observance, and law-enforcement. Members of legislative bodies, from town councils to Congress, are among those who need to think of the probable consequences of action and inaction, seeking relevant knowledge and adjusting their behavior accordingly. This does not necessarily mean that individual legislators must all make themselves experts on every measure on which they vote. Inevitably some will follow the lead of others whom they trust. But through a committee system or otherwise, legislators have an obligation to see to it that desirable legislation is considered and that harmful legislation is avoided.

One of the problems is whether to speak of a mistake or of irresponsibility when something goes wrong, the difference being that irresponsibility implies some kind of moral delinquency whereas a mistake does not. The answer, of course, depends on circumstances, but the circumstances may be ambiguous enough to leave observers with a choice between the labels. Think, for example, of the action of Congress some years ago that led to the savings and loan scandal, costing the taxpayers billions of dollars. What Congress did was extend the guarantee of the Federal Deposit Insurance Corporation to larger deposits without requiring savings and loan associations to follow acceptable standards in making loans. When many of them then became over extended and were unable to repay deposits, the federal government had to take over the burden. Did Congress simply make a mistake, or was it irresponsible?

This kind of question can be raised endlessly. For example, how should we judge the annual deficits of the federal government? Do they result from sound policies? from mistakes? from irresponsibility? If they are explained in terms of sound policy or mistakes for a few years, how about if they keep occurring year after year? Is it responsible behavior if those of one generation seek their own comfort by borrowing money that later generations have to pay back? To the extent that irresponsibility is involved, who is to be blamed? Does the democratic system, or do institutional arrangements, encourage irresponsibility?

Law observance is a duty for everyone. To ignore this duty, violating law either systematically or capriciously, is to act irresponsibly. I will note exceptions in a moment but want first to emphasize the rule. The greater the proportion of people who are irresponsible about law observance, the greater the danger to the social order and the more government is undermined.

These generalizations apply in every field in which government operates. Providers of health care in connection with Medicare or Medicaid are irresponsible if they charge for services that they did not perform or that they performed unnecessarily; defense contractors are irresponsible if they falsify reports of tests of weapons; manufacturers are irresponsible if they violate the law in disposing of dangerous chemicals; automobile drivers are irresponsible if they violate the law by driving under the influence. Even a shoplifter is irresponsible in failing to respect property rights and in challenging the government in connection with its duty to protect them.

Law enforcement needs to occur responsibly, too, meaning that enforcement must occur on as consistent a basis as possible, but with due regard for the rights and interests of all those affected. To enforce law against some while winking at violations of the same law by others would be irresponsible, and so would arbitrary arrests. So would actions taken ostensibly to enforce law but actually to harass. When Senator Joseph McCarthy made charges that he could not prove about alleged communist infiltration into the federal government after World War II, he was surely being irresponsible. And every now and then a congressional committee conducts investigations in such a way as to raise the question of whether it is engaged in responsible inquiry or irresponsible harassment.

Above I mention exceptions to the rule that the law is to be observed. The better statement perhaps is that the requirement of law observance varies in its urgency, for laws differ in importance. The record shows that if people drive cars five or ten miles above the speed limit, the heavens do not fall. It is possible too that, where law enforcement is a problem, the solution lies not in more vigorous efforts at enforcement but in changing or repealing the law. This is what happened in connection with the Eighteenth Amendment, prohibiting the sale of liquor, and some argue that this is what should happen in connection with the prohibition of the sale of certain drugs.

A few violate the law as a matter of conscience, believing the law to be wrong, which puts government in a dilemma. On the one hand, a government that wants to encourage moral behavior needs to be sensitive to moral protest; but on the other hand it cannot maintain its authority if it permits everyone to decide which laws to obey. In the case of conscientious objectors, they won the day, government changing the law so as to give them the choice of public service other than military service. The government has not, however, acted similarly with respect to those who withhold a portion of their income taxes so as to avoid supporting the armed forces; nor would it permit you to withhold the portion of your tax that might otherwise help pay the salary of a member of Congress with whom you disagree. In general, though with qualification, the proposition stands that duty and responsibility call for the observance of the law.

Problems relating to duty and responsibility are complicated by the fact that legislators (in truth, most people) are torn by conflicting values, in which case differing judgments about duty and responsibility may be appropriate, depending on the value considered. Members of Congress, for example, have a variety of legitimate concerns: for the well-being of the whole country, for the well-being of the people of their own state or constituency; and for their own prospects of re-election. And concern for their own prospects of re-election implies a concern for the interests of various persons and groups who provide campaign contributions and votes. The problem is to adjust responses to each of these concerns so as to minimize or avoid irresponsibility in relation to the others.

Questions like those raised here concerning people who make and administer the law can also be raised about candidates for election. Like those who eventually serve in Congress, candidates are likely to be torn by a concern for different values. On the one hand, they need votes and so are highly motivated to make appeals that they think will win votes. On the other hand, they presumably want to be honest and to avoid promises that they cannot fulfill or that would lead to harm. Different persons respond differently to these considerations. The temptation to pander to voters is strong and may well lead to irresponsibility. Think, for example, of candidates who inveigh against taxes, knowing full well that they cannot reduce them without cutting programs that ought to be maintained. Tax increases may even be necessary.

It is interesting to contemplate the fact that we do not allow anyone to practice medicine without a license testifying to proper training and competence, but we have no comparable requirement in the political field. The question is what proportion of those who run for public office, or who serve in public office, are irresponsible in claiming an ability to diagnose social ills and prescribe remedies.

You can go on and ask, if you wish, whether it would be compatible with democracy to adopt a system for licensing those qualified to tend to the health of the body politic.

■ Self-Support and Self-Fulfillment

The principal reason why the subject of duties and responsibilities has come to the fore in the United States concerns the welfare program, and the feature of that program that gets the most attention concerns teenage mothers and deadbeat dads. The charge is that these mothers and dads are irresponsible, giving little or no thought to the consequences of what they do. The boy enjoys the pleasure of the moment and then goes on to other conquests, giving no thought to the question of who will support the babies his girlfriends produce. And like as not the teenage mother, who has little chance of supporting the baby anyway, drops out of school and thus makes it all the less likely that she will be able to provide support. Mother and baby become dependent on welfare. Welfare, as it is said, provides not only a safety net but a way of life.

In a society that assumes that people should be self-supporting and that parents (both the father and the mother) are morally obligated to support their children, this behavior is plainly irresponsible. But the prevailing view is that others would be neglecting their moral duty (would be irresponsible) if they allowed babies or anyone to starve. Thus a dilemma. What is the responsible response to irresponsibility?

David Norton takes the view that it is not enough that people should support themselves. In addition, he says, "the basic moral responsibility of every person is to discover and progressively actualize his or her innate potential worth" (Norton 1991, 110–15). Moreover, he goes on to argue that if individuals have this responsibility then society has a corresponding duty: to see to it that conditions exist that make self-fulfillment possible.

Norton mumbles on the meaning of this for government. Surely it means that government must provide, or at least contribute toward, the education necessary to help people discover and develop their talents. In practice, government responds to this obligation by making elementary and secondary education free, and governments in the more advanced countries subsidize higher education. The progressive introduction of free higher education is one of the obligations assumed by states that ratify the international Covenant on Economic, Social, and Cultural Rights.

Not only is education essential to self-fulfillment, but so is health; and in most of the advanced countries governments accept responsibilities in this field just as they do in the field of education.

■ International Affairs

The question of the duties and responsibilities of individuals with respect to international affairs becomes sharpest in time of war. In World War II, and to a lesser extent in the Korean War, a substantial consensus prevailed: it was everyone's duty to support the government against the enemy. Precisely what "support" meant for different people was a question. At the minimum, nothing was to be done to aid the enemy. At the maximum, those conscripted were to serve in the armed forces. In between these extremes, conceptions of duty and responsibility varied.

Questions about the meaning of duty and responsibility became acute in connection with the war in Vietnam. In some eyes, this was a war like all others, to be prosecuted through to victory. In other eyes it was at least an unwise war, and perhaps an unjust and immoral war, from which the government should extricate itself as soon as possible. Members of the two groups naturally had different conceptions of duty and responsibility. Those in the first group thought that everyone had a duty to rally around the flag. In their eyes, even those who personally opposed the war should do nothing to avoid conscription into the armed forces but should fight if called up; and others should give patriotic support. Members of the second group, though rarely if ever intending to aid the enemy, wanted as a minimum to avoid being conscripted; and many of them felt that it was their duty and responsibility to agitate against the war, hoping to minimize the harm done. The differences illustrate the point that the dictates of duty and responsibility are not always clear. People on both sides were conscientious and reasonable.

In principle, regardless of judgments about Vietnam, it ought to be recognized that duty, and a sense of responsibility for the well-being of the country, might dictate opposition to the government or to specific policies. Virtually everyone would agree, for example, that citizens of Germany who sought the defeat and downfall of Hitler were manifesting a high form of patriotism, seeking to do their duty and exercise their responsibility in the best interests of their country and humankind. And the same is true of those who fought against communism. Behavior that a Hitler or a Stalin would regard as treasonable might well be regarded by others as reflecting a praiseworthy sense of responsibility.

In the early 1990s a number of developments abroad raised questions about US duties and responsibilities in the world. Saddam Hussein of Iraq committed aggression against Kuwait. Strife in Somalia threatened hundreds of thousands of people with starvation. Bosnian Serbs, with help from Serbia, went to war against the Muslims of Bosnia, seeking "ethnic cleansing" in territory that they regarded as properly Serbian and aiming at independence or union with Serbia. A military dictatorship in Haiti violated human rights so egregiously and in general followed such oppressive policies that large numbers of Haitians sought to flee, most of them heading for the United States in boats or ships of questionable seaworthiness. In Rwanda fighting broke out between the two main ethnic groups, the Hutus and the Tutsis—fighting that took on a genocidal character. What duties and responsibilities, if any, did these developments entail for others?

In every case, people disagree about the appropriate answer. The same principles apply as with respect to the duty to help others, discussed above. An international and worldwide analogy exists to criminal law. Everyone all over the world has certain rights, and ultimately everyone all over the world has a degree of obligation to protect everyone else in the exercise of their rights. But the obligation is stronger with respect to immediate neighbors than with respect to those far away, and the practical possibility of giving effective help without undue risk or cost varies tremendously.

For example, what duties and responsibilities does a bystander country have when international aggression occurs? Everyone can agree that, at least as a rule, the aggression should be condemned: there should be no attempt to change international boundaries by force and no attempt to deprive other countries of their independence. Everyone can agree that the same principle that applies to domestic crime should apply to international crime: a common interest exists in seeing to it that the law is observed. Left unchecked, crime among countries may come to engulf us all, just as is the case within countries. But the possibilities of practical action must be considered in the one case as in the other; and so must the possible risks and costs.

When Saddam Hussein committed aggression against Kuwait, the United States went to Kuwait's aid, but more out of concern for a set of special national interests than out of a belief in selfless duty. The United States has not accepted the principle that it must take military action against any aggressor anywhere. For humanitarian reasons, the United States intervened militarily in Somalia and sent in foodstuffs and other materials with a view to minimizing starvation and alleviating distress; but then it got involved in the local strife among the rival clans, and some American soldiers were killed. The episode drove home the point that government has responsibilities to its own citizens and needs to take them into account when deciding what international responsibilities it has and how to respond to them. In other words, estimates of potential risks and costs need to be taken into account in connection with decisions about help to others.

With respect to Bosnia, Haiti, and Rwanda, countervailing considerations are relevant. On the one side, as just indicated, governments have responsibilities to their own citizens—to their lives and their property. Action abroad does not come free. It has to be paid for with dollars collected in taxes, and it may be paid for with lives. Further, the record of states when they intervene abroad, whether to settle foreign quarrels or to respond to humanitarian needs, is not one of unmixed success. Such interventions tend to be plagued by more or less ignorance of the local situation and local attitudes and also by the tendency to let ulterior motives of a self-regarding sort intrude into an otherwise altruistic enterprise. Given the record of Western imperialism, its former victims are suspicious of anything suggesting its renewal. Moreover, difficulties like those in Bosnia, Haiti, Rwanda, and Somalia do not suggest that a quick fix is a likely possibility. A foreign country (like the United States) that intervenes with the very best of intentions may well find itself in a situation from which it cannot withdraw for many years, perhaps not for decades. And a prolonged effort would run the risks of arousing the same kinds of local resentments and opposition that imperialism stimulated.

Where duty and responsibility lie in the face of such complex and contradictory considerations is difficult to say. It is natural for those concerned with duty and responsibility to want to bring an end to "ethnic cleansing," to a despotism that drives people to desperation, and to genocide, but prudence gives pause.

■ Review

Theories about the sources of duties and responsibilities are similar to theories about the sources of rights. If you concede that another person has a right, the logical implication is that you have a duty to respect the right. And you may have a duty, alone or through government, to protect and help others in the exercise of their rights.

Duties and responsibilities attend law making, law observance, and law enforcement. To act responsibly, those who make and administer or enforce the law need to be informed about the relevant values and attentive to them. The prevailing consensus is that everyone has a duty to observe the law, although exceptions to this rule are also recognized.

Responsible people are concerned about the consequences of their choices. Issues concerning responsibility have arisen in the United States, especially in connection with the increase in the number of teenagers who become mothers and fathers when they either do not or cannot support their offspring, or perhaps themselves. In some eyes, a sense of responsibility requires making those choices that are most likely to lead to self-fulfillment.

Questions concerning duties and responsibilities arise in international affairs. Is it to be assumed that citizens have a duty to support the government in war, regardless of the nature of the government and regardless of the war? Is it a national duty to help and protect foreign governments and peoples in the exercise of their rights?

■ Reading

Aaron, Henry J., Thomas E. Mann, and Timothy Taylor, eds. (1994) *Values and Public Policy*. Washington, D.C.: Brookings.

Anderson, Digby, ed. (1992) *The Loss of Virtue. Moral Confusion and Social Disorder in Britain and America*. London: Social Affairs Unit, National Review Book.

Arkes, Hadley (1986) *First Things. An Inquiry into the First Principles of Morals and Justice*. Princeton: Princeton University Press.

Bellamy, Richard, ed. (1993) *Theories and Concepts of Politics. An Introduction.*New York: Manchester University Press.

Wilson, James Q. (1991) *On Character*. Washington, D.C.: AEI Press.

Why Democracy Develops and Succeeds or Fails

People generally want a share in decisions affecting them. Democracy has done best when it has developed incrementally.

Political stability is precarious when the population divides into a small, rich upper class and impoverished masses.

No one can say with complete assurance why democracy develops or why it succeeds or fails. Explaining great historical developments and events is among the most difficult tasks that scholars face. Chance—good and bad luck—plays a role, manifesting itself, for example, in the fact that some persons are born and live in circumstances that lead them to the ideas that they entertain. It is difficult to say how much of a role chance plays, however, for circumstances may call forth the persons and the ideas that are appropriate to the time. Causal conditions play a role, but it is not always easy to distinguish a causal relationship from a chance correlation. Causal chains go back and back, leaving it uncertain where the effort to explain should stop.

Democracy is relatively new in history. In Britain it developed over a number of centuries, parliament gradually expanding its powers at the expense of the monarch, and the people gradually gaining the rights that go with democracy, including the right to vote. Americans may think of the United States as a democratic country since 1776 or 1789, but in the early decades, suffrage being limited, government was accountable to only a portion of the people.

In Arend Lijphart's view, "Not a single democratic government can be found in the nineteenth century, and it was not until the first decade of the twentieth century that in two countries, Australia and New Zealand, fully democratic regimes with firm popular control of governmental institutions and universal adult suffrage were established" (Lijphart 1984, 37).

Thus, though rooted in earlier developments, democracy has come to flourish mainly in this century, the victories of the countries of the North Atlantic in the two world wars, and more recently in the cold war, being crucial. Classifying 186 countries at the beginning of 1993, Freedom House describes seventy-five as both free and democratic and twenty-four others as "formally" democratic though only partly free. The two groups combined make up more than half the states of the world. Thirty-four countries have become democratic (at least formally so) only since the end of the cold war. How well these new democracies will develop, and how stable they will be, remains to be seen.

Robert A. Dahl, drawing on the writing of a number of others, has analyzed the conditions that seem relevant to the rise of democracy and to its success or failure. Instead of democracy, however, he speaks of public contestation, participation, and polyarchy. Public contestation refers to legal and open competition for control over government. It implies a right to oppose the government—to organize a loyal opposition—and it may occur within an oligarchy or within and among greater and greater portions of the population as the right of participation is extended. (An oligarchy is government by the few, and so is an autocracy.) Full democracy exists when public contestation is free and when the right to participate (for example, to vote) is universal. A polyarchy is a regime that is "substantially popularized and liberalized, that is, highly inclusive and extensively open to public contestation" (Dahl 1971, 8).

Dahl (1975, 133–61) identifies the following as "conditions favoring public contestation and polyarchy":

a. Historical sequences
b. Concentration in the social and economic order
c. The level of socioeconomic development
d. Equalities and inequalities
e. Subcultures, cleavage patterns, and governmental effectiveness
f. Foreign domination
g. The beliefs of political activists

I am adopting Dahl's pattern of organization but am modifying it in several respects, especially on the basis of the work of Dankwart Rustow and Samuel P. Huntington. To minimize the danger of confusion, I will speak of democracy where Dahl uses the term *polyarchy*.

■ Historical Sequences

Dankwart Rustow preceded Dahl in emphasizing the historical factor. His focus is on problems of political modernization more than on democracy as such, but some of his findings are relevant to the question under scrutiny here. In a book published in 1967 Rustow names "countries such as the Philippines, Lebanon, Chile, Costa Rica, and Uruguay that can be said to have attained relatively stable democratic systems" (Rustow 1967, 228–33). The list is ironic in that democracy was destroyed in all of the countries named except Costa Rica in the dozen years after Rustow wrote, only to be restored later in all of them except Lebanon.

Nevertheless, it is of some interest to note what Rustow identifies as the historical antecedents of democracy. First, "a history of anywhere from 40 to 130 years of administrative and educational modernization." Second, the enjoyment of "a stable geographic context." Third, "a tradition, dating back at least one, two, or three generations, of parties that provided some organic link between rulers and subjects, and that were able to involve progressively larger groups in the political process." And fourth, bitter conflict between major social or political groups in the early years of the development toward democracy, the conflict terminating in such a way that "the vital interests of no major part of the community were destroyed."

Theorizing on the basis of this record, Rustow suggests that democracy develops out of oligarchic or autocratic regimes in which "the traditionalists have accepted the necessity of modernization" and have reconciled themselves to "the inevitability of greater equality." Democracy "requires that conflicting interests be expressed rather than suppressed [and] that the participants acquire experience in the arts of settling conflict." It requires "a relative abundance of skilled administrative and political personnel," so that alternation in office becomes possible. And since democracy involves the ever-present possibility of changing rulers, it requires "a continuing sense of identity among the subjects," with a substantial measure of mutual understanding and responsiveness.

Elsewhere in his book, Rustow emphasizes the need for "sequence rather than simultaneity" in the development of the modern nation-state (Rustow 1967, 123–32). As he sees it, the three basic ingredients of such a state are unity (a sense of belonging together), authority, and equality. Unity is obviously important to any kind of effective and stable government, including democracy. Authority is the very essence of government; in its best form it implies a bureaucracy skilled in giving impartial public service and dedicated to the rule of law. Equality is necessary with respect to rights of participation. According to Rustow, both authority and participation must grow fairly slowly and cumulatively over a period of several generations. The expansion of modern state services in communications, in education, in social welfare, and in economic planning requires a steady growth of trained personnel; an over-ambitious pace is likely to lead to problems. Similarly, a reliable expansion of the circle of political participants must proceed step by step.

Eric Nordlinger expresses similar views. His concern is with the development of political systems toward democracy in a nonviolent, nonauthoritarian, and stable way. The variables he takes into account are the sequence in which the successive steps or stages come and the speed with which they come. He argues that the prospects for democracy are best when the sequence is as follows: first a sense of national identity, then the "institutionalization of a central government," and only thereafter the emergence of mass parties and a mass electorate. Moreover, he argues that any attempt to take these steps in rapid fashion is likely to lead to violence and repression, making the achievement of democracy more difficult (Nordlinger 1968, 500).

Britain and the United States both fit the pattern that Rustow and Nordlinger describe. In Britain, over a period of centuries, monarchs were compelled to share their power in greater and greater measure with an aristocracy. The "institutionalization of the central government" then occurred; that is, a bureaucracy developed, and the roles of parliament and the executive were clarified. Finally, the aristocracy was compelled to acquiesce in the enfranchisement of larger and larger portions of the people, until universal adult suffrage was reached. The gradual incorporation of people in the political system was accompanied by the development and spread of political skills, understandings, and mutual trust, keeping the system tolerable for a high proportion of those involved.

Viewed from another perspective, what happened in Britain and the United States (and for that matter in a number of other countries) is that an *élite* agreed on the institutional arrangements for democratic government and on the related fundamental rules and principles before the suffrage was extended to a very large portion of the population. This suggests the hypothesis that the chances for democracy are best if constitutionalism is allowed to become firmly established before universal suffrage is introduced.

If the hypothesis is sound, the question remains why it is sound. The answer may be that the prospects of democracy are greater if the upper class has the opportunity to develop the attitudes and skills on which democracy depends, and becomes committed to its rules and principles, before others with conflicting interests are enfranchised. When the others are enfranchised, they may take advantage of their power and enact legislation for their own benefit; and it may then be a touch-and-go question whether the upper class will continue to support democracy. No person or group or class can be expected to give loyal and lasting support to a political system that continually operates against its interests.

Samuel P. Huntington's theme with respect to the historical background of democracy is somewhat different. It is that the *nature of the traditional society* tends to determine future possibilities. If the traditional society was bureaucratic and highly centralized, its modern successor is most likely to be centralized and authoritarian. Conversely, if the traditional society was "more pluralistic in structure and dispersed in power"—as in a feudal system—its modern successor is more likely to be a pluralistic democracy (Huntington 1968, 176).

The historical record suggests an explanation of the breakdown of democracy in most of the former colonies that have become independent since World War II. They lacked an historical buildup toward democracy, to say nothing of a tradition of democracy. They simply had democracy conferred upon them. In a number of cases the conferral followed agitation in the colony for "one man, one vote and majority rule," but in most cases "one man, one vote" turned out to be "one man, one vote once," and "majority rule" turned out to be authoritarian rule by a member of the race that was in the majority. Perhaps the historic conditions favoring democracy were not there; perhaps the pace of change was too fast.

As chapter 20 indicates, debate on the above points is in progress in Asia. One question concerns the relationship between the Confucian tradition and democracy. The Confucian tradition emphasizes the community, conformity, and hierarchy, not liberty, equality, and fraternity. The ruler is to be virtuous and to promote the happiness of the ruled, and members of the educated élite may feel it their duty to criticize the ruler who fails in his duty, but such criticism is not protected. The idea of individual or human rights is not a part of the Confucian tradition. Law is designed to uphold the state, not to protect the individual. Confucian doctrine thus suggests authoritarian government, not democracy, which makes it understandable why even Asians who are favorably disposed toward democracy raise questions about the wisdom of attempting to introduce it in short order without qualification. Moreover, a considerable portion of the population is illiterate. No wonder that the Chinese who are unhappy with the authoritarian rule of the Communist party think of democracy not so much in terms of equal participation by all the people as in terms of rule by a "democratic" elite.

■ Concentration in the Social and Economic Order _____

Concentration exists in the social and economic order when *control* is in the hands of the few—control over wealth, over violence, and over the government itself.

Instead of speaking of control, Dahl speaks of *access* and of *sanctions*. In this context *sanctions* are measures that impose costs of some sort; they are penalties or deprivations.

Dahl's generalization is that "the circumstances most favorable to competitive politics exist when access to violence and socioeconomic sanctions is either dispersed or denied both to oppositions and to government. The least favorable circumstances exist when violence and socioeconomic sanctions are exclusively available to the government and denied to the oppositions" (Dahl 1975, 137–38).

This suggests that if the few control wealth and violence they are also likely to control government. Conversely, a pluralistic social order is most favorable for competitive politics.

The idea of *a pluralistic social order* should be distinguished from the idea of *a plural society* described earlier. A *pluralistic social order* is one in which political and economic power is divided among a number of groups—economic, religious, ethnic, and geographical. Membership in these groups is cross-cutting; that is, any set of persons may find themselves in the same group when their concern is for one interest and in different groups when their concern is for another. They align themselves one way for economic purposes, another way for religious purposes, still another way for ethnic purposes, and so on. The same two persons may be in the same group and thus allies in one connection and be in different groups and thus opponents in another connection. Members of all groups have access to the political system and engage in both cooperation and competition in shaping public policy. They share a sense of membership in and loyalty to a common society.

In contrast, a *plural society* consists of distinct communities that cherish and want to preserve their separate characteristics—that is, their race, language, religion, culture, or sense of nationality. A kind of voluntary apartheid (separateness) exists, in that, except in the marketplace, relationships among people rarely cross communal lines. People in the various groups may or may not all have access to the political system. The sense of membership in a common society is weak or nonexistent.

The opposite of a pluralistic social order is one that is centrally dominated—dominated by one person or one relatively small group. It is *monistic*.

The record of agrarian societies illustrates the relationship between social and economic circumstances on the one hand and political developments on the other. If an agrarian society divides into a small landholding class and a mass of dependent peasants, it is rarely democratic. In contrast, if it is characterized by a mass of free farmers, it may well be. The United States and Canada have been countries of free farmers. El Salvador has been a country of great landowners. This is one of the reasons why those who support democracy seek land reform in countries like El Salvador.

The record of commercial and industrial societies is more complex. Private ownership of the means of production and distribution is obviously compatible with democracy, as the record of the United States illustrates. In fact, wherever democracy flourishes, it is associated with full or substantial emphasis on private ownership and the market. Whether this is a necessary condition of democracy is uncertain. Countries classified as democratic vary considerably in the extent to which government participates in economic life.

The crucial consideration may relate not to ownership but to control. Dahl's view is that if the direction of the economy is decentralized, no matter what the form of ownership, "a pluralistic and hence a competitive regime can exist," whereas if the direction of the economy is highly centralized, this is unlikely (Dahl 1975, 141).

Private ownership obviously does not guarantee democracy, as the record of so many right-wing dictatorships attests. Most of them leave private ownership substantially untouched while ruling in an authoritarian way.

Note that we are dealing here with tendencies, not with absolutes. The claim is that certain conditions are favorable to democracy, or make it possible or likely, not that they assure its existence.

The dispersion of *command over violence*, or the absence or weakness of land armies, is also favorable to the development and success of democracy. A central ruler may then have difficulty establishing or maintaining authoritarian control. The voice of the people is likely to be stronger when power relationships make rebellion a possibility. It is possible to argue that parties and elections are substitutes for armies and battles, the substitution being most likely when the weapons of the time make each person about as powerful as every other person.

Eighteenth-century Britain provides an illustration. Its military power was concentrated mainly in the navy, and control over its small land forces was dispersed among the local gentry. Moreover, a man with a musket was about as powerful as any other man. If this did not make the king as prudent as he should have been, it nevertheless imposed limits on arbitrary rule.

Modern armed forces are under centralized control and are equipped with expensive and powerful weapons that seem to assure political control to any person or group willing and able to use them ruthlessly. Moreover, governments generally seem to have the advantage even when the political struggle is conducted with bombs and small arms, as long as determination and a willingness to be ruthless are maintained. In general, then, the contemporary situation with respect to command over violence is not favorable to democracy.

Nevertheless, command over violence does not stem entirely from the possession of weapons. The attitudes of people are important. Perhaps a few rulers can go on being ruthless even when they believe that they have lost a moral claim to authority, but most cannot. They need a moral conviction that they are right. Those who lose that conviction lose their fervor and may accept change. Otherwise disaffection is likely to develop. Members of the armed forces may become unreliable as they swing to the view that the rulers are out of tune with the needs of the time. The masses of people may shift from cowering submission to defiance. And domino effects occur: that is, the course of events in one country is influenced by the course of events in others.

In saying the above, I have in mind developments in both South Africa and the communist world in the late 1980s and early 1990s. In South Africa the white élite abandoned the view that the domination of one race by another was morally justified. In other words, they abandoned the view that their own political control and the exclusion of blacks from participation in the political process were morally justified. This meant an acceptance of the view that they were presiding over an immoral system. They had the military means to preserve their rule for many years, although no doubt at the cost of increasing, and increasingly violent, opposition. Instead of attempting this, they negotiated an abandonment of their dominant role and accepted democracy.

Something similar happened in the Soviet Union and in eastern Europe. It was not a reduced supply of weapons that induced the Soviet government to drop its policy of maintaining communist dictatorships in the countries of eastern Europe, nor was it a reduced supply of weapons that induced the governments there to give up rather than fight. Democracy surged ahead more because of pervasive changes in attitudes than because of changes of a material sort relating to weapons.

■ Level of Development

The record indicates a correlation between democracy and *level of socioeconomic development*.

Examining transitions to democracy since the Portuguese dictatorship ended in 1974, Huntington says that they were "most likely to occur in countries at the middle and upper-middle levels of economic development." But the correlation was loose. Huntington goes on to note that ten of the countries in question had per capita GNPs of less than $300, that the corresponding figures for nine others were between $500 and $1,000, and that for two it was over $1,000. Moreover, a number of countries at the same general level of economic development remain undemocratic (Huntington 1991, 61–62).

Several assumptions underlie the theory that level of socioeconomic development is important to transitions to democracy. Given such development, more people are better educated and better informed about choices potentially open to them. With development, the middle class becomes larger, and a smaller and smaller portion of the population live at the margins of existence, which means that more people are more secure, less threatened by the compromises and accommodations that democracy entails, and can take more interest in politics and give more time to it than those living in desperate circumstances.

Another theory emphasizes one of the points made just above, that the *level of literacy and education* is important to the development of democracy. Illiterate people can no doubt participate in politics effectively on the basis of knowledge gained via the radio and TV, but literacy and education nevertheless facilitate communication. They thus facilitate and may well enhance participation in social and political life and make it more likely that a pluralistic social order will develop.

At the same time, one must be cautious about generalizations on this subject. At the end of World War I, Britain, France, Germany, and Italy were not far apart in their level of socioeconomic development, but the first two remained democratic while the second two endorsed Nazism and fascism (to be discussed in chapter 25). And in the early 1970s Chile had an economy among the most highly developed in Latin America, yet it became a dictatorship.

■ Equalities and Inequalities

Consideration of equalities and inequalities overlaps with the earlier point relating to concentration in the social and economic order, for concentration implies inequality of some kind. The relevant equalities and inequalities may be of various sorts; they may relate to income, wealth, knowledge, skills, zeal for work, race, language, religion, and so on. The distribution of resources in such categories correlates reasonably well with the distribution of political resources and skills and of satisfaction and discontent. Those who have greater income, wealth, status, knowledge, and zeal for work, and those who command the dominant language, belong to the dominant race, or adhere to the dominant religion are likely to have greater political influence and power. The differences may or may not be due to deliberate discrimination. Among those who adhere to the same religion, inequalities may stem from differences in status, some claiming and being conceded special knowledge of the divine will.

Extreme differences militate against the development or preservation of democracy. We have already noted the point with respect to agrarian societies dominated by large landowners. In industrial societies, the inequalities are not likely to be so extreme, and industrial societies usually display a measure of flexibility, making concessions to appease the deprived—concessions having to do, for example, with trade union rights, collective bargaining, unemployment insurance, efforts to maintain full employment, social welfare measures, and the like. Such concessions tend to reduce inequalities and to increase the political power of those hitherto deprived. At the same time, in most societies it is obvious that the deprived tend to join the privileged in accepting, and perhaps in approving, substantial inequalities.

Inequalities based on race, language, and religion show up in subcultures and cleavage patterns, to which we now turn.

■ Subcultures and Cleavage Patterns

Cultural and racial homogeneity and heterogeneity affect the prospects of democracy.

This problem has been mentioned earlier. A homogeneous society is a unified society, its members speaking the same language, sharing the same religion, regarding themselves as members of the same nation, and belonging to the same ethnic or racial group. A heterogeneous society is a plural society—divided by language, religion, sense of nationality, ethnicity, or race.

The prospects for democracy are clearly best in a homogeneous, unified society. Heterogeneous societies face special problems, the extent of the problems varying with the depth of the divisions. If the various segments are suspicious and distrustful of each other, and above all if they are historical enemies, as is all too frequently the case, the problems are likely to be acute, and democracy in its usual form may not develop or be maintained.

As Dahl puts it, "Any dispute in which a large section of the population of a country feels that its way of life or its highest values are severely menaced by another segment of the population creates a crisis in a competitive political system. Whatever the eventual outcome may be, the historical record argues that the system is very likely to dissolve into civil war or to be displaced by a hegemony, or both" (Dahl 1975, 152). The more deeply divided a society is, the more difficult it is for democracy to develop or survive.

The history of the treatment of blacks in the United States illustrates problems stemming from heterogeneity. For many decades, even after blacks were freed from slavery, many whites found it unacceptable to admit them as participants in the political system. Democracy was thus limited. Important steps have been taken, especially during and since the 1960s, to assure blacks full rights of participation, but the process is not yet complete.

Democracy in Lebanon has been destroyed by social cleavages based on religion. Cyprus illustrates comparable problems. It got independence in 1960 on the basis of a democratic constitution, but differences between the Greek and Turkish elements in the population—differences of language, religion, and national affinity, coupled with differences stemming from a history of communal struggles—led to the collapse of the democratic system within a few years.

Dahl names three interrelated conditions as essential if a heterogeneous society is to develop and maintain democracy. First, no subculture is to be " 'indefinitely' denied the opportunity to participate in the government—i.e., in the majority coalition whose leaders form the 'Government' or the Administration." Second, each subculture must be provided with a relatively high degree of security. Each must be assured that it will have full opportunity to maintain its distinctive characteristics and that its distinctive interests will get full consideration. Third, the government must be regarded as effective in coping with the country's major problems.

As indicated earlier, the first two of these conditions can be met in various ways; for example, by arrangements guaranteeing the representation of each significant subculture in the different parts of the government, including the executive, or arrangements that give the subcultures a veto on certain kinds of change. The third condition is common to all governments, but is added because of the possibility that what is done to meet the first two may tend to reduce the government's effectiveness.

The first two conditions call for substantial departures from the usual rules of democracy. They raise questions about equal treatment, discussed in chapter 8, and about self-determination, to be discussed in chapter 12.

In mentioning religion above I am assuming that a country is more likely to be democratic when people adhere to the same religion than when they are religiously divided. Disputes between Protestants and Catholics make democracy difficult in Northern Ireland, and disputes between Hindus and Muslims make it difficult in India.

Religion may involve difficulties for democracy in another way, too. Think, for example, of the view of the more fundamentalist Muslims that life should proceed according to the rules of the Qur'an. It is shari'a law that should prevail. Given this view, the question is who decides which passage in the Qur'an to regard as the most relevant and who should interpret this passage. By the same token, the question is who decides what shari'a law requires in the specific situation confronted. If people decide these questions for themselves, then the incompatibility with democracy, if any, is limited: democracy does not tell people on what basis they should make up their minds. But if the mullahs or ayatollahs or anyone else give political advice and claim to do it in the name of God or on the basis of any other transcendental authority, they are challenging democracy. In truth, they are challenging the right of anyone but themselves to rule. They are the ones who know the will of the Lord, and what mere mortal should be permitted to challenge that will?

In *Modern Islamic Political Thought*, Hamid Enayat recognizes the problem. "By upholding the Sharī'ah," he says, "Islam affirms the necessity of government on the basis of norms and well-defined guidelines, rather than personal preferences" (1982, 129). Those Muslim thinkers who face the question of the compatibility of Islam with democracy, he further says, normally come up with the open admission that the two are irreconcilable (1982, 135). Huntington points out that "between 1981 and 1990 only two of the thirty-seven countries in the world with Muslim majorities were ever rated 'free' by Freedom House in its annual surveys" (Huntington 1991, 307). The two were Gambia (for two years) and the Turkish part of Cyprus (for four years).

The problem of the relationship between religion and democracy is not limited to the Muslim countries. Although a strong correlation exists between Western Christianity and democracy, Christian fundamentalists pose challenges to democracy. Those who believe in the inerrancy of the Bible and who claim to know what God and the Bible require are calling implicitly for authoritarian, theocratic rule. The point is illustrated by the bumper sticker: "God said it, I believe it, that settles it!" And it is illustrated by the question "why bother to pay attention to anyone else's ideas if we've already heard from God?"

■ Foreign Influences

The question of whether democracy develops and survives is not always answered simply on the basis of domestic conditions. The actions and policies of foreign governments may be crucial. Democracy would surely have been set back had the Central Powers won World War I or had Hitler, Mussolini, and Hirohito won World War II. Conversely, the fact that democratic powers won these wars strengthened the cause of democracy everywhere.

Foreign influence is explicit and obvious in the fact that from the end of World War II until 1989 the Soviet Union made the development or restoration of democracy impossible in eastern and southeastern Europe. In contrast, the United States and Britain regarded anything other than democracy as unacceptable in the countries that they occupied at the close of World War II.

After World War II the United States mixed its concern for democracy abroad with a determination to prevent communists from coming to power in additional countries. And it seemed to give more emphasis to stopping communism than to promoting democracy, giving support in numerous instances to undemocratic if not antidemocratic leaders who were also anticommunist. Whether it thus impeded or prevented the development or preservation of democracy is a controversial question. In any event, in principle it is clear that the political system of a country may be more a function of the influence and activities of foreign powers than of domestic circumstances.

■ The Beliefs of Political Activists _____

Beliefs relating to democracy help determine whether it will develop and endure. Democracy rests on a set of rules and principles, and its existence and persistence depend on their acceptance. People—at least a substantial portion of them—must believe in democracy; they must believe that government ought to be responsive and accountable to them; they must believe that it is best to select public officials in competitive elections and must believe that the elections should be and are fair. They must believe in human rights.

Further, people—at least a substantial portion of them—must regard compromise as acceptable. Adamant, nonnegotiable demands and fanatical devotion to the dictates of some faith or ideology are inimical to democracy. Political competition must be based on a reciprocal understanding that whoever wins will maintain the rules, permitting the defeated to win later if they can; that is, there must be trust and confidence that the various political leaders and movements share a fundamental acceptance of democratic principles.

Democracy is in danger if those who control the government attach prime importance to undemocratic values. In a number of instances persons and parties that have come to power democratically have made democracy a sham, perhaps by harassing or imprisoning or killing their opponents, curtailing free speech, or rigging whatever elections they hold. In a number of other instances they have explicitly set democracy aside. Especially when the masses of people and the mass organizations in a society are less than fully committed to democracy, or when the people are so badly split that no democratic government gets solid and stable support, it is easy for political leaders to attach paramount importance to their own continuation in office. Sham democracy or no democracy is the likely result.

Beliefs about democracy that prevail within the military are likely to be especially important. In many countries military leaders have at their disposal the means of seizing political power. A number of considerations are likely to influence their decision whether to do so, and if they do it a number of considerations will influence the nature of their rule and their attitudes toward maintaining their power indefinitely. Their response to the question of whether democracy is desirable is among the considerations.

■ Security and Peace

Finally, a proposition might be added to Dahl's list: that security and peace are favorable to democracy. A preoccupation with foreign threats and dangers and with war is unfavorable to respect for free speech, competitive elections, and legislative deliberation. Whether justifiably or not, fear of a foreign enemy tends to strengthen a military outlook and the belief that authority should be concentrated in one or a few hands. Defeat in war may have varied effects, depending at least in part on the policies of the victors.

■ Review

The division of the world between democratic and authoritarian regimes raises the question of why democracy develops and why it succeeds or fails. Various considerations and theories figure in the answer:

1. Historical sequences. Some patterns of historical development are more favorable to democracy than others.
2. Concentration in the social and economic order. Democracy has the poorest prospects when control over wealth and violence is in the hands of the few.
3. Level of development. Democracy seems to correlate with a certain minimum level of well-being and with a certain level of education.
4. Equalities and inequalities. Equalities are favorable to democracy, and inequalities are unfavorable.
5. Subcultures and cleavage patterns. The more deeply divided a society, the more difficult it is for democracy to develop or survive.
6. Foreign influences. A foreign power may affect domestic struggles, playing a major role in determining whether democracy develops and survives.
7. The beliefs of political activists. Beliefs favorable to democracy are crucial to its development and survival.
8. International security and peace are more favorable to democracy than foreign threats and war.

■ Reading

Dahl, Robert A. (1975) "Governments and Oppositions," in Greenstein and Polsby (1975).

Greenstein, Fred I., and Nelson W. Polsby, eds. (1975) *The Handbook of Political Science*. Vol. 3, *Macropolitical Theory*. Reading, Mass.: Addison-Wesley.

Huntington, Samuel P. (1991) *The Third Wave: Democratization in the Late Twentieth Century*. Norman: University of Oklahoma Press.

Huntington, Samuel P., and Jorge I. Dominguez (1975), "Political Development," in Greenstein and Polsby (1975).

Lijphart, Arend (1977) *Democracy in Plural Societies*. New Haven: Yale University Press.

Pinkney, Robert (1994) *Democracy in the Third World*. Boulder: Lynne Reinner.

Przeworski, Adam (1991) *Democracy and the Market*. Cambridge: Cambridge University Press.

Rustow, Dankwart A. (1967) *A World of Nations. Problems of Political Modernization*. Washington, D.C.: Brookings.

Schumpeter, Joseph A. (1942) *Capitalism, Socialism, and Democracy*. New York: Harper & Row.

Sisk, Timothy D. (1992) *Islam and Democracy*. Washington, D.C.: United States Institute of Peace Press.

Sorensen, Georg (1993) *Democracy and Democratization. Processes and Prospects in a Changing World*. Boulder: Westview Press.

Usher, Dan (1981) *The Economic Prerequisite to Democracy*. New York: Columbia University Press.

Violence and Revolution

Violence lies in the background, if not in the foreground, of political struggles.

"I am sure the country is behind us."

The threat of violence is rapidly advancing from background to foreground in this Indian cartoon. Even as they flee, the leader of the Indian government, Mme. Nehru, assures her cabinet that the country supports them.

The threat or use of violence (or force) is a regular feature of government, and it is an option for those who challenge government, perhaps as an aspect of revolutionary struggle. Moreover, domestic struggles may become international, for foreign governments sometimes become involved. My object now is to describe and explain the role of violence in domestic politics and to inquire into its justifiability.

The violence of government is an aspect of its need to coerce. It must coerce if it is to enforce the law. Moreover, it must be prepared to coerce if it is to maintain itself against a disloyal opposition—that is, against persons who believe that they could govern better than those in office and who would seize control if they could. In advanced democratic countries, the coercion may seem to be no more than a background possibility, manifested perhaps by nothing more than a police officer cruising in a car. But in some connections police officers must be ready to shoot, and behind them must be others who are also ready to shoot. The total military power of the government must be available to support the police. To maintain itself, government must command more force and violence than any challenger.

It is sometimes said that what distinguishes government from other organizations is its monopoly on legal violence. No other organization is free to use force or violence. The statement is true, but it involves an ironic twist in that it describes a situation that government itself brings about: while claiming the right to use violence itself, government prohibits other organizations from doing the same. Further, as I will note shortly, in using violence, government does not always stay within the rules that it has fixed. Its own violence may be illegitimate.

Despite the law and the power behind it, those who challenge government sometimes resort to violence. They engage in riot, sabotage, and murder; they resort to terrorism; they rebel or try to seize power in any of several ways. Violence lies in the background (if not in the foreground) on both sides of political struggles. It is farthest in the background in stable democracies and most in the foreground in dictatorial and authoritarian systems.

■ What Counts as Political Violence? What Is Repression?

Coercion counts as violence when its purpose or effect is to damage, to destroy property, or to intimidate, restrain, injure, or kill. It may be either legal or illegal, though when it is legal some prefer the word *force* rather than the word *violence*. Violence is political when its purpose or effect concerns the organization, the leadership, the policies, or the survival of government.

The definition rules out the idea of "institutional" or "structural" violence. For example, it rules out such statements as the following: "The impoverishment of the majority of the inhabitants in Latin America represents a form of violence embedded within the very structure of current economic practices." To use the word in this way is to confuse its meaning. It may be wrong to impoverish as well as to kill, but it is surely bad practice to describe such different kinds of actions by the same word.

Repression is the use of governmental coercion to weaken, control, or eliminate actual or potential opponents.

■ Governmental Force and Violence

Governments use (or threaten) force and violence not only in normal police actions but also in extraordinary and unconventional ways. If they choose, they use the police—and thus potentially the violence of the police—to harass and intimidate opponents. They may declare martial law or proclaim a state of siege, in which case they free themselves from some of the restraints in their own laws having to do with arrest, imprisonment, and execution. They routinely deny the use of torture, but, especially in the case of dictatorial and authoritarian regimes, it is clear that most of them engage in it, whether sporadically or regularly.

Prisoners sometimes die in the hands of the police, and it is clear that the explanation is sometimes political. Some are killed deliberately and some die of torture carried too far. Political prisoners sometimes commit suicide—perhaps as a desperate escape from torture.

Apart from deaths inflicted in the course of enforcing law or handling prisoners, some governments arrange murders or are accomplices to them. This is most evident in connection with governmental terror and "dirty war," to be described in a moment; but the calculated murder of individuals occurs, too. It surely occurred in 1994 in Haiti as a beleaguered military dictatorship tried to hold on to power. It may even occur outside the country. Colonel Qaddafi, head of the government of Libya, has made himself infamous in various ways —among them by sending hit men to kill opponents who had fled abroad for refuge.

Official violence sometimes occurs on such a scale and with such disregard of the law that it is described as terror. When government seeks to enforce the law, and even when it resorts to murder, it is discriminating in selecting the victims, and the victims are relatively few in number. When terror develops, the arrests and killings are more widespread, and discrimination in the selection of victims loses in relative importance. Further, the requirements of due process get little attention. Specific persons or classes of persons may be picked out for elimination, but people also become victims haphazardly. A major purpose is to inculcate fear and anxiety in the whole community—to make everyone cower. In truth, however dramatic and deplorable the killing of people may be, the psychological effect on those not killed may in a sense be even more important. Fear that they might be next induces most of them to lie low, which is just what the government wants.

When killing by a government becomes so extensive that it amounts to terror, it is difficult to conceal. The name of Stalin—the dictator of the Soviet Union from the late 1920s to his death in 1953—is identified primarily with his terror and his purges. He killed people by the millions, among them a high proportion of his own colleagues in the Central Committee of the Communist party; and he sent millions of others into slave-labor camps—the Gulag Archipelago—where a considerable portion of them died.

In recent years governmental terror has been more prominent in some of the Third World countries. The communist regime of Pol Pot in Cambodia and governments in several of the African countries (most notably Equatorial Guinea and Uganda) have made themselves especially notorious.

The terms *dirty war, death squads,* and *the disappeared* have come into use with respect to Latin America. "Dirty war" is waged by authoritarian, right-wing regimes, perhaps military dictatorships, against opponents of the center and the left. The very fact that it is called "war," even if dirty, reflects a bias, for the term *war* implies the existence of enemy soldiers whom it is legitimate to kill, whereas a "dirty war" has nothing legitimate about it. It is dirty in the sense that it is conducted by illegal methods, with no public avowal of what is being done and no acceptance of responsibility for specific deeds.

The underlying circumstance is that opponents of the government—generally on the left, and perhaps including communists—seek change and themselves engage in demonstrations, rioting, and violence to bring it about. Members of the government and supporters of the government refuse to change policies sufficiently to allay discontent but despair of preserving order and preventing change if they act within the law. Their solution to the problem is to identify persons who, in their eyes, somehow threaten the social order, and "death squads" then see to it that these persons are killed or simply disappear.

Dirty war developed in Chile in the 1970s and has been waged in some degree in at least nine other Latin American states as well. Argentina is one of the nine. Between 1976 and 1979, guerrillas seeking the overthrow of the military dictatorship are said to have killed about seven hundred persons. In retaliation, death squads eliminated somewhere between six thousand and twenty thousand (Stohl and Lopez 1984, 54, 63).

The military dictatorship in Argentina discredited itself in several ways—especially by suffering defeat in an effort to seize the Falkland Islands—and then gave way to a civilian, democratic regime. That regime faced a dilemma. A concern for justice dictated that many of those who had been in high governmental office, and many of the officers in the armed forces, be tried and punished for illegal kidnappings and killings. But the new civilian government could not count on the support of the military if it prosecuted any large proportion of the accused and would thus risk overthrow if it took vigorous action. The result was a weak compromise. The government prosecuted and imprisoned a few of those who were guilty, including three former presidents, but then adopted a full-stop amnesty, bringing prosecutions to an end. Uruguay followed the same policy.

El Salvador and Guatemala are also prominently identified with dirty war. In El Salvador in the two years leading up to the elections of 1982, some thirty thousand civilians were killed for political reasons, mostly by government troops (Stohl and Lopez 1984, 12). Guerrilla attacks against the government, military defense by the government, and the activities of death squads characterized El Salvador from then until 1992, when the two sides signed a UN-sponsored peace accord that survives precariously. The course of events in Guatemala has been similar. In 1987 the Guatemalan press reported over a thousand cases of political violence, almost half of which were killings. In a three-month period ending in February 1988, 450 persons were killed and 60 disappeared.

Many of the dirty deeds of dirty war are committed by members of the police or security services, who at least ostensibly act in their private capacity, or they may be committed by private citizens. The situation is reminiscent of the lynching of blacks in US history. The lynching was generally done by men who were outside government or who acted unofficially, but they knew that there would be no governmental action against them. In this sense, government became an accomplice to what they did. At the very least the Latin American governments have been accomplices in the dirty wars, and in many cases it is clear that hit lists were compiled or approved in the highest offices.

Since World War II the word *genocide* has come into common use. The central feature of genocide is an attempt to destroy an ethnic group as such, killing its members not because of anything they have done but simply because of their ethnic or racial character. Genocide occurred long before anyone thought to coin the word—as suggested by the view of some nineteenth-century Americans that the only good Indian was a dead Indian. The first horrible instance of genocide in this century was the massacre of Armenians by the Turks during World War I. On the basis of a deliberate decision of the government, something like 800,000 Armenians were killed (Kuper 1981, 105).

By a similar deliberate decision the Nazi government of Germany sought, during World War II, to exterminate the Jews and certain other groups—the most sweeping program of genocide in history. The program led to the death of some six million persons (Kuper 1981, 124).

Since World War II most of the governments of the world have ratified a treaty outlawing genocide, yet it goes on. And massacres occur that may or may not count as genocide. Following an unsuccessful effort by communists to seize power in 1965, the government of Indonesia hunted down and killed all the communists it could find—anywhere from 200,000 to over a million of them. Later Indonesia engaged in a massive slaughter of the people of East Timor (Kuper 1981, 152, 175). When Bangladesh seceded from Pakistan, Pakistani soldiers hunted down Bengalis and killed up to three million of them whether or not they had taken up arms. The killing went on until India intervened and put a stop to it (Kuper 1981, 79). Massacres of genocidal proportions also went on in the central African countries of Rwanda and Burundi in the 1970s. In Rwanda the dominant Hutu people sought to kill off the Tutsi minority, and in Burundi the roles of the two tribes were reversed. The bloody, genocidal struggle between the Hutus and the Tutsis in Rwanda resumed in 1994.

Implicit in what is said above is the fact that governments engage in force and violence for reasons in addition to their own self-preservation. We will take up these reasons more fully later in the chapter.

■ Antigovernmental Violence

Violence against the government takes varied forms, among them assassination, kidnapping, sabotage (e.g., bombing), riots, hijacking, armed uprisings (e.g., rebellions and revolutions), and the staging of *coups d'état*. A coup d'état (or, more simply, a *coup*) is a relatively bloodless seizure of power, usually by military leaders.

In the early stages of their efforts, antigovernment groups ready to use violence are generally unable to get control of territory in which they are reasonably secure. They thus have to act on a hit-and-run basis. Perhaps they set off a bomb. Perhaps they rob a bank. Perhaps they hijack an airplane or kidnap, holding hostages until some demand is met. Every dramatic event staged calls attention to the existence of the group and to its broader goals.

Assassination and attempts at it are not uncommon. In the early 1980s assassins took the lives of the heads of government in Egypt (Sadat) and India (Indira Gandhi) and made an attempt on the life of Margaret Thatcher, prime minister of Britain. (An attempt also occurred on the life of President Reagan, but it was not politically motivated.) The great care that is taken to protect prominent political figures, especially the principal governmental leaders, testifies to the danger under which they live.

As in the case of governmental violence, antigovernmental violence may take on the characteristics of *terrorism*. Terrorists may aim at a particular governmental official because they think he deserves punishment or because they fear his policies, but they do not confine themselves to such targets and are not restrained by the usual moral rules (let alone the law) concerning the use of violence. When they set off bombs or hijack an airplane, for example, they do not ordinarily have

specific victims in mind. Their victims usually turn out to be totally innocent persons, killed or maimed or held hostage arbitrarily. Moral questions thus become acute—questions that will get attention later in the
chapter.

Assassination, sabotage, kidnapping, and hijacking are unlikely to
lead directly to revolution. If revolution is the object, the dissident group
needs to deprive the government of popular support and to gain such
support itself; and it needs control of territory. Further, the dissident
movement needs both the kind of leadership and the kind of program
that large portions of the public can support. It needs to be careful lest
it alienate the public by killing the innocent.

When enemies of the government control territory, which implies that
people in the territory give them substantial support, they can go beyond furtive acts of violence and wage civil or revolutionary war, fighting battles that are more or less like those fought in international war.

Confusion is generally greater in civil than in international conflict. In
international war it is usually clear who is on which side, and third states
can be neutral. In civil conflict, people choose sides or attempt to straddle
the fence. Others may or may not be sure what choice any one person
has made. Neither the government nor those trying to bring about its
downfall ordinarily have much sympathy for those who try to stay on
the sidelines; and people get killed by the rebels if they are suspected
of loyalty to the government or killed by the government if they are suspected of aiding the rebels. Moreover, those acting against the government often disagree with each other about strategy and tactics, and
members of one faction may kill members of another in an effort to en-
sure that the right decision is made. When people are willing to use violence to keep or gain political control, or to save or change a social order, they tend to regard human life as unimportant.

Coups d'état are distinctive as a method of transferring control over
the government. Coups are ordinarily staged by members of the armed
forces. One bold person may decide that it is his duty to save the country from a government that is somehow intolerably deficient. He must
rally others to his banner, and if at all possible he assures himself in advance that other members of the armed forces will not fight against him.
He is then likely to order troops loyal to him to surround one or more
central government buildings and to seize radio and TV stations. He arrests leaders of the government and announces that he has taken over.
If resistance occurs, some killing follows; but the hope and expectation
of anyone staging a coup is that fighting and killing will be limited.

Sometimes a coup is the work of a conspiratorial group—perhaps the
leading officers of the armed forces—rather than of one person. They
presumably make sure in advance that their action will get general support from the military and from what they regard as respectable civilian

elements. They select the new president or prime minister, perhaps from within their own group, and may replace him later if a need for change arises.

Over a number of years, coups have been the normal means of transferring power in most of the Third World. In South America democratic procedures seem to be returning to favor—partly because the military rulers have done so badly and have lost so much support that they are willing to withdraw, leaving the problems to others. Elections have also become more common in sub-Saharan Africa, but respect for their outcome is precarious.

The objective of a coup, like the objective of revolution, is the seizure of political control. In contrast, the objectives of other forms of antigovernmental violence vary. The violent individuals may simply want to advertise their cause, demonstrating to the government and to the public that they exist and that they are determined to achieve certain goals. They believe, it is said, in "propaganda of the deed" (or as it is also said, in propaganda of the dead). They may seek immediate policy concessions. They may want to demonstrate to the people that the government is unable to maintain law and order, or to provoke the government into adopting indiscriminate measures of repression, hoping that such measures will deprive it of public support. They may want to get rid of specific enemies. Or they may seek objectives relating to the struggle itself—for example, to maintain the morale of the group, to get money to support the group's activities, or to bring about the release of imprisoned comrades.

An assessment of the consequences of antigovernmental violence is ordinarily difficult. To what extent is the effectiveness of a government impaired by its need to look to its own security and survival? How well can a government official do her job when she fears that an assassin may be lurking around the corner or that a bomb may explode when she starts her car? If an assassinated leader is replaced by someone representing approximately the same constituency, what is gained? How much do measures of defense against terrorists impair the quality of life for the general population and therefore affect their support of the government and the social order?

A government that in effect must withdraw into a fortress is not in a good position to get its job done, let alone to play an imaginative role in contributing to progress.

■ Why Force and Violence?

It is easier to explain governmental than antigovernmental violence. When governments use violence, they are ordinarily responding to what they perceive as a challenge, whereas when others use it against the government they are ordinarily taking the initiative. Why do they do it?

Explanations have long been offered in terms of the *frustration/ aggression theory* or in terms of a variant, the *relative deprivation theory.* Those advancing the first of these theories hold that a frustrated (thwarted) person can be expected to commit some kind of aggression; and one of the possibilities is that the aggression will be directed against the source of the frustration. Thus, a government that frustrates people may lead them to some kind of antigovernmental aggression.

The variant focusing on relative deprivation is identified with a book by Ted Gurr entitled *Why Men Rebel* (1970). The theme of the book is that a sense of relative deprivation explains antigovernmental violence. People develop a sense of relative deprivation when the values that they enjoy fall short of expectations that they think are reasonable. Discontent grows, and the discontented may resort to violence.

These theories are plausible, but difficulties attend them. Various studies show that frustration does not necessarily lead to aggression (at least to overt aggression) and that aggression may occur without any prior frustration (Lupsha 1971, 96). And it is equally clear that feelings of relative deprivation and antigovernmental violence have no predictable relationship to each other.

Probing into the problem, Peter A. Lupsha arrives at "righteous indignation" or "moral outrage" as the factor that plays the crucial role (Lupsha 1971). He defines indignation as a sense of wrath evoked by unworthy or unjust treatment. The indignant person has a sense of what is right, a sense of the requirements of justice. She makes a judgment about the moral legitimacy of some action or practice. She may herself be the victim of a wrong, or she may be indignant over the treatment of someone else.

Now, it is clear that righteous indignation is like frustration and a sense of relative deprivation in that it does not always lead to violence. For a variety of possible reasons, the righteously indignant may take no concrete action at all or may seek remedies in nonviolent ways. Further, it is clear that some of those who resort to antigovernmental violence do so for reasons that have little or nothing to do with indignation. Nevertheless, Lupsha's explanation obviously applies to a high proportion of those who engage in illegal violence.

In resorting to violence the righteously indignant person attaches overriding importance to a value that he himself selects. He implies that it is paramount over other values and that he is justified in taking virtually any action to promote or uphold it, including the killing of the innocent. In his eyes, his conception of justice and of the permissible means of promoting it supersedes any contrary judgment. It is an arrogant position, though a position that many have taken. It is an outlook associated with fanaticism and intolerance.

Others may or may not agree with the judgment of the righteously indignant person, and different judgments may give rise to the use of different language—thus the statement that one person's freedom fighter is another person's terrorist. To describe persons as freedom fighters is to imply that their violence is understandable and perhaps that it should be condoned or applauded or supported. At least they are fighting for a good cause (freedom), whatever their methods. In contrast, to describe a person as a terrorist is to avoid any note of approval; if anything, it implies a condemnation.

Righteous indignation presupposes commitment to a cause. Perhaps it is simply a commitment to honesty in government. Perhaps it is a commitment to support the existing social order or to restore a social order of the recent past. Perhaps it is a commitment to bring about reform or revolution. Perhaps it is a commitment to achieve some kind of political goal for a colony or an oppressed minority (for example, autonomy or independence). Perhaps it is a commitment to maintain or change relationships between racial, linguistic, religious, or national groups.

Most of the likely commitments are ideological. I will describe the relevant ideologies in later chapters. *Nationalists* have employed violence again and again. The central tenet of nationalism is that the members of the nation should be united in a political entity with a distinctive status— usually independence. And nationalists are ordinarily prepared to fight for that status if need be. Algerian and Vietnamese nationalists did so after World War II. Later the Ibos fought to free themselves from Nigeria, but failed. The Bengalis fought to free themselves from Pakistan, and (with India's help) succeeded. The Tamils of Sri Lanka are engaged in violent struggle in an effort to gain either autonomy or independence. Since the defeat of Iraq in 1991, Kurdish nationalism has come to the fore again, different Kurdish factions in Turkey and Iraq fighting against each other as well as against what they regard as foreign oppression. Little is heard from the Kurds in Iran.

Ethnonationalism—the ideology of a segment of the population of a country identified by race, language, or religion—may lead to violence. In the United States race has figured in the Civil War, in decades of lynchings, and in urban rioting. In Indonesia people of Chinese ancestry have been the victims of racial massacres. People along the east coast of Africa whose ancestors came from India have been similarly persecuted. The racial struggle in Zimbabwe is over, "majority rule" having been established (that is, rule by blacks, who comprise some 97 percent of the population). The racial struggle in South Africa, at least the armed struggle, also seems to be over, whites having accepted electoral and other arrangements that make blacks full and equal participants in the political process.

Ethnonationalism centering on religion tends toward violence. Leaders who consider themselves close to God or god may believe that they are released from the moral rules that have a purely earthly origin. They can kill with special unction. Moses showed the way when, in connection with the golden calf episode, he asked the children of Israel which of them were with him on the side of the Lord and then ordered them to kill the rest.

In our time religious differences are central to the violence of Northern Ireland. They are central to the violence in Israel, Palestine, and Lebanon, where Jews, Christians, and Moslems are at each other's throats, and they lurk in the background of Saddam Hussein's aggressions. They have contributed to the fighting on Cyprus between the Greeks (Orthodox Christian) and Turks (Muslim). They led to the death of millions of persons when Pakistan split off from India in 1947—Muslims killing Hindus and vice versa. Within independent India they divide Hindus from Muslims and Hindus from Sikhs and have led to sporadic communal rioting and fighting among them.

A sense of separate ethnic identity sometimes develops that is akin to ethnonationalism but is called *tribalism*. It is found in most of the countries of Africa south of the Sahara. Some of them have managed their tribalism in a more or less accommodating way—Kenya, for example. Others have allowed tribalism to lead to genocidal practices. Rwanda and Burundi are mentioned in this connection above. In Uganda the two principal rulers of the 1970s and 1980s, Amin and Obote, both used their power to favor and protect their own tribes and to kill off and oppress members of other tribes.

Whenever members of one tribe or nation migrate into territory that has historically belonged to another, the stage is set for violence. Relationships between the European peoples and the Indians of the Western Hemisphere after 1492 are evidence of this fact. So is the treatment of the Chinese in Indonesia and of the Indians in East Africa, mentioned above. So are the troubles of Assam, a state in the northeast portion of India into which Bengalis have been moving from Bangladesh. Native peoples generally resent intruders, above all when the intruders are numerous enough to seriously adulterate the local culture and perhaps to get significant political power. This has been the case in Assam, with the result that the native Assamese have taken to violence to drive the intruders out, or at least to deny them citizenship and the right to vote.

Other ideologies are also powerful. Marxism-Leninism is in tatters now, but for many decades it was a clarion call for revolution. Liberals are sometimes revolutionary, ready to use violence to advance their cause. Both the American and French revolutions attest to this fact, though both stemmed from additional considerations as well. In dictatorial countries yet today, some liberals think of violence as a means of throwing off the dictatorial yoke and establishing democracy. And where liberalism already prevails, those who support the system may be willing to use force or violence, if need be, to maintain it. Progressive liberals are more inclined than many others to attach great value to human rights, including the right to life, and to seek alternatives to violence in pursuing their goals.

Conservatives, too, may employ violence, as the dirty wars of Latin America attest. Seeing what they regard as civilization threatened with destruction, some of them feel justified in resorting to the most extreme measures to save it.

People resort to violence not only because of ideological differences but also because of differences relating to practice. Everyone involved may endorse the same principles—for example, that government should operate efficiently and honestly—but those out of power may claim that those in power are corrupt or are otherwise failing to live up to their declared principles. And then those out of power may resort to violence, perhaps staging a coup, to see to it that principles to which all subscribe are in fact upheld.

■ The Morality of Force and Violence

In asking why people resort to violence, in the above section, I have already touched on the moral issue. Now I want to focus on it.

With respect to governmental violence, the usual presumption is that government is entitled to adopt and enforce law. Even if government and law are somehow deficient, the presumption is that they should nevertheless be tolerated until change can be brought about in a peaceful and legal way. To defy the law is in some degree to shake the foundations of the social order, and to resort to antigovernmental violence is to invite violence in return. This general attitude is associated especially with democracy, the feeling being that even a bad government should be tolerated until it can be voted out of office.

This position reflects a preference for orderly, predictable relationships, which are what law promotes. At the same time, order and predictability are obviously not the only values relevant to political behavior. And judgments on moral issues are bound to vary, depending on the set of values assumed.

Governments provide us with a possible set of relevant values when they ratify the international covenants on human rights. The covenants are legal instruments, but they also reflect a degree of consensus on the requirements of morality. I say a degree of consensus rather than complete consensus, because many of the words expressing the rights are open to more than one interpretation.

The covenants naturally permit governments to enforce the law, but they impose limits on the means that may be employed. The Covenant on Civil and Political Rights acknowledges that everyone has a right to life (that is, a right not to be killed arbitrarily) that binds even government. Further, it lays down a number of rules concerning arrest, trial, and punishment. According to the definition given at the beginning of the chapter, governmental force that violates these rules would be illegitimate violence.

To be sure, as noted earlier, the Covenant permits a government to declare a state of siege and thus suspend the rules, but it specifies that this may occur only "in time of emergency which threatens the life of the nation." And the Covenant specifies that the provisions having the most to do with violence—those concerning the right to life and freedom from torture—are never to be suspended. Moreover, the claim of a government that it faces an emergency that threatens the life of the nation is in principle subject to international review.

What this suggests is that by international agreement governmental force that violates the Covenant can be considered illegitimate and immoral.

Unfortunately, no such neat basis exists for judging the morality of antigovernmental violence. Suppose that a government is violating human rights. Suppose that it denies the right to vote or refuses to hold elections; suppose that it commits genocide; suppose that it follows discriminatory racial policies; suppose that it refuses to honor the right of a people to self-determination; or suppose that, as in Haiti in recent years, a narrow oligarchy controls government and follows repressive policies that keep large portions of the population in ignorance and poverty. Do such violations of human rights by the government justify antigovernmental violence? Are there moral limits, and, if so, what are they?

Obviously, many people have decided that such violations of human rights by governments justify antigovernmental violence. The thirteen American colonies adopted the Declaration of Independence and fought a revolutionary war in vindication of a whole set of rights, including the rights to equal treatment and representative government. Violence is recurrently used, and is widely approved, against governments that refuse to hold elections; otherwise change and progress might be extremely slow. Surely most people would agree that violence against the Nazi government was morally justifiable, including violence directed against Hitler personally and against his leading collaborators; in other words, those who commit genocide are surely fair targets themselves.

When the law provides for racial discrimination, as it once did in the United States and South Africa, many conclude that antigovernmental violence is justified—whether or not it is prudent. Experience shows that it is reasonable to presume (though the presumption is potentially rebuttable in individual cases) that every assassin and every antigovernment terrorist thinks of himself as serving a high and worthy moral cause.

Generalizations about the justifiability of antigovernmental violence are difficult and hazardous. One possibility is to adopt a standard comparable to the one that governments have adopted in ratifying the covenants on human rights. That is, when antigovernmental violence is contemplated or judged, the crucial question might concern the likely consequences for the equal enjoyment of human rights. Only if the probability is high that the violence would promote such equal enjoyment would it be judged moral.

That test is potentially helpful, but it is by no means an unerring guide. What promotes human rights in the short run may not promote them in the long run. It is always possible that the effort to eliminate one evil may lead to a new and greater evil. People sometimes accept, or are urged to accept, the devil they know in preference to one that theoretically lurks over the horizon. This is characteristic especially of one of the varieties of conservatism.

Among the difficult questions—wherever violence is contemplated or used—is the question of the legitimate target. In international war, one of the long-established rules (often violated) is that the deliberate killing of civilians is to be avoided. Such killing is excusable only if it occurs as an incidental side effect of an attack on a legitimate target and only if the number killed is not disproportionate to the military gain. A comparable principle might well apply to violent domestic political struggles. An effort to apply it, however, raises the question of the appropriate domestic counterpart of the international distinction between the soldier and the civilian. If we think of attitudes and activities that range from simple acquiescence in an oppressive dictatorship through membership in the civil service to full political support, at what point does a person lose "civilian" status?

And the principle that "civilians" are to be spared leads to the question of how absolute the principle is. In struggling against Israel, if Palestinians had selected as targets only those persons directly responsible for their plight, few targets would have been open to them. Perhaps they should therefore have limited themselves largely to nonviolent means, unpromising as those were bound to be. What they in fact did was to reject the standard that "civilians" are to be spared. They hijacked airplanes knowing that a high proportion of the passengers had no connection at all with the struggle, and they set off bombs that were at least as likely to kill the innocent as the guilty. Then, in the *intifada*, they shifted their strategy, depending on the throwing of stones at police and at military personnel serving Israel.

Though all actions are subject to moral judgment, the moral issue is of relatively little significance in connection with many coups d'état. Coups that occur against governments in black Africa, for example, are sometimes based simply on the claim that the ousted government is inefficient or corrupt, failing to address itself effectively to the country's problems. Each person who seizes power decries the failures of the ousted government, and then a few months or years later someone else seizes power for approximately the same reasons. Some may be more effective in handling governmental problems than others and more inclined to respect human rights, but differences are not always clear-cut.

■ Foreign Participation

Violence in domestic politics often has international ramifications. The world is interdependent enough that what happens within any country is bound to be of interest to both the government and private parties in one or more other countries. Some kind of foreign involvement is especially likely when the domestic situation is tense or seemingly unstable. One or both sides in the domestic struggle may seek foreign support, or foreign support may be volunteered. Or a government wanting to intervene may do so in response to an invitation from an alleged government that it itself has set up.

Both the Soviet Union and the United States illustrate the possibilities. In the closing stages of World War II and thereafter the Soviet Union took a special interest in developments in eastern and southeastern Europe, installing communist-controlled governments in each of them; and for more than forty years Moscow stood ready to respond to any appeal for help from local communists; when necessary it located domestic communists willing to make the appeal. It intervened militarily in East Germany (1953), in Hungary (1956), and in Czechoslovakia (1968); and its reputation for willingness to intervene intimidated and deterred people of the region who otherwise might have risen up to throw the communist governments out.

The United States likewise stands ready to intervene abroad, or to extend military assistance, in certain situations. It intervened in Grenada, throwing the government out and installing a different one. In El Salvador and Guatemala it gave support even to governments waging dirty war, and in Nicaragua it gave support to counterrevolutionaries. It intervened in Panama to oust a dictator. In 1994 it negotiated an "intervention" in Haiti.

In general, each side in a violent domestic struggle has a fair chance of obtaining support abroad. When domestic violence or the threat of it puts the existence of a government at stake, the crisis is unlikely to remain purely domestic for long.

One implication is that violence in domestic politics may be somehow related to violence in international politics. The field of international politics is addressed in Part III.

■ Velvet Revolution

In the late 1980s, and above all in 1989, profound changes, including revolutionary changes, occurred in the communist world with a minimum of violence, raising the question of how this could have happened. First the

Soviet leader, Gorbachev, called for structural changes (*perestroika*) and openness (*glasnost*) in the Soviet Union. Then he replaced the Brezhnev doctrine with what his spokesman called the Sinatra doctrine. The Brezhnev doctrine was that, if need be, the Soviet Union would intervene militarily in eastern Europe to keep communist governments in power. The Sinatra doctrine was the opposite: that the countries of eastern Europe could do it their way—could choose the kinds of political, social, and economic systems to maintain. In adopting the Sinatra doctrine, the Soviet Union renounced a policy of intervention.

Changes began in Poland even before the adoption of the Sinatra doctrine, and after its adoption all of the governments in eastern Europe that had been upheld by Soviet power collapsed. In a remarkably short period of time communist governments fell in East Germany, Hungary, Czechoslovakia, Bulgaria, and Rumania. Except in Rumania, where the dictator and his wife were executed and where some fighting occurred, the process was peaceful. The transformation was especially quick and smooth in Czechoslovakia, and it is to it that the term "the velvet revolution" especially applies.

Historians will be seeking to explain the developments for decades to come, and the explanation will surely turn out to be complex. I will deal with it mainly in chapter 19. The main point that I want to make here is that communists generally lost faith in their moral right to rule. That rule had been based on a belief that Marxism-Leninism is a science and that those schooled in the science knew and could serve the true interests of the people. The corollary was that capitalism served the interests of the bourgeoisie and was based on the exploitation of the proletariat.

As the years went by, it became increasingly clear that the Marxist-Leninist diagnosis and prescription were wrong. Even in the minds of the faithful, Stalin's heinous policies must have raised the question of whether communism was really in the interests of the people. Then the failings of the Soviet economy became clearer and clearer. Life got marginally better for the Soviet people, but it improved much more for people in the advanced Western capitalist countries. Promises that the Soviet Union would catch up with and surpass the West became mockery. Further, when noncompetitive "elections" led to the claim that 98 percent of the people supported the communists, the fraud was obvious to everyone.

In the countries of eastern Europe, especially in those with the greatest contacts with the West, the relative failure of the communist governments was all the more apparent. As the Czechoslovak leader Václav Havel put it, the governments and peoples of the Soviet world were living a lie when they took or tolerated the view that communism was serving the interests of the people and had their support.

The record in foreign affairs is probably significant, too. Through the years the communists made much of the claim that the capitalist world was threatening and that they needed to put great emphasis on the Red Army to deter and defeat aggression. The result was that an extraordinarily high proportion of the resources of the Soviet Union went to the armed forces. But then it became clear that the West was not really threatening and that the Soviet Union was hampering its own economic progress by its emphasis on guns at the expense of butter.

The combination proved fatal. The communists themselves tended to become demoralized, unable to escape the overwhelming evidence of their failure. As some of them put it, events deprived them of a moral right to lead. Such an attitude is obviously not a good basis for an effort to maintain power by force—especially when, in addition, opposition to communist control and disillusionment with communism came to pervade the armed forces and the general population.

When the Soviet Union signaled that it would no longer use its military power to uphold the communist regimes in eastern Europe, therefore, a general consensus quickly developed on the need for drastic change. The unheard-of then occurred, as successive communist governments peacefully surrendered power. Only in Rumania did the dictator seek to hold on. The surrenders were no doubt speeded and eased by signs that succeeding governments would, as a rule, let bygones be bygones, prosecuting very few. Thus, something very much like a voluntary abdication occurred. Like the whites of South Africa, the communists in the Soviet Union and eastern Europe came to the view that the regimes over which they presided were not morally defensible, and so they gave up without much of a struggle.

■ Review

This chapter concerns violence in domestic politics, used by governments and against governments. And it notes that one or both sides in a domestic struggle may get support from abroad.

Governments must coerce if they are to enforce law. In most countries most of the time enforcement occurs in legitimate ways with little or no illegal violence. But in some countries some of the time government resorts to illegitimate violence or becomes an accomplice in it. Governmental leaders have on occasion arranged to have individual opponents killed. In critical times a government may declare a national emergency and thus suspend some of its own laws concerning arrest, trial, and punishment. On rarer occasions, governments have resorted to terror or have engaged in or tolerated "dirty war." A few governments have resorted to genocide.

Antigovernmental violence occurs, too: assassinations, sabotage, riots, terrorism, coups d'état, and revolutions.

No theory explains antigovernmental violence reliably enough to make it predictable. The most helpful theories focus on frustration and aggression, on feelings of relative deprivation, and on righteous indignation. Righteous indignation is likely to be associated with an ideology—perhaps liberalism, perhaps Marxism-Leninism, perhaps nationalism or ethnonationalism, perhaps a religion.

Violence, both governmental and antigovernmental, raises moral issues. One possible general test is whether the use of violence tends to promote or to undermine the equal enjoyment of human rights.

Those engaged in domestic political struggles often find it possible to get support from abroad. Thus, domestic and international politics get intertwined.

Revolutions—mostly velvet revolutions—have occurred in eastern Europe, demonstrating that profound change can sometimes be nonviolent.

■ Reading

Bushnell, P. Timothy (1991) *State-Organized Terror: The Case of Violent Internal Repression.* Boulder: Westview Press.

Crenshaw, Martha, ed. (1983) *Terrorism, Legitimacy, and Power. The Consequences of Political Violence.* Middletown, Conn.: Wesleyan University Press.

Goldstone, Jack A. (1986) *Revolutions: Theoretical, Comparative, and Historical Studies.* San Diego: Harcourt Brace Jovanovich.

Kegley, Charles W., ed. (1990) *International Terrorism: Characteristics, Causes, Controls.* New York: St. Martin's.

Kuper, Leo (1977) *The Pity of It All: Polarisation of Ethnic and Racial Relations.* Minneapolis: University of Minnesota Press.

Laqueur, Walter (1987) *The Age of Terrorism.* Boston: Little, Brown.

Long, David E. (1990) *The Anatomy of Terrorism.* New York: Free Press.

Stohl, Michael, ed. (1988) *The Politics of Terrorism.* 3d ed. New York: Marcel Dekker.

Stohl, Michael, and George A. Lopez, eds. (1984) *The State as Terrorist. The Dynamics of Governmental Violence and Repression.* Westport, Conn.: Greenwood.

———— (1988) *Terrible Beyond Endurance? The Foreign Policy of State Terrorism.* New York: Greenwood.

Wardlaw, Grant (1989) *Political Terrorism: Theory, Tactics, and Counter-Measures.* 2d ed. New York: Cambridge University Press.

THE INTERNATIONAL SYSTEM

*W*hat does "sovereignty" mean, and what are its implications? What are nationalism and imperialism? What groups are entitled to self-determination, and what may they determine? What kinds of rules and practices are associated with diplomacy? Where does international law come from, and what good does it do? What are the functions and powers of the United Nations, the World Court, and other international organizations? Why is it so difficult to eradicate war and the intervention by one state in the affairs of another? What rules and principles govern international economic relations, and what kinds of problems arise? If nations are entitled to self-determination, how about minority nationalities within countries?

PART III

THE INTERNATIONAL SYSTEM

Sovereignty, Nationalism, Imperialism, and Self-Determination

CHAPTER

12

A political entity is sovereign if it is free to make and enforce law as it sees fit, subject only to the requirements of international law.

This 1938 Herblock cartoon shows that Hitler's Germany has already annexed Austria and was about to gobble up Czechoslovakia. Imperialism denies sovereignty, nationalism, and self-determination.

All states claim to be sovereign, and it is sovereignty that makes them eligible to join the United Nations and to have diplomatic relationships with other states. Thus, the first question for this chapter concerns the meaning of *sovereignty*.

Sovereign states are also referred to as "nations." The practice leads to confusion, but at least it calls attention to the central role of *nations* and *nationalism* in world affairs. Thus, the second question for this chapter concerns the meaning and significance of these terms.

Imperialism and anti-imperialism have both figured prominently in the international system for many decades, suggesting the third question: what is imperialism, and why has it engendered anti-imperialism?

Finally, both of the international covenants on human rights declare that all peoples have a right of *self-determination*, and this right wins almost universal acclaim. But who count as "peoples," and what may they determine?

■ Sovereignty

From a legal point of view, *sovereignty* is a status. A political entity that is free to make and enforce law as it sees fit, subject only to the requirements of international law, is said to possess sovereignty or independence. In other words, where law-making and law-enforcing authority is unlimited, except by international law, there sovereignty resides. The fact that sovereigns are subject to international law implies that they have a status permitting them to enter into relations with each other, conducting their own foreign relations.

You can think of a sovereign as standing on a line across this page. The upper part of the page is the field of international law, and the lower part the field of domestic law. The sovereign is on the line between the two fields, limited by regulations in the upper field but free to do as she pleases in the lower field. However, the line is not permanently fixed. As international law develops—for example, through treaties about the protection of human rights—the line cuts across the page at a lower point. According to this conception, sovereignty is not given away or divided when international law expands, but its significance is reduced, for the realm of action in which the sovereign has a free hand is smaller.

Political orators in the United States tend to attribute sovereignty to the various states. Thus, they speak of "the sovereign state of Pennsylvania." Now, neither Pennsylvania nor any of the other forty-nine states is sovereign in the sense of the definition given above. Most obviously, they are not independent, for federal law is enforced within their territory, the federal Constitution limits their law-making power, and they are not free to conduct their own foreign relations. So what sovereignty is intended to mean in this context is uncertain; it should probably be classified as pure hyperbole.

The Charter of the United Nations says that the UN is based on the principle of the sovereign *equality* of its members. Thus, the idea of *equality* is added to the idea of sovereignty, but in what sense are sovereign states equal? Obviously not in their wealth or power, and not even in their rights, for their rights differ in many ways. For example, the Charter itself names five states as permanent members of the Security Council and gives them a veto—which sets these five apart from all other states.

True, when the rights of states differ it is in the realm of treaty law ("particular" law), not in the realm of general law. The very idea of "general" international law is that it applies equally to all states. Where general law is involved, the principle of reciprocity prevails—the principle that a state that claims a right for itself will concede it to others. For example, when the Soviet Union put Sputnik into orbit in 1957, no rule existed about jurisdiction in outer space, the question never having arisen. But Sputnik implied a Soviet claim that it was free to send an object over the territory of other states. Given the rule of reciprocity, the Soviet Union then had no basis for protest when the United States and some other states put objects into orbit that went over Soviet territory. Thus, the rule that outer space is open to all, like the high seas, was established. But you should not read too much into the rule of reciprocity, for it is simply a rule that states have equal rights except where special action creates differences.

A similar sort of relationship exists between the rule of equality and voting. The principle of the sovereign equality of states involves a presumption that where voting occurs, each state has one vote. But again exceptions occur, as in the Security Council and in a number of other international organizations, like the World Bank.

Perhaps the main significance of sovereign equality is that each sovereign state, whatever its rights may be, is as much entitled as any other state to have them respected. And one of the implications is that each state may veto any change in its rights.

What is good and bad about sovereignty? Its principal justification is that it provides a framework within which each country can govern itself as it sees fit, maintaining its own culture, customs, and possessions, free from foreign control. In other words, it theoretically provides a framework within which strong and weak states can exist side by side, each preserving its distinctive characteristics and values.

The great problem is that states use their sovereignty to prevent the development of international institutions and practices that would make peaceful change possible. It is significant that nothing quite comparable to sovereignty exists in domestic politics. We do not speak at all of the sovereignty of individual persons, and although we speak of their equality, we do not interpret the idea of equality in such a way as to prevent the development of government or to prevent majority rule. Even though individuals have equal rights under the law, they have no choice but to submit to legislative, executive, and judicial institutions. An individual may perhaps be able, in one way or another, to influence what these institutions do, but his right to equal treatment does not imply a right to veto change. We speak of the consent of the governed, but in fact people have no choice but to consent—and then to accept whatever change government legitimately decides upon.

At the international level, in contrast, the principle of sovereign equality is interpreted to give states a choice. They can veto any change in their rights, and they can refuse to endow international institutions with significant powers.

The principle of sovereign equality thus impedes the development of strong international institutions and reinforces the status quo. Each state can veto change in its own rights, and other states have no right to impose change. But all history shows that the status quo does not endure forever, and, in some cases, if states cannot achieve change in a legal and peaceful way, they may resort to ways that are illegal and violent, as Iraq did in 1990. In other words, the principle of sovereign equality makes intervention or war likely.

Intervention is the dictatorial (probably military) interference by one state in the affairs of another. The victim has a choice whether to regard the act of intervention as an act of war.

States have tried to shore up their sovereignty by making intervention and war illegal. But they create an impossible situation when they rule out violence without agreeing to alternative peaceful means of bringing about change. This is not to say that all the changes that powerful states want are justified. In fact, a considerable proportion of the acts of intervention that have occurred and of the wars that have been fought have been designed to achieve ends that no imaginable set of international institutions would have endorsed. Nevertheless, although sovereignty provides a framework within which self-government can occur, it also impedes the development of international institutions that would make intervention and war less likely.

■ Nationalism

Nationalism relates to the idea of the *nation*—a word that quickly leads to confusion, for *nation* is regularly used as a synonym for (sovereign) *state*. For example, we speak of the United *Nations* as the main *international* organization. But the word *nation* also has another meaning, and it is the other meaning that underlies the idea of nationalism.

According to the other meaning, the existence of a *nation* depends upon attitudes. The people involved must share sense of solidarity—a common feeling or will, a sense of oneness, of unity, of common purpose. They must recognize the existence of common bonds and common interests that set the national society apart. They must believe that they have more in common with each other than with people in foreign countries. They must "feel that they belong together in the double sense that they share deeply significant elements of a common heritage and that they have a common destiny for the future" (Emerson 1960, 95). They must have a conception of a *national self* with collective purposes that are to be advanced and protected.

It is not essential, of course, that every single person in the state have these attitudes. The population of most states is heterogeneous, with people thinking of themselves as belonging to different ethnic, racial, or national groups. Some of them may have more of a sense of solidarity with their kin abroad than with others in the country where they live— for example, the Kurds, who are divided among Iran, Iraq, and Turkey but whose loyalty tends to go to the Kurdish nation. Moreover, some who have the same characteristics as other members of the nation may reject nationalist attitudes. For a nation to exist, however, a high proportion of those involved must share the kinds of attitudes described.

How they develop these attitudes is another question. It is somewhat more likely to happen if people have certain characteristics in common— mainly language, religion, and race. But sometimes people share such characteristics without developing a sense of nationhood, and sometimes they develop a sense of nationhood even in the absence of those characteristics. Governments usually try to inculcate a sense of nationalism and patriotism through the educational system and in other ways. And patriotic persons and groups supplement the efforts of government. Shared dangers, shared struggles, and shared triumphs, perhaps along with shared sacrifices, are also likely to play an important role.

Given the idea of a *nation*, I can now speak of the main variety of *nationalism*. I call it nationalism of the European kind. It consists of a set of beliefs: (1) that a nation exists, more or less as described above; (2) that the nation should be an object of loyalty, with individual persons as good nationalists, ready to make sacrifices if need be for the nation; and (3) that the nation should be united politically and enjoy a distinctive political status. Sometimes the status sought is a degree of autonomy and self-government within a multinational or imperial framework. More commonly the status sought is sovereign independence, as described above.

"My country, may she ever be right, but my country right or wrong" is a manifestation of the second of these attitudes. And a multitude of historical events are manifestations of the third. In the first part of the nineteenth century, what are now Italy and Germany were both divided into a number of sovereignties, but the forces of nationalism transformed them into united nation-states. After World War I the map of central and eastern Europe was completely redrawn in response to demands for national independence. When Moscow abandoned its repressive policies in that area in 1989, it was simply taken for granted that Germany would be reunited; and minority national groups in most of the states of the region began demanding some kind of change in their status. The Soviet Union and Yugoslavia have gone out of existence, many of their constituent parts achieving sovereignty, some of them fighting with neighbors over the question of where the boundary lines should be. Czechoslovakia has divided peacefully into its Czech and Slovak parts. Korea remains divided, but good nationalists in both the north and the south are determined somehow to bring that division to an end. It is possible to argue that no set of beliefs on earth are more powerful and have had as much influence over the course of modern history as the beliefs associated with nationalism.

Nationalism leads us to a paradox. The logical counterpart of the idea that the nation should be a state is that the state should consist of one and only one nation. But nationalists do not always accept this logic. They often have sought greatness and glory for the nation, and, like Mussolini and Hitler, they have tended to conceive greatness and glory in terms of domination over territory and people. Thus, nationalists generally want to preserve the territorial integrity of the state even if this means keeping some other national group in subjection. And so conflicts of nationalism occur as one national group strives for independence or to join its kinfolk in an adjacent state while another national group tries to hold on to the territory to which it considers itself historically entitled. And nationalism has time and again led to *imperialism* as those who want the nation to be great seek to prove its greatness by conquering foreign nations and peoples.

This leads to another meaning of the word *nationalism*. References to "African nationalism" and to "Arab nationalism" are common, even though there is no African or Arab nation in the same sense that there is a German or French nation. What initially united the African and Arab peoples, respectively, in a kind of nationalism is the fact that they were victims of European imperialism. Europeans conquered them or otherwise got control over them, and the Europeans were whites who, in the light of racial and cultural differences, tended to hold their colonial subjects in contempt.

Not surprisingly, the subject peoples developed deep and bitter resentments and came to share a determination to free themselves from imperial control. So what is called African and Arab "nationalism" began essentially as an anti-imperialist, anticolonialist movement. What future exists for this variety of nationalism now that colonialism is substantially ended remains to be seen. Some black Africans and some Arabs continue to use the concept, dreaming of the political unification of the black African and the Arab peoples, even though they do not comprise a nation in the European sense.

■ Imperialism

I spoke above of *imperialism* and now want to focus on that term. It is defined variously. The simplest definition is that imperialism is the process by which empires are created, maintained, and perhaps extended. And an empire is a sovereign political organization or structure in which a dominant state rules over (or by formal arrangement exercises a significant degree of control over) subordinate units ordinarily inhabited by alien peoples.

In connection with overseas imperialism, illustrated preeminently by the British Empire of times past, the subordinate units were dependencies, perhaps colonies or protectorates. When an empire occupies a great land mass, as in the case of the Austro-Hungarian Empire of the period before World War I and as in the case of the Soviet Union until 1989, constituent units are not spoken of as colonies or dependencies, though in a number of cases they might well be.

By a slight extension, a relatively powerful state is imperialistic if it imposes an unequal relationship on a foreign people or state. Britain was thus imperialistic when it imposed unequal treaties on China in the nineteenth century, and the Soviet Union was imperialistic when, after World War II, it imposed communist governments on the peoples of eastern and southeastern Europe and compelled these governments to join with it in a military alliance.

Imperialism is also defined as extranational expansionism. As long as expansionism is directed toward the unification of a nation, it is regarded as a manifestation of nationalism. When expansionism goes beyond the confines of the nation and brings about the subordination of alien people, it is said to manifest imperialism.

These definitions have much in common. They make an imposed inequality in political relationships (subordination) the basic feature of imperialism. When I use the term I assume this meaning.

Imperialism is given other meanings, too. Lenin treated it essentially as a stage of history in which capitalist powers are allegedly driven by economic forces to seek to expand their political control. He considered it an inevitable stage, though he did not explain why some capitalist powers (for example, Switzerland) never enter it.

Hans Morgenthau described any policy as imperialistic if it aims at a reversal of the order of power; for example, an effort by the number two country to become number one would be an imperialistic effort.

In the usage adopted by many, above all in polemical situations, any kind of policy followed by a rich and powerful state in relation to a poor and weak state is an imperialistic policy. According to this definition the United States is automatically imperialistic whenever it deals in any way with a Third World country. This usage makes *imperialism* an epithet and not a word that is useful in discriminating thought.

As noted above, overseas imperialism aroused resentment and gave rise to anti-imperialist or anticolonialist nationalism. It aroused resentment in part because of the belief of subject people that they were being exploited economically. They found it easy to blame their relative backwardness and their relative poverty on their foreign rulers, forgetting that the gap between their level of well-being and the level of well-being in advanced countries was at least as great before the foreign rulers arrived.

Even more important as a cause of their resentments was the humiliation flowing from the unequal status imposed upon them—a humiliation made all the more galling by the racism of the whites, who tended to assume their own superiority and to impute inferiority to subject peoples. Writing when European imperialism was in its terminal stage, Rupert Emerson—referring to colonies in Africa—spoke of "the humiliation [that] runs so deep as to be almost beyond repair. What is involved is . . . a charge of inherent inferiority against a race as a whole" (Emerson 1960, 382, 426). Emerson quoted another commentator as saying that "people do not like being exploited, but they can put up with it. What they cannot put up with is being considered inferior"(Emerson, 1960: 382, 426). The comment of Nehru in India was that Franklin Roosevelt stopped too soon in enunciating only four freedoms during World War II; he should have added a fifth: freedom from contempt.

■ Self-Determination

Nationalism and imperialism both stimulate demands for *self-determination*.

Self-determination is identified historically with Woodrow Wilson, who, at the end of World War I, championed the idea that *nations* have a right of self-determination—an idea that turned out to have a major influence on the peace settlement. It led to the breakup of the Austro-Hungarian Empire and to other changes in the political map of Europe, as noted earlier.

Since World War II, the references have been not so much to *national* self-determination as to the self-determination of *peoples*. Both international covenants on human rights declare that "all peoples have the right of self-determination. By virtue of that right they freely determine their political status and freely pursue their economic, social, and cultural development." People all over the world appeal to the right and proclaim it endlessly. Self-determination has become a shibboleth that all must pronounce if they want to be counted among the virtuous.

The United Nations provides a major platform for champions of that right. As colonies and other dependencies became independent after World War II, they joined the UN and used it as a forum in which to denounce imperialism. The General Assembly established a committee, which came to be called the "Committee of Twenty-Four," that probed into the plans and practices of imperial countries, prodding them to allow self-determination to have full sway. In 1960 the General Assembly adopted a Declaration on the Granting of Independence to Colonial Countries and Peoples, in which among other things it affirmed that "inadequacy of political, economic, social or educational preparedness should never serve as a pretext for delaying independence."

The assertion of the right of self-determination raises several questions: What choices do "peoples" have? That is, what are the acceptable outcomes of an exercise of the right of self-determination? Who comprise a "people"? Can the right of self-determination be exercised more than once?

As to the acceptable outcomes, note that the resolution of the General Assembly was on "the granting of independence," as if independence is the only possible outcome. Later, in a more sober mood, the General Assembly acknowledged other possible outcomes: "free association or integration with an independent state" or "any other political status freely determined by a people."

A few dependencies have chosen an outcome other than independence. The Cook Islands, for example, chose to remain associated with New Zealand rather than become independent, and two groups of Pacific islands (the Northern and Southern Marianas) chose commonwealth status in association with the United States. From the point of view of the United States, Puerto Rico has made the same choice, though it is unclear whether the choice is definitive. Relatively few Puerto Ricans want independence. The main political struggle is between those who want to maintain roughly the present commonwealth status and those who want Puerto Rico to become the fifty-first state.

Who comprise a people is a more difficult question, made difficult by the fact that independence (secession) is regarded as the usual or normal outcome of an exercise of the right to self-determination. States have proved themselves able to face secession where overseas dependencies are concerned, and Russia seems to have more or less reconciled itself to the break-up of the Soviet Union. But generally states abhor the idea of losing any of their metropolitan territory. The history of the United States illustrates the point. According to that history, it was glorious for colonies to secede from an empire, but thereafter it was impermissible for any state to secede from the union. Despite obvious divisions in the population, the oath of allegiance speaks of the United States as "one nation, indivisible."

Either of two strategies might be followed to minimize the possibility that an acknowledgment of the right of self-determination might lead to demands for secession. One of the strategies is to define the term *peoples* in a restrictive way; and this is the dominant strategy in the United Nations. The claim is that the term *a people* applies to the entire population of a sovereign state and to the entire population of a dependency but that it does not apply to any segment of the population of either. This is obviously arbitrary, but it also obviously protects the territorial integrity of existing states and dependencies.

A different strategy rests on a proposition already advanced more than once: that rights are not to be regarded as absolute. Every right needs to be considered and applied with due regard for other rights that may be affected. And it is legitimate to take the view that established states (and dependencies that are political units?) have a right to maintain their integrity and other vital interests.

Given that understanding, it becomes possible to concede that various segments of the population of a state or dependency may be *peoples* with the right of self-determination. If a segment constituting a people then wants to exercise its right in such a way that the right of the state to maintain its integrity is affected, a conflict of rights occurs; and in such a case, it is not necessarily foreordained which right will prevail or how the conflict will be resolved. Some kind of political compromise may need to be sought, the most likely possibility being that the group that ideally prefers independence will instead be given autonomy, or at least some kind of special status, within the state. This in fact frequently happens, whether or not as an explicit application of the right of self-determination.

The right of self-determination has had, and presumably will continue to have, important consequences. I have already noted its effects after World War I. At the close of World War II fewer than 60 states existed; now the figure is over 180. India got its independence in 1947, and in the following years a number of other grants of independence occurred. In the 1960s they came in a flood, and by the end of that decade the British, French, Belgian, and Dutch empires were substantially dissolved. The Portuguese Empire collapsed in 1974, and Namibia finally got its independence from South Africa in 1989. In 1989 and during the next few years the major constituent units of the Soviet Union all got their sovereignty, and so did the constituent units of Yugoslavia. A number of extremely small colonial territories remain, and more and more microstates are coming into existence as they get independence, too. Overseas imperialism is substantially gone.

The remaining multinational states and continental empires are threatened. Canada shows fissures. Most of the states of Africa are potentially vulnerable. India and Pakistan have fought wars over the question of self-determination for Kashmir, and peoples elsewhere in India are possible sources of demands.

If you want to think through the problems that demands for self-determination sometimes create, you might line up the considerations that would need to be taken into account if African Americans or Hispanics, or the two groups combined, were to become dominant in New

York City or Chicago and were to demand the right of self-determination. And having identified the considerations, you might develop an argument supporting your preferred solution to the problem. Or you might think of the problem if, just after a rich oil field was discovered off the Scottish shore, Scotland had invoked a right of self-determination, aiming to gain a greater economic advantage from the oil than it could while remaining a part of the United Kingdom.

The reasons for the triumph of the idea of self-determination are complex. Prior to World War I the chance that a movement for self-determination would succeed was generally so remote that championship of the idea would have been quixotic. After World War II, however, the situation changed, and hope of success brought the idea to the fore.

The hope had several bases. One was the fact that the war had weakened the imperialist powers. Japan was defeated, and Britain, France, Belgium, and Holland faced needs and problems at home that left them less inclined to give priority to imperial concerns. Moreover, many people in the imperialist countries had a change of heart, losing their will to rule and even coming to believe that imperial rule was wrong. They concluded that they had no moral claim to continued imperial authority. After all, the denial of democracy that is inherent in imperialism contradicts the political beliefs that prevailed in the European imperialist countries.

Further, the idea that it was good to bear "the white man's burden" for the benefit of subject peoples lost its appeal. It became clear even before World War II that, in general, colonies were in fact a burden and not a boon. The common allegation is that the imperial countries exploited the colonies, and some exploitation occurred. But the reverse was also true: the net economic benefit gained by the colony was often greater than the net economic benefit gained by the imperial power. And when a colony rebelled, costs to the imperial power skyrocketed.

After World War II, first in Vietnam and then in Algeria, France faced major colonial rebellions and in each case was finally compelled to grant independence. France's experience implicitly warned other imperialist powers that they faced similar possibilities. Ironically, the threat was all the greater, at least in some of the dependencies, because of the success of the imperial countries in contributing to their economic and educational development; it would have been easier to maintain imperial control if the colonies had been left completely untutored and backward. Further, colonial powers faced pressures from the United States, whose anticolonialist and democratic tradition put it generally on the side of colonies seeking independence.

And so the imperial powers gave way, giving independence in sweeping fashion, even to political entities that had very few people with the education and experience that successful governance requires. The constitutions conferred on the new states were regularly democratic, but in almost all of them democracy soon went by the board and rule by native authoritarians came to replace imperial rule. The people exchanged one master for another, in many cases getting worse government than they had had, though at the hands of rulers who accepted them as equal human beings. In more recent years, however, democracy has been restored in some of them.

I should stress a point that is implicit in what has already been said: that the *peoples* who have the right of self-determination include the population of sovereign states. After all, it would make no sense to say that the peoples inhabiting a colony have that right, but that they lose it as soon as they become independent. And it would make no sense to say that the right has no relevance to states far removed from colonial status. For sovereign states the right of self-determination is the same as the right of exclusive jurisdiction, or, more generally, the right to manage their own affairs without intervention from the outside. Thus, the idea of self-determination is a weapon against intervention as well as a weapon against imperialism.

The prevailing view, whether justified or not, is that a people may exercise its right of self-determination only once. This view tends to reduce the instability to which the idea of self-determination might otherwise lead; and it tends to reinforce the claim that the idea has no relevance to segments of the population of a political unit that has exercised its right.

■ Review

Sovereignty denotes a status—the status of an entity that is subject to international law but supreme over domestic law. A sovereign state is an independent state, bound by international law but otherwise free to govern itself as it sees fit. Sovereign states are said to be equal, meaning principally that they are equally entitled to have their rights respected. Sovereignty gives those who enjoy it an opportunity to govern themselves as they see fit; at the same time it impedes the development of strong international institutions.

Nationalism calls for loyalty to the nation, and a nation is a body of people with a strong sense of solidarity—a common feeling or will, a sense of unity, a common purpose. They must "feel that they belong together in the double sense that they share deeply significant elements of a common heritage and that they have a common destiny for the future." Nationalism is perhaps the strongest ideology extant.

Imperialism is a process by which empires, or unequal political relationships, are established, maintained, and perhaps extended.

Self-determination is the right of a nation or people. Problems arise over the questions of who constitute a nation or people, what the outcome of self-determination may be, and whether the right of self-determination may be exercised more than once.

■ Reading

Alan, James (1986) *Sovereign Statehood: The Basis of International Society*.Boston: Allen & Unwin.

Birch, Anthony H. (1989) *Nationalism and National Integration*. Boston: Unwin Hyman.

Breuilly, John (1993) *Nationalism and the State*. Manchester, UK: Manchester University Press.

Connor, Walker (1994) *Ethnonationalism: The Quest for Understanding*. Princeton: Princeton University Press.

Doyle, Michael W. (1986) *Empires*. New York: Cornell University Press.

Gottlief, Gidon (1993) *Nation Against State. A New Approach to Ethnic Conflicts and the Decline of Sovereignty*. New York: Council on Foreign Relations.

Greenfeld, Liah (1992) *Nationalism: Five Roads to Modernity*. Cambridge: Harvard University Press.

Ignatieff, Michael (1994) *Blood and Belonging: Journeys into the New Nationalism*. New York: Farar, Straus, and Giroux.

Mayall, James (1990) *Nationalism and International Society*. New York: Cambridge University Press.

Pfaff, William (1993) *The Wealth of Nations: Civilization and the Fury of Nations*. New York: Simon and Schuster.

Tamir, Yael (1993) *Liberal Nationalism*. Princeton: Princeton University Press.

Diplomacy and International Law

On rare occasions governments may look for a fight, but ordinarily they seek relationships that are peaceful, stable, and predictable.

A wry look at diplomacy after World War II. Diplomats seek a stable relationship among their countries while an atomic bomb of unknown magnitude measures the world for destruction.

195

Small states that are remote from each other may have little reason to communicate, but the larger states with extensive interests, and most neighbors, find communication important. Each state wants, at a minimum, to ward off harm to its interests and may seek somehow to promote them. To facilitate communication, states establish diplomatic relations, the first subject of this chapter.

On rare occasions governments may look for a fight, but ordinarily they seek relationships that are peaceful, stable, and predictable. Law is the principal means of achieving this end, just as it is the principal means of assuring peaceful, stable, and predictable relationships among persons and groups within countries. Further, even when states fight, they have found it desirable to have laws—the laws of war.

I did not say much about law in the chapters that dealt with domestic politics, for we all know about it and know that it plays a significant role. Knowledge of international law, however, is not so common, and some of those who know about it tend to scoff at it—a tendency that I want to challenge. Thus, international law is the second subject of the chapter.

■ Diplomacy

The communication system that states establish with each other is based on *recognition*—recognition of the state itself as a sovereign entity and recognition of the right of a person or set of persons to speak for the state. Both sorts of recognition may involve problems. At the moment, for example, a set of Serbs in Bosnia claim to be a government, and so do a set of Muslims; and other countries are in disagreement about the proper response. Problems have existed about the government of China ever since 1949, when the communists completed their conquest of the mainland and when the Nationalist government fled to Taiwan. The communists in Peiping and the Nationalists in Taiwan both claimed to be the government of all of China, creating a problem that has not been resolved yet today.

Given mutual recognition, the larger and richer states regularly establish diplomatic relations with each other and with a considerable portion (possibly with all) of the smaller and poorer states as well. This ordinarily means that states establish diplomatic missions in each other's capitals—usually embassies, headed by ambassadors. And the common practice is for diplomatic missions to be accredited to the major international organizations.

As agents of the sovereign state that sends them, diplomats are to have the freedom that the accomplishment of their mission requires. This means that they have diplomatic immunity; save in rare circumstances, they are not under the jurisdiction of the police in the country that receives them. If they behave unacceptably, the remedy of the receiving government is to send them home or ask that they be recalled. And the premises of the diplomatic mission are likewise held to be extraterritorial—outside the jurisdiction of the receiving government.

Many of the smaller and poorer states have so little need to communicate with the rest of the world, or find diplomatic missions so expensive, that they accept diplomatic relationships only with a select list of other states. In effect, they may conduct their diplomacy mainly at the United Nations, where virtually all are represented. Some of the very smallest or poorest entrust the task of representing them abroad to a friendly power.

Sometimes one state severs diplomatic relations with another, usually to protest some feature of its behavior. But even then the need to communicate may be so great that a circumvention is used. Thus, the United States severed diplomatic relations with Cuba in 1961, but the need to communicate was such that sixteen years later it arranged to reopen the embassy in Havana as the "American interest section" of the Swiss mission there; and Cuba reopened its embassy in Washington as the "Cuban interest section" of the Czechoslovak mission. Diplomatic relationships were not formally renewed, but official lines of communication were restored.

Diplomatic missions are not the only channels of communication. Increasingly, high governmental officials are communicating with each other by telephone and in personal meetings. When many governments are involved, the tendency is to communicate through conferences.

The most spectacular conferences have been peace conferences, notably the conference at Versailles following World War I. "Summit" conferences—attended by heads of state or heads of government—have become common, with the principal persons at the summit attended by "sherpas"—their foreign ministers or other advisers. The largest and most extended conference in history occurred after World War II—a conference meeting intermittently over many years to get agreement on the law of the sea. Meetings of the General Assembly of the United Nations are conferences, and so are the hundreds of other meetings associated somehow with international organizations. I will say more about them in the next chapter.

Communication among governments leads to understandings and agreements, which may take any of various forms. The more formal of them are put in writing. For example, consultations and conferences may lead to the issuance of a communiqué recording the outcome. Governments may exchange *notes*, each specifying what it will or will not do or affirming some principle or rule; or they may formally conclude a *treaty* that a representative of each government signs and that each government then ratifies in accordance with the requirements of its constitution.

The usual rule is that treaties come into force whenever instruments of ratification are exchanged (or perhaps when they are deposited with the secretary-general of the United Nations). If many states are involved, the usual practice is to stipulate that the treaty will come into force only when a certain number have ratified.

Treaties and less formal agreements among states may or may not specify the period of years during which they are to remain binding. Ways of terminating treaties exist, but states are not legally free to denounce them at will. Many treaties include an article providing for termination. For example, the article may permit the parties to give notice and then free themselves from the obligation a year later; perhaps this right to give notice becomes effective only after a specified number of years have passed.

If one party violates a treaty, the other party may cease to observe it, too. And sometimes a state can free itself by appealing to the principle of *rebus sic stantibus*—the principle that the binding quality of a treaty depends on the continuation of circumstances vital to its original acceptance. This principle is vague and open to abuse.

Sometimes diplomats are idealized as champions of international peace, but this reflects a misleading view of diplomacy. The object of the diplomat must be to serve the government that appoints her, acting within the limits of the instructions that it gives. Of course, most governments most of the time want peace, but at times they put prime emphasis on some other goal—perhaps a propaganda triumph, or the destabilization of some other government, or victorious war—and the diplomat must adjust her behavior accordingly.

Broadly speaking, diplomacy depends on persuasion and coercion. States find it relatively easy to resolve a dispute if they are agreed on the relevant rules and principles, for the problem then is simply to ascertain the relevant facts and to apply reason and argument. Where accepted rules and principles do not provide a basis for resolving an issue, one side may offer rewards of some sort to induce the other side to oblige, or it may threaten or impose penalties. At the extreme, each side may calculate the probable outcome and the probable costs of war and then may choose between peaceful settlement and war, depending on what the calculations show. The terms of a peaceful agreement may thus reflect calculations of the probable outcome if war were to occur. Of course, it is vital that the side threatening war be able to make the threat credible. If one side threatens war and the other regards the threat as a bluff, a war that neither side wants may ensue.

Third parties may become involved in efforts to resolve a dispute. They may serve a mediating role, conveying messages back and forth between the disputants. They may attempt conciliation, not only conveying messages but making suggestions themselves. If the dispute is over the application of law to the issue at hand, the parties may resort to arbitration or adjudication. In arbitration, the parties appoint members of an arbitral tribunal and argue their cases before it, agreeing in advance to accept its award as binding; the tribunal is obliged to make the award on the basis of respect for law. Adjudication is similar, except that it takes place before a permanently established international court.

■ International Law

International law is defined as a body of rules and principles that states regard as binding on themselves and for violation of which they are habitually held responsible by international procedure.

As the definition suggests, states regularly accept the idea that international law exists and that they are bound by it. No state takes a contrary position. And states are generally also agreed on the importance of the principle of the rule of law.

How does the law come into existence? The answer is suggested in the statute of the International Court of Justice, established after World War I and reconstituted after World War II. The statute lists *the evidences or sources of the law* that the court should apply, putting them in four categories.

First, the court is to apply relevant *treaties*. A treaty may simply record the agreement of the parties that some rule is already a rule of law; or a treaty may create new law. As a rule, a treaty binds only the states that ratify it, but when a high proportion of the states of the world ratify the same treaty, some speak of *international legislation* that binds even the few states that do not ratify. A treaty is also sometimes called a "convention," "charter," "covenant," "pact," or "protocol."

Second, the court is to respect *custom*. Just as the practice of governmental agencies in Britain, especially the practice of the courts, gave rise to common law, so the practice of governments gives rise to international law. When different governments or courts or other public agencies face the same issue a number of times over a period of years and regularly appeal to the same rule in resolving it, that rule is said to become a rule of *customary law*. One of the obvious questions is how many precedents it takes to make a customary law.

Third, the court is to apply *"the general principles of law recognized by civilized nations."* If enough states incorporate a given principle or rule in their domestic law, that rule or principle is said to transfer automatically to the international field.

Fourth, the court is to apply *rules established in earlier judicial decisions and rules revealed by the work of scholars.*

Given such sources or evidences of law, it follows that uncertainties often exist about it. Even a treaty may be worded in a vague way, leading to argument over its meaning. Evidence found in international practice may be meager or inconsistent, and the other kinds of evidences of law likewise have obvious potential inadequacies. Moreover, in connection with a great many issues it turns out that two or more rules of law may be potentially applicable, giving each contending party some kind of a basis for its claim. Further, the law is not static. It changes and develops. And when an apparent deviation occurs, different persons and different agencies may make different decisions on the question of whether newly developed law permits what the old law prohibited.

These problems lead to difficulties that should not be minimized, but they are not unique to international law. They exist in the domestic field, too, providing employment for lawyers and keeping courts busy.

International law has traditionally been divided into three categories: *the law of peace* (prevailing between states that are at peace with each other); *the law of war* (prevailing between belligerents); and *the law of neutrality* (prevailing between belligerents and neutrals).

The law of peace is naturally the most voluminous, covering various topics. It provides rules for identifying persons subject to law. Who or what may have rights and duties under international law? What kind of an entity counts as a state? What counts as a government? For example, suppose that a group of persons claims to be the government of a new state, carved out of the territory of an old one. It says it has seceded. Are there rules to go by in deciding whether to concede the claim? May an international organization such as the United Nations have rights and duties under international law? How about a colony or a protectorate? How about you personally?

The law of peace includes rules relating to the succession of states and governments. When the Philippines got its independence from the United States, did it automatically succeed to any of the rights and duties of the United States? When one government or administration succeeds another—for example, when Clinton succeeded Bush—does the new government have all the rights, and must it assume all the obligations, of its predecessor?

One of the basic rules of international law is an implication of the idea of sovereignty. In the previous chapter, I equated sovereignty with independence—freedom from foreign control. And I gave a more formal definition: that sovereignty denotes the status of an entity subject to international law but supreme over domestic law.

My present point is that, being supreme over domestic law, each sovereign state has exclusive jurisdiction (the exclusive right to state and enforce law) within its own domain. The law of the United States, for example, does not apply in Canada, nor is the United States free to send a police officer to make an arrest in Canada or to cross the border for any purpose without Canada's consent.

For this reason and others it is important to know the extent of each state's domain—another of the subjects covered in international law. In the case of a maritime state, how far out on the surface of the sea does exclusive jurisdiction extend? May a state exercise jurisdiction on the surface of the sea beyond its sphere of exclusive jurisdiction? How about rights to oil under the continental shelf, and how about those manganese nodules on the deep sea bed? Does an uninhabited rock jutting out of the sea count as an island, and can a state have jurisdiction over that rock and over a surrounding portion of the sea? In case a boundary river shifts its course, does the boundary shift with the river? Who has jurisdiction over aircraft flying over a state? Who has jurisdiction over orbiting satellites? What rules and principles relate to the question of whether any state may claim jurisdiction over part or all of the surface of the moon?

The law of peace includes rules relating to recognition and to the establishment and conduct of diplomatic relations, referred to above.

The law of peace also concerns itself with the status and treatment of persons. Suppose that an American couple living in Canada has a baby. Is the baby a US citizen? a Canadian citizen? What are the respective rights and obligations of the various parties? If a French woman marries a German man, does the marriage affect her citizenship? In case a government believes that its citizens are being denied justice in a foreign state, what, if anything, may it legally do? May a government draft a foreign student into its armed forces?

I note above that international law changes and develops. The greatest change in recent decades concerns human rights. The general view before World War II was that individual persons had no rights under international law. Even when citizens of one state were denied justice in the territory of another, the theory was that the offense was not against them but against the state from which they came. Each state had a right to expect that its citizens abroad would receive justice.

But World War II gave human rights a central place on the international stage. The Charter of the UN obliges members to promote them, which has a twofold meaning. On the one hand, the assumption is that each human being has rights that all members of the UN are bound to promote. On the other hand, the assumption is that each state is accountable to other states for its policies relating to human rights. States still sometimes claim that the treatment of persons under their jurisdiction is a matter of exclusively domestic jurisdiction, but that view is plainly wrong. The Charter requires all members of the UN to promote human rights, and more than half the states of the world have ratified the covenants on human rights, accepting an obligation to respect the rights enumerated. I asked above whether you personally have rights under international law, and the answer is that you do.

States have supplemented the provision of the Charter concerning human rights with a number of treaties, above all the just-mentioned covenants. The European countries have gone farther than others in that in addition to ratifying a European Convention on Human Rights they have set up an international commission and an international court concerned with the enforcement of human rights. If you lived in France, for example, and believed that the French government was failing to respect one of your rights, you could appeal to the Commission, and in certain circumstances to the Court. In fact, many people have done this. Private citizens have arraigned their government before these international bodies again and again, and adverse judgments against governments are not at all uncommon. Moreover, governments generally change their ways when they are found guilty.

The European states have obviously not been deterred by the thought that the acceptance of international obligations concerning human rights would somehow infringe on their sovereignty. They want assurances that their neighbors will respect human rights and are willing to give assurances in return. They do not want a repetition of Hitler's crimes.

Do violations of human rights justify foreign intervention? The rule generally proclaimed is against intervention. Thus, in 1970 the General Assembly of the UN adopted a resolution declaring that "no state or group of states has the right to intervene, directly or indirectly, for any reason whatever, in the internal or external affairs of another state." But what if government breaks down, as in Somalia in 1992, leaving large numbers of people threatened with starvation? What if civil strife has a genocidal character, as in Rwanda in 1994? What if the hardships of life and the repressive measures of the government are so severe, as in Haiti in 1994, that large numbers of people seek refuge abroad, becoming burdens to neighbors? Should not humanitarian intervention be permissible? Should it perhaps not be a moral obligation when violations of human rights are especially egregious? If individual countries have no right to intervene unilaterally, how about intervention that gets the formal approval of an international agency such as the United Nations or the Organization of American States? Whatever your answer to these questions, you will be able to construct a good argument in its support. The law needs to be clarified, and so do the rules of morality.

International law concerns itself with the *peaceful settlement of disputes*. What are the differences between political and judicial methods of settlement? What rules govern the arbitration of a dispute (referred to above)? Under what conditions may the International Court of Justice or any other international court render judgment in a dispute?

Suppose that one state violates the rights of another. What may the injured state legitimately do? Through the early 1980s the Soviet Union was taking military action in Afghanistan, and in 1989 the United States sent armed forces into Panama. Did either or both of the intervening countries violate the law? In case a state intervenes illegally in the affairs of another or goes to war in violation of the law, what may other states legitimately do? In 1984 the Reagan administration assisted "contras" using the territory of Honduras as a base for military forays into

Nicaragua aimed at bringing about the overthrow of the Sandinista government there. What legal questions are thus raised, and how should they be answered? In what circumstances, if any, is resort to war legal?

Once war breaks out, the *laws of war* come into operation. They fall into two main categories: laws regulating the conduct of hostilities and laws concerning the treatment of persons and property in occupied territory. Laws in the first of these two categories lead an especially precarious life, for they tend to become obsolete as new weapons come into existence and as new ideas about strategy and tactics develop. Even so, laws and moral rules concerning the conduct of hostilities are in fact acknowledged. The question, as well as the question of resort to war in the first place, is explored in a fascinating way by Michael Walzer in *Just and Unjust Wars* (1977).

During war between any two states, how are the rights of third states affected—states that want to remain *neutral*? Each belligerent is likely to want to cut off trade, and perhaps travel as well, between the enemy and neutrals, but under what conditions is interference with the normal pursuits of a neutral legitimate?

Why do states develop international law, and why do they normally observe it? They develop it for roughly the same reasons that they develop domestic law. It is a general rule of human life (to which there are exceptions, of course) that people prefer the orderly and the predictable to the chaotic and the arbitrary. They want to know where they stand and on what they can count. They have interests that they want to protect and promote, some of them so fundamentally important and so widely shared that they have come to be classified as rights; and people would rather have rules defining what is permissible and impermissible than to have confrontations every time their interests clash with those of other persons. The references here are to people and to persons, but the statements apply to states as well.

The law created by a treaty is called *particular* because it binds only the parties. Most of international law, however, is *general* because it binds all states. And in connection with general international law, as I noted in the preceding chapter, the *rule of reciprocity* applies. No state claims a right that it is unwilling to concede to others, and each accepts the law in the expectation of reciprocal behavior on the part of others. The ideal is to arrange things so that the benefits of adhering to the rule of reciprocity are greater than the benefits of rejecting it.

Not that the law is always fair, any more than it is always fair within countries. Even general international law, like law within the state, is sometimes biased, but it applies to all states nevertheless. It would be potentially disorderly and chaotic, for example, to have no standard rule about access to oil under the continental shelf. If a country claims the right to exercise jurisdiction over the continental shelf adjacent to its territory, it is expected to concede the same right to other countries with respect to the continental shelf adjacent to their territories.

One of the current problems concerning international law stems from the fact that so much of it developed before the breakup of empires. Many former colonies are not sure that they want to accept every aspect of laws that they had no share in making. Communist governments tended toward the same attitude for many years, but in the late 1980s Gorbachev in particular came down firmly in support of the idea of handling international relationships on the basis of law.

The definition of international law given at the outset of this section requires that states be habitually held responsible for violating it. If they are not habitually held responsible for violating a rule or principle, it does not count as law. But in the absence of a central executive, how is the violator held responsible?

Self-help is the traditional method of enforcing international law. Each state is its own police officer; that is, each state can apply *sanctions*, taking measures designed to induce the other state to observe the law. The potential sanctions cover quite a range, from verbal remonstrances at one extreme to war at the other. In between, the most likely possibilities concern diplomatic and economic relationships. Thus, the injured state may recall its ambassador from the capital of the offending state, or seize any of its assets to which it has access, or suspend all trade with it.

Self-help is not the only possibility. A state whose rights have been violated may get support from a third party, as Afghanistan got help from the United States following the Soviet invasion of 1979. The third party that gives help may be formally an ally, or it may give help as a member of the United Nations—a possibility that will be discussed in the following chapter. A war for the defense of a victim of aggression— like the war against Iraq in 1991 to liberate Kuwait—is the ultimate sanction of international law.

A World Court exists to which states may resort when they have a dispute over the meaning of the law. A few regional courts, including a European and an inter-American court on human rights, also exist separately. The various courts are not organized in a hierarchy, which means that no arrangement exists for appealing against an adverse judgment to a higher court.

The World Court is the International Court of Justice, located at The Hague in the Netherlands. It consists of fifteen justices elected for nine-year terms by the General Assembly and the Security Council of the United Nations. The justices are supposed to represent the principal legal systems of the world.

The court could theoretically be a powerful body in connection with the enforcement of law, as the courts of the United States are, but in fact it plays a modest role. The states establishing it specified that it must respect their sovereignty, which means, among other things, that it can accept jurisdiction over a case only if both parties give their consent. As noted earlier, the states of Europe permit private persons to arraign them before international bodies on a charge that they have violated human rights, but they insist on the rule that the World Court consider a case that another government brings against them only if they consent.

This rule is not as limiting as it might seem. Governments give their consent not only *ad hoc* (that is, after a dispute has arisen) but also in advance. If they give it in advance, they may do it in either of two ways. One is to accept the so-called optional clause in the Statute of the Court. If a state that ratifies the Statute goes on to accept the optional clause, it thereby promises to submit future disputes of certain types to the court. The second way to give advance consent is to insert in a treaty or other agreement a provision that any disputes that arise over its meaning are to be referred to the Court.

When consent is given in advance, the possibility is created that a state may be obliged to accept the jurisdiction of the Court even though, at the time, it would prefer not to do so. The United States was caught in this way in 1984 when Nicaragua claimed that the United States was violating its rights under international law. The United States had accepted the optional clause in 1946, but held that it was not bound by it in relations with Nicaragua, because Nicaragua's acceptance of the clause had been incomplete.

The Court ruled against the United States on this point and (in 1986) on most of the complaints that Nicaragua made. Later, when the Security Council of the United Nations considered a resolution calling for full compliance with the decision of the court, the United States took a defiant stand, vetoing the resolution. The United States thus put itself in the paradoxical position of defying the law as interpreted by the Court while at the same time proclaiming its support for the idea of the rule of law.

In addition to considering disputes that arise between states, the Court may give *advisory opinions* on legal issues on the request of any of various international agencies.

In practice, the number of cases referred to the Court is not large. The only ones suitable for judicial settlement are those in which the parties are in dispute over the meaning or application of the law: both are willing to abide by the law but disagree on what the law requires. Disputes of this sort arise, of course, but they are not numerous and rarely play a major role in international politics. International politics is plagued more by general tensions and by issues that arise over discretionary policies than by disputes over the requirements of law. It is also plagued by demands for change in the law, or for other kinds of change regardless of the law. Thus, in taking up arms the Bosnian Serbs sought a change in the law. They had no chance of getting what they wanted through the Court.

Furthermore, a state may refuse to submit a dispute to the Court because it does not want to risk an adverse judgment. And the Court still suffers as a result of a decision it made in 1966 in a case concerning South Africa's policies of apartheid in Namibia (then called South West Africa). It ducked the issue, dismissing the case on technical grounds, and it thus alienated a great many governments and political leaders, making them less inclined to utilize its services.

In thinking about the role of the International Court of Justice, you should remember that only a small portion of the public issues that arise within countries are settled by the action of a court. Most are settled by political rather than judicial means. In democracies, they are fought out in elections and in legislative bodies, with the winner given the right to decide how the problem should be resolved. In authoritarian systems, procedural arrangements for handling problems may or may not be spelled out, but in any event judicial settlement is not to be assumed. Judicial settlement is appropriate when the question concerns the interpretation or application of existing law, not when the action in dispute is admittedly legal or when the demand is for a change in the law.

No formal arrangement exists for enforcing the judgments of the International Court of Justice once they are made, the assumption being that the parties will voluntarily comply; and they usually do. If they do not, self-help again becomes the rule, though a possibility exists that the Security Council might exercise one of its powers—the power to declare that a refusal to comply is a threat to the peace. When the Security Council finds a threat to the peace or an act of aggression, it may go on to order the application of sanctions against the offending state. I will describe this possibility in the next chapter.

Given the extent to which the international legal system depends on self-help, it must be classified as relatively primitive and it is bound to be unsatisfactory. The point here is not that international law is fully effective, serving all the functions of law in stable, advanced countries, but rather that international law exists, traditionally providing a basis for international relationships.

Various international organizations, most prominently the United Nations, concern themselves with the development and observance of law among states and with international cooperation more generally. They and their activities will be the subject of the next chapter.

■ Review

Although states are sovereign and independent, they have common concerns and thus need channels of communication. Diplomacy provides a major channel. The establishment of diplomatic relations depends on mutual recognition. Governments that recognize each other and that have much business to conduct ordinarily establish diplomatic missions in each other's capital and communicate in other ways.

All states consider themselves subject to international law. It comes into existence in various ways, notably through explicit agreements (for example, through treaties) and through the development of custom. It includes rules applicable in times of both peace and war. It is enforced first of all on the basis of self-help, each state being its own police officer. Friendly and allied governments may help a state uphold its legal rights, and so may the United Nations and the International Court of Justice.

■ Reading

Barston, R. P. (1988) *Modern Diplomacy.* New York: Longman.

Boyle, Francis Anthony (1985) *World Politics and International Law.* Durham, N.C.: Duke University Press.

Franck, Thomas M. (1990) *The Power of Legitimacy Among Nations.* New York: Oxford University Press.

Henkin, Louis (1995) *International Law: Politics and Values.* Boston: Martinus Nijhoff

Levi, Werner (1991) *Contemporary International Law: A Concise Introduction.* Boulder: Westview Press.

Moynihan, Daniel Patrick (1990) *On the Law of Nations.* Cambridge: Harvard University Press.

Wallace, Rebecca M. M. (1992) *International Law: A Student Introduction.* 2d ed. London: Sweet & Maxwell.

Watson, Adam (1982) *Diplomacy: The Dialogue Between States.* London: Eyre Methuen.

International Organizations

Is it sensible to speak of the United Nations as a world government?
Why or why not?

Columbian cartoonist Gonzalo Aganta shows a top-hatted man on the
right seeking to stop war. Is he analogous to the United Nations?

209

International organizations have played a greater and greater role in world affairs since the Napoleonic Wars. More than six hundred of them are in existence. They have purposes that are either specific or general, and they are either limited or potentially universal in membership. Specific purposes are usually identified by the organization's name—for example, the International Bureau of Weights and Measures and the Universal Postal Union. Some of the general-purpose organizations that are limited in their membership are regional—for example, the European Union and the Organization of American States. The United Nations is the one general-purpose organization with potentially universal membership.

International organizations do not have jurisdiction over territory or people; that is, they do not enact and enforce law against individuals, nor do they tax individuals. To the extent that they engage in activity within the territory of a state, they do it with the consent of its government. They get their financial support from governments, which make voluntary contributions or agree on the rules for calculating the assessments. In other words, international organizations accept and respect the sovereignty of the member states. Membership in them is voluntary.

I will begin the treatment of international organizations with a statement about the League of Nations and then devote a major section of the chapter to the United Nations. Among the regional organizations, I will focus on the European Union and the Council of Europe. Finally, I will describe a selected list of international organizations that are specific rather than general in the purposes that they pursue.

■ The League of Nations

The League of Nations was established at the close of World War I. Woodrow Wilson had styled that war both as "a war to end war" and as "a war to make the world safe for democracy"; and he conceived the League as the principal means of attempting to realize those goals.

So far as war and peace are concerned, the central feature of the League was an arrangement for *collective security*, that is, an arrangement in which states act collectively to provide security for each other. The constitution of the League was called a Covenant, and in it the members agreed not only to *respect* but also to *preserve* each other's territorial integrity and political independence. The theory was that if a potential aggressor saw that the combined military might of the rest of the world would be arrayed against him, he would decide not to attack; in more recent language, he would be deterred. And peace would be preserved.

The arrangement and the supporting theory both looked appealing, but they had a fatal flaw. The flaw is made plain by a comparison between domestic and international politics. In domestic politics, government normally has overwhelming power that it can bring to bear against any challenger; but this is rarely possible in international politics. Think of the problem that an international organization would face if it tried to mobilize overwhelming power against the United States.

During the period of the League of Nations, as in most periods of modern history, a number of states were so powerful that an international organization had little chance of intimidating them or deterring them by threats of force. It is one thing to enforce law within a country against individuals like you and me and another thing to enforce it internationally against a whole country, most obviously if that country is big and powerful. Moreover, the more powerful countries, especially if they are adversaries, may not see eye to eye about enforcing the law even against a weak state. On the contrary, one or another of them may champion the cause of any state, even a weak one, that will line up with it on international issues. These truths are not as obvious now that the Soviet Union has collapsed, but the current situation is unusual.

The problems to which these considerations point soon showed up in the League of Nations. In fact, they showed up even before it got under way, for the United States, repudiating Woodrow Wilson, refused to join. It refused to join for several reasons, among them the belief in the Senate that the country should not obligate itself to *preserve* the territorial integrity of states all over the world.

Further, it developed that other states were unwilling to live up to the obligation. In 1931 Japan invaded Manchuria, which theoretically should have led all League members to spring to the defense of China. But the defense of China meant war, and Japan was powerful. The outcome was that members of the League limited themselves to saying "tut-tut" and wagging a finger. Later, when Mussolini (Italy) attacked Ethiopia, they decided through the League to apply economic sanctions; but they carefully limited the sanctions to those unlikely to provoke war with Italy or drive it into an alliance with Hitler's Germany. And the limited sanctions did not work. One League member conquered another and made it a colony.

Thus, when Hitler made his successive moves toward war, including the annexation of Austria, the subjection of Czechoslovakia, and finally the attack on Poland in 1939, the League played no significant role. It did not keep the peace, and those who finally decided to act against Hitler's aggression did not think it worthwhile to do it in the name of the League. The League was simply irrelevant to the war.

As World War II turned out, the aggressors were defeated and individual leaders on the defeated side were tried for their violations of the law, a number being either executed or imprisoned. The war thus illustrated *collective self-help* in upholding the law, but it did not illustrate *collective security* as envisaged in the League Covenant.

During and after World War II, leaders in the United States had guilt feelings about US isolationism between the wars, including the refusal to join the League of Nations, tending to believe that perhaps World War II could have been averted had the United States involved itself in the effort. And they were determined that the country should play a fuller role thereafter in efforts to keep the peace. Thus, they joined in formulating what became the Charter of the United Nations. The organization got under way in 1945, with the United States among the fifty-one original members.

■ The United Nations: Structure and Functions

The major organs of the United Nations are the Security Council, the General Assembly, and the Secretariat.

The Security Council consists of fifteen members and meets on call. The Charter names five states as permanent members: the United States, the Soviet Union (now replaced by Russia), Britain, France, and China. That arrangement has become anachronistic and invidious in that certain other states (notably Germany, India, and Japan) seem to belong in the same general category but are denied the same status. In addition to the permanent members, the Security Council consists of ten other members elected by the General Assembly for two-year terms.

Each member of the Security Council has one vote. Members may propose resolutions, which are classified as either *procedural* or *substantive*. Nine votes are enough for the adoption of a resolution, but on *substantive* matters the negative vote of a single permanent member is a *veto*. The question of whether a resolution should be classified as substantive or procedural is itself substantive, so the United States or any other permanent member can first veto an effort to classify a resolution as procedural and then veto the resolution itself.

The Charter does not impose on members an obligation like the one in the League Covenant to preserve each other's territorial integrity. But it authorizes the Security Council to take any of several kinds of action with respect to disputes or to situations that might lead to international friction. Further, it authorizes the Security Council to make a finding that a threat to the peace exists or that a breach of the peace or act of aggression has occurred. And if the Security Council makes such a finding, it may go on to order members of the United Nations to apply sanctions, that is, measures aimed at inducing the observance of law. The sanctioning measures that the Security Council may order range from the severance of diplomatic relations with the guilty state through economic embargoes and boycotts to military action.

The General Assembly consists of representatives of all member states (185 in 1994), each state having one vote. It meets annually and in special session and may discuss any question relating to the purposes of the organization. More particularly, it may "recommend measures for the peaceful adjustment of any situation, regardless of origin, which it deems likely to impair the general welfare or friendly relations among nations." Note that it can discuss and recommend. The Charter does not authorize it to enact or amend law, as do the legislatures that operate within countries. It does in fact make a few decisions that have binding force (for example, with respect to budgetary assessments), but the main point, nevertheless, is that it has little power.

Like the Security Council, the General Assembly acts by considering resolutions. They are classified as *important* and *other*. Those that are *important* require a two-thirds vote for adoption, and those in the *other* category can be adopted by a simple majority. The Charter itself lists some questions that are to be considered *important* and specifies that additional questions may be placed in this category by a majority; in other words, a majority may require that a resolution be so classified that a two-thirds vote is necessary.

The Secretariat is the civil service of the United Nations. A secretary-general is at its head, appointed by the General Assembly on the recommendation of the Security Council. In addition, the Secretariat consists of some 14,000 persons recruited from around the world, with the more important positions shared out on a quota basis among the various countries and regions. About half of the members work in New York, where the General Assembly and Security Council normally meet, and the rest work in various offices around the world, mostly in Geneva, Switzerland, where they occupy the old building of the League of Nations.

The secretary-general is the chief administrative officer of the UN, and he also serves in a political role that I will describe in a moment. Members of the Secretariat perform a variety of functions. They provide the services needed for meetings and conferences of the UN. They translate and distribute the necessary documents. They do research and assemble information and knowledge. They administer various programs (for example, programs designed to promote the development of the less developed countries), and they administer the organization itself, recruiting its employees, managing its funds, and so on. And they perform other tasks.

The regular budget of the UN runs to about $1.4 billion per year, and to raise the money the General Assembly assesses members on an agreed-upon scale, the United States and Japan accepting the highest assessments, 25 and 12.45 percent of the total respectively. Some 83 of the 185 members have the minimum assessment: 0.01 percent.

When costs connected with peacekeeping are added to the regular budget, the grand total comes to over $5 billion per year. The US assessment for peacekeeping costs is 30.8 percent, but in 1995 Congress said it would provide only 25 percent. In addition to the assessments, members are invited in various connections to make voluntary contributions.

In the fall of 1993 only sixty-six of the members had paid their assessments in full. Forty-five had paid nothing at all. Although paid up in 1993, the United States has since become a major delinquent. The UN faces a chronic financial problem.

■ Peacemaking, Peacekeeping, and Peace Enforcement

According to the Charter, the first purpose of the United Nations is to promote international peace and security. In pursuit of that purpose it seeks to help in peace-making and peacekeeping, and on occasion it has engaged in peace enforcement.

The secretary-general, the Security Council, and the General Assembly all involve themselves in peacemaking. The secretary-general may urge either the Security Council or the General Assembly to take a matter up, or he may act on his own. If he acts on his own, he may do it in person or through others to whom he delegates authority. The lines of action potentially open to him range from facilitating communication (perhaps by arranging meetings or serving as a letter carrier) to proposing terms of settlement. In addition to his powers of persuasion and his moral authority, he may seek support for his proposals from governments. In connection with the fighting in Bosnia, for example, the secretary-general appointed a former US secretary of state, Cyrus Vance, to be his agent in helping to establish peace.

Perhaps the most notable peacemaking efforts of the General Assembly and Security Council have related to the Middle East. It was the General Assembly that in 1947 enacted a resolution calling for the partition of Palestine, and it was the Security Council that adopted resolution 242 suggesting basic terms for an Arab-Israeli settlement.

Efforts at peacekeeping have been more common. These efforts occur when parties are in a tense relationship but nevertheless want to maintain peace between themselves, even if temporarily. Given the tension, the danger is that some kind of an incident will trigger hostilities that neither side really wants. With the consent of both sides, then, the UN provides a peacekeeping force, perhaps locating it in a buffer zone, the hope being that it can help keep the situation under control. Peacekeeping forces are not expected to fight. Instead, they simply withdraw if one party requests it or if war breaks out. One of the many illustrations of UN peacekeeping is found in Cyprus, where neutral observers for years have helped Greeks and Turks avert or manage dangerous incidents.

Peace enforcement has occurred less frequently and less successfully. From the establishment of the UN until the later 1980s, the major members were locked in a cold war that precluded friendly collaboration in peace enforcement. The veto in the Security Council alone made action to deter or defeat aggression unlikely. The five permanent members could all block action against themselves, and in addition, each of the five could veto action that might be especially beneficial to an adversary; further, each could block action that would go against the interests of a friend and ally or of a state whose friendship and support it sought.

The result was that during the cold war the United Nations, like the League of Nations before it, was on the sidelines in connection with the major threats to the peace. To be sure, the Security Council authorized action when North Korea invaded South Korea in 1950, but President Truman had already acted on his own; and support from the Security Council is not to be credited to its effectiveness but rather to the fact that the Soviet Union was inept enough to be boycotting its meetings when the matter came up.

The Security Council did not find a threat to the peace or breach of the peace when China and India fought each other, or India and Pakistan; nor did it make such a finding in connection with any of the wars involving Israel, or the war in Vietnam, or the Iraq-Iran war, or the war over the Falkland Islands. And the Security Council sat by helplessly during the major crises in Soviet-US relations—over Berlin and over Khrushchev's secret efforts to install nuclear missiles in Cuba.

The odd fact is that prior to Gorbachev's reversal of Soviet policy in 1987, the Security Council found threats to the peace only when racial discrimination was the fundamental issue. This first happened in 1965 in connection with Southern Rhodesia, a British colony with a population that was 95 percent black. When the white supremacist government there illegally declared the country independent so as to avoid "majority rule," Britain requested the Council to find that the situation thus created was a threat to the peace. The Council obliged, ordering the mandatory application of economic sanctions, which continued to be applied until the white regime finally gave up some fifteen years later and Southern Rhodesia legally gained independence as Zimbabwe.

The Security Council made a comparable decision in 1977 as one aspect of an intense international campaign against the government of South Africa because of its policies of apartheid. The Security Council declared that the continued acquisition of arms and related matériel by South Africa constituted a threat to the peace, and it ordered an arms embargo. These sanctions were lifted only in 1994, after democratic elections in South Africa.

New possibilities are open to the UN now that the cold war is over and the Soviet Union has broken up. The changed situation made it possible for the Security Council to order sanctions against Iraq when it invaded Kuwait in 1991. Whereas in earlier years the Soviet Union would surely have vetoed any dispatch of US troops to the Arabian peninsula, Russia was willing to have this happen. And China, which remains a communist power, did not object. Twenty-eight UN members joined the United States in crushing Iraqi forces and freeing Kuwait.

Similarly in 1992 and 1993 the Security Council found it possible to adopt a number of measures, including the imposition of economic sanctions, aimed at bringing fighting in the area of Yugoslavia to an end. It ordered an arms embargo against Somalia (where civil war threatened to have international ramifications) and authorized the use of force to establish a secure environment for humanitarian relief operations. And it called for an air traffic embargo against Libya and economic sanctions against Haiti.

At the same time, it should be acknowledged that, although the end of the cold war permits the UN to be more active in the realm of peace enforcement, what it can do is limited. The permanent members of the Security Council still have a veto, and if a problem arises they can be expected to use their veto to prevent action against themselves or their major interests. And even when the permanent members agree in principle on action, what each one does is more likely to be a function of its interpretation of its national interest than a function of its sense of obligation under the UN Charter. Peace enforcement succeeded against Iraq because the United States, pursuing its national interest, made it succeed. Neither the United States nor any other major power regards it as vital to terminate the hostilities in the area of Yugoslavia, and so they go on.

The UN Charter reflects a presumption that aggression is wrong and that it should be deterred or defeated. The General Assembly has wavered on this principle in connection with what some call wars of national liberation, but it is reasonable to say that the presumption stands. It rests on a belief that the world community has an interest in deterring or defeating aggression, just as within countries everyone has an interest in deterring crime and bringing criminals to justice. But though states generally accept this position in principle, they take a variety of considerations into account in deciding what action to take, if any, on behalf of the principle.

These statements apply to the United States as well as to other states. Given that the United States is among those that are unwilling to commit themselves to military action against any aggression anywhere, the question is what considerations it should take into account in making a decision on the matter. I suggest the following:

1. Is the presumption sound that the aggression is wrong, or is the aggression to either excused or approved on the ground that the war being waged is just?
2. How probable is it that action against the aggression can be successful? At what cost? What counts as success?
3. How probable is it that if the immediate act of aggression is allowed to succeed, other such acts would follow? Is it a choice between acting now and acting later?

4. How great is the possibility that armed action against aggression, even if successful, would bring new and greater dangers or evils into existence?

5. Apart from the general interest of the United States in the preservation of law and order in the world, what more specific interests of the country are at stake, and how important are they?

6. How much weight should the United States give to the record and the characteristics of the victim of aggression? Suppose, for example, that the victim is itself a notorious violator of international law with a record of contempt for human rights. Is it as much entitled to aid as another victim of a more virtuous sort? Note that following Iraq's attack on Iran some years earlier, the United States did not spring to the aid of Iran.

7. How great is the possibility that an adequate degree of success could be achieved by measures short of armed action; for example, by economic sanctions?

8. What are the pros and cons of acting unilaterally v. acting under the auspices of the UN? Should the United States make its willingness to act contingent on the willingness of other states to share the burdens?

Suppose that the president has taken the country so far down the road to war that a refusal to follow his lead would undermine the credibility of US foreign policy for years to come. In that case another question arises:

9. Even if the case for armed action looks doubtful, should it occur and be supported as a means of avoiding national humiliation?

Differing circumstances may make the proper reaction to aggression a matter of judgment rather than a matter of rigid rule.

■ Human Rights

The United Nations has made, and is making, significant contributions in the field of human rights.

Prior to World War II, international action with respect to human rights was rare. The League Covenant contained no general provision on the subject, those who formulated the Covenant even refusing to go along with a proposal by Japan directed against racial discrimination. But attitudes changed, and abhorrence of Hitler's policies led to the inclusion in the United Nations Charter of a provision requiring members to promote human rights without distinction as to race, sex, language, or religion.

One of the early acts of the General Assembly was the establishment of a Commission on Human Rights, whose first major task was to seek agreement among members of the United Nations on what to count as human rights. The result was an enumeration in the Universal Declaration of Human Rights, adopted by the General Assembly in 1948. In 1966 the General Assembly went farther, adopting two covenants, enumerating civil and political rights in one and economic, social, and cultural rights in the other. It has also adopted a number of more specialized conventions, including one on racial discrimination. These documents have been mentioned in earlier chapters. The covenants have been ratified as treaties by almost two-thirds of the states of the world.

These various documents are significant in that, in principle at least, they register a widespread international consensus about what is permissible and impermissible in the field of human rights. Moreover, the very process of developing the documents has served to promote consciousness of the problem around the world. The question of respect for human rights has been brought to the fore in both domestic and international politics to an extent unprecedented in history, and a basis has been provided for international scrutiny of policies that not many decades ago were of purely domestic concern.

The Charter requires members to *promote* respect for human rights but not actually to respect them; and it does not provide for international *enforcement*. Publicity is the principal weapon. Any of several UN agencies can inquire into human rights practices, condemn guilty states, and put a spotlight on them. The UN Commission on Human Rights receives periodic reports from members concerning their relevant practices and adopts resolutions that tend to be velveted but that nevertheless get attention. The US Department of State releases a report each year on practices relating to human rights around the world, and various nongovernmental organizations (for example, Amnesty International) concern themselves with human rights.

Results are sometimes achieved. Governments do not like to be publicly condemned, and criticisms in the UN stand a fair chance of encouraging and strengthening domestic critics and opponents of guilty regimes.

In addition to publicity, other weapons are potentially available. The Security Council can find that the violation of human rights is a threat to the peace, which is approximately what it did in the Rhodesian and South African cases mentioned above. For years the General Assembly, taking the stand that the racial policies of South Africa made its government illegitimate, refused to seat its delegates. The United States threatened to withhold aid, and has actually withheld it, from governments engaging in a persistent pattern of gross violations of human rights, and it has urged the World Bank and other international institutions to deny loans and other aid to such governments. On a number of occasions, the UN has sent in observers to monitor human rights practices, and especially to monitor elections. (The Universal Declaration proclaims a human right "to vote and be elected at genuine periodic elections. . . .")

In 1993 the General Assembly finally created a new post of High Commissioner for Human Rights. The holder of the post is to coordinate the human rights activities of the UN and to seek greater respect for human rights around the world.

■ Other UN Activities

The UN engages in a number of additional activities. It maintains the office of the High Commissioner for Refugees, which mobilizes assistance for those who flee abroad. It administers an aid program for the less developed countries. It is involved in environmental issues. It promotes the development and codification of international law. It gives small countries a forum where they get a hearing not available to them elsewhere. It brings together political leaders from all over the world who presumably gain greater knowledge of the attitudes of other persons, and of the rights and interests of other states, and perhaps a greater inclination to respect them. It provides the more experienced delegates, especially delegates from the more advanced countries, with an opportunity to educate the less experienced delegates and socialize them in the ways of international diplomacy.

■ An Appraisal

The United Nations is necessary. If it did not exist, it (or something very much like it) would surely be created. The problem of war and the problems of international cooperation in the pursuit of common ends need to be attacked, and not simply in ivied halls and national capitals. In terms of any standard of judgment that is at all relevant, and particularly in terms of economic, human, and cultural costs, war should not be an instrument of public policy, and any institution that contributes toward a reduction in its incidence, or shows even a modest promise of doing so, justifies itself. Similarly, the problems of economic well-being and progress call increasingly for international consultation and cooperation. Even if the UN had achieved nothing, the lessons learned from the failure would make the efforts associated with it worthwhile, contributing somehow to a better organization of humankind than the one that now prevails.

What has already been said is enough to establish the point that the UN has justified its existence. A point implicit in what has been said, however, deserves emphasis: that the UN serves as a formulator and champion of international principles and standards that are of vital importance. The Charter itself gives legal status to a set of moral rules basic to human progress, and the Charter is supplemented in this respect by numerous resolutions of the General Assembly and numerous treaties such as the covenants on human rights. Activities associated with the UN implant these moral rules in the consciousness of governments and peoples all over the world.

Not only does the UN formulate and champion principles and standards but it also throws a spotlight on problems, inducing governments and people all over the world to focus on them together. Even when no solution is found, lessons are learned that make future successes more likely.

Despite all of the above, the UN has engendered widespread disappointment in the United States and in the Western world. The cold war is a major part of the explanation, for the two sides in that war had fundamentally conflicting objectives that tended to paralyze the UN and many other international organizations.

The great expansion of the membership in the UN since 1960 is another part of the explanation, for most of the new members, coming from the Third World, tended either to be hostile toward the United States or to adopt different priorities. The Third World countries tended to be hostile because of a strong inclination toward socialism, an inclination that Daniel Patrick Moynihan attributes to the London School of Economics, where so many of their leaders were educated. The socialist thesis was that the Third World countries, almost all former dependencies, were victims of imperialism, relatively less developed not because of circumstances internal to them but rather because of foreign exploitation and oppression. The tendency was to forget that the Third World countries were less developed before they became dependencies.

Very few of the Third World countries had ever been dependencies of the United States, but the United States was the leading capitalist power and therefore was a prime object of socialist criticism and resentment. In contrast, the commitment of Third World leaders to socialism disposed them to vote with the Soviet Union and to refuse to criticize it, accentuating tendencies in the United States to look upon the UN with skepticism and misgiving.

As to priorities, the Third World countries tended to be preoccupied with white racism, inducing the General Assembly to devote a striking proportion of its energies to denunciations of South Africa and to denunciations of white "imperialist" countries for not acting more decisively against South Africa. Moreover, perhaps in order to win Arab votes for denunciations of South Africa, Third World states tended to join Arab states in denunciations of Israel.

On top of these factors leading to disappointment with the UN is the general intractability of the problems that it faces. The states of the world are sovereign and jealous of their sovereignty—more concerned with their own interests (usually short-term interests) than with the common interests of humankind. They like decentralization, for it permits them to manage their own affairs as they please. They resist the idea of subordinating themselves in a wider community. Given attitudes like this, the development of global international institutions is bound to be slow.

The breakup of the Soviet Union and the collapse of communism improves the prospects of the United Nations, as it does of the world as a whole. The Russian government seems to want to be a constructive partner in managing the affairs of the common home, to use Gorbachev's words. This will surely make for a more effective United Nations.

Abba Eban, writing when the Soviet Union was still intact and when Third World countries tended to vote in the General Assembly in accordance with their socialist inclinations, raised the question of whether the whole United Nations system is not based on the wrong principle. The choice, as he put it, is between the "diplomatic principle" and the "parliamentary principle." "The diplomatic principle," according to Eban, "tells me that I need my adversary's agreement. The parliamentary principle tells me that I do not need his agreement; I can secure his defeat and humiliation by a majority vote" (Eban 1983, 280).

In the United Nations, Eban pointed out, the parliamentary principle had put the diplomatic principle to rout. The member states voted! They adopted resolutions critical of the richer and more powerful countries, and then adopted others condemning those same countries for not doing what they had been called upon to do. And they imposed what amount to taxes!

Rather than contrast the diplomatic and parliamentary principles, others call for change in the voting rules. Weighted voting is one of the possibilities, but it requires agreement on the criteria for assigning weights. Should states have votes in proportion to their military power? in proportion to their GNP? in proportion to their per capita GNP? in proportion to the amount they are expected to contribute to the UN budget? in proportion to their population? No consensus has developed about the matter. The smaller and poorer states, even if dictatorial at home, tend to champion what they call "democracy" in the UN—one state, one vote, and majority rule. Others comment that it is an odd democracy that gives as much voting power to Grenada as to China.

In 1986 the US Congress forced the issue, at least in part. It demanded that, where "budgetary consequences" are concerned, voting power be allocated according to budgetary assessments. Otherwise the US contribution to the UN budget would be reduced. Thus threatened, the General Assembly gave way, strengthening the budgetary role of a committee that had already been operating by consensus—meaning that a single negative vote blocks action. The richer countries, including the United States, are regularly represented on this committee, so in effect they have been given a veto on expenditures. Or, as Eban would say, the diplomatic principle has been made dominant. The arrangement is informal—a kind of "gentlemen's agreement"—but it seems to be working. Thus, in 1993, the United States finally paid up on its dues, and Russia went far in the same direction.

Given the veto in the Security Council, the problem created by the rule of one state, one vote is not so great there. Even so, the stature of the Security Council is not enhanced when, as was the case some years ago, over half the members were small states contributing only 0.25 percent of the UN budget.

This is not to say that a shift to the "diplomatic principle" or to weighted voting would enable the UN to flourish. Many of the problems that beset international politics are simply intractable. Agreement with the adversary is sometimes impossible. But a strategy based on realism is less likely to discredit an organization than a strategy that gives illusory command to weak and poor countries simply because they have the votes.

■ Regional Organizations

Various regional organizations exist: the Organization of American States, the Organization of African Unity, the Arab League, the Association of Southeast Asian Nations, the European Union, the Council of Europe, and others.

I focus here on Europe, and especially on the European Union, which is distinctive in two main respects. In the first place, it is a union of peoples and not simply an agency of the various governments. Major institutions of the Union can act on their own authority, independently of any instructions from governments. In the second place, the Union provides more fully for genuine international legislation on the basis of (qualified) majority rule than most international organizations.

The existence of the Union reflects the fact that European peoples have special incentives to reduce the dangers and ills that accompany the absence of an overarching government. They share a common civilization (common values, the Christian religion, and so on), but their history is nevertheless one of intermittent war, culminating in the catastrophic wars of this century and the horror of the Holocaust. The urge to put an end to war among themselves and to prevent any other regime like Hitler's from coming to power is strong. The desire has also been strong to safeguard themselves against the Soviet Union and the intolerance and fanaticism of communism—a motivation that is less significant now that even the communists recognize that their god has failed. In any event, the peoples of Europe are seeking to solve, or at least to alleviate, their problems through economic and political integration.

The European Union, called the European Community until 1993, is the principal expression of this hope. Its original six members were France, Germany, Italy, and the Benelux countries (Belgium, the Netherlands, and Luxemburg), and they have been joined by Austria, Denmark, Finland, Greece, Ireland, Portugal, Spain, Sweden, and the United Kingdom. Other states, most notably the formerly communist states of eastern and southeastern Europe, seek to join.

The immediate, specific goal of the Union is the establishment of a single market—free trade and the free movement of capital and labor among the members—a goal that has political and social implications. Pursuit of this goal culminated in 1987 in the adoption of the Single European Act expanding the role of the various institutions of the Union and naming 1992 as the year by which a single common market was to be achieved. And in fact it has substantially been achieved. The Act also fixes monetary union as a goal, and it calls formally for cooperation with respect to foreign and security policies. Further, it recognizes a need for "cohesion," that is, for financial support for the members most likely to suffer in free-market competition, which means financial support for the poorest members. At the same time, the Union is plagued by the problem of farmers, especially the farmers of France, who are accustomed to protection from foreign competition and who are therefore threatened by free trade.

No one can yet be sure how far the movement toward integration will be carried. Although agreeing with each other sufficiently to be members and to seek a single market, the states involved differ on how far and how fast to go with respect to the more distinctly political arrangements. A few (notably Britain) are especially sensitive to questions of sovereignty, and all subscribe to the principle of subsidiarity: that matters should be handled at the lowest feasible level.

The four main institutions of the European Union are a Commission, a Council, a Parliament, and a Court of Justice.

The Commission consists of twenty persons who are chosen by agreement among the member governments but who are neither to seek nor to take instructions from any government or any other body. They are to act in the general interest of the Union, proposing measures to the European Parliament and the Council and seeing to their execution once they are approved. The Commission is thus the chief initiator of legislation and has executive powers. On the basis of the legislation enacted, it issues rules that member states are to follow and then issues additional instructions concerning the application of the rules in particular cases. Moreover, the rules and instructions come in relatively large numbers—for example, over six thousand of them in 1991 alone. The Commission represents the Union in its external affairs. Its president is generally regarded as the leading figure in the organization.

If the Commission believes that a member is not living up to its obligations, it may request an explanation or justification; and if the explanation or justification is inadequate, the Commission may issue a reasoned opinion with which the offending state is bound to comply. A failure to comply leads to a referral of the issue to the European Court of Justice. In 1991 the Commission issued 259 reasoned opinions, and they led to the referral of 73 cases to the Court. Judgments of the Court are binding and are generally implemented, but in some instances compliance is slow.

The Council of the European Union consists of cabinet ministers from the different governments—different sets of ministers, depending on the problem being considered. The Council is the principal legislative body of the Union, though it adopts legislation only on the recommendation of the Commission and only after consulting the European Parliament.

A system of weighted voting prevails. France, Germany, Italy, and the United Kingdom each have ten votes. Others have lesser numbers, down to two for Luxembourg. The Council operates on the basis of a "qualified" rather than a "simple" majority, the precise number of votes required to adopt resolutions changing as new members are added. The general principle is that approximately three-fourths of the votes give a "qualified" majority, which means that approximately one-fourth of the votes can block action. A smaller number of negative votes can get action suspended for a "reasonable period" during which greater consensus is sought. This latter arrangement is a concession to Britain, which, as indicated above, is jealous of its sovereignty and wants to keep it as easy as possible to apply the brakes to the movement toward integration.

The European Parliament has 626 members. They are not appointed by governments, as in the case of the General Assembly of the UN, but rather are elected directly by the voters of the different member countries. Germany has 99 seats, and the next three most populous states have 87. Others have lesser numbers, down to 6 for Luxembourg. The rule of one state, one vote is thus rejected, but representation is not strictly proportional to population, either, for the smaller the population of a country, the more it is relatively overrepresented.

Together with the Council, the European Parliament draws up the budget of the Union. Union funds come in part from member governments, which are assessed in proportion to their GNP.

The Maastricht treaty of 1992 significantly enlarges the powers of the Parliament, and the Parliament has expressed its intention to use the power of the purse to "help the Community develop." Nevertheless, it remains weak in comparison with domestic parliaments in democratic countries. Theoretically, it can force the resignation of the members of the Commission by a two-thirds vote of censure, but it has never exercised this power. Members of the Commission and the Council are expected to attend the sessions of Parliament and to respond to questions put to them.

The integration of states in the European Union calls for extensive domestic adjustments. For example, the tax policies must be coordinated, for differences might confer unfair advantages or disadvantages on the economic enterprises of different countries. And the members have adopted a Social Charter and accompanying protocols. They agree that a single market is not an end in itself but a means toward the achievement of a greater end: ensuring a maximum of well-being for all in accordance with Europe's tradition of social progress. On this basis the protocol enumerates the social rights of all persons, such as equal and nondiscriminatory treatment, freedom of movement, the improvement of living and working conditions, social security, and so on. Members are to adjust their policies and laws accordingly. Such international pressure with respect to what are ordinarily domestic matters is rare. One wonders in what circumstances, if any, the United States would find it acceptable. It goes without saying that only democratic states are welcome in the European Union.

In addition to the Council described above (the Council of the European Union), a Council of Europe exists, with thirty-two members as of 1993. Since its establishment in 1949 it has recommended nearly 200 treaties and conventions for ratification dealing with various economic, social, and cultural subjects. Best known of them, and probably most important, is the Convention for the Protection of Human Rights and Fundamental Freedoms (1950), modeled after the Universal Declaration of Human Rights and ratified as of 1990 by twenty-three states, from Iceland to Turkey.

In addition to spelling out human rights and binding the parties to respect them, the convention provides for enforcement action. Individual persons who believe that their rights have been violated can arraign the accused government and get a judgment by which the government is bound. The enforcing agencies have been a Commission and a Court, but a decision of 1993 calls for the merger of these institutions. A large proportion of the ratifying states, including all of the major powers of western Europe, have in fact been arraigned, and it is not uncommon for judgments to go against them.

The Council of Europe preceded the European Union in sponsoring a Social Charter. Ratifying states (sixteen of them as of 1990) declare their intention to protect a set of rights like those in the Covenant on Economic, Social, and Cultural Rights. The European Union's Social Charter, mentioned above, is similar, but it binds ratifying states to prompt implementation. One of the objectives is to reduce disparities in the treatment of labor in the different countries.

European regional organizations fall short of political union, but they nevertheless indicate that quasi-governmental activity goes on at the international level. It is no longer sensible, if it ever was, to assume that the study of politics can reasonably be limited to the domestic level.

It would become tedious to describe the other regional organizations. None of them have gone as far as the European states in giving their international institutions functions that are suggestive of government.

■ Special-Purpose Organizations _____

In addition to the intergovernmental organizations pursuing general purposes, a large number of others pursue special purposes. Most of them deserve and get little public attention; for example, the International Olive Oil Council. A very few, such as the Organization of Petroleum Exporting Countries (OPEC), make decisions that shake the world. I will describe a few of the more prominent organizations for purposes of illustration.

The Universal Postal Union (UPU) operates on the basis of a constitution that concerns the structure, powers, and responsibilities of the Union and on the basis of a convention that sets forth the rules and principles for operating the international postal service. The member states meet periodically in congresses at which a majority may amend the convention; any member that objects to the change may withdraw from the organization, but the benefits of membership are such that this rarely happens.

The World Health Organization (WHO) also has a special purpose and is also potentially universal in membership. Members meet periodically in a World Health Assembly, which adopts regulations concerning sanitary requirements and the prevention of disease and establishes standards relating to the safety, purity, and other qualities of drugs. These regulations and standards become binding on all members except those that specifically "contract out."

A considerable portion of the work of the WHO takes the form of training programs, advice, and technical assistance to member states. It assists governments in improving their health services. It seeks the cooperation of governments in efforts to eradicate diseases, and in the case of smallpox it has come close to complete success. It concerns itself with environmental hygiene and public health. It promotes research and the dissemination of the results of research to professional and lay groups.

The International Labor Organization (ILO) concerns itself with the treatment of labor and with trade unions all over the world, engaging in studies relating to the health, safety, and welfare of workers, sponsoring treaties that members are invited to ratify, checking on the observance of the rules contained in the treaties, and making recommendations. The Governing Body has set up a Committee on Freedom of Association, authorizing it to take up complaints concerning the right of workers to organize; the complaints may be made by one government against another or by an organization of workers or employers; and numerous such complaints are in fact made and investigated, leading the accused government in a substantial portion of the cases to change its law or its practice. The ILO is distinctive in that, though intergovernmental, its leading organs include nongovernmental representatives. In the annual conference, delegates named by workers and by employers join delegates named by member states.

Controversy of a political sort arises in connection with the International Labor Organization just as it does in a number of other specialized organizations. In 1977 the United States withdrew. It had been offended by the appointment of a Soviet citizen as one of the six assistant directors general. It pointed to what it called "the erosion of tripartite representation"—the point being that the delegates from communist countries who were supposed to represent the workers and employers were under the thumb of the various communist parties. It pointed to what it called "a selective concern for human rights." This had to do not only with undue communist influence in the ILO but also with the "British revolution" described earlier, leading to socialist and anticapitalist/imperialist attitudes and an unwillingness to be critical of communist countries.

The United States pointed also to the disregard for due process in condemning countries, the reference being to the claim that the ILO had joined many other organizations in ill-considered or extreme denunciations of Israel and South Africa. And it pointed generally to an increasing politicization of the organization in taking actions that had little or no relevance to its central purposes.

In 1980 the United States rejoined, taking the view that the ILO had made progress in solving the problems that had led to the withdrawal.

The United Nations Educational, Scientific, and Cultural Organization (UNESCO) aims "to contribute to peace and security by promoting collaboration among the nations through education, science, and culture in order to further universal respect for justice, for the rule of law and for human rights and fundamental freedoms." It is concerned with education at every level, giving advice and technical assistance to governments and cooperating with governments and other international organizations in the execution of individual projects. It sponsors a Convention Against Discrimination in Education. It has special programs relating to the natural sciences, the social sciences, and the humanities. The General Conference of UNESCO meets annually, and subordinate committees and groups meet, each for a brief period, throughout the year.

Even more than the ILO, UNESCO has been a center of controversy. A movement developed in it in the 1970s that the more-advanced democratic countries regarded as an attack on the freedom of the press. In addition, UNESCO and some of the other international organizations are criticized for the poor quality of their personnel and their inefficient and wasteful administrative practices. The personnel referred to are those in the permanent secretariats. It is essential that they be recruited in reasonable proportion from the various member states, and it has become customary for governments to recommend their nationals for service. All too often, in selecting those to recommend, governments have taken the opportunity to get rid of incompetents or to give out plums without considering the question of competence. In the case of UNESCO, a long-time director-general—a Third World figure who had some of the attitudes associated with the "British revolution"—came under severe criticism for inefficiency and wastefulness and was eventually replaced.

These various problems concerning UNESCO led the United States to withdraw from the organization in 1985. The statement issued at the time of the withdrawal spoke of UNESCO's "endemic hostility toward the institutions of a free society" and of its "politicization" and "mismanagement." Britain and Singapore also withdrew. The Clinton administration is said to be considering the question of rejoining, although anything that involves expense has come to be looked on with a jaundiced eye.

On several occasions the United States has threatened to withdraw from other organizations, too, if resolutions directed against Israel were adopted.

It should be acknowledged that Third World states are not the only ones to bring political considerations into the work of the specialized organizations. The United States itself has been voting in institutions of the "Bank Group" (see below) against giving help to governments guilty of a consistent pattern of gross violations of human rights. In so doing, it should be added, the United States is seeking to uphold generally approved international standards, which is not the case in connection with the politicization that the United States criticizes in such organizations as the ILO and UNESCO.

The "Bank Group" and the International Monetary Fund (IMF) are important among the agencies with specialized purposes. The "Bank Group" consists of the World Bank itself, plus the International Finance Corporation (IFC) and the International Development Association (IDA). The IFC is an affiliate of the bank, but it is legally separate and has its own staff. The IDA is a subdivision of the bank, extending credits to the poorer countries.

The Bank makes long-term loans to governments for a variety of purposes, the overarching purpose being described as "sustainable poverty reduction." Loans go in the main to the less developed countries. In the fiscal year ending in mid-1993, for example, the Bank loaned almost $24 billion, the sharpest increase being in loans to governments in what was the Soviet Union and its sphere. The bank has a professional staff of more than 2,500 persons. It gets its capital both from member countries and by borrowing (selling bonds); the IDA operates mainly on the basis of grants from the wealthier member countries. The Bank operates on near-commercial terms and is likely to make a profit, but the IDA, though collecting a small service fee, charges no interest. The expectation is that all loans will be repaid, though the IDA's loans may not come due for up to fifty years.

The IFC deals mainly with private businesses in developing countries, lending them money and buying their stock.

The emphasis of the Bank is on supporting projects designed to help meet "basic human needs" and on development aimed at general benefit for the population of the borrowing country. Countries that borrow must meet the conditions that the Bank fixes, both to qualify for the loan initially and actually to get the money thereafter, which means that an international agency is having effects on domestic policies. Staff members participate in dialogues with the representatives of governments wanting to borrow, examining the application of general principles to problems the government faces and joining in efforts to identify specific projects that are feasible and worthwhile.

The Bank publishes World Development Reports and country economic reports that presumably influence thinking about the kinds of policies to pursue and the kinds of projects to undertake for the sake of development. It helps build institutions within recipient countries, for development includes growth in relevant capabilities in both the public and the private sector.

The Bank is among the international organizations that provide for weighted voting. Each member has 250 votes plus one vote for each $100,000 of capital that it subscribes. The result is that the number of votes for the various members ranges from 293 for Botswana to 64,980 for the United States. Botswana casts 0.1 percent of the votes cast, and the United States almost 23 percent.

The purpose of the IMF is to promote international trade by fixing rules and taking action relating to exchange rates among the currencies of different countries. The subject is too complex to be pursued here. Among other things, countries sometimes get into balance of payments difficulties; they buy abroad more than they sell and borrow more than they can pay back on schedule. In such situations, they may seek help from the IMF, which fixes conditions on which it is willing to extend help. Depending on how desperate a country's need is, important features of its economic life may in effect be dictated by the international agency.

Some students of specialized international organizations have developed the idea of *functionalism*, with which you should be familiar. The idea is that the collaboration of states in special purpose organizations, presumably non-political, will gradually build up international contacts and cooperative attitudes to the point where thoughts of war simply fade away.

The record provides little support for the idea. Though the major special-purpose organizations make indispensable contributions to human well-being, they should not be expected to solve political problems. In truth, instead of relegating those problems to the back burner, the special-purpose organizations themselves tend to become forums in which the political struggle goes on. All the signs are that politics is universal and eternal.

■ Alliances

Two alliance systems confronted each other during the cold war. The Soviet Union was so dominant in its system, based on the Warsaw Pact, that no notable international organization developed, so none needed to be disbanded when the Soviet Union broke up and the cold war came to an end. In contrast, although the United States has played the leading role in the North Atlantic system, it has sought to coordinate the allied efforts through an international structure—the North Atlantic Treaty Organization (NATO). NATO provides a central command structure and has concerned itself with burden sharing and questions of strategy. Sixteen states are party to the treaty, including the United States, Canada, nearly all the states of western Europe, and Greece and Turkey.

With the ending of the cold war and the collapse of the Soviet alliance system, one of the possibilities was that NATO should disband, too. What justifies its continued existence? The issue is open to debate. Perhaps the best argument is twofold. On the one hand, NATO provides a basis for the continued involvement of the United States in the affairs of Europe, making it less likely that historical European frictions will lead to another major war. On the other hand, surprisingly enough, NATO provides a link between its members and the former members of the Soviet alliance system: they want to join. But this involves problems. Given nationalist rivalries in eastern and southeastern Europe and potential problems about the location of boundaries, members of NATO are reluctant to extend guarantees of security. Moreover, they do not want to act on the assumption that Russia is a threat, for this would be offensive in Moscow. The result is that the NATO states have invited the others to become "partners for peace," with no decision made about long-term relationships, and twenty-two of them have accepted the invitation. Eighteen of the twenty-two, including Russia, are former Warsaw Pact countries. "Partners" commit themselves to "transparency" in their own military affairs (that is, to sharing information) and to the democratic control of their armed forces; and they participate in NATO planning and training activities, with future participation in peacekeeping activities and in peace enforcement among the possibilities.

■ Review

The international system includes international organizations serving purposes ranging from the specific to the general and with memberships ranging from the limited to the universal.

The League of Nations, existing between the two world wars, was the first general-purpose organization aiming at universal membership. Its principal purpose was to keep the peace through a system of collective security, but governments proved unwilling to accept the risks and sacrifices that this involved.

The United Nations replaced the League. Membership in it is nearly universal. It consists of the Security Council, the General Assembly, and a Secretariat headed by a secretary-general. Peacemaking, peacekeeping, and peace enforcement are the primary functions, but the UN is also notable especially for its activities relating to human rights. Members are jealous of their sovereignty but nevertheless permit action by either a simple or a two-thirds majority, except that in the Security Council the five permanent members all have vetoes. The Security Council is primarily responsible for peace enforcement. The General Assembly may discuss a wide variety of matters and adopt resolutions that are in effect recommendations.

The European Union is the strongest and most prominent of the regional organizations, although a number of others exist. Numerous special-purpose organizations exist, such as the Universal Postal Union, the World Health Organization, and NATO.

■ Reading

Baehr, Peter R., and Leon Gordenker (1994) *The United Nations in the 1990s*. 2d ed. New York: St. Martin's.

Coate, Roger A. (1994) *U.S. Policy and the Future of the United Nations*. New York: Twentieth Century Fund Press.

Forsythe, David P. (1993) *Human Rights and Peace: International and National Dimensions*. Lincoln: University of Nebraska Press.

Mingst, Karen A., and Margaret P. Karns, eds. (1995) *The United Nations and the Post-Cold War Era*. Boulder, Colo.: Westview.

Pinder, John (1991) *European Community. The Building of a Union*. New York: Oxford University Press.

Riggs, Robert E., and Jack C. Plano (1994) *The United Nations. International Organization and World Politics*. 2nd ed. Pacific Grove, Calif: Brooks-Cole.

Roberts, Adam, and Benedict Kingsbury, eds. (1993) *United Nations, Divided World: The UN's Roles in International Relations*. 2d ed. Oxford: Oxford University Press.

Rochester, J. Martin (1993) *Waiting for the Millennium. The United Nations and the Future of World Order*. Columbia, S.C.: University of South Carolina Press.

Weiss, Thomas G., David P. Forsythe, and Roger A. Coate (1994) *The United Nations and Changing World Politics*. Boulder: Westview Press.

White, N. D. (1993) *Keeping the Peace*. New York: Manchester University Press.

War and Intervention

It is difficult to imagine anything so likely to transform life on earth as a third world war fought with nuclear weapons.

"YOU MEAN YOU WERE BLUFFING?"

7/7/65

Dan Wright imagines the aftermath of nuclear war, with a darkly ironic twist.

233

Scarcely any feature of political life is more important than war and preparation for war. This chapter begins with a brief elaboration of that theme and goes on to ask briefly about the incidence of war (who fight, and how often?) and its costs. Most of the chapter, however, is devoted to two further topics: (a) the causes of war and the factors contributing to the preservation of peace; and (b) just and unjust war. Questions about intervention (dictatorial interference by one state in the affairs of another) come up at several points.

■ The Importance of War

Perhaps none of the activities in which governments engage is the most important by all the potentially relevant criteria, but surely war and the preparation for war are among the most important. No other governmental activity has done so much to shape the course of political history, and probably no other has had more general and profound effects on the lives of so many people. And no other has produced so many deaths.

War has played an important role in the birth, growth, and extinction of states. The United States itself was born in revolution. War in Europe made the Louisiana Purchase possible, vastly expanding the national territory. War against Mexico made possible the annexation of Texas and the Southwest. The Civil War determined whether the Union would survive. The Spanish-American War led to the annexation of Puerto Rico, the Philippines (later freed), and various Pacific islands. World War II led to a special relationship between the United States and the Pacific island groups that Japan had controlled.

War has played a comparable role in the histories of most other countries. The principal exceptions are the many states that have come into existence since World War II—formerly dependent territories that have become independent. The question of the role of war in connection with the freeing of these territories is too tangled to pursue. Suffice it to say that war and the threat of war played a direct role in a few cases (Algeria, Indochina) and an indirect role in others.

Both the Austro-Hungarian and the Ottoman empires went out of existence as a result of World War I. That war enabled Estonia, Latvia, and Lithuania to become independent, and World War II enabled the Soviet Union to extinguish their independence; and now that the Soviet Union has broken up, they have become independent again. Both Germany and Korea were divided as a result of World War II (with Germany now peacefully reunited), and both Palestine and Pakistan were divided in later wars.

In addition to its role in the birth, growth, and extinction of states, war has been fateful to ideologies, cultures, and civilizations. Mussolini's Fascism and Hitler's National Socialism were destroyed through war.

Communism got its big start when the Russian government was so weakened by war (World War I) that power, as Trotsky said, lay in the streets. And World War II enabled the Soviet Union to extend communism to the countries of eastern and southeastern Europe. Further, World War II was among the factors making the victory of the communists possible in China and Yugoslavia, and eventually in Indochina.

The sweep of history provides many more illustrations. War played a vital role in the spread of Christianity and Islam and a vital role in determining their geographical limits. Military power, if not war in the usual sense, enabled the European peoples to make their colonial conquests all over the world. Among other things, the Aztec and Inca civilizations disappeared as a result.

In sum, it would be difficult to exaggerate the historical role of war and preparation for war. And it is difficult to imagine anything so likely to transform life on earth as a third world war fought with nuclear weapons.

■ The Incidence and Costs of War

Scholars have found it surprisingly difficult to develop reliable knowledge of the incidence and more especially the costs of war. What to count as war and what costs to attribute to it are problems; and once these problems are resolved, others arise concerning the availability and reliability of data, followed by still others of a methodological sort.

Jack S. Levy has made the most recent serious attack on the problems (Levy 1983). He focuses on the period beginning with the sixteenth century and limits himself to wars in which the great powers have been involved, not counting civil or colonial wars. He focuses on the whole set of these wars and also on a subset of them, the subset consisting of those wars in which at least one great power fought on each side.

On this basis Levy arrives at various findings: wars have declined in frequency and have been getting shorter in duration. Thus, the number of nation-years of war has been declining, but in terms of other kinds of measures, "wars involving the Great Powers have changed little over time." The other kinds of measures include battle-connected deaths of military personnel. With respect to them Levy's conclusion is "that the most violent periods . . . have become even more violent, and the most severe Great Power wars have become more severe, but in general [considering the ratio of battle-connected deaths of military personnel to total population] there has been no significant increase in the total losses of life from wars involving the Great Powers or from Great Power wars" (Levy 1983, 116, 123, 125, 129, 135).

These findings are significant but limited. They speak only of battle-connected deaths of military personnel, not of all deaths caused by war; and they say nothing of other kinds of effects of war, good or bad—

nothing about the effects of war on particular countries or on human progress. And though the findings take into account the use of nuclear weapons at Hiroshima and Nagasaki, they give no basis for predicting the costs of an unrestricted nuclear war.

Assuming some clear answer to the question of what to count as war, questions about the incidence of war become easier to answer. Under any plausible definition, virtually all states that came into existence prior to World War II have been belligerents in the period that Levy covers. War is not distinctive to any one political outlook or ideology. Again, however, the significance of the point is limited, for it does not distinguish between states that bring war on and states that fight in self-defense. The record indicates that democracies are much less likely than autocratic regimes to initiate war.

The coming of nuclear weapons and the rockets with which to deliver them threatens to transform war. Even the fission bombs (A-bombs) dropped at Hiroshima and Nagasaki make the biggest bombs previously dropped seem like firecrackers in comparison, and fusion bombs (H-bombs) developed subsequently have no theoretical limit to their destructive power. Moreover, in addition to explosive power and heat, nuclear bombs release lethal radiation—in varying amounts depending on circumstances. And some fear that a number of nuclear explosions might throw enough smoke, dust, and debris into the upper atmosphere to screen out the sun and lead to "nuclear winter," thus adding another catastrophe to the catastrophe already caused.

Rockets that can deliver nuclear warheads at speeds in excess of 17,000 miles per hour are as important to the nuclear revolution as the nuclear warheads themselves. After all, given enough time and the absence of an effective defense, airplanes dropping conventional bombs can inflict unlimited destruction. The great difference associated with the delivery of nuclear bombs by rocket is the speed with which the damage can be done and the impossibility of defense.

In conventional warfare those responsible for waging war have time to become aware of damage and loss of life, and the tendency is to somehow bring war to an end when it seems to be getting prohibitively expensive. In contrast, the timely termination of nuclear war may not be possible. With nuclear bombs delivered by rockets in great numbers, tens of millions of people might be killed within the first hour or two, and everything that the war is supposed to defend might be destroyed before either side becomes fully aware of what is happening. It is instructive that those thinking and writing about nuclear war speak of "Mutual Assured Destruction" and use the acronym MAD.

■ Why Wars Occur

Wars occur for various reasons. Here I will (1) briefly recall points already made, mainly in chapter 11. Then I will focus on (2) the desire for self-preservation and security, (3) nationalism and self-determination, (4) upholding and promoting an ideology, (5) economic considerations, and (6) concern for prestige and pride.

A Recollection of Points Made Earlier

Both in the preceding chapter and in chapter 11 I noted that within countries governments do their best to maintain an overwhelming preponderance of power against any challenger. They maintain police and armed forces. They may or may not permit individuals to possess weapons, but they prohibit the formation of private armies. Those against whom the law is to be enforced are (if possible) kept weak and helpless against the police and military power of government.

Internationally this is not possible. Given the system of sovereign states, and given the great power of some of them, law and order (peace) has to rest on a very different basis. It has to rest on the voluntary choices of individual governments and on such enforcement action as one state or set of states can threaten or take against another. Whereas police action within a country can ordinarily occur without any significant disruption of the peace, the equivalent of police action at the international level is likely to mean war. And if the police action were taken against the United States or any of the major countries, it would mean major war.

I also noted in chapter 11 that within countries, through educational systems and otherwise, governments have the opportunity to inculcate attitudes that make for unity and peace, including attitudes of loyalty to the political system, whereas no real counterpart of this possibility exists at the international level. Further, within countries, governments have the opportunity to forestall or allay discontent by making timely changes in law and policy, whereas the possibility of this is restricted at the international level by the principle that sovereign states may veto changes in their rights. To put this thought more crudely, within countries governments have the opportunity to impose changes that allay the discontent of those who might win in civil war, and if this happens war can be avoided; among countries timely action to allay discontent is more difficult.

It is also implicit in what is said earlier that within countries disputes about the requirements of law—disputes about rights and duties—are somewhat less likely to arise than among countries; and institutions for handling them without threats of violence are more fully developed.

Self-Preservation

With rare exceptions, states are determined to preserve themselves with their territorial integrity intact. From this basic proposition much else flows.

Concern for self-preservation leads to a concern for *security*, and a concern for security leads to a concern for power relationships. History gives states little choice about this. To be sure, some weak states have survived for a long time. They gain safety from the rivalries of the stronger states or from the belief that they are not worth conquering. But time and again, too, weak states have failed to survive, as the above sketch of the role of war in history suggests. Anyone skeptical about the importance of power relationships might contemplate the fate of the American Indians.

Concern for power relationships is often spoken of as a concern for a *balance of power*. The expression is a loose one, for *balance* has several meanings. Sometimes it denotes an equilibrium, as when a scale is brought into balance by adjusting the weights, or when a mobile or chandelier is balanced through the interrelationships of a number of parts. Sometimes it denotes a remainder—an amount left over when one sum is deducted from another, as when one speaks of a bank balance; this means that *balance* may designate disequilibrium rather than equilibrium and that the balance may be more favorable to one party than to another. The upshot, found in actual usage, is that *balance of power* may designate simply the distribution of power, whatever the distribution may be.

Perhaps the best statement is that every state seeking self-preservation wants power relationships to be such that aggression against it could not succeed. The underlying assumption, of course, is that another state will not attack unless it has a reasonable prospect of winning.

A state can seek the desired power relationship through both domestic and foreign policies. Through its domestic policies it can adjust the strength of its own armed forces to the desired level. Through its foreign policies it can seek friends and allies, it can seek international agreements on the level of armed power to be maintained, and it can try to create or maintain situations that other states find acceptable, giving them no reason to attack.

One of the paradoxes of international politics is that, though measures aimed at self-preservation may contribute to it, they may also have opposite effects. Relationships among some states are plagued by distrust. Both sides may say that the measures they are taking are purely defensive, but each may suspect that the other has (or will develop) ambitions that involve a threat of aggression.

Thus, domestic measures taken, or alliances made, to promote national security may be interpreted abroad as threatening; and any state that feels threatened is likely to try to improve its relative power position. A spiraling arms race may develop, together with a race to win and keep friends and allies. Such a race is likely to accentuate tensions and may do about as much to bring war on as to ward it off.

Moreover, as we note below, once war begins, distrust about the future policies of a victor tends to lead other states to join in the war to make it as sure as can be that the peace settlement will be compatible with their interests.

Oddly enough, policies of self-preservation sometimes raise questions about the location of boundaries. Precisely what is to be preserved? Disputes over territory, or over the extent of jurisdiction, still occur. India and China fought a brief war in 1962 over a disputed boundary. China's relations with the Soviet Union were plagued by disputes over islands that are forever appearing and later disappearing in boundary rivers, and presumably Russia and China will face the same problem. Argentina and Britain fought in 1981 over the Falkland Islands, both claiming to be the legitimate sovereign. North Korea attacked South Korea in 1950, claiming rightful jurisdiction over the entire peninsula. Libya claims jurisdiction over the Gulf of Sidra, whereas the United States claims that most of the gulf is part of the high seas. In 1994 a boundary dispute led to hostilities between Peru and Ecuador. Tensions exist among several states, including China and the Philippines, over the ownership of the Spratly Islands. And so on. Methods short of war are available for resolving such disputes, but often the parties are unwilling to accept a method that might lead to the rejection of their claims.

Self-preservation is, of course, not the only goal that states pursue. At one time or another, most countries have attached enough importance to some other goal that they have been willing to risk their own survival. Hitler and Mussolini both did this, and more recently so did Saddam Hussein. Further, the relative power of states is difficult to calculate without the actual test of war, so what one state regards as a power relationship that provides security another may regard as a relationship that gives opportunity.

Nationalism and Self-Determination

I have already discussed nationalism and self-determination in chapter 12. Here my only object is to link the subject to war.

I noted that the central tenet of nationalism is that the nation should be united as a distinct political entity, usually as an independent state. And I noted that the right of a people to self-determination is, among other things, its right to determine what its relationship with other peoples should be.

If the nation is not already united, nationalists want to bring unification about. Thus, in the nineteenth century Garibaldi and Cavour wanted to bring about the unification of Italy, and Bismarck wanted to bring about the unification of Germany. In each case, this meant that one or more states into which the nation was divided had to go out of existence, and in each case war was necessary to bring this about. Garibaldi rallied Italian nationalists against other Italians; and Cavour fought not only other Italians but also Austria-Hungary, which controlled part of Italy. Bismarck had to fight Austria-Hungary and France in turn, neither of which wanted Germany united.

World War I got its start in nationalism. In 1914 Serbia existed as an independent state, but it did not include all Serbs; some were in the Austro-Hungarian Empire. Seeking somehow to bring about the unification of all Serbs in one Serbia, a Serbian nationalist assassinated an Austrian archduke in Sarajevo. Austria-Hungary then went to war against Serbia.

What might have been fought out as a minor war between these two states then got transformed into world war because of balance of power considerations: one state after another decided to enter the war rather than allow its possible future enemy to win and thus presumably strengthen itself. Russia did not want Austria-Hungary to strengthen itself by defeating Serbia. Germany did not want Russia to strengthen itself by defeating Austria-Hungary. France and Britain did not want Germany to strengthen itself by defeating Russia. So they all went to war, and eventually the United States joined in, at least in part on the basis of the same kind of considerations. Secretary of State Lansing expressed the thought, saying that if the oligarchy in Germany were allowed to win, it would then turn upon the United States as its next obstacle to imperial rule over the world and that it was "safer and surer and wiser for us to be one of many enemies than to be in the future alone against a victorious Germany."

World War II developed in a comparable way. Hitler had a number of aims, but among them was a nationalist desire to unite all German people in a greater German Reich. This meant that he sought to annex territory in neighboring states that was inhabited by German-speaking people. And he had other ambitions, too. He annexed both Austria and the German-speaking part of Czechoslovakia without war, but when he attacked Poland, Poland fought back; and other states joined in on the basis of the same kind of considerations that had led to the spread of the war between Austria-Hungary and Serbia.

As noted in chapter 12, nationalism also sometimes leads to war—to civil war or a war for independence—when a people under alien control claim their right to self-determination and attempt to secede. Thus, the Algerians and the Vietnamese both fought after World War II to get independence from France; and the Bengalis of Bangladesh fought to get independence from Pakistan. The Ibos of Nigeria likewise fought but were defeated. The Chechens seek independence from Russia. And guerrilla war is going on in Sri Lanka as the Tamils seek a separate state. Most of the countries of the world contain peoples that might theoretically claim a right to self-determination and thus create at least the danger of war.

The countries of western Europe apparently all accept their current boundaries, but this is far from the case in the area of what was Yugoslavia. War goes on between the Serbs and Muslims of Bosnia, and both Croatia and Serbia are more or less involved. Tensions exist between Greece and the Macedonian part of what was Yugoslavia. The current leaders of Germany promise to respect the Polish border, but even they cannot be sure what territorial ambitions their successors may pursue two or three decades hence: some day, if Germany is no longer restrained by its allies, it may seek to reclaim what it regards as its historical borders. Issues have already come to a boil over the treatment of a Hungarian minority in Rumania and over the treatment of Turkish people in Bulgaria, and no one familiar with the appeals of nationalism can be sure that other issues over the treatment of minorities and over the possession of historically disputed territory will not develop.

Upholding and Promoting an Ideology

Principles and theories—ideologies—sometimes lead to domestic violence and international war. Think, for example, of the Middle East. There religion mixes with nationalism and other considerations to explain the intermittent wars in which Israel and its neighbors have been involved since World War II—Israel trying to take territory occupied for centuries by Muslims, a former prime minister claiming a right to do so because God gave the territory to the Jews in biblical times. Religion also mixes with nationalism to explain the struggle between the Greeks and Turks on Cyprus, the Greeks being Christian (Greek Orthodox) and the Turks Muslim. This struggle has an international aspect in that Greece and Turkey are involved.

Apart from nationalism, communism and anticommunism are the principal ideologies that gave rise to the danger of war from the end of World War II until the late 1980s. Several countries intervened in Russia after the revolution of 1917, hoping to destroy the Bolshevik regime. Partly for ideological reasons the Soviet Union imposed communism on the countries of eastern and southeastern Europe at the close of World War II, and later it intervened in some of them to keep communist regimes in power. Beginning in 1979 it fought to establish and maintain a communist regime in Afghanistan, finally withdrawing only in 1989. The Soviet Union and other communist states supplied arms to local "anti-imperialist" movements in several states, thus fostering revolution and accentuating the danger of international war. In large part to prevent the extension of communism the United States fought major wars in Korea and Vietnam and has intervened elsewhere as well—notably in the Dominican Republic, Grenada, and Nicaragua. Ideological antagonisms have been basic to the tensions between East and West.

Economic Considerations

Marxists explain war largely in economic terms and make a seemingly plausible case when they stick to abstract theory. But those who approach the question empirically, examining the course of events leading to the outbreak of specific wars, rarely if ever come up with a predominantly economic explanation. More often than not, in fact, those with a relevant economic stake exert their influence for peace rather than for war.

The most that can be said correctly is that economic considerations have in a number of instances led a powerful state to intervene militarily in the affairs of a weak state. Thus, in the early decades of this century the United States intervened (that is, interfered dictatorially) in several of the countries of the Caribbean and Central America for economic reasons. Such action, however, has come to be generally condemned; and the interventions that have occurred in more recent decades are not to be explained to any significant degree in these terms.

Economic considerations focusing on oil are obviously involved in the action of Iraq against Kuwait and in the reaction of the rest of the world. Historians will no doubt be arguing for many years to come whether the economic considerations were dominant.

Concern for Prestige and Pride

Prestige is reputation that suggests importance, authority, or ascendancy; it suggests a capacity and a will to promote and defend vital interests. A state with prestige commands respect, if not deference; its voice is heard, and its wishes command attention. The prestige of a state may by itself provide a shield for its interests, inducing other states to act warily and not to offer any challenge. Conversely, a state lacking prestige can expect no more than minimal consideration and risks being scorned. It may find that its choice is between submission and war or some other form of struggle.

Pride is sometimes thought of as a deadly sin, but people also speak of "just pride"—well-founded gratification with one's status and role, one's position or achievements. The factors contributing to pride encompass and go beyond those contributing to a sense of honor. The opposite of pride is shame or humiliation, and of course the opposite of honor is dishonor. Pride and honor are everywhere valued. Among other things, people want to be proud of any association or group with which they are identified, including their government and their country; and they want to avoid shame, humiliation, and dishonor.

Given such definitions, governments must be concerned with their prestige and with the basis that they provide for pride or shame. A government that has prestige must seek to maintain it, and a government that has little or none must seek to acquire it. Similarly, a government in which people take pride is in a more solid and secure position than a government that inspires shame or accepts humiliation.

These considerations necessarily influence decisions concerning peace and war, though proof of the relationship is difficult to establish. Political leaders have sometimes explained their actions in terms of maintaining national honor, but rarely if ever have they admitted that they acted out of a concern for prestige or pride. Surely, however, they have often done so. Among other things, some of the wars fought to gain and maintain colonies are to be explained in part in these terms, for the domination of alien peoples long served as a basis for prestige and pride. Greatness was found in empire. That is no longer as true as it once was, for the domination of alien people is now widely seen as contradicting the principles of democracy and violating the rights of the dominated; so viewed, it is a source of doubt and guilt and shame.

The Cuban missile crisis of 1962 provides as good an illustration as any of the influence of concern for prestige and pride. It did not result in war, but it included an acceptance by the United States of a risk of war. In 1962 the Soviet Union was discovered to be building a missile site in Cuba. Since the Soviet Union was acting in cooperation with the government of Cuba, it was acting within the law. Nevertheless, President Kennedy did not hesitate to take the view that the completion of the site was unacceptable to the United States. In effect he imposed a partial blockade on Cuba, calling it a "quarantine," and he threatened to sink any Soviet ship that attempted to carry anything relating to missiles through the blockade. Further, he demanded the dismantling of the site and the removal of missiles from Cuba.

Various explanations of Kennedy's stand are possible. I believe that concern for the prestige and pride of the country, although perhaps not consciously recognized, was a major, if not the dominant, factor. More specifically, I believe that underlying the reasons publicly given for the stand was an assumption of which few were fully conscious: that the prestige and pride of the country required that it enjoy a special status and play a special role in the Western hemisphere.

I am sure that concern for prestige and pride played a major, if not the dominant, role in motivating the space program that developed in the 1960s, especially the manned lunar-landing program, and this motivation surely played a major role in the Cuban missile crisis, too. In truth, I believe that it plays a greater role in human affairs generally than is commonly realized (Van Dyke 1964, chaps. 8 and 9).

The claim of the United States to a special status and role was implied in the Monroe Doctrine of 1823, prohibiting any extension of European power in the Western hemisphere. Various presidents emphasized the doctrine and elaborated on it, leading some people to rank it with the Constitution and God as an object of devotion. It was bad enough that

Castro's Cuba, located not many miles off the Florida coast, had aligned itself with Moscow; it would be worse—an intolerable challenge to our primacy in the hemisphere—for the Soviet Union to have a missile base there. Our prestige throughout the world would plummet, and our pride would be destroyed.

The humiliation would be all the greater and all the more mortifying because only a few years earlier the Soviet Union had been able to gloat via the electronic signals broadcast by *Sputnik*, which it had put into orbit ahead of any comparable achievement by the United States. Of course, nuclear missiles could have reached targets in the United States more quickly from Cuba than from bases within Soviet territory, but it is doubtful whether this was a crucial consideration. It was the threatened blow to our prestige and pride that was intolerable.

So Kennedy accepted the possibility of war, and Americans have generally commended him ever since for his handling of the crisis. Khrushchev, in contrast, accepted humiliation. Not many months thereafter he lost his job, and the Soviet Union began a military buildup to reduce to the minimum any chance that it might have to accept a similar humiliation again. The Soviet Union was also concerned about its prestige and pride.

Instead of speaking of a concern for prestige and pride, Francis Fukuyama, referring to the views of Hegel, speaks of a "struggle for recognition" as a crucial factor in history. This struggle, he says, reflects "the prideful and assertive side of human nature that is responsible for driving most wars and political conflicts. . . . The 'struggle for recognition' is evident everywhere around us . . ., [providing] a useful and illuminating way of seeing the contemporary world (Fukuyama 1992, 144–45).

■ Nuclear War

When the United States dropped nuclear bombs on Hiroshima and Nagasaki at the end of World War II, it did not need to fear retaliation. Japan had no such bombs and probably could not have delivered them against US targets anyway.

The United States no longer enjoys a nuclear monopoly. The Soviet Union had both A-bombs and H-bombs by the early 1950s. Subsequently, Britain, China, France, and India also exploded nuclear devices, and Israel, Pakistan, and South Africa are thought to be capable of doing so. Further, most of these countries have demonstrated rockets capable of putting objects into orbit, which means that they could send nuclear warheads (however accurately or inaccurately) toward targets anywhere in the world. Now that the Soviet Union has broken up, Ukraine and Kazakstan are both nuclear powers of sorts. A war in which any of thesecountries becomes involved might be a nuclear war. And other countries (North Korea?) seem likely to join the nuclear club.

This creates what almost everyone regards as a horrifying prospect. With the breakup of the Soviet Union and the more cooperative policies of Russia, nuclear war between Russia and the United States seems to be out of the question, but it is nevertheless instructive to imagine what such a war would entail. It would surely bring utter catastrophe, destroying everything that the war was intended to defend or promote. Neither side could expect to win in any reasonable sense. The two societies would both come to an end as operating systems, with tens of millions of people dead and with the living, as Khrushchev once said, envying the dead. The prospect is so dreadful that, after Hiroshima and Nagasaki, no country has used nuclear weapons in war, and both the United States and the Soviet Union made it clear on various occasions that they wanted to avoid any turn of events that might bring on nuclear war.

The above refers to *unrestricted* nuclear war, each side firing nuclear weapons in considerable numbers. *Limited* nuclear war is also a theoretical possibility. Its costs would obviously vary, depending on the limits observed. The problem is that no one can be sure that a war in which nuclear weapons are used would remain limited. Many believe that any use of nuclear weapons would lead to unlimited escalation.

Why then maintain nuclear weapons? Obviously, most states are getting along without them. Why don't the states that possess nuclear weapons give them up either unilaterally or by general agreement? The answer has a number of parts.

One part of the answer is that, though it is theoretically possible to give up nuclear weapons, it is not possible to expunge knowledge of how to make them. And in a crisis the state that could first arm or re-arm itself with nuclear weapons would gain a breathtaking, probably a decisive, advantage. Rather than risk such a possibility, the nuclear powers prefer to keep nuclear weapons on hand.

The second part of the answer is related to the first. Parties to an agreement on nuclear disarmament would inevitably be tempted to hide rather than destroy some weapons; and they would be tempted to make nuclear weapons in secret. Mutual suspicions would thus be inevitable, and the problem of allaying them would be severe. The obvious solution is a system of international inspection, but the question is whether a system that would be acceptable would also be reliable.

The third part of the answer is that an agreement among some states on nuclear disarmament might leave the way open for other states to remain or to become nuclear powers. If Russia and the United States were to agree on nuclear disarmament, what would China do? And what is the chance that Brazil, Iran, Libya, or North Korea might choose to go nuclear and find it possible to do so? Iraq's effort to arm itself with nuclear weapons was among the factors galvanizing the world against it following its invasion of Kuwait.

The fourth part of the answer is related to the third. Not only is there a possibility that additional states might become nuclear powers, perhaps some of them with rogue governments, but it is also thinkable that criminal elements would get control of nuclear devices. What would happen if the kind of people who bombed the World Trade Center in New York or the headquarters of a Jewish group in Buenos Aires had one or more nuclear weapons at their disposal? The possibility of this is suggested by the fact that weapons-grade nuclear material from which bombs could be made has been showing up in Germany, evidently spirited out of some part of the former Soviet Union. It is uncertain how a government could use nuclear weapons if faced with a threat by private nuclear terrorists, but cautious governments are not likely to accept nuclear disarmament until and unless they can be confident that they will not be confronted by a nuclear challenge from any source.

The fifth part of the answer asks about the balance (distribution) of power once nuclear disarmament is achieved. If reliance on conventional forces will put a state at a disadvantage, it faces a special problem. Should it accept nuclear disarmament in the expectation that it can overcome its disadvantage in conventional forces, or should it insist on retaining some nuclear weapons?

The sixth part of the answer addresses the fact that no state has gone out of existence because it lacked nuclear weapons, which might be taken to indicate that others could relieve themselves of their burden and place themselves within a nuclear-free zone. But if governments with nuclear weapons have refrained from brandishing them against governments without them for four decades, does this give reliable assurance for the future? If Saddam Hussein had nuclear weapons, would you trust him not to use them? Further, have the nonnuclear states really been without nuclear protection? If China, for example, were to threaten to use nuclear weapons against nonnuclear Japan, it would have to face the possibility that either the United States or Russia might go to the defense of Japan. And that is a possibility that should give China pause. I do not mean to say that nonnuclear countries necessarily get safety from rivalries among nuclear powers. Afghanistan obviously did not. But to assume that nonnuclear powers lack protection from nuclear weapons is not sound either.

Instead of seeking complete nuclear disarmament more or less at once, states might theoretically divide the problem up and seek to solve it in successive steps, requiring a satisfactory experience with a limited agreement before taking the next step. This is in fact what they have been doing, but the steps so far taken have been short; and the chance that they will take enough more steps to complete the course is at best uncertain.

Given the limited nature of the agreements so far made, the main nuclear powers are seeking such safety as they can get by maintaining a capacity to retaliate. Winston Churchill expressed the thought years ago when he spoke of the prospect that "safety will be the sturdy child of terror, and survival the twin brother of annihilation." The idea is that security depends on maintaining a second-strike capacity, thus preventing any other state from profiting by striking first. A second-strike capacity is a capacity to absorb the worst damage that a nuclear enemy can inflict and still have enough nuclear power left to inflict unacceptable damage on him in return. A first-strike capacity, in contrast, is the capacity to knock the other side out in one blow, leaving it incapable of significant retaliation. Reference was made above to MAD—Mutual Assured Destruction. MAD would presumably occur if one state attempted a first strike that fell short of a knockout, followed by a retaliatory second strike from the victim.

Werner Levi has written a book entitled *The Coming End of War* (1981). He sees signs in several developments that international war is ceasing to be an acceptable and useful method of handling problems. In the first place he takes the view that states, especially the developed states, have become so interdependent in every way—economically, culturally, scientifically, technologically—that war among them would be much more disruptive and costly than ever before. In the second place, he especially stresses the potential costs of nuclear war and the lack of any assurance that nuclear states would fight war without using their nuclear weapons. In the third place, he points to the development of methods of decision making within countries that give greater assurance of rationality—that is, greater assurance that the ends pursued by governments will be compatible with each other and greater assurance that the means employed will be suited to the ends. And in the fourth place, he points to improved methods of handling disputes—methods more compatible than war with the values of civilization.

Levi thinks that "developing states with relatively simple needs can still afford to fight wars" but that developed states cannot. Among the developed states "the premium is . . . upon the exchange of goods, services, capital, labor, knowledge, and the sharing of other human achievements, not upon mutual destruction. . . . Peaceful cooperation is no longer a luxury. It now is a matter of selfish national interests" (Levi 1981, 94, 99, 101).

Levi's argument is intriguing. Whether rulers can stop using a method that they have employed throughout history remains to be seen. The record since World War II, including the war undertaken against Iraq in 1991, indicates that wars will continue to be fought, and that great powers will be involved, although it does not indicate that the great powers will necessarily fight each other. Further, it is possible that nuclear weapons will not be employed, provided the side that is winning does not seek to impose such draconic terms of peace that the loser resorts to a nuclear strike in desperation.

■ Just and Unjust Wars

My basis for discussing this subject is Michael Walzer's *Just and Unjust Wars: A Moral Argument with Historical Illustrations* (1977). The book is fascinating.

Note that Walzer presents a *moral* argument, and he deals with both war as such and the methods of waging it. Along with governments and scholars all over the world, Walzer rejects the view that in resorting to war states leave the realm of morality behind. "All is fair in love and war" is a false statement. States do not, by going to war, escape moral rules and moral judgment. Everything they do or fail to do, in time of peace and in time of war, can be judged good or bad, right or wrong.

At the same time an obvious tension exists between war and respect for the requirements of morality. A state that is fighting desperately, perhaps for its very existence, inevitably faces powerful temptations to forget about morality if it can gain significant advantage thereby. Moreover, insofar as the methods of waging war are concerned, tension is increased by the development of new weapons. Fundamental moral rules endure, but questions about their meaning and application are bound to arise as new weapons and new strategies come along. Governments succumb to temptations and make questionable interpretations often enough that the tendency to scoff at the idea of moral requirements is widespread. Nevertheless, the very hypocrisy of states with respect to the requirements of morality is an acknowledgment of those requirements.

Inquiring into just and unjust wars, Walzer accepts an underlying presumption that *states and individuals have a moral right (and, for that matter, a legal right) to live in peace.* No state or person has a right to attack another without good reason. It is wrong—immoral—to kill arbitrarily, wrong to take arbitrary action that forces a state to fight for its existence and forces individuals to risk their lives.

The expressions *without good reason* and *arbitrarily* appear above. The view was long dominant that a just cause gave good reason for war—that a war fought in a just cause was not arbitrary. That view has been largely superseded by another: that it is *wrong to initiate a war (wrong to commit aggression)*, regardless of the justice of the cause. States believing that they have a just cause are to pursue it by means other than war.

This latter view has come to be incorporated in international law. In the Kellogg Pact of 1928, states renounced war, promising never to seek the settlement of disputes except by pacific means. It was largely on this basis that, after World War II, certain Nazi leaders were convicted of a conspiracy against the peace. The Charter of the United Nations reaffirms the obligations of the Kellogg Pact, expressing a world consensus on the requirements of morality and law. Self-defense is permissible, but the initiation of war is wrong.

It is easy enough to state these rules, but it is often difficult to decide what they require in specific circumstances. The principal difficulties arise in connection with fear for the future and in connection with military interventions that are not intended to initiate war.

Fear for the future sometimes leads to preemptive attack or to preventive war. The distinction between *preemptive* and *preventive* is not always clear. Both involve anticipations. If one state is already taking steps directed toward an attack, but the prospective victim manages to get in the first blow, that first blow is said to be *preemptive*. If one state thinks that another is going to attack sometime and decides that it is better to fight now than later, the war is said to be *preventive*.

The question is whether the state that launches the preemptive attack or preventive war is to be condemned as the aggressor, and the answer depends on how sure it is that the attack is coming. If state A begins the series of actions necessary for attacking B and announces that it is doing so in order to attack B within a week, no one will blame B if it can manage to get in the first blow.

But the situation is rarely that clear. Egypt came close to behaving in the way described in 1967, and when Israel then in fact got in the first blow, most of the world classified Israel's action as preemptive rather than aggressive. But no one can be sure that Egypt would in fact have attacked. And when the events feared are farther in the future and more uncertain, the case for preventive action becomes weaker.

Before the Soviet Union got nuclear weapons, for example, would the United States have been justified in destroying Soviet nuclear facilities? After the Soviet Union got such weapons, would the Soviet Union have been justified in preventing China from doing so? In 1981 Israel in fact destroyed a nuclear facility that Iraq was building, and judgments divide on the question of whether Israel's action should be condemned as aggressive or excused as preventive. A desire for revenge is surely among the factors motivating Iraq ever since.

Judgments similarly divide with respect to the action of the United States in the Cuban missile crisis; the United States threatened to sink Soviet ships approaching Cuba, lest the missile bases under construction be made operational. Surely an attack on the United States was still too remote to justify describing American action as preemptive. Whether it should be excused as preventive is open to argument.

Similar problems arise about the military intervention of one state in the affairs of another—an action that obviously borders on war. Is such intervention ever justified? If so, in what circumstances?

Walzer approves it in three kinds of circumstances. The first two both reflect the emphasis that Walzer places on the right of peoples to self-determination. He approves intervention in support of struggles for national liberation, going back to 1848 to get his illustration—when Hungary sought liberation from the Hapsburg monarchy of Austria. And in the name of protecting the right of self-determination he also approves intervention by one state designed simply to counterbalance the effects of an improper intervention by another. Third, he approves humanitarian intervention—for example, intervention to put an end to genocide in another state.

Intervention in these kinds of circumstances entails obvious dangers. The populations of most states include minorities that might readily be classified as "peoples" entitled to self-determination. The continued existence of most states, or at least the territorial integrity of most states, is therefore potentially threatened by the right of peoples within them to self-determination. And when Walzer approves intervention to uphold that right he invites great risk that one state may champion self-determination within another for its own ulterior purposes. Similarly, the record shows that governments claiming that their interventions are humanitarian tend also to be pursuing some ulterior interest of their own.

The presence of these dangers does not necessarily mean that Walzer's position is unjustified, but it does mean that intervention is suspect and that an intervening government faces a heavy burden in seeking to justify what it does.

Walzer asks not only about the morality of war—and of intervention that might lead to war—but also about the morality of methods of fighting. Here one of the basic principles, developed long ago, is that the only legitimate targets are those of a military nature. With this principle goes another: that it is permissible to employ only those methods and those weapons that promote the legitimate ends of the belligerent without excessive or disproportionate destruction of life or property.

These principles lead to problems. Which possible targets are of a military nature and therefore fair game? And when are costs to be judged excessive or disproportionate?

So far as persons are concerned, the relevant generalization is that combatants are fair targets and noncombatants are not. But who counts as a combatant? The rules are reasonably clear with respect to the treatment of enemy soldiers, though difficult questions arise. Questions that are all the more difficult arise with respect to the occasional fighter—the guerrilla who takes up arms for a short time and then melts into the civilian population. And questions also arise about the treatment of the family or the village that provides food or shelter for the guerrilla.

Property is sometimes a legitimate target—the factory producing guns, for example, and the truck that transports the guns. But if a city includes several factories, or if it serves as a transportation hub for matériel (all sorts of military equipment and supplies), does the city become a legitimate target?

In an age of nuclear rockets, the question is especially portentous. Among the relevant rules is one already mentioned: that noncombatants are not legitimate targets. It has always been the case, of course, that attacks on legitimate targets might have unintended side effects, including the killing of innocent civilians. But so long as the killing of civilians was a side effect and not a deliberate purpose, it was accepted as an inevitable though regrettable feature of war, provided that the number of deaths was not disproportionate to the prospective military gain.

A qualification was established long ago with respect to efforts to starve the enemy out by besieging a city or blockading a country. Sieges and blockades were recognized as legitimate methods of warfare, even when directed as much at noncombatants as at combatants; and it went with a siege that noncombatants who sought to flee could be forced back lest their departure enable the defending forces to hold out longer.

With the development of bombers, the temptation to drop bombs on cities became irresistible. During World War II, Germany, Britain, and the United States all did it, their efforts culminating in the nuclear bombing of Hiroshima and Nagasaki. And the morality of the policy has been debated ever since. Although claims were advanced that the cities were centers of military production and transportation and thus legitimate military targets, the claims were weak. Moreover, a reasonably good case can be made for the view that the death and destruction meted out by the bombing of cities, especially Hiroshima and Nagasaki, were disproportionate to the military gains.

Suppose, however, that the bombing of German cities was essential to prevent a German victory. Facing this kind of possibility, Walzer places great stress on *the right of a political community to survive*, preserving its "common life," and he holds that a "supreme emergency" justifies a refusal to abide by the rules. He says that if the heavens are (really) about to fall, a country is justified in resorting to any means to save itself. Of course, the claim that the heavens are about to fall is suspect. Violation of the rules is not to be justified easily. Belligerents can do what they think they must, but history places the burden of justification on the belligerent who sets the rules aside.

What are the implications for nuclear war? The decisive consideration relates more to the interests of states than to principle. Mutual Assured Destruction—mutual suicide—is not an attractive prospect. As long as a prospective victim maintains a second-strike capacity—a capacity to retaliate in a devastating way—it would be against the interests of any other state to initiate an attack. Principles, however, are relevant, too, and the relevant principles are stated above: that noncombatants are not legitimate targets, that the death and destruction caused by an attack on them are not to be disproportionate to the military gains reasonably anticipated, and that the burden of justification is on the side that fails to abide by the rules. A placement of the burden of justification, of course, will neither bring people back to life nor give comfort to the survivors of a nuclear attack.

■ Review

This chapter treats the importance of war, its incidence and costs, the causes of war and the conditions of peace, nuclear war, and just and unjust wars.

War and preparation for war are among the major activities of states. The costs are difficult to determine, but in proportion to the population and wealth of states, they apparently have not changed much over a considerable period. They would increase catastrophically, however, if nuclear weapons were to be used on an unrestricted basis.

Some of the conditions that make for peace within countries are absent at the international level: a police force with overwhelming power, an opportunity to inculcate loyalty to an international system, and a means of assuring change so as to allay discontent.

States seek self-preservation—security. This leads to a concern for power relationships, including the balance of power; and it sometimes leads to wars over the extent of the self—for example, over disputed boundaries. The peoples of the world have come to champion nationalism and self-determination, both of which carry with them risks of war. Other ideological commitments—for example, to religion or to communism—sometimes also lead to war. Economic interests might do so, too, though Marxists and others tend to exaggerate their importance. Concern for prestige and pride likewise plays a role.

Although general agreement exists that unrestricted nuclear war would be catastrophic, nuclear powers have plausible reasons for not accepting nuclear disarmament and relying instead on deterring aggression by maintaining second-strike capacities. For various reasons it is plausible that World War III will never be fought.

Wars can be classified as either just or unjust. The presumption is that no person or state has a right to attack another; that is, aggressive war is wrong. Problems arise, however, over the question of when preemptive or preventive action is justified; and problems arise about the justifiability of military interventions that involve a risk of war.

The question of justice and injustice comes up not only with respect to war itself but also with respect to methods of waging it. The central principle is that attacks are to be directed only at military targets and not at noncombatants, but various problems arise in applying this principle in concrete circumstances.

■ Reading

Betts, Richard K., ed. (1994) *Conflict After the Cold War: Arguments on Causes of War and Peace.* New York: Macmillan.

Brown, Seyom (1987) *The Causes and Prevention of War.* New York: St. Martin's.

Ceadel, Martin (1987) *Thinking About Peace and War.* New York: Oxford University Press.

Craig, Gordon A., and Alexander L. George (1990) *Force and Statecraft: Diplomatic Problems of Our Time.* New York: Oxford University Press.

Jervis, Robert (1985) *The Logic of American Nuclear Strategy.* Ithaca, N.Y.: Cornell University Press.

Mueller, John E. (1989) *Retreat from Doomsday: The Obsolescence of Major War.* New York: Basic Books.

Nye, Joseph S., Jr. (1986) *Nuclear Ethics.* New York: Free Press.

Schraeder, Peter J., ed. (1989) *Intervention in the Nineteen Eighties: U.S. Foreign Policy in the Third World.* Boulder: Lynne Rienner.

Walzer, Michael (1977) *Just and Unjust Wars. A Moral Argument with Historical Illustrations.* New York: Basic Books.

The International Economic Order and Foreign Trade Policies

Why are some countries rich and others poor?

Governments are sometimes agents of business in seeking to open up foreign markets. Here H. Payne questions Clinton's efforts to open up the market for American automobiles and automobile parts in Japan.

International affairs include economic as well as political relationships. Governments concern themselves with foreign trade and commerce, wanting it to proceed in a way that will promote domestic prosperity and well-being—raising the question of what policies this concern suggests.

Governments have additional concerns, too—among them a concern for support from various interest groups, which suggests another question: What does and should happen when the desires of such groups go against the interests of the country as a whole?

Questions also come up about relationships between foreign trade and commerce and the promotion of political goals in foreign affairs. What can be done relating to foreign trade and commerce to influence the foreign or domestic policies of other states? More specifically, how effective can economic sanctions be in deterring or defeating aggression or in pressuring another state to change its domestic policies?

Finally, questions arise because some countries are richer and more developed than others. How are these differences to be explained? Do they result from the exploitation of one set of states by another set? When the richer and more developed states are importuned to help less fortunate states, what do they do, and what should they do?

This chapter explores the above questions, with a focus on market economies.

■ Foreign Trade and Domestic Goals

The Argument for Free Trade

When economists assume, as they generally do, that the government's goal is domestic prosperity and well-being, they endorse free trade. That is, they recommend (perhaps with some qualifications) that government keep its hands off international trade and commerce, permitting private enterprises to do business across boundaries as they please. They generally recommend against tariff and other trade barriers aimed at protecting the home market or at protecting the jobs of those who might be adversely affected by imports.

The argument for free trade is complex. The basic proposition is that, given free trade, the doctrine of comparative advantage operates: Each country produces and exports whatever it can produce most advantageously; further, each country imports whatever it could produce only at a comparative disadvantage, if at all.

The smaller the country, the more obvious the argument. It would be preposterous for a small country to attempt to produce everything it needs. If economies of scale are to be enjoyed, a large market is imperative—almost always a larger market than individual small countries can possibly provide. Imagine, for example, an effort on the part of Grenada to produce its own automobiles.

In the argument for free trade, it is *relative advantage* that counts. To illustrate, assume two countries—A and B—and two products—computers and textiles. Country A can produce both products more cheaply than country B, but its advantage in producing computers is twice as great as its advantage in producing textiles. It should therefore concentrate on producing computers and let country B produce textiles.

Theoretically, trade might be conducted on a barter basis—so many computers for so many yards of textiles—but that is rarely practical. Money is ordinarily involved. Each country has its own currency, and let us assume that merchants in each country price what they have to sell in terms of their national currency. The foreign buyer of each product must acquire the currency in which it is priced. Thus, the currencies themselves are bought and sold, and the price at which they are bought and sold is called the exchange rate.

Suppose that, at the prices asked and at the exchange rate prevailing, country A wants to import many yards of textiles, but country B has relatively little interest in buying computers. Various possibilities are then open. One of them is that the merchants involved adjust their prices. Those selling textiles may raise their prices, hoping to increase their profits; and those having difficulty selling computers reduce their prices. These changes alone may stimulate trade and, we assume, benefit both parties.

Another possibility is similar but more general: the change in the prices of textiles and computers may be an aspect of change in price levels in the two countries. Money flowing into the country that sells textiles makes the price level there go up; and money flowing out of the country unable to sell its computers makes the price level go down. So again, mutually profitable trade is stimulated.

A shift in the exchange rate is another possibility. If the demand for textiles is high, the demand for the currency in which they are priced must also be high; so in a free-market situation the price of that currency rises. And at the new exchange rate the demand for textiles presumably goes down, while the demand for computers goes up.

The above paragraphs concern, among other things, what is called the *terms of trade*—the terms on which the products of the two countries are exchanged—how much of one product it takes to pay for a given amount of the other product. And the above paragraphs also concern the *balance of trade*—how the amount of money that a country collects for its exports compares with the amount that it spends for its imports.

If receipts for exports do not cover the costs of imports, various methods of handling the problem exist in addition to those mentioned above. For example, the country may simply borrow what it needs—hoping to be able to export enough later to pay off the debt. And the country that has more foreign currency than it needs to pay for its imports may simply invest the surplus abroad. It leaves in abeyance the question of re-patriating either its profits or its capital.

In any event, given all these (and other) methods of handling problems in international trade, the free-trade argument is that government should just keep its hands off. The merchants of the trading countries will come to terms with each other, and mutually beneficial trade will occur. International competition will supplement domestic competition in requiring efficiency and stimulating innovation. The result is a higher level of prosperity and greater progress.

A few qualifications on the free-trade argument are common. One is that government may need to interfere in order to have a secure source of products that would be vital in time of war; perhaps such products need to be manufactured within the national boundaries even if they then cost more than imports would.

Another qualification is that government may also need to interfere to prevent the *dumping* of products on the domestic market—that is, to prevent the importation of goods that foreign producers are selling at prices lower than they charge at home. If the foreign producer could be counted on to dump on a regular, continuing basis, it would be advantageous to the receiving country; but this is not to be expected. The dumping may be a strategy designed to ruin producers in the receiving country and thus leave the foreign producer in control of the market. Or the dumping may be sporadic, tending to render domestic production unprofitable and thus to leave the receiving country without a stable source of supply.

A case can also be made that governmental intervention in foreign trade and commerce is justified to protect *infant industries* from foreign competition. Given such protection, the argument is, the infant industry may develop and become competitive, whereas without the protection it would be unable to get started at all.

In principle, the infant-industry argument is strong, but problems arise. An industry that could get started satisfactorily without protection may nevertheless claim to be "infant" and so may get unjustified protection. And protection once granted may be difficult to withdraw.

A case is sometimes made for using tariffs not so much to protect domestic producers as to discourage the use of a product and/or to produce revenue. For example, some argue that the United States should impose a tariff on imported oil, making its use relatively costly and thus encouraging people to shift to alternative sources of energy and at the same time bringing revenue to the government.

Problems with Free-Trade Theory

The principal question about free trade is whether it is reasonable to expect the flexibility, fluidity, and rationality that the theory assumes. Although free trade may benefit the country as a whole, it does not necessarily benefit each individual producer or firm. The profits of a given enterprise may depend on protection from foreign competition. Theoretically, entrepreneurs might recognize that they must either produce more efficiently or go out of business, but what they are more likely to do is appeal to the government for protection; and they can probably strengthen their appeal by saying that in addition to their own profits many jobs are on the line. As likely as not, they will also claim that the survival of their industry is important to national defense.

Further, when a recession or depression confronts government with special problems, the temptation is strong to resort to protection. Almost everyone assumes that government should play a role in promoting full employment, and the protection of an industry from foreign competition is one way to protect the jobs of those who work in the industry. Moreover, governments can also act in various ways to control or regulate the exchange rate, thus facilitating or impeding international trade. And they may influence the international flow of capital by their fiscal policies and by actions affecting the interest rate.

Since protection is often vital to those it helps, they are likely to be vigorous in pursuing it; and since the costs are widely dispersed, those harmed are unlikely to act to defend themselves. The pressures on government thus come disproportionately from the side of those seeking protection, which means that those in office or seeking election face a difficult problem. They presumably realize that in general and in the long run, the country will be more prosperous if free trade is maintained. But in the short run, if they stand up for free trade, they may fail to get elected or re-elected.

Most notoriously, pressures for protection have come from farmers. The European Union follows a "common agricultural policy" that involves subsidies, above all for the farmers of France. Japan succumbs to pressures from rice farmers and gives them protection. And the United States follows comparable policies, in part because of the same kind of pressures and in part to make up for the disadvantage American farmers are under because of the subsidies and the special protection that their competitors get.

Another problem arises because of what Mancur Olson calls "rigidities"—rigidities that slow up and may even prevent adjustments relating to foreign trade. Merchants are under various constraints with respect to the prices they charge, and they may not be able to adjust prices as quickly as they should. Influenced perhaps by their own business communities, governments commonly see disadvantages in fluctuating exchange rates and seek to keep them stable. Labor is really not as mobile as free-trade theory assumes. To solve the problems accompanying free trade, workers should be able to shift from one line of work to another and from one locality or region or even country to another.

In practice such mobility is rarely realized. The new line of work may require skills that the worker has difficulty developing, and people are often reluctant to move when they are not sure of a job at the new location and when moving entails leaving friends, relatives, and familiar surroundings. Moving becomes especially difficult when a change of language and customs is involved, and moving across international boundaries is in some cases virtually out of the question. Some countries restrict or prohibit immigration. Further, if one government refuses to accept free trade, and above all if it deliberately seeks special advantage for itself in international economic relationships (e.g., if it seeks "to export unemployment"), others are likely to feel that they must adopt protective measures as a matter of self-defense.

Free trade raises questions, too, about social legislation and about the protection of the consumer and the environment. Suppose that one country imposes a tax to maintain a social security system, is stringent about matters of health and safety, and is rigorous in protecting the environment. Another does little or nothing about these matters. Merchants in the state that is lax thus have an automatic advantage in trade, and merchants put at a disadvantage are likely to appeal to their government for some kind of protection.

To a degree, domestic producers get protection naturally, without governmental action. Natives and long-term residents of a country have advantages over foreigners, especially when different languages and, perhaps, sharply different cultures are involved. Then the question is how much foreign merchants are motivated to overcome the natural disadvantage that they face and how effective they are in doing it. This factor clearly operates in connection with trade between the United States and Japan. And the Japanese are more inclined to learn English than Americans are inclined to learn Japanese.

Responses

What is said above points to a contradiction. On the one hand, free-trade theory is rationally persuasive, yet on the other hand it leads to practical problems. The outcome is indecisive. Tariffs as a means of protecting the local market have lost favor, even if they have not entirely disappeared; but nontariff barriers to trade have come to the fore. And while taking some measures aimed at freeing trade on a global basis, states are at the same time tending toward the development of special trading blocs.

The nontariff barriers take various forms. The United States insists on one kind of barrier when it asks Japan to accept "voluntary" limitations on the number of automobiles it exports. Subsidies to farmers, mentioned above, count as a nontariff barrier to international trade, as do subsidies or bailouts or special help to ailing producers of any sort. Antidumping measures, even if justified, count as barriers to trade, and so do cumbersome and dilatory procedures for clearing imports through customs. Regulations designed (ostensibly or actually) to protect consumers may be more burdensome to foreign than to domestic merchants. Salvatore speaks of such nontariff barriers as "the new protectionism" and says that as much as 50 percent of world trade is now affected by it (1993, 1).

Sometimes it is difficult to say whether a policy should count as a subsidy and therefore as a nontariff barrier to trade. For example, in sponsoring research and development relating to military aircraft the United States has indirectly aided the manufacturers of civilian aircraft, and in sponsoring research relating to agriculture it has helped US farmers in their competition with the farmers of other countries.

As for the formation of trading blocs, the European Union and the North American Free Trade Agreement (NAFTA) are the principal illustrations. In each case the member states are removing obstacles to trade with each other while allowing the obstacles to remain in place where trade with nonmember states is concerned.

At the same time, most of the states of the world are parties to the General Agreement on Tariffs and Trade (GATT), which aims to reduce trade barriers on a global basis. And the latest revision of the agreement, following the so-called Uruguay round, provides for the establishment of a World Trade Organization that will monitor the policies that the parties follow.

The argument for free trade also leads to another question: does free trade have a built-in bias? Some who focus on Third World countries claim that it does, helping the rich get richer at the expense of the poor. I will take this issue up toward the end of the chapter.

Though governments are unavoidably tempted to give either protection or subsidies to producers threatened by foreign competition, they must consider the possibility that if they do so, they invite retaliation. Other governments may play the same game. Thus, in trying to help one set of domestic producers by protecting them against foreign competition, a government risks hurting another set who seek to sell in foreign markets. Moreover, apart from inciting retaliation, a country that reduces its imports is likely to hurt its own export trade, for foreigners who are deprived of a market for what they produce have less money with which to buy goods that they would like to import.

The choice that governments make in the face of such cross-pressures is not a foregone conclusion, but the temptation to endorse protection against foreign competition, or to provide subsidies, is obviously strong.

■ Foreign Trade and Foreign Policy Goals _____

Domestic considerations are not alone in influencing policies concerning foreign trade. Considerations relating to the goals of foreign policy are also often taken into account.

Relative Military Power

Sovereign states are generally concerned about their relative military power, and they may regulate their foreign trade with this concern in mind. One of the goals of the United States, for example, is to avoid strengthening enemies or potential enemies. Thus, the law authorizes the president to decide what items are of strategic value and to permit their exportation only on the basis of a license; and in granting the license, the government can impose whatever conditions and restrictions it pleases. Other states follow similar policies.

Problems arise. What kinds of materials and products should be listed as "strategic"? How about computers, for example? And if the decision is that the big mainframe computers are "strategic," how about personal desktop computers? How about computer programs? Many questions of this sort must be answered, and differing judgments are inevitable, which may be especially troublesome when allies try to coordinate their policies.

Economic Pressures on Other States

In addition to being concerned about their relative power positions, governments also sometimes want to influence the foreign or domestic policies of other states, and they may seek to do so by bringing economic pressures to bear. Especially when they act alone, however, the prospects of success are ordinarily not bright.

In the early 1990s the United States and a number of other countries cut off trade with Haiti in an attempt to bring a military dictatorship to an end, but economic pressures proved to be inadequate. The dictator finally gave up in 1994, agreeing to the peaceful entry of US troops into the country, but only after the United States threatened an invasion. In 1993 President Clinton announced that he would not renew most-favored-nation treatment for China unless China improved its human rights record. But China refused to oblige, and Clinton faced the prospect that if he carried out his threat he would throw many Americans out of work who were producing goods for the China trade. And so he backed down.

The embargo that President Carter imposed on the sale of grain to the Soviet Union after the invasion of Afghanistan underscored US objections to Soviet policies, but it is uncertain whether any other purpose was served. To a considerable extent Moscow was able to find alternative sources of supply—for example, buying wheat from Argentina instead of the United States. When Reagan became president, he called off the embargo.

The effects of the US embargo on trade with Cuba are also uncertain. The principal question is how much the embargo had to do with Cuba's decision to align itself with the Soviet Union. In any event, the Soviet Union stepped in with aid for Cuba, and it got Cuban support in the international arena as long as the aid continued to flow. Whether it would have had such support in the absence of the US embargo cannot be known.

Soviet aid, continued until the breakup of the Soviet Union, helped counteract the effects of the embargo. Since then the deterioration of the Cuban economy has speeded up, and Castro has caused difficulties for the United States by allowing Cubans to head for Florida in small boats and rafts. Whether the economy will deteriorate enough to bring about Castro's downfall remains to be seen.

I have noted already that the Security Council of the UN ordered an embargo on the shipment of matériel to South Africa, and the General Assembly refused to seat South African delegates on the ground that they had been sent by an illegitimate government. Some governments imposed additional sanctions. For example, black African governments refused to allow South African planes to fly over their territory. Private organizations and individuals supplemented these official measures, boycotting South African products, urging American business concerns to get or stay out of South Africa, and urging investors to divest themselves of stock in companies doing business there. The sanctions helped drive home to the white South Africans the censure of the world, and the white South Africans finally negotiated an end to the apartheid system, but no way exists for determining the relative contribution of economic pressures and other factors in bringing about this result.

International Sanctions

At various other points, I have already mentioned economic sanctions imposed by the Security Council. The first of the cases concerned Southern Rhodesia, a British colony where a small white minority controlled the government and sought to block changes that would lead to black political control. The Security Council found that this action threatened the peace, and it recommended (and later ordered) the application of sanctions. It selected limited measures at first, but in succeeding months and years it extended them to call for the virtually complete economic isolation of Rhodesia.

Rhodesia was landlocked, which suggests that the enforcement of the sanctions should have been easy, but in fact it was not. The attempt to cut off trade meant that private enterprisers could make high profits by finding ways to evade the restrictions, and many sharpened their wits to do so. Moreover, many governments, though perhaps voting for sanctions or endorsing them publicly, found it easy to turn a blind eye to evasions. Why should they prevent their citizens from making money, especially citizens who supported them politically?

Apart from that consideration, some governments were simply too inefficient to enforce the sanctions effectively. The Portuguese colony of Mozambique bordered on Rhodesia, and so did South Africa, and neither Portugal nor South Africa saw good reason to cut off trade across their territories to and from Rhodesia. Despite the sanctions, trade continued on a substantial scale.

The crucial turn of events came in 1974 when the Portuguese Empire collapsed. The new government of Mozambique—controlled by blacks—had no sympathy for the racist whites of Rhodesia. Its most important action was to allow the use of its territory as a base for guerrillas who launched attacks across the border, but it presumably also sought to clamp down on Rhodesian trade through its ports. Finally the white Rhodesian regime gave up, and Rhodesia became Zimbabwe under a government dominated by blacks. The economic sanctions no doubt contributed to the outcome, but it is difficult to say how much.

More recently, the Security Council ordered the application of economic sanctions against Iraq, having found it guilty of aggression against Kuwait, and apparently their application was fairly complete. But the judgment after several months was that economic sanctions could not be relied upon to induce an Iraqi withdrawal from Kuwait, and so the Security Council authorized the military action that then occurred. The Security Council has also ordered economic sanctions against both Haiti and Serbia, with indecisive results. In the case of Haiti, the Security Council went on to authorize military action.

Instead of attempting to use economic relationships as a stick, states may use them as a carrot, offering economic rewards for certain actions or policies. When explicit bargains are made, the payoff is presumably clear. In contrast, when one state follows a benevolent policy toward another in the general hope of getting diplomatic support in return, it may or may not be possible to say how effective the economic carrot is.

■ Rich and Poor Countries

Why are some countries rich and others poor? In different terms, why are some "advanced" and others "less developed"? And what can and should be done, if anything, to promote the development of the Less Developed Countries (LDCs)?

The problems that these questions reflect are illustrated in tables 16.1 and 16.2. Both show growth in per capita GNP (gross national product), the first table focusing on groups of countries and the second on a selected list of countries.

For present purposes the most striking feature of the tables is the poor record of the low- and middle-income countries—the forty-two countries with a per capita income of $675 or less in 1992. Several sets of countries, especially those in the Middle East and North Africa, have been losing

Table 16.1   Growth of GNP Per Capita, Average Annual Rates

Country Group	1980–92
Low- and middle-income countries	0.9
Sub-Saharan Africa	−0.8
East Asia & Pacific	6.1
South Asia	3.0
Middle East & N. Africa	−2.3
Latin America & Caribbean	−0.2
High-income countries	2.3
World	1.2

SOURCE: World Bank, *World Development Report 1994* (New York: Oxford University Press, 1994), p. 163

Table 16.2   Growth in GNP Per Capita, Average Annual Rates, 1980–92

Argentina	0.9	Kenya	0.2
Bolivia	−1.5	Korea (South)	8.5
Brazil	0.4	Malaysia	3.2
Chile	3.7	Mexico	−0.2
China	7.6	Nicaragua	−5.3
Costa Rica	0.8	Nigeria	−0.4
Ecuador	−0.3	Philippines	−1.0
Egypt	1.8	Portugal	3.1
El Salvador	0.0	Singapore	5.3
Ethiopia	−1.9	Sweden	1.5
France	1.7	Switzerland	1.4
Ghana	−0.1	Tanzania	0.0
Greece	1.0	Thailand	6.0
Hong Kong	5.5	Tunisia	1.3
Hungary	0.2	Turkey	2.9
India	3.1	United Kingdom	2.4
Indonesia	4.0	United States	1.7
Italy	2.2	Venezuela	0.8
Japan	3.6	Zimbabwe	−0.9

SOURCE: World Bank, *World Development Report 1994* (New York: Oxford University Press, 1994), pp. 162–63

ground. The average per capita growth rate in the low- and middle-income economies from 1980 to 1992 was 0.9 percent, while in the high-income countries it was 2.3 percent. The great exception was China, with a growth rate of 7.6 percent. Among the upper middle-income countries South Korea was outstanding, with a growth rate of 8.5 percent, and among the high-income countries Hong Kong and Singapore did especially well, with growth rates of 5.5 and 5.3 respectively.

In 1992 the per capita GNP in the low-, middle-, and high-income countries was $390, $2,490, and $22,160 respectively.

Few questions relating to the international economic order raise more controversy and lead to such confusion as the question of why so much difference exists in rates of growth and in the level of the per capita GNP achieved.

One view is that "the system" is biased and that fundamental, if not revolutionary, change is necessary to set things right. The most recent expression of this view is the demand for a New International Economic Order (NIEO). From another viewpoint the poor countries are poor for a variety of reasons having to do with their own characteristics and policies, and the solution (insofar as there is one) depends on them.

Appropriate terminology for this discussion is in transition. Until the break-up of the Soviet Union, the advanced countries, mainly of western Europe and North America, were thought of as constituting the First World, the Soviet Union and other communist states as the Second, and the less developed countries the Third. Whether it should be assumed that the Second World still exists, and which countries now compose it, is a question. I will continue to speak of Third World countries, otherwise known as LDCs. With a few exceptions, the LDCs are former colonies. Most of those in Latin America obtained their independence early in the nineteenth century, and almost all of the others have achieved it since World War II—mainly since 1960. Since most of the Third World countries are located in the Southern Hemisphere, relations with them are described as North-South relations.

The System Is Biased!

Those blaming the system for the poverty of the LDCs advance any of several arguments. The oldest and most widely known is the Marxist-Leninist argument. It concerns the nature of capitalism, which developed first in Europe and enabled several of the states of Europe to establish empires. The argument is that the capitalist system, based on the private ownership of property and the profit motive, leads to the division of society into classes, with the owning class (the bourgeoisie) controlling not only the economy but also the polity. Given its ownership of the means of production, it exploits the workers; and given its control of government, it oppresses them. Moreover, it is driven to extend its economic and political power abroad, becoming imperialistic; and it exploits and oppresses the colonized populations, retarding their development, just as it exploits and oppresses the domestic proletariat.

The relevance and the appeal of this argument are diminished now that no sizable colonies are left and now that Marxist- Leninists (communists) have been so discredited by the obvious failings of the governments and economies they have controlled. But the failings of the communists do not prove the virtue of the capitalists. It is to be expected that many of those who have been influenced by Marxist thought would persist in believing that imperialist countries owe restitution to the peoples of the Third World for the alleged wrongs of the past and would continue to complain that the exploitation of the LDCs persists even in the absence of direct political controls. If imperialism is gone, it is easy to claim that neoimperialism continues.

The trouble is that Marxists satisfy themselves with what is superficially plausible without being able to muster substantial evidence in support of their theory. After all, the peoples who became subject to European imperialism were "less developed" when the imperialists first arrived. They were already poor. Europe did not make them poor. If they have not developed as fast as they might have wished since the arrival of the imperialists, this does not prove that they would have developed any faster had the imperialists never come.

No sensible person claims that exploitation never occurs, whether at home or abroad. Of course, what constitutes "exploitation" and what constitutes a fair arrangement is a question on which people may differ, but exploitation no doubt occurs in some cases, whatever the definition. Nevertheless, economic relationships can be mutually beneficial and are especially likely to be when they are voluntarily established and maintained. A few Third World countries—Ethiopia and Thailand, for example—largely or entirely escaped colonialism, but it is unlikely that they are better off economically because of that fact. It is arrogant to speak of the "white man's burden," but the record shows that in a material sense colonies generally gained more from their mother countries than vice versa.

Noncommunist Marxists are torn. On the one hand, they are suspicious and distrustful of capitalists from the more advanced countries (for example, the multinational corporations); but on the other hand, they know that they need the help of capitalists if they are to develop their countries as speedily as possible. They must either borrow money or attract direct investments, and to do either they must treat capitalists and property respectfully.

Those blaming "the system" for the poverty of the Third World states have developed another argument, referred to as "dependency theory," identified primarily with a Latin American economist, Raul Prebisch. Addressing itself only to the question of why the poor states are poor, dependency theory is much more limited in its scope than Marxism, but its answer to the question it poses is similar to the Marxist answer.

As the name indicates, dependency theory holds that the economies of poor states are dependent on the economies of the richer states, doing no better than the dependency relationship permits. And the relationship is allegedly biased in that the terms of trade are regularly more favorable to the advanced countries than to the LDCs. In other words, price levels favor the advanced countries, permitting them to sell dear and buy cheap. The bias allegedly traces back to colonial times and continues today.

Dependency theory goes on to contend that the bias stems from differences in power, mainly the kind of power that comes from industrialization, command of technology, and wealth. Given such power, free enterprisers from the more advanced countries are said to have an advantage even within a Third World country in exploiting its resources and so can dictate advantageous terms for coming in and doing it. Among other things, they demand freedom to repatriate their profits rather than reinvest them in the country where they are made. Thus, a constant drain occurs ("exploitative," of course).

Further, dependency theory claims that Third World countries tend to produce agricultural products and raw materials that they are not equipped to process (that is, to prepare for their ultimate use); and it claims that those producing these raw materials in different Third World countries generally find it impossible to organize so as to control their marketing arrangements or to bargain collectively. The Organization of Petroleum Exporting Countries (OPEC)—a *cartel* of countries that produce oil—is the possible exception, although even it has had trouble keeping its members in line.

In contrast, firms in the advanced countries face little or no competition with each other in dealing with a given Third World merchant or government. Thus again, those from the advanced country have an advantage and can impose terms that are inequitable but that Third World merchants have little choice but to accept. Moreover, the needs of the advanced country allegedly have priority in determining the direction that development in the Third World country should take.

In addition, the Third World country that seeks to industrialize is said to suffer disadvantages like those leading to the infant-industry argument. Protection for the infant industry in one Third World market, however, is not enough; that market is too small. If the Third World country is to develop, it needs access to markets in the more advanced countries, but tariffs and other protective measures have traditionally kept them out, condemning them to enduring poverty.

Thus, the set of countries that got the jump on others in industrializing has a permanent advantage; and they exploit it in such a way that the gap between them and the poor countries becomes wider and wider. Writers speak of the "Matthew effect," a reference to the biblical verse saying that to him who hath shall be given, and from him who hath not shall be taken away.

As with Marxism, dependency theory is appealing. It looks plausible, and many endorse it with passion. But those who try seriously to support the theory with concrete evidence, or who try to test the theory against the evidence, come out with mixed results. Some dependency theorists think they have established their case, but critics point to one or another kind of inadequacy in the evidence and dismiss the case as unproved.

We cannot resolve the argument here, but the negative case appears to be the strongest; that is, the results of serious inquiry "provide little evidence either for the Matthew effect as commonly propounded or for the idea that dependence on foreign investment inhibits growth" (Jackman, in Seligson 1984, 212. Cf. Grubel 1981, 108–15).

A much simpler theory is that *the poor are poor because they are poor*. In other words, poverty is self-perpetuating. Relatively fewer of the people who live in poor countries can get the education and training necessary for progress, and they do not have the money with which to make money. Market economies respond to the purchasing power of those with money, not to the needs of those without it. So the uneducated and the poor are left farther and farther behind.

Again the theory looks plausible, but, as already noted, some Third World countries are improving their lot faster than the rich, raising the question of why other Third World countries cannot do the same. Further, some economists take the view that if "the system" has a bias, it favors small states (Grubel 1981, 88).

It's Their Own Fault!

In contrast to those who blame "the system" for the plight of the LDCs are those who explain it by citing circumstances relating distinctively to them. Most notable is the view that *some cultures are simply not favorable for economic progress*. Various combinations of a number of possible characteristics and choices may explain the slowness of development.

Just as the early economic progress of the people of western Europe is sometimes explained in terms of the Protestant ethic, so is the slowness of development elsewhere sometimes explained in terms of the lack of any such ethic. Perhaps people deliberately emphasize leisure rather than work. Perhaps they think that manual labor is beneath their dignity. Perhaps they are disease-ridden. Perhaps they lack the discipline that is required if offices and factories are to operate on regular hours. Perhaps they feel no need for achievement. Perhaps they are bound to support so many needy relatives that they do not gain much for themselves through personal achievement and cannot build up the capital on which the expansion of a business enterprise rests. Perhaps they are so preoccupied with religion and their fate in the next world that they neglect possibilities in this world. Perhaps they are so corrupt that stable and trusting economic relationships cannot develop. Perhaps they are tradition-bound, fearing innovation or not thinking of the possibility. Perhaps they are not forward-looking, not willing to accept self-denial and exercise patience in the hope of future benefit. Perhaps their language has only limited currency, not giving them access to the knowledge recorded in the major languages. Perhaps they attach little value to education and are even illiterate and unskilled. Perhaps they do not have a sufficient number of persons with suitable education and training to operate even minimal government effectively, yet despite this have attempted central planning and have botched the job. Perhaps the problem is not so much a lack of resources as a failure to use available resources wisely: too much spent on the military, and too much spent on luxuries for a dictator or on projects whose main function is to massage his ego. Perhaps, for whatever reasons, they have failed to develop a political order that is broad and stable enough to provide a framework within which economic development can occur.

The claim that "the system" is to blame for the poverty of the Third World is called into special question by the fact that the records of the Third World countries have varied so much. If "the system" were to blame, you would expect that all Third World countries would do badly; but while many have languished, some have flourished. The economies of Hong Kong, Singapore, and South Korea have boomed over a period of many years, and Japan has been so outstandingly successful in developing itself that it does not even count as a Third World country. What these countries have done raises the question of whether it is "the system" that prevents others from doing the same.

No one has entirely sure answers to questions about the timing and rate of development. Why did not the ancient Greeks invent the steam engine? Why did not the Incas develop a written language and invent the printing press? Why did the Industrial Revolution occur in Europe, and why did it not first occur somewhere else? Factors have obviously been at work in the world other than "the system" associated with capitalism.

It is obvious, too, that quite apart from "the system," the resources available to people have something to do with the rate and extent of their development. No one is surprised that the Eskimos did not lead in the Industrial Revolution or that their standard of living is low.

It is also obvious that those who fell behind cannot reasonably expect to catch up overnight. After all, the relative affluence of the richer countries is the result of several centuries of development. Perhaps others who start from approximately the level at which the Europeans started can aspire to develop more rapidly, but changing the level of education and the skills, habits, and outlook of masses of people is necessarily a slow process, above all when the political system itself is unstable, inefficient, or corrupt.

The Demand for a New International Economic Order (NIEO)

Despite all these questions and uncertainties, governments of the LDCs leave no doubt that, in their view, their economic problems stem at least in part, if not entirely, from a biased system, and they are strident in their demand for change. They formalized the demand in resolutions that the UN General Assembly adopted in 1974: a Declaration on the Establishment of a New International Economic Order, a Program of Action, and a Charter of Economic Rights and Duties of States. They complained that "the developing countries, which constitute 70 percent of the world's population, account for only 30 percent of the world's income." And they asserted that it had "proved impossible to achieve an even and balanced development of the international community under the existing international economic order."

The resolutions of the General Assembly express demands, not pleas or recommendations. The language employed is the language of rights and duties—principally the rights of the LDCs and the duties of the advanced countries. In the years following the adoption of the resolutions, the LDCs and others began talking of the "right to development," implying that the more advanced states have the duty to take action responding to that right. This of course raises the question of what makes X a right and who decides (see chapter 7).

The NIEO that is demanded is not to be entirely new, for the resolutions reaffirm some of the principles of the existing order. But through the documents runs a consistent demand for change for the special benefit of the LDCs. The terms of trade are mentioned again and again, action being demanded in various fields to make them more favorable to the LDCs. This implies governmental efforts relating to either price levels or exchange rates or both. In several connections, too, the demand is for preferential treatment of developing countries with respect to access to markets in the advanced countries—for example, preferential tariff rates; and the advanced countries are warned not to expect any reciprocal concessions.

The resolutions refer vaguely to the right of the LDCs to "restitution and full compensation" for past exploitation and the depletion of their human and material resources. International commodity agreements are called for—presumably agreements like that of the OPEC cartel concerning oil—the purpose being to regulate the flow of the commodity onto the market to maintain high prices. The huge international debt of some of the LDCs is recognized in the call for negotiations looking toward any of several actions designed to alleviate the burden, including the cancellation of the debt. And the advanced countries are asked to expand their programs for extending financial aid. They had earlier been asked to devote 1 percent of their GNP to aid, 0.7 percent coming from governments.

Responses to the Demand for an NIEO

In general, the advanced states see no need for an NIEO. After all, the new order would not be for their benefit, and it is scarcely to be expected that they would accept the view that "the system" is biased.

However, they have a variety of possible reasons for concern about poverty in the LDCs. One, shared to varying extents by different persons, is simply a feeling of moral obligation to help the less fortunate. This feeling seems to be especially strong in countries inclined toward socialism, and it is presumably a major explanation of the relative generosity of Norway and Sweden. The egalitarianism that influences their domestic policies carries over into the international field.

To cite moral reasons is to leave open the question of how much to give and precisely to which country and for what kind of purpose. The needs of the Third World countries are endless. France solves the problem in part by confining its aid largely to its own former colonies.

To cite moral reasons—or to cite almost any other reason, for that matter—is also to leave open the question of what to do if the political system of a Third World country is so unstable or inefficient or corrupt as to undermine confidence that aid would be used effectively. Similarly, those who believe that economic growth is most likely to occur in a free-enterprise system are bound to look skeptically at aid to a government that rejects free enterprise. Why should aid be given if it will only be wasted?

Supplementing moral reasons for aid, or as an alternative to them, self-regarding reasons may operate. The object may be to win the diplomatic competition for the friendship and support of another state, or to contribute to the strength or stability of a friendly government, or to shore up the position of a particular leader or party in a friendly state. Either economic or military aid, or both, may be given for such reasons.

A donating country may have an interest in a specific bargain: a certain kind or amount of aid in return for any number of possible quid pro quos—ranging, for example, from the right to establish a military base in the receiving country to the promise of a supporting vote on a given issue in the General Assembly.

A point implicit in the above should be made explicit. Within democratic countries the poor have a possible method of commanding attention to their needs: they have the vote. A political party that wants to win an election may have to make promises to the poor or may have to be able to point to a record of concern for the interests of the poor. At the international level the counterpart is weak. Poor states have votes in the United Nations, of course, but the political and legal consequences of that are limited.

Within countries, too, the poor may turn to crime, riot, or rebellion. Here again the international counterpart is weak, but a Pakistani author, Mahbub Ul Haq, looks forward to a time when it will be stronger. He thinks that the time is coming when the poor countries can wring concessions from the rich. He expects "a dramatic shift in the balance of power." He points to demographic trends indicating that the rich countries will "shrink in the next few decades to less than 10 percent of the total world population." He expects that the poor countries will get nuclear weapons and that "once the power of the rich is neutralized, the minority will begin to realize how dependent it is on the goodwill of the majority." He expects that the developed countries will become increasingly dependent on natural resources imported from the developing countries and increasingly dependent on them as markets for their products. He thinks that the common resources of humankind, like those on the ocean beds and in space, are going to acquire ever greater importance, putting the poor countries in a stronger position.

Asserting that "the real bargaining power of the poor lies in their ability and their willingness to disrupt the life styles of the rich," Haq predicts that in due course the rich will have to weigh the costs of disruption against the costs of accommodation, just as the upper classes have had to do in the more advanced countries. And he cites a former president of the World Bank as coming to the same judgment: "'it is only a question of time before a decisive choice must be made between the political costs of reform and the political risks of rebellion'" (Haq 1976, 170–80).

It is difficult to imagine that a Third World government would explicitly threaten an advanced country with a nuclear strike, for it would thus invite the advanced country to get in the first blow or at least to retaliate. But, facing such a possibility, advanced countries might be inclined to make concessions simply to minimize the danger. Moreover, if terrorists wanting to champion the cause of the Third World got hold of a nuclear bomb, who knows what might happen? Imagine the problem, for example, if terrorists should at some time declare that they have planted a nuclear bomb in Washington, D.C., and that they will explode it unless the United States adopts a policy of restitution.

The advanced countries have in practice responded variously to Third World demands. One of the themes (suggestive of dependency theory) is that the advanced states can best help the less advanced by keeping their own economies in high gear. Almost all of them give preferential tariff treatment to the LDCs without asking for concessions in return. Tariff barriers remain, however, and are significant. A World Bank report indicates that the United States, for example, is "saving" about 116,000 jobs in the textile industry by its tariffs—at a cost of $1 to American consumers for every seven cents gained by American workers. And of course the "saving" of jobs in the United States means that fewer jobs are available in an LDC, some of which have a comparative advantage in the making of textiles.

In addition, the advanced countries all have aid programs, and so do most of the states in OPEC. In 1991 the governments of Denmark, Finland, the Netherlands, Norway, and Sweden all gave more than 0.7 percent of their GNPs, the goal recommended by the General Assembly. The United States gave 0.2 percent, next to the lowest percentage given by the twenty countries represented in the Development Assistance Committee. In the total amount given in 1991, however, the United States was in the lead.

On the whole, the response to the demand for an NIEO has been meager; and that is not surprising, especially in light of the uncertainty about what the mainsprings of development are.

Growth Records and Their Significance

Figures relating to growth records, given earlier in this chapter, are significant, but they do not by any means tell the whole story. The Pakistani author cited above illustrates the point. Pakistan, he says, experienced a "healthy" growth rate in the 1960s. (According to the World Bank, the per capita GNP growth rate was 2.5 percent from 1965 to 1987.) Nevertheless "unemployment increased, real wages in the industrial sector declined by one-third, the per capita income disparity between East and West Pakistan nearly doubled, and concentration of industrial wealth became an explosive economic and political issue" (Haq 1976, 32).

In other words, Pakistan's efforts to promote development involved a Matthew effect within the country: the rich got richer, and the poor got poorer. Of course, some find this acceptable, but those inclined toward egalitarianism do not. The lesson that Haq draws from Pakistan's experience is that emphasis must be placed directly and explicitly on "the satisfaction of basic human needs" rather than on meeting the demands of the market. "We were taught to take care of our GNP, as this will take care of poverty. Let us reverse this and take care of poverty, as this will take care of the GNP."

No one who surveys international economic relationships and foreign trade policies is likely to conclude that they are generally satisfactory. Exactly how the problems should be handled, however, is a question with many answers.

■ Review _____

This chapter concerns government and economic life at the international level. Questions about international economic relations arise both when a government seeks to promote domestic prosperity and when it pursues certain foreign policy goals.

So far as domestic prosperity is concerned, the argument for free trade is most compelling. Given free trade, the assumption is that considerations of comparative advantage govern behavior. Each country specializes in the production of, and exports, whatever it can produce at the greatest comparative advantage; and it imports other products.

But problems arise. Within a country, people who are hurt by foreign competition tend to seek some kind of governmental help (tariff protection, for example), and they may have sufficient political influence to get it. Moreover, the theory of free trade assumes that labor is more mobile than it may in practice be.

Relevant foreign policy goals include those relating to military power, to economic pressures on other states, and to promoting the development of the less developed countries (LDCs). Governments may regulate foreign trade to reduce their dependence on it, to strengthen friends and allies, and to weaken (or avoid strengthening) others. They may impose economic sanctions to induce foreign states to change their behavior. And they may adopt policies designed to aid the LDCs.

Controversy attends the problem of the LDCs. According to one school of thought, the whole international economic system is unfairly biased against them, and thus a New International Economic Order (NIEO) is called for. According to another school of thought, the LDCs are less developed because of their own history and their own characteristics, and thus what is mainly needed is domestic change on their part.

Rates of development in different countries vary considerably. The differences are accounted for at least in part by differences in the characteristics and in the policies of the governments involved.

■ Reading

Baldwin, Richard E. (1994) *Towards an Integrated Europe*. London: Centre For Economic Policy Research.

Bhagwati, Jagdish (1988) *Protectionism*. Boston: MIT Press.

Bhagwati, Jagdish (1990) *The World Trading System at Risk*. Princeton: Princeton University Press.

Gilpin, Robert (1987) *The Political Economy of International Relations*. Princeton: Princeton University Press.

Hunt, Diana (1989) *Economic Theories of Development. An Analysis of Competing Paradigms*. New York: Barnes and Noble Imports.

Lawrence, Robert, and Charles Schultze, eds. (1990) *An American Trade Strategy: Options for the 1990s*. Washington, D.C.: Brookings.

Oxley, Alan (1991) *The Challenge of Free Trade*. New York: St. Martin's.

Salvatore, Dominick. (1993) *International Economics*. 4th ed. New York: Macmillan.

————, ed. (1993) *Protectionism and World Welfare*. New York: Cambridge University Press.

Weisband, Edward, ed. (1989) *Poverty Amidst Plenty: World Political Economy and Distributive Justice*. Boulder: Westview Press.

Self-Determination for Peoples Within Countries?

Government is difficult and may be impossible in deeply divided societies.

'I Don't Care What the Lion Said!
You Are White—With Black Stripes!'

In Rhodesia, Ian Smith's government was a white government ruling a population that was more than 95 percent black. Subjected to economic sanctions, the white government eventually capitulated, accepting "majority rule."

277

The chapters of Part III deal with "the international system," but one of the subjects covered—self-determination—has implications for domestic politics, too. If colonies have a right of self-determination, how about nations within multinational states? How about distinctive ethnic communities? Must domestic politics necessarily be oriented toward individual persons? May the actors be collective entities?

The argument of this chapter is that an individualistic approach to politics is not always the most suitable. To develop the argument, I must distinguish between homogeneous and plural societies and between individualism and communalism. I do this in the first two sections of the chapter. Then I look at a selected set of plural societies, identifying the special problems they face and describing and appraising the special rules and arrangements they have adopted to cope with their problems.

■ Homogeneous and Plural Societies _____

The distinction between *homogeneous* and *plural* societies can be made most easily by setting up imaginary models.

Imagine one society in which everyone, or almost everyone, belongs to the same race, speaks the same language, adheres to the same religion, and shares the same culture. They may divide into social classes, but no serious divisions are based on ethnic or racial characteristics. Such a society is *homogeneous*.

In contrast, imagine another society in which the population divides into distinct communities based on race, language, and religion, the divisions being so deep that their elimination in any foreseeable future is out of the question. The divisions are mutually reinforcing and not cross-cutting. That is, those of the same race also speak the same language and adhere to the same religion, so that each community is set apart from the others by the combined set of characteristics. (If the divisions were cross-cutting, people would end up in different groups depending on the characteristic considered.) The members of the various communities attach importance to their differences, identifying themselves primarily with their own community and viewing members of other communities with suspicion, distrust, and hostility. The communities are historical enemies. Such a society is *plural*. A plural society, in other words, consists of a number of distinct homogeneous societies.

These models are at the extremes. Actually, societies range along a scale, with all sorts of gradations and variations between the extremes. Those found toward the one end of the scale tend to be called homogeneous even if they are not completely so, and those found toward the other end tend to be called plural even if they do not have all the characteristics that mark the extreme. A great many countries find themselves toward the plural end of the scale. *Plural* societies are also sometimes called *deeply divided* societies.

■ Individualism and Communalism _____

The prevailing ideology in the United States is individualistic. It assumes that the individual, and not any kind of community, should be the basic unit in domestic politics. According to the ideology, almost every adult should have the vote, and the "majority" (plurality?) should rule. When people are divided up for purposes of representation, the boundary lines should be geographic, with no attention paid to differences of race, language, religion, or culture.

Thus, representation is to be for persons as equal human beings, not for ethnic, racial, or cultural communities. If people choose to guide their behavior by communal considerations—for example, if they choose their places of residence in such a way as to create Latino barrios—they are free to do so, but this must occur in the private realm and is not to be provided for or encouraged by law. In the realm for which government is responsible, ethnic and racial communities are to have no status or recognition. Egalitarian individualism is to prevail. Underlying the ideology is the tacit assumption that communal differences are irrelevant to politics or can be made irrelevant. The arrangements that the individualist favors tend to encourage people to jump into the melting pot and (to mix a metaphor) come out homogenized.

Communalism is concerned only with plural societies, having no relevance to societies that are homogeneous. Those espousing communalism think it implausible that the kinds of political arrangements suitable for homogeneous societies will also be suitable for plural societies; on the contrary, the closer a society is to the plural extreme depicted above, the less suitable do they expect individualistic arrangements to be.

The communalist may in principle be just as concerned as anyone else with the fate of the individual, but she holds that the interests of the individual can sometimes be best protected and advanced through the community of which she is a part.

The argument is that the further a society goes toward the plural extreme, the more likely it is that individualism, if it is attempted, will turn out to be not only unsuitable but also deceptive. Given self-consciousness about differences of race, language, religion, or culture, people cannot be expected to ignore these characteristics when they vote or when they engage in many other kinds of activities. They will tend to vote for their own kind and to favor their own kind whenever they have a choice.

Thus, even if individualism is nominally maintained, a majority community, if there is one, will be able to control government and build up a system of privilege for itself. And once in control, it may seek to preserve its control indefinitely, perhaps by setting democracy aside. What is ostensibly an individualistic system becomes in effect communal, and the dominant community uses government as an instrument of continued struggle with other communities. If one community alone cannot obtain these results, it may form a coalition with one or more others and gang up against the rest. In any event, the result is an unjust system, and minorities will have no reason to give it their loyalty or support.

The communalist does not claim to have a panacea. In any society that approaches the pluralist extreme, governing is bound to be difficult. In truth, such a society may come close to being ungovernable, and the solution might be to break it up into two or more states. But sometimes that is not possible, and a way of handling the problem while keeping the state intact is needed.

The communalist says that since the different communities are going to act as self-conscious collectivities anyway, this might as well be provided for. The main guiding principle should be that each community over a certain size should be guaranteed a share in governmental power, no one community being allowed to have full control. No community is to have a basis for the view that government is simply the tool of a competing, if not hostile, community. Everything possible should be done to promote cooperation among the communities and to prevent domination by one of them. The specific devices employed to assure the sharing of power will differ, depending on circumstances. The most probable devices are identified in the description of actual problems and practices described in the remainder of the chapter.

The communalist also endorses a second guiding principle—that each community should enjoy autonomy insofar as possible. The emphasis is on decentralization. Each community should manage its own affairs, insofar as they can be set apart, with the proviso that each shall give due regard to the rights and interests of the other communities.

■ Belgium

Belgium divides into language communities. The two main ones are the Flemish, who speak Dutch, and the Walloons, who speak French. A German-speaking community also exists, but is small. For more than a century after Belgium came into existence (in 1830), French was the dominant language, with Dutch looked upon as a language for peasants, all the more disdained because it was used in a number of dialects and lacked a standard form. Flemish people who wanted to get ahead needed to learn French.

The Flemish thus faced a handicap and suffered humiliation. Further, they gradually lost out territorially through the expansion of the capital, Brussels, as Walloons moved in and as Flemish people shifted to French. Increasingly the Flemish developed an ethnic consciousness and pride—a nationalist spirit—and increasingly they became resentful. Being the larger of the two communities, they gained political strength with the introduction of universal manhood suffrage about the time of World War

I and gained more when women were also enfranchised. They might theoretically have become dominant in government, or they might have sought independent statehood for themselves. Rather than risk any such outcome, the Walloons made concessions, culminating in a major constitutional reform in the 1960s.

The simplest and sharpest illustration of *communalism* in Belgium is the requirement that, not counting the prime ministry, the cabinet must be divided half-and-half between French-speaking ministers and Dutch-speaking ministers. In other words, the cooperation of leaders in each community must be obtained if a government is to be formed. And the agreement is that the two communities are also to be represented equally within the civil service. Equality of opportunity for individuals and selection according to merit are thus partially abandoned in favor of an arrangement that averts the humiliation of either community and assures them both that government will give consideration to their interests. Further, each community has a council that manages its own cultural affairs, including its educational system. Struggles continue over the question how far to carry this devolution.

The population of Brussels includes both Flemish and Walloons, and both Dutch and French have official standing. In the rest of the country, however, linguistic separation is the rule, and Belgium follows the *principle of territoriality*, not the *principle of personality*. This means that the language of the region is the required language for all public purposes; business must be conducted and school must be taught in that language. Bilingualism is rejected. People who move across a language boundary are expected to take up the language of the region into which they move. Boundary lines are not to be shifted as people move back and forth.

Thus, guarantees are provided against the subordination of one community to the other; each community is assured a share in governmental power and assured of its cultural survival. Official recognition of the communal differences no doubt reinforces them to some extent, but the chance that the differences would disappear is in any case remote.

■ Cyprus

Cyprus is an island in the eastern Mediterranean, south of Turkey. When it gained independence from Britain in 1960, 78 percent of the population were Greek-speaking and Greek Orthodox, 18 percent were Turkish-speaking and Muslim, and the remaining 4 percent divided into various linguistic and religious groups. The two main communities were historical enemies. Unlike the situation in Belgium, they were not geographically concentrated. Individual villages might be either Greek or Turkish, but no line could be drawn that would divide the island into Greek and Turkish parts.

Britain faced a problem when it granted Cyprus independence. If it had simply provided for "majority rule" on Cyprus, the Greeks would have dominated the government. Moreover, they might have chosen *Enosis*; that is, they might have chosen to merge Cyprus into Greece, thus making the Turks a still smaller percentage of the whole. To these prospects the Turks on Cyprus objected vigorously, and they had the backing of the government in Turkey.

The result was a constitution that provided for communalism. In accordance with the constitution, the Greeks and Turks registered on separate electoral rolls, those neither Greek nor Turkish being invited to cast their lot with one or the other of these communities. Those on the Greek roll elected the president of Cyprus, and those on the Turkish roll the vice president. Ministerial posts, seats in the House of Representatives, and posts in the civil service went to members of the two communities on a 7–to–3 ratio, and membership in the armed forces was divided 6 to 4. The smaller community was thus conceded disproportionate representation, a not-unusual arrangement. The theory presumably was that the larger community could adequately defend and promote its interests even if it was relatively underrepresented and that the smaller community needed to be overrepresented in order to have a chance to do the same.

In the House of Representatives, Greek and Turkish members voted separately on tax measures, and concurrent majorities had to be obtained; in other words, for this purpose the two communities were weighted equally and each had a veto. The High Court of Justice consisted of two Greeks, one Turk, and one neutral person with two votes, the neutral person being selected by agreement between the Greek president and the Turkish vice president. Each community elected a communal chamber, authorized to tax and to exercise governmental powers "in all religious, educational, cultural and teaching questions" as well as in questions "where the interests and institutions are of a purely communal nature." The five largest towns had parallel municipal governments, with coordinating bodies to supervise activities that needed to be carried on jointly.

Thus, the constitution (as long as it was observed) reassured the Turks against domination by the Greeks, guaranteeing them a share in political power; and it provided for some devolution of governmental powers to the two communities so that each could manage its own distinctive affairs.

The arrangement lasted for three years and then broke down. Distrust and hostility between the two communities was too deep to be bridged. The Greeks seized power in 1963 and governed by themselves. Then in 1974 Turkey intervened militarily, occupying a portion of the island. Subsequently, a sorting of populations occurred, with Greeks moving out of the area that the Turkish armed forces controlled and Turks moving out of the area left in Greek hands.

What the eventual settlement will be is uncertain. "Majority rule" in a unitary system is obviously out of the question. Negotiations have been in progress, looking toward some kind of federal arrangement giving each community a degree of autonomy.

Lebanon has had a problem comparable to that of Cyprus. From 1945 to 1975 it operated on the basis of a pact among its different religious communities, assuring each of them a share in governmental power. Then the arrangement broke down in civil war and, later, foreign intervention.

■ New Zealand

About 15 percent of the population of New Zealand are Maoris, descended from people who lived there before the Europeans arrived. If Maori voters were lumped in with the rest on an individualist basis, they would theoretically risk exclusion from parliament, for people of European extraction could outvote them in every district.

New Zealand long ago decided to assure the Maoris representation. To accomplish this, it registers voters on separate electoral rolls—a Maori roll and a general roll. Maori voters choose the roll on which to register, and seats in parliament are reserved for them in proportion to the number who register on their separate roll.

It happens that relationships between the Maoris and their fellow citizens of European extraction are good. Intermarriage is common. About half of the Maoris choose to register on the general role, and a few are elected to parliament from predominantly European constituencies, so Maoris hold seats in addition to those especially reserved for them.

New Zealand's policy can perhaps be more fully appreciated if we think of a comparable arrangement in one of the states of the United States—for example, an arrangement that permits Indians or blacks or Mexican-Americans to register on a separate roll and to elect their separate representatives to the state legislature or to Congress. In the United States, this would be considered a denial of the equal protection of the laws.

■ Fiji

The population of Fiji is 46 percent Melanesian, 50 percent Indian, and 4 percent European and other. Ancestors of the Indians lived in India, most of them migrating to Fiji as indentured laborers to work in the sugarcane fields. Britain was the imperial power.

The Melanesians and the Indians differ sharply—in race, language, religion, lifestyle, level of education, and motivation for progress of the Western sort. As a rule, the Indians are more advanced and more determined to get ahead. Little intermarriage occurs. Intercommunal tensions exist and have been increasing, but are less acute than, say, on Cyprus.

As the imperial power, Britain long ago confirmed the Melanesians in their communal ownership of 83 percent of the country's land, reserving it inalienably for them, meaning that it cannot be sold. The continuation of the culture and lifestyle of the Melanesians depends on their relationship to the land.

As in Cyprus, Britain faced a problem when preparing to grant independence to Fiji. If it had followed an individualistic policy, it would have provided for "majority rule" in a unitary state. But the Melanesians opposed any such arrangement, fearing that the Indians would then get control of government and revise the laws concerning land ownership. The Indians (perhaps looking forward to the same possibility) preferred individualism and sought "majority rule," but made a concession as a means of inducing Britain to grant independence.

The result was a complex communal arrangement. Voters registered on one of three separate rolls—for Melanesians, Indians, and others, respectively. Those on each roll had an assigned quota of seats in the House of Representatives: the Melanesians and the Indians twenty-two each and the others eight.

The Senate consisted of persons appointed by the governor-general on advice from communal sources. The arrangement was such that the Melanesians ended up with sixteen of the twenty-two seats, or 73 percent.

In both the House and the Senate, special majorities were required for the enactment of certain kinds of measures, which meant that the Melanesians could block certain kinds of change. For example, a bill that altered any provision of a variety of laws having to do with Melanesian land, customs, or customary rights could be enacted only if supported by not less than three-quarters of the members of the House and by at least six of eight senators appointed on the advice of the Melanesian Great Council of Chiefs.

The communal arrangement, which operated with reasonable success for seventeen years, did not regulate the distribution of posts in the cabinet or the composition of the armed forces. Melanesians regularly controlled the cabinet—until 1987, when the Melanesian prime minister, accepting the results of an election, conceded a majority of the cabinet posts to Indians. This led a Fijian officer to stage a coup, set the constitution aside, and establish a dictatorship. A new constitution is under discussion and is expected to strengthen the Melanesian hold on the government.

It is easy to pick out individual features of the original Fijian arrangement that are at best questionable, and those dedicated to an individualistic system of "majority rule" would have to condemn the whole arrangement on principle. American courts would find that the arrangement denies the equal protection of the laws.

However, a moral and intellectual defense of a grant of quota representation to ethnic communities is possible. It starts with the argument stated earlier that the well-being of individuals often depends not only on their own personal efforts but also on the continued existence of the community to which they belong. Without community their religion is likely to be undermined, their language may come to be used less and less, communication among them may be reduced, and their culture may be adulterated and transformed. In general, their way of life may come to an end.

It is not surprising, then, that people come to cherish their communities and want to preserve them. Preservation cannot be assured, however, if it depends on the individual decisions of a great many people. Especially in the case of the indigenous, it has been proved time and again, in country after country, that they do not have whatever it takes to defend and advance their interests in personal competition with more advanced people. If they are to defend themselves, it must be (at least in part) through the community. The community as a collectivity must have status and rights, both moral and legal, and it must be able to maintain the arrangements on which its continued existence depends.

When differences between communities are moderate, these considerations are not necessarily decisive. Individuals may be able, without undue cost, to accept the changes that a melding of the communities brings. But in deeply divided societies the destruction of the weaker community may be devastating to its members, ruining their lives and perhaps the lives of their children and grandchildren after them. Measures designed to enable distinctive communities to preserve themselves and to protect their interests are thus not surprising.

A realistic approach to the problem suggests that in deeply divided societies we ought paradoxically to regard individualism as well as communalism as communal weapons. The community most likely to achieve dominance through individualism is likely to champion it, and the weaker or smaller or less dynamic community is likely to favor communalism.

Dangers thus lurk in both individualism and communalism. Individualism may be a cover for a strategy of communal dominance, and communalism may prolong and even accentuate divisions in a population. I take it for granted that those seeking an equitable arrangement would hold to the principle that the legitimate interests of all communities deserve equal consideration and that the rights of individuals should be maintained insofar as they are compatible with reasonable safeguards for the community. The problem is to arrive at a balance of conflicting rights and interests that is fair and reasonable.

■ Malaysia

After World War II, Britain, the imperial power, organized the states of the Malay peninsula into a federation and in 1957 granted them independence as Malaya. A part of Borneo was later added, and so (briefly) was Singapore; and Malaya was renamed Malaysia.

Forty-seven percent of the population of Malaysia are Malays, 34 percent are Chinese, and 9 percent are Indians. The rest are mainly indigenous peoples in the Malaysian part of Borneo. The various groups differ sharply in language, religion, and culture, if not also in race. And they are self-conscious about the differences, maintaining a lively sense of their separate identities.

The Chinese and Indians are virtually compelled to learn Malay, for it has been made the language of instruction in the schools. But no melting pot operates—ethnic and cultural differences are too deep. Malays remain Malays, Chinese remain Chinese, and so on. As in Fiji, the different groups differ in level of development and determination to get ahead. The Chinese and Indians have long been in the lead in the economic and commercial life of the country and in the professions. They are mainly urban, whereas the Malays are mainly rural.

Tensions exist among the communities. The Malays, already there when the Chinese and Indians came in as immigrants, consider themselves to be the *bumiputra*—the sons of the soil. This implies a claim that the country really belongs to them and that the immigrants and the descendants of the immigrants are outsiders if not intruders.

The Malays are especially sensitive to the presence of the Chinese—jealous of their relative prosperity and fearful of their potential political power. The Chinese in turn are fearful for their fate—their fears reinforced by the fact that fellow Chinese in other countries of the region have been treated like the Jews were historically treated in Europe—harassed, persecuted, and even massacred.

When Britain formed Malaya, it did not include Singapore, for Singapore was predominantly Chinese, and its inclusion would have exacerbated Malay fears. Later the Malays themselves agreed to the inclusion of Singapore, but they did so under various safeguards and soon reversed their action.

The Malays, Chinese, and Indians each have their own political party. The three parties have never had a legal monopoly, but other parties have been unable to challenge them successfully. Apparently the dominant view in each community is that it must present a united front to the others.

In the years leading to independence the three parties worked out a set of agreements and understandings that came to be called a constitutional contract, and it has been substantially observed ever since. In effect, the contract accepts the claim of the Malays that they are the *bumiputra*. It does this by declaring that the Malays are entitled to a "special position." At the same time it says that the "legitimate interests" of the others are to be respected.

These expressions appear in the constitution and are given a reasonably clear meaning. On the one hand, the Malays, by virtue of their "special position," have the leadership in politics and government. Malay rulers head the government of every state, most of them by heredity. They elect one of their own number to serve as king for five years. He in turn supervises a system of preferences for Malays, to be described below. The prime minister is always a Malay. As noted above, the Malay language is the language of instruction in the schools and the national language—although English is also freely used. And the religion of the Malays (Islam) is the state religion.

On the other hand, the recognition of the "legitimate interests" of the Chinese and Indians means mainly that they are conceded the leading role in the economic life of the country. They are also assured a share in politics and government, if only as junior partners. They are free to preserve their language and religion, though without the governmental support enjoyed by Malay and Islam. And they are assured of some relaxation of rules restricting the grant of citizenship to immigrants and the descendants of immigrants.

For electoral purposes the parties that formulated the constitutional contract belong to what was long called an "Alliance" and is now called a "National Front." They regularly agree in advance on a common slate of candidates in parliamentary elections. Bargaining occurs, but in the bargaining the Malay party has the upper hand, so it may in effect decide how many seats to allocate to its allies. And, though the combined parties face opposition, they always win.

Malays and the natives of the Borneo states enjoy preferential treatment in several connections. By constitutional requirement the king reserves for them a reasonable proportion of (a) positions in the public service, (b) scholarships and like benefits, and (c) licenses for certain businesses that can be conducted only on the basis of licenses. One of the results is that Malays dominate in the upper ranks of the civil service.

Tensions among the communities led to racial rioting in the capital of Malaysia, Kuala Lumpur, in 1969, and the rioting in turn led to emergency rule for a few years and to constitutional and legal changes strengthening an ordinance prohibiting sedition. Though strengthened, the ordinance is still vague, as laws against sedition usually are. It permits criticism of the government aimed at change but prohibits speech that "has the tendency of stirring up hatred, contempt, or disaffection." Thus, the government is left free to punish criticism of those aspects of the constitutional contract that are most beneficial to the Malays.

As in the other cases of a departure from individualism and "majority rule," judgments can well differ about Malaysia's arrangements. Individualists might wish to chip away at them, especially at the system of preferential rights for Malays; and the more extreme individualists would condemn the arrangements entirely. It is obviously a question of whether the Chinese and Indians should be obliged to make the concessions they have made in order to get the kind of treatment to which they ought to be entitled in any case. And it is obviously a question of whether the Malays are entitled to special rights just because their ancestors got there first.

Those willing to balance the different rights and interests may make a less critical judgment. After all, Malaysia has a plural, and not a homogeneous, society. Despite efforts to make Malay the common language, the different communities seem likely to maintain their separate identities indefinitely. Whether or not one approves every feature of the communal bargain that has been reached, it seems likely that it has kept communal friction and strife below the level that it would otherwise have reached.

Although predictions would be hazardous, and although frictions have been increasing among the Malays themselves, Malaysia's arrangements should probably be rated as successful so far. With the exception of the rioting of 1969 (which was confined to one city), the country has been stable, and the general level of well-being has been rising at a substantial rate. Adherence to the constitutional contract has been voluntary, all parties apparently believing that they benefit from it more than they would benefit from any alternative, or at least that the risks entailed in pursuing an alternative are too great to be accepted. Though the Malays have enjoyed special concessions, they have in general exercised their power in a restrained way, maintaining a variety of democracy. A pragmatic test (Does it work?) and a balancing of the various individual and communal rights and interests that are at stake both give arguable basis for a favorable judgment.

■ South Africa

The population of South Africa is racially divided: 72 percent black, 16 percent white, 9 percent colored, and 3 percent Asian. In absolute numbers, there are 21 million blacks, 4.5 million whites, 2.6 million coloreds, and 0.8 million Asians. The coloreds are mainly mulattoes, and the Asians are mainly people whose ancestors came from India. Of the whites, 59 percent speak Afrikaans (derived from Dutch) and are called "Afrikaners," and the remainder are English-speaking. The dominant view among the whites is that they comprise one nation despite linguistic and related differences.

The blacks divide into a number of different tribes or nations, speaking diverse languages; and they vary in the extent to which they have given up their traditional cultures for the culture of the whites. A considerable portion of the blacks and coloreds speak either Afrikaans or English in addition to their native languages and belong to one or another of the Christian churches.

When the Europeans arrived in South Africa, they were technologically more advanced than the few blacks who were there, just as their counterparts who went to North America were more advanced than the

Indians. In a cultural sense, too, the Europeans and the natives were far apart. Claiming territory as their own and needing government, the Europeans set one up on a separate basis, as the Pilgrims did, and they continued their political monopoly after the course of events brought blacks under their jurisdiction. *Apartheid* (separateness) developed partly as a matter of social convention and partly as a matter of law. The National party, which came to power in 1948, made the policies of apartheid more fully a matter of law. At a time when the rest of the world was swinging away from racial discrimination, South Africa went in the other direction.

The apartheid system, at its fullest extent, can be described as follows. Over the last decade or two, the features described have been eliminated one by one, their elimination culminating in the election of the black leader Nelson Mandela as president in 1994.

1. Political control by whites only, with members of the other races historically accepted as citizens but denied the vote and denied eligibility for public office.
2. A requirement that all persons be officially classified by race and that members of each race live only in designated geographical areas. The relevant legislation permitted the government to relocate people to get the different races into the areas designated for them; in the language that has come to be used in relation to what was Yugoslavia, the legislation permitted "ethnic [or racial] cleansing." Further, it provided for limitations on freedom of movement, especially the freedom of blacks to remain in an area other than the one where they were entitled to live. The relevant legislation also provided for homelands, or Bantustans, to be described below.
3. Segregated education, with more and better educational opportunities available for whites than for the other races.
4. A variety of measures relating to employment and trade unions, putting whites in a privileged position and keeping the others at a disadvantage—and permitting trade unions to gain additional privileges for whites through collective bargaining.
5. A prohibition not only of interracial marriage but also of interracial sex.
6. Segregated sports. No mixing of the races on the same team, and no competition across racial lines.
7. Rules like those associated with Jim Crow in the United States—for example, rules making race the crucial factor governing access to transportation facilities, hotels, restaurants, theaters, swimming pools and public beaches, post office windows, drinking fountains, park benches, and so on.
8. Various measures enabling the government to enforce its policies. Some of the measures were common to law enforcement every-

where, but some were special. Among the special measures was one requiring blacks to carry passbooks with them at all times—books identifying them and their place of employment. Thus, a black found where he or she had no legal right to be could be jailed or expelled.

Among the special measures were some that permitted the government to silence or imprison any person and to outlaw any organization engaging in activities it found intolerable. And without benefit of law it appears that the government eliminated some of its opponents by having death squads kill them.

9. A homeland system. The system was based on the fact that long ago the government set aside over 100 pieces of territory (13 percent of the total area of the country) as reserves for the blacks—more or less analogous to Indian reservations in the United States. Under the National party, the government engaged in a process of consolidating and grouping these pieces of territory, ending up with ten homelands (bantustans), one for each of the "nations" into which the black population was said to divide. Only three of the homelands consisted of one block of territory. The others consisted, in each case, of from two to ten separate, noncontiguous blocks—enclaves within what the whites called the "white" area.

Policies of apartheid included the promise of self-government and eventual independence to each of the black homelands. In fact, the government declared four of them independent and claimed that they were sovereign states. Other homelands that were offered independence declined it, not being willing to foreswear their stake in the country as a whole.

About half the blacks of South Africa lived outside the homelands—in what the whites called the "white" area even though the whites were a numerical minority in it. The government's theoretical solution to the problem of these blacks was ingenious, but even those putting it into effect were too embarrassed by it to argue that it was a good solution. It was based on an extreme form of the *bumiputra* doctrine, with the whites as the *bumiputra*.

The "solution" rested on the assumption that the so-called white area really belonged to the whites and that the blacks living in it were temporary sojourners (guest workers), permitted to be there so long as they served white needs. The further assumption was that no matter where the blacks actually lived, they really belonged in the homeland with which they had ancestral or linguistic ties.

Pretending to take these assumptions seriously, the government stripped blacks of citizenship in South Africa when their homeland became independent and arranged for that homeland to confer citizenship on them. The blacks thus became aliens in the country where they lived and presumably had no more claim than other aliens to suffrage and other political rights. In the end, all blacks in the "white" area were to become aliens even if they were born there and had lived there all their lives; and they were to become citizens in homelands that they justifiably viewed as irrelevant. It is as if the Afrikaners, though continuing to live in South Africa, were told to exercise their political rights in the Netherlands.

The reasons for policies of apartheid are fairly clear. Race consciousness was basic, supplemented by a sense that the population of South Africa divides into culturally distinct nations. From the white point of view during the period of apartheid, South Africa did not comprise one community or one people that happened to be divided. Rather it consisted of a set of separate communities and was thus a multinational state, a plural society—not at the extreme described in the model at the beginning of the chapter, but close to it. The whites who spoke for the government talked in we/they terms, not in terms of "one nation, indivisible."

A major assumption going with the white political monopoly was that, if universal suffrage existed, votes would be cast largely on a racial basis, with whites voting for whites, blacks for blacks, and so on. In other words, the assumption was that in the secrecy of the voting booth, voters would discriminate racially. And the implication was that a one person, one vote system, with "majority rule," would lead to domination by the blacks, which was a prospect that whites long found unacceptable.

Nevertheless, the whites were in an impossible position. If they had been convinced of the moral justifiability of their policies, they might perhaps have maintained their dominance indefinitely, but (with exceptions, of course) they came to recognize that they were presiding over an unjust society. Further, the whole world loudly proclaimed the same view. Prodded by delegates from other African countries, the UN General Assembly thundered out condemnations relentlessly. The communist dictatorship in Moscow was no doubt morally worse, but even it was not excoriated as insistently and as stridently as the government of South Africa. South Africa became known as the skunk of the world. Further, the whites of South Africa faced the prospect of escalating domestic violence as blacks became more and more inclined to rebel against the injustice that they suffered. Whites just to the north, in Rhodesia, had tried to preserve their dominance, only eventually to fail, and whites in South Africa faced the same prospect of eventual failure.

Oddly enough, the collapse of the Soviet Union probably affected the course of events in South Africa. A significant portion of the leadership of the African National Congress (the principal organization of blacks) was communist, and had the Soviet Union been flourishing it would have put wind in the sails of communists all over the world, including South Africa. And surely the whites of South Africa would have held out to the bitter end if they had expected that not simply blacks but black communists would become dominant following their abdication or defeat. But the collapse of the Soviet Union dimmed the prospects of communists everywhere, and it made socialism less appealing. This meant that whites could accept a political revolution in South Africa without necessarily dooming themselves also to a social and economic revolution.

Thus, the prime minister of South Africa, F. W. de Klerk, initiated talks with the African National Congress, releasing its leader, Nelson Mandela, from prison. And Mandela proved to be moderate enough that negotiations could proceed. He spoke in 1991 of the "fears of the whites" and of the need for "structural guarantees" against the "domination of whites by blacks." Moreover, he and the African National Congress modified their earlier calls for certain socialist policies and shifted their emphasis to reliance on a free market. The upshot is what is fairly called a "negotiated revolution," the terms of which are incorporated in an interim constitution that is to be in effect for five years.

The central feature of interim constitution is the termination of explicit and avowed racial discrimination in public affairs and the assurance of full civil and political rights to all on a democratic basis. More particularly, all adult citizens are enfranchised regardless of race and are eligible to serve in public office. Nothing in the constitution gives explicit recognition to racial differences. Nominally, at least, South Africa is to be a nonracial society.

But implicitly the constitution permits the representation of races. It does this by providing for proportional representation, which enables voters to group themselves by race if they choose and then gain representation in proportion to their voting strength. And the constitution protects each party against racial defection by specifying that members of parliament who cease to belong to the party electing them are to lose their seats and be replaced by someone else from the original party list.

Further, the constitution provides for power sharing by the parties, which is a euphemism for power sharing by the races. During the interim period when the constitution is to be in effect, portfolios in the cabinet are to be allocated proportionately to the various parties, provided they win at least 20 of the 400 seats in parliament; and the second-largest party (or any party that wins at least 80 seats) can name an executive vice president. Moreover, apart from the constitutional arrangement, Mandela spoke during the electoral campaign of granting "grace-and-favor" cabinet portfolios to leading opponents in smaller parties. He champions the idea of a Transitional Government of National Unity and Reconstruction.

It goes without saying that the interim constitution brings to an end the legal division of South Africa into white and black areas. The nominally sovereign bantustans have been reincorporated into South Africa.

The country is divided into nine provinces, implying a certain amount of decentralization. But power resides overwhelmingly in the central government.

In the elections of 1994, Mandela was elected president. Many of the coloreds of the Western Cape apparently voted for white candidates, but apart from that the various parties got scant support across racial lines. As anticipated, de Klerk became vice president. Both the parliament and the coalition cabinet operate on the basis of majority rule, which gives control to the blacks, but Mandela's assurance is that the majority will rule "in a consensus-seeking spirit." During the five years of the interim constitution, the parliament is to formulate a permanent constitution, a two-thirds vote being required for its adoption. Whether power sharing will continue remains to be seen. In Zimbabwe, just to the north, the arrangement under which whites had assured seats in parliament lasted only for the seven-year period originally specified.

Mandela's government faces difficult problems. At the very least, the preferential treatment of whites and discrimination against other races is to end. But this means some degree of redistribution. For example, it is to be assumed that a government in which blacks have the lead will want to provide better schooling for blacks, but the probable implication is that it will have to reduce its support for the education of whites. And the government is likely to face this kind of necessity in almost every sphere of activity. If it does too little for the blacks it may lose their support and fail to get re-elected. But, though the whites are no doubt reconciled to the prospect that some redistribution will occur to their disadvantage, the more their interests and their standard of living suffer, the more disaffected they are likely to become. In other words, the blacks face the risk of killing the goose that lays the golden eggs. More literally, the risk is that many of the whites will be driven to leave the country, as many of the whites in Zimbabwe have done. It is hard to get away from race in seeking to solve the problems of a society that has long been racist.

■ Conclusion

In giving prominence to the idea of self-determination at the end of World War I, Woodrow Wilson was thinking of nations and parts of nations that were within one of the European states, mainly in the Austro-Hungarian Empire. And as the idea of self-determination was applied at the end of World War I, it involved the secession of a number of national minorities from the states of which they had been a part. The Austro-Hungarian Empire broke up entirely, and various minorities seceded from both Russia and Germany. Further, since World War II, those seeking independence for colonies have obviously assumed that the exercise of the right of self-determination would normally mean secession from empire.

This record colors thought about self-determination for peoples within the state. Political leaders are ordinarily determined to maintain the territorial integrity of the states over which they preside and so resist the thought of self-determination for segments of the population of the state. But the right of peoples to self-determination does not necessarily mean a right to secede. That depends on circumstances. If states have a right to maintain their territorial integrity, as is usually assumed, the fact must be taken into account in interpreting the right of self-determination, for all rights are to be interpreted with due regard for other rights that may be affected. And one of the ways of balancing the two kinds of rights is to rule out secession but to give effect to self-determination in other ways.

Individualism has little to offer on this problem. In Belgium and in the other countries used as examples in this chapter, those seeking solutions to the special problems of plural societies have had to supplement, modify, or abandon individualism and to provide special status and rights for ethnic and racial communities. One of the solutions they have repeatedly chosen is to give distinct peoples an assured role in government, and another is to give them a measure of autonomy.

■ Review

The argument of this chapter is that individualism is unsuitable for plural societies and that it may need to be modified to include some form of communalism.

A plural society is one that is deeply divided, with ethnic or other distinct communities permanently set apart from each other.

Given a society so divided, the theory is that the interests of the individual can best be promoted and protected through the community of which she or he is a part.

A number of countries illustrate the problem and suggest possible solutions. Belgium legally recognizes language communities; among other things, it guarantees each main community a certain degree of representation in government. Cyprus attempted a similar but more elaborate scheme, only to find that the divisions between its communities were too great to overcome. New Zealand permits the Maoris, and Fiji requires members of each community, to register on different electoral rolls; the separate communities then have guaranteed roles in government. In Malaysia the dominant political parties are communal parties; they cooperate in running the government with due concern for communal interests.

South Africa has a plural society that presents an extremely difficult problem. The whites have historically assured preferential treatment for themselves and have discriminated in draconic ways against nonwhites.

Now they have negotiated a transfer of control. Although the interim constitution does not explicitly provide for communalism, it permits it implicitly. And the question is how the communal system will work now that blacks instead of whites have preponderance.

■ Reading

Adam, Heribert (1993) *The Opening of the Apartheid Mind: Options for the New South Africa*. Berkeley: University of California Press.

Buchheit, Lee C. (1978) *Secession. The Legitimacy of Self-Determination*. New Haven: Yale University Press.

Connor, Walker (1994) *Ethnonationalism: The Quest for Understanding*. Princeton: Princeton University Press.

Halperin, Morton, and David J. Scheffer (1992) *Self-Determination in the New World Order*. Washington, D.C.: Carnegie Endowment for International Peace.

Horowitz, Donald L. (1985) *Ethnic Groups in Conflict*. Berkeley: University of California Press.

———— (1991) *A Democratic South Africa? Constitutional Engineering in a Divided Society*. Berkeley: University of California Press.

Lijphart, Arend (1984) *Democracies: Patterns of Majoritarian and Consensus Government in Twenty-One Countries*. New Haven: Yale University Press.

Ottaway, Marina (1993) *South Africa. The Struggle for a New Order*. Washington, D.C.: Brookings.

Van den Berghe, Pierre (1981) *The Ethnic Phenomenon*. New York: Elsevier.

Van Dyke, Vernon (1985) *Human Rights, Ethnicity, and Discrimination*. Westport, Conn.: Greenwood.

IDEOLOGIES

By an ideology I mean an action-oriented political theory—a set of fundamental and general beliefs that guide people in deciding what to support and what to oppose.

Ideologies differ in the central issue on which they focus. Nationalism, described in chapter 12, focuses on the question of how humankind should be divided for purposes of government. Liberalism, conservatism, libertarianism, socialism, and communism all focus on a different question—the question of government and its role. What kind of government is best? What functions should we assign to government and what should we leave in private hands? Why?

The question of what kind of government is best is not an issue in US life today. We have a democracy and are committed to it. The chapters of Part II are devoted to its different aspects.

In contrast, questions about the functions of government arouse heated argument, and the argument gets confused and confusing because of the vagueness of the terms central to it, such as the term liberal.

The object of the chapters that follow is to clarify both the meaning of the terms and the arguments for and against the stands that people take. Where appropriate, the chapters focus on specific foreign countries; otherwise they relate mainly to the United States.

Classical and New Liberalism

Classical liberalism was mainly a reaction against extensive governmental interference in economic life.

HIGH PLACES IN GOVERNMENT LIKE STEEP ROCKS ONLY ACCESSIBLE TO EAGLES AND REPTILES

Published April 1836, by the proprietor H. R. Robinson, 48 Courtland St. New York

Opposition to the growth of the power of the federal government has been a persistent theme in American history. This 1836 cartoon places George Washington at the summit, thus putting the federal government in a good light, but those currently trying to reach the summit or descending from it are depicted as unsavory.

Classical liberalism developed in Great Britain and became the dominant ideology both there and in the United States through most of the nineteenth century. It was based on the writings of Thomas Hobbes (d. 1679), John Locke (d. 1704), Adam Smith (d. 1790), Jeremy Bentham (d. 1832), John Stuart Mill (d. 1836), Richard Cobden (d. 1865), and others. Ideas associated with classical liberalism were shared by the Founding Fathers of the United States, especially James Madison.

Classical liberals were individualists. More particularly, they put the focus on the liberty of the individual. They were in substantial agreement about some aspects of the meaning of individualism, but as time went on they disagreed increasingly about others, the central question dividing them being the role of the state: What functions should it perform? What should be left to individuals and private associations? Why?

Struggle over these questions led in Britain to the development of "new" liberalism, differing from classical liberalism in that it assigned a greater role to the state in promoting well-being. It was this modified form of liberalism that Franklin D. Roosevelt took up and extended in combating the Great Depression. His kind of liberalism—progressive liberalism—then dominated American political life until the election of Ronald Reagan in 1980.

■ Laissez-Faire

Although the seeds of classical liberalism were planted earlier, it was mainly a reaction against the political system and the governmental policies of eighteenth-century Britain. That system was more authoritarian than democratic, and the government was incompetent and corrupt—an instrument in the hands of a small class of persons, used by them to promote their own advantage. Their policies involved extensive interference in economic life—granting legal monopolies, restricting imports, regulating wages, and so on.

These policies, known as policies of mercantilism, benefited favored persons but limited the freedom and the opportunities of others. Moreover, they reflected little or no concern for the prosperity of the country as a whole (Rosenberg 1979, 23–24). Adam Smith, author of *The Wealth of Nations* (1776), was especially critical, and he sought to reduce the role of government and shift emphasis to the individual.

In today's terminology, what Smith sought was a free market. As Jacob Viner says, Smith's doctrine was that "economic phenomena were manifestations of an underlying order in nature, governed by natural forces. . . . Smith's further doctrine was that this underlying natural order required . . . a system of natural liberty, and that in the main public regulation and private monopoly were corruptions of that natural order" (Viner 1928, 116).

Smith assumed the private ownership of property and the profit motive; that is, he assumed a capitalist system. People should be free to enrich themselves—free to produce what they pleased and free to buy and sell property, products, and services as they pleased. Smith championed the principle that each person should be regarded as the best judge of his interests and should have the freedom to pursue them. With exceptions to be noted later, government should keep its hands off. In the main, laissez-faire should be the rule.

Not that Smith credited private persons with attempting always to promote the public good. On the contrary, he was scathing in his comments about those engaged in private enterprise: "People of the same trade seldom meet together, even for merriment and diversion, but the conversation ends in a conspiracy against the public, or in some contrivance to raise prices." But Smith wanted to hold the conspirators in check mainly by emphasizing competition. Given competition, the actions of those engaged in private enterprise would be guided as if by an "invisible hand" to promote the public good.

John Stuart Mill's position was similar, at least in one period of his life. He urged a presumption against governmental interference "in the business of the community." Laissez-faire, he held, "should be the general practice: every departure from it, unless required by some great good, is a certain evil" (Mill 1965, 945).

■ The Liberties and Rights of Individuals

Championship of liberty and laissez-faire rested on assumptions about the actual and ideal characteristics of individuals, and these assumptions in turn had implications for governmental policies. In the main, they reinforced demands for limited government.

Classical liberals, like some others, found it convenient to conjure up an imaginary state of nature—a state of affairs preceding the formation of government. They assumed that in the absence of government everyone—or at least all men—had unlimited liberty. Actually, they made liberty virtually unlimited by defining it as what exists in the absence of restraint and by thinking only in terms of governmental restraint: no government, therefore no restraint, therefore unlimited liberty.

But unlimited liberty made the state of nature intolerable. A war of all against all developed, and, as Hobbes put it, life tended to be solitary, nasty, brutish, and short. To get greater security for life and property, men entered into a social contract, establishing government and thus giving up some of their liberties in order more surely to enjoy the rest.

Now, if everyone in the state of nature had unlimited liberty, the implication was that they were politically equal—even if some were stronger or richer than others. So the idea of political equality was included in the contract. The slogan came to be that everyone should count for one, and no one should count for more than one: when voting occurred, each man should have one vote, with all votes weighted equally.

This in turn had implications. The rule of equality required limitations on government. It would not do to say that all men were equal for political purposes and then allow government to treat them differently for no good reason. The presumption had to be for a rule of law, with all persons subject to the same law and enjoying equality before the law. And the presumption had to be for the honest administration of the law, with public officials incorruptible.

The importance of this point is reflected in the assertion of the Declaration of Independence that all men are created equal and by the French revolutionary appeal for liberty, equality, and fraternity. Moreover, the French Declaration of the Rights of Man demanded that distinctions based on birth be eliminated and that careers be open to all according to their talents.

Since government came into existence on the basis of a social contract, it followed that government rested on the will of the people and was limited by that will. Thus, the right to participate in government was one of the tenets of classical liberalism. You can argue, as Hobbes did, that those accepting the social contract agreed simply to turn powers over to the sovereign, but you can also argue, as others came to do, that government must rest continuously on the will of the people, which means that it must be democratic. And it was this second view that prevailed. Pursuing liberal ideals, Britain, the United States, and a number of other countries not only permitted people to organize political parties as they pleased but also took successive steps toward universal suffrage.

Classical liberals found it easy to translate the idea of natural liberties into the idea of natural rights, with the implication that these rights are aboriginal, not acquired from government. And since government did not confer the rights, it could not take them away. On this foundation rests the classical liberal prohibition of certain kinds of governmental action, as indicated in the US Bill of Rights: Congress shall not abridge freedom of speech or of the press, or the right of the people to assemble. It shall not prohibit the free exercise of religion. It shall not resort to unreasonable searches and seizures. It shall not deny due process of law. Support for such prohibitions is a feature of classical liberalism and has become a feature of various contemporary ideologies, too.

Further, the rights that are protected are inalienable. You might agree to give them up, of course. You might even agree to become someone else's slave. But no court would enforce any such agreement. Courts would take the view that you retain your right to liberty despite any renunciation on your part.

■ Qualities of the Model Liberal Person _____

Emphasizing the liberties and rights of individuals, classical liberals went on to assume that individuals have certain characteristics, significant for various reasons. Among other things, some of them are significant because they call for limitations on the role of government. And they are significant because they, at least most of them, have come to be features of other ideologies, too.

Classical liberals assumed that people have a capacity to reason and can act rationally and responsibly. People can select the purposes to pursue and the strategies to employ in pursuing them. People are the best judges of their own interests and are motivated primarily by self-interest. They are potentially self-reliant, and, although government should provide them with various services, such as the protection of their life and property, it should as a rule do nothing that might undermine their self-reliance. Government should respect the rule that people are to reap the rewards of their choices and accept the burdens. It would be shameful, except perhaps in unpredictable emergencies, for an adult to become dependent on charity, whether the charity of others or of the government (Galston 1988, 128).

Note the assumption above that the individual should be goal-seeking, identifying purposes or values or interests that she wants to protect or promote and deciding on the strategy to employ. And note the further implication that the classical liberals expected change and progress. Goal-seeking persons may of course seek simply to preserve the status quo, but ordinarily they want improvement of some sort. They are likely to innovate. They want to build a better life.

Classical liberals also wanted the model liberal person to be autonomous. That is, he should be capable of making up his own mind and prepared to advance good arguments in support of the choices he makes. He should be able to formulate and defend a coherent program of action and then carry it out without depending on the guidance of others. Or, if he does rely on the judgment and advice of others, he should be able to give good reasons for doing so. The presumption is that he should obey the law and thus accept the guidance of the state, but his obedience should be reasoned, not blind. The opposite of the autonomous, rational person is the person who lacks a mind of his own, who submits routinely to the directions of others or makes choices on an arbitrary and unthinking basis and is unable to justify them.

Wanting liberty for herself, the model liberal concedes it to others. This implies an acceptance of the prospect that people will differ in their choices, and this in turn implies a commitment to tolerance. Government and law should give equal respect to persons regardless of the ideology or religion or fundamental belief system that they endorse. The classical liberal thus expects diversity and accepts the idea of pluralism. She may be intolerant only of intolerance.

Finally, the classical liberal extols equality of opportunity, although, like others, he rarely says what equality of opportunity means. At a minimum it necessarily means that government must refrain from discriminating arbitrarily against some persons and arbitrarily giving preferential treatment to others, but this minimal definition leaves fundamental questions unanswered. Is the absence of governmental discrimination enough to assure equality of opportunity? If a person is disadvantaged because of past discrimination, does she have equality of opportunity? What if she is born with handicaps? Does the person born into poverty have equality of opportunity with the person born into wealth? How about the baby who dies within the first year? How about those in ill health? How about those thrown out of work through no fault of their own?

■ The Functions of Government _____

Although classical liberals agreed on the rule of laissez-faire, they did not agree on the interpretation of the rule. If the rule were given an extreme interpretation, it would call for the elimination of government. No responsible person went to this extreme, but some went far toward it, urging what has come to be called minimal government.

Richard Cobden went toward this extreme. He gained fame especially through his objections to tariffs, but he stood out generally for a relatively strict hands-off governmental policy.

> His view was that there should be no interference by the State in our domestic concerns. He believed that individuals should be left to themselves to make the best of their abilities and circumstances, and that there should be no attempt to equalise the conditions of life and happiness. To him, accordingly, protection of labor was quite as bad as protection of trade. . . . To him all factory legislation was as bad as the institution of tariffs (Joseph Chamberlain, quoted by Greenleaf 1983, 2:33).

He no doubt agreed with Goldsmith's couplet:

> How small, of all that human hearts endure,
> That part which laws or kings can cause or cure.

Herbert Spencer (d. 1903) was the most extreme of the advocates of laissez-faire. He above all others is identified with the idea of social Darwinism—the idea that, just as evolution occurs in the natural world on the basis of the survival of the fittest, so it should occur in the social and economic world. He opposed any "scheme of coercive philanthropy." If government "taxes one class for the benefit of another, it exceeds its functions." Each able-bodied person "ought to receive the benefits and the evils of his own nature and consequent conduct" (Spencer 1898, 2:17, 377). Spencer thus opposed any public relief for the indigent or any other kind of government interference in what he regarded as nature's plan. From his point of view,

> the poverty of the incapable, the distresses that come upon the imprudent, the starvation of the idle, and those shoulderings of the weak by the strong, which leave so many "in shallows and in miseries," are the decrees of a large, far-seeing benevolence (Spencer, in Greenleaf 1983, 2:77).

Spencer's views were like those of a compatriot who at mid century had denounced any pampering by government, asserting that it made people worse rather than better. Dependence on government was a "moral disease" that had to be eradicated. The Irish famine was God's judgment on an undeserving and indolent people, His way of teaching them a lesson. Their death by starvation was a painful but necessary discipline, essential to secure a greater good (Greenleaf 1983, 2:44).

Spencer asked his readers to imagine two societies, otherwise equal. In one the superior are allowed to retain the entire proceeds of their labor; but in the other the superior are required to hand over part of these proceeds for the benefit of the inferior. He simply assumed that "the superior will thrive and multiply more in the first than in the second" (Greenleaf 1983, 2:79).

Spencer was so extreme in his opposition to government that he did not want it to provide for education, carry the mail, build a public sewage system, or issue currency. What he wanted is sometimes called a night watchman state.

Criticisms of Spencer's position will come, implicitly and explicitly, later, but consider some questions now. To what extent is a social and economic order to be regarded as "natural" rather than as an outcome of choices that people make? If it reflects choices, and if it leaves a substantial portion of the people starving or destitute, are the choices wise? Do the successful owe their success in any degree to the social order within which they operate, and if so do they have obligations with respect to its preservation and improvement? Are those who are well-off financially necessarily superior, and are those in need necessarily inferior? Might a whole society gain by throwing a lifeline to those in distress? Given an enterprise that is likely to be advantageous to a society, is it to be assumed that the profit motive will induce private persons to undertake it?

■ A More Beneficent State

Cobden and Spencer had allies in their extreme views, but they did not dominate the field. Most classical liberals, while endorsing laissez-faire, gave it a more relaxed interpretation, wanting laissez-faire as a general rule but admitting numerous exceptions.

Adam Smith was in this category, endorsing laissez-faire but also as-signing important duties to government. He listed three duties that government should perform and then added others here and there through his writings. The three were: "First, the duty of protecting the society from the violence and invasion of other independent societies; secondly, the duty of protecting, as far as possible, every member of society from the injustice or oppression of every other member of it, or the duty of establishing an exact administration of justice; and, thirdly, the duty of erecting and maintaining certain public works and certain public institutions" (Smith 1976, 2:687–88).

Let us examine the import of these duties in turn.

National Defense

Many others joined Adam Smith in assigning to government the duty of protecting society from the violence and invasion of other societies. Even Herbert Spencer held that the "true function of the State is that of guarding . . . citizens against aggressions, external and internal."

But what is the chance that a night watchman state could give effective protection against external aggression? Does not the assignment of this function to government open the way to a range of activity without clear limits?

It is inconceivable that in today's world a government could provide for national defense and still be as limited as the more extreme advocates of laissez-faire expect. World War II, for example, was widely referred to as "total," and the governments of all the major belligerents conscripted men (an ultimate denial of liberty) and largely abandoned laissez-faire, taking command of the national economies and mobilizing economic resources according to their conception of the need. The point is so obvious that I need not elaborate on it.

But I should point to a troublesome question. The waging of war is necessarily a collective enterprise. Public purposes supersede private purposes, above all in connection with conscription but also in other connections, such as the collection of taxes to pay for defense. Thus, extreme advocates of laissez-faire are in a dilemma: to preserve the laissez-faire system they must accept some degree of collectivism. And if they accept the idea that national defense is a public good that justifies an abandonment of laissez-faire, they raise the question of whether other public goods, such as the promotion of health or the reduction of poverty or the stimulation of the economy, justify a similar response.

Protecting People from Harm

John Stuart Mill joined Adam Smith in holding that the protection of people from harm is one of the duties of government. In *On Liberty* he asserted that "the only purpose for which power can be rightfully exercised over any member of a civilized community, against his will, is to prevent harm to others. His own good, either physical or moral, is not a sufficient warrant" (Mill [1859] 1956, 13).

The views of Smith and Mill on the use of government to protect people from harm have extensive possible ramifications. The line between protecting people from harm and promoting their good is not easy to draw, but even if we give a narrow interpretation to the principle that Smith and Mill endorsed we still have important functions for government to perform.

Most obviously, the functions include the enforcement of criminal laws and the provision of courts in which private persons may file civil suits.

The functions also include a range of activities designed to protect consumers from the conspiracies by entrepreneurs to which Adam Smith referred. Implicitly Smith rejected the idea of *caveat emptor* (let the buyer beware), and people have generally rejected it. Departures from the principle, many of them dating from the nineteenth century, are too numerous to list. You are familiar with most of them already. They concern such subjects as honest weights and measures; pure food and drugs; regulations having to do with sanitation and hygiene; truth in advertising; licensing requirements (which, among other things, presumably give consumers some degree of assurance that those licensed have the expertise that they claim); the formation and operation of corporations; and the regulation of banks. If classical liberalism poses any question, it is not whether to observe the rule of *caveat emptor* but how far to go in rejecting it.

Monopolies pose a problem that classical liberals treated differently, but some favored governmental action to prevent them from developing or to break them up. The reason is obvious: monopolies destroy the competition on which the case for economic liberalism rests. The United States adopted antimonopoly (antitrust) legislation long before either new or progressive liberalism came along.

What have come to be called *externalities* are relevant here. *Externalities* are the consequences of an action for persons who are not party to it; and they may be the consequences of inaction. They are side effects— neighborhood effects. They may be generally beneficial, as when the owner of a property beautifies it and others enjoy what he does, but they may also be harmful, as when a farmer uses a pesticide that poisons the drinking water in a nearby city.

It is with harmful externalities that we are here concerned. Many of our activities produce them. Every time you drive your car, the exhaust pollutes the atmosphere, the noise pollutes the environment, and the presence of the car on the highway contributes to congestion. If you build a filling station on a lot in a residential area, you reduce the attractiveness of adjacent property for residential purposes. If you cut down a tree to get the lumber, you reduce nature's capacity to absorb carbon dioxide. If you use aerosol, you contribute to the destruction of the ozone layer. If you throw away a newspaper, you add to the problem of disposing of waste. And so on and on.

In declaring that government has a duty to protect people from harm done by others, including harmful externalities, Smith and Mill espoused a principle that is widely endorsed. Even those generally inclined today toward minimal government are likely to grant that government is needed as a device to deal with harmful externalities (Tullock 1970, vi; Friedman and Friedman 1980, 214). Different metaphors are used to clinch the argument. One of them is that liberty for the wolf means death for the sheep: too much liberty for some may be fatal to the vital interests of others.

Public Works and Public Institutions

The third duty of governments, according to Adam Smith, is to erect and maintain public works and public institutions. All governments do this in some degree. For example, all develop and maintain a system of roads and highways, and they may go much farther than that in providing systems of transportation and communication. The United States has a system of national parks and forest preserves. It operates a postal system. It sent men to the moon, and expects to send some to Mars. Public institutions may include educational institutions; in fact, Adam Smith called for a universal system of public education. And so on. The aphorism that that government is best that governs least seems odd when we look at the numerous functions that governments undertake on the basis of the principles that Adam Smith and other classical liberals endorsed.

I might note too that John Stuart Mill in his later years went far toward the abandonment of laissez-faire, adopting positions suggestive of state socialism (Greenleaf 1983, 2:112–21).

■ Successes

The benefits that have come from classical liberalism are difficult to assess, for reasons that will become clearer as we proceed. It is often uncertain whether to credit a given policy or measure to classical liberalism; and all countries that have been influenced by classical liberalism have also been influenced by other ideologies, notably socialism and new or progressive liberalism. The social and political orders in all of the advanced countries have mixed pedigrees.

Nevertheless, the achievements of classical liberalism are clearly substantial. It provided a basis for the development of both democracy and capitalism, which have done better than all rival systems. It was in the heyday of classical liberalism that the industrial revolution unfolded. Great advances occurred in standards of living, and in most eyes the cultural achievements associated with classical liberalism were outstanding, too. The fact that new and progressive liberalism succeeded classical liberalism in Britain and the United States, respectively, does not suggest that classical liberalism was a failure. It contributed to, and set the stage for, the greatest expansion of human welfare that history has known.

■ Problems

Although classical liberalism is associated with progress, it is also associated with problems. In Britain, where classical liberalism flowered, relatively few got rich, and a vast gulf persisted between them and the poor. Those who owned the factories controlled the jobs on which others depended. Competition between employers in search of labor was somehow less intense than competition among workers in search of jobs, with the implication that the employers were in a better bargaining position than the workers. Unconscionable exploitation occurred—men, women, and even children working for long hours at low pay, perhaps in circumstances that were unhealthful and hazardous. Unemployment was not uncommon, and there was no unemployment insurance. Neither was there health insurance or provision for old-age pensions. Britain had a Poor Law designed to provide for paupers, but it provided for them in a meager way, and the deliberate effort was to make the receipt of public charity humiliating.

Furthermore, through the period of classical liberalism—in both Britain and the United States—owners and employers were generally more influential politically than workers, and they used their influence to secure the adoption of favorable policies: outlawing trade unions or strikes; prohibiting picketing; prohibiting one trade union from acting to reinforce the strike of another; prohibiting closed shops; prohibiting boycotts; prohibiting trade unions from making political contributions. Or, if they did not succeed in getting trade unions outlawed, they might at least ward off governmental interference with their freedom to fire workers who became trade union organizers, or ward off police interference when they arranged to have organizers beaten up. When issues between labor and management arose, government was not likely to be neutral.

But while using government in various ways to promote their own economic interests, owners and employers generally opposed its use to protect the common people against the hazards of life. If untrammeled individualism left a high proportion of individuals in miserable circumstances, that was simply an aspect of the competitive struggle rather than an intolerable situation calling for ameliorative measures. And through the period when classical liberalism was dominant, little attention was paid to the possibility that government might follow policies designed to stimulate and maintain economic growth.

■ New Liberalism

The classical liberals included not only the social Darwinists on the right wing but others ranging toward the left. Those on the right were extreme individualists, advocates of a minimal state. Those on the left were more willing to use government as a means of promoting well-being—promoting it directly by measures aimed at helping specific individuals in distress and promoting it indirectly by measures aimed at promoting general prosperity. In these terms Hobbes himself was on the left, having held that the indigent "ought not to be left to the Charity of private persons; but to be provided for . . . by the Lawes of the Commonwealth" (Moon 1988, 87). Similarly, as suggested above, John Stuart Mill came to endorse governmental measures to promote welfare. He held it "right that human beings help one another" and thought it "highly desirable that the certainty of subsistence should be held out by law to the destitute able-bodied, rather than that their relief should depend upon voluntary charity" (Moon 1988, 137).

Enough others shared these views that the British parliament in the nineteenth century adopted a number of measures aimed at mitigating the harshness of the economic circumstances in which large numbers of people lived, and toward the end of the century the changes became significant enough that people began speaking of "new" liberalism. By the time World War I broke out, new liberalism was triumphant.

The change was motivated partly by compassion, partly by principle, and partly by pragmatic considerations. The reasons for compassion were plain to many of those who witnessed child and sweated labor, unsanitary and hazardous working conditions, bad housing, unemployment, unequal opportunities, widespread poverty, and other conditions associated with laissez-faire. Not that the classical liberals on the right desired or wanted to preserve such conditions, but the measures that they were willing to adopt, if any, were long-run and indirect. New liberals looked for quicker and presumably surer results and so resorted to more direct measures.

The operating principle concerned the core belief in the liberty of the individual. Recall that the classical liberals assumed that liberty is what exists in the absence of restraint and that they tended to think only of restraint by government. T. H. Green was among those who reacted against this conception, and for obvious reasons. After all, the definition leads to the conclusion that a person who does not have a dime in her pocket is free to stay at an elegant hotel and eat at a gourmet restaurant. Or, to reverse the image, the prince and the pauper are both free to sleep under a bridge.

Green proposed a different conception: freedom should be conceived affirmatively—as "a positive power or capacity of doing or enjoying something worth doing or enjoying" (Greenleaf 1983, 2:130). According to this conception, a person is free to get an education only if it is somehow possible for him to do it. Freedom exists only if it can be exercised. It assumes the possibility of choice.

You can get to the same point by a different route. You can accept the classical negative definition of freedom and go on to conclude that for some it has little worth. It has little worth, for example, to the uneducated and unskilled, to those in poverty, and so on.

Whichever of these views you accept (and I am inclined toward the second), the next question is whether government can and should take action to make freedom meaningful or to give it worth. Perhaps government should provide education or operate an employment service or offer old-age pensions or give other aid in the name of enhancing either freedom or the worth of freedom.

Pragmatic considerations suggesting new liberalism were of several sorts. First, laissez-faire liberalism left the talents of a considerable portion of the population undeveloped. Progress might be expanded and speeded if government adopted programs attacking this problem. Second, laissez-faire liberalism left a large portion of the people impoverished; economic development might be speeded and made fuller if their purchasing power were enhanced. And third, laissez-faire liberalism led to discontent, with people increasingly attracted to political parties other than the Liberal party. Marxist socialism was gaining ground, and the progressive Conservatives (to be described later) were championing a program of social amelioration.

New liberals went in the direction that these various considerations suggested. They adopted measures that seem meager and halting by today's standards but that were bold and challenging according to the standards of the time—measures aimed at regulating and supplementing the operations of the market so as to bring about better conditions of life for the masses of the people.

Thus, in 1908 the Liberal government sponsored a modest scheme for old-age pensions, which Colin Cross describes as "a turning point towards the creation of the future Welfare State" (Cross 1963, 67). And the next year, anticipating Lyndon Johnson by almost sixty years, it called for a "war against poverty." Lloyd George looked forward to the "time when poverty, wretchedness, and . . . human degradation . . . will be as remote to the people of this country as the wolves which once infested its forests" (Cross 1963, 102).

And so the welfare state developed. In the midst of World War II the British Liberal party adopted a resolution declaring that it was determined to use the power of the state to overcome ignorance, squalor, idleness, and want (Freeden 1986, 367). And then at the end of the war came the Beveridge report, liberal in nature although not sponsored by the Liberal party. It argued that "want was a needless scandal due to not taking the trouble to prevent it," and it called for governmentally sponsored social insurance and social security programs to protect people from several of the major hazards of life "from the cradle to the grave."

In the meantime, developments had occurred in the study of economics that led to another kind of expansion of the role of government. Recall that when Adam Smith listed the duties of government, he said nothing of a duty to keep the economy of the country in high gear, and the idea that this might be its duty was slow to develop. Little was said about it until the Great Depression struck the world in 1929.

Then students of economics saw possibilities in the monetary and fiscal policies that government pursued. By regulating the amount of money in circulation and by adjusting its taxing and spending policies, government could maintain a stable and growing economy and a desired price level. It followed almost automatically in the minds of the new liberals that government should take advantage of these possibilities.

Thus, in addition to performing the three duties that Adam Smith had listed, government should pursue a fourth: it should seek to do good. It should promote welfare and well-being by both direct and indirect means. The direct means include not only public education, which Adam Smith endorsed, but regulations having to do with working conditions and labor/management relations, employment services, unemployment and old-age insurance, and so on. The indirect means include efforts to stimulate the economy and keep it running in high gear, the theory being that this will be good for all. A rising tide lifts all boats.

Britain's new liberalism set the path that Franklin Roosevelt was to follow in the United States. Meanwhile, however, Karl Marx and others reacted to the objectionable features of laissez-faire capitalism in a different way, as we will see in the next chapter.

■ Review

Classical liberalism developed mainly in nineteenth-century Britain and became "new" liberalism by the time of World War I. Reacting against the governmental interventions associated with mercantilism, it called for laissez-faire. It also endorsed equality of opportunity and called on government to respect natural liberties and rights—mainly the civil and political rights. Further, it upheld a conception of the model person: rational, goal-seeking, autonomous, self-reliant, tolerant, and open to change and progress. Liberals tended to seek support for their views through assumptions relating to an imaginary state of nature.

Classical liberals varied in the degree of emphasis that they put on laissez-faire. Herbert Spencer was the most extreme, wanting a night watchman state. Others, including Adam Smith, assigned duties to government that gave it a more significant role—duties relating to national defense, to protecting people from harm, and to the erection and maintenance of public works and public institutions.

The laissez-faire system enjoyed great success, but it also posed problems in that it produced unfair inequalities, leaving so many in squalor and with their talents underdeveloped. Concern about these problems led to the development of "new" liberalism, which called on government to promote social welfare and to take measures to keep the economy in high gear.

Those going toward the extreme in interpreting laissez-faire tend to define liberty as what exists in the absence of restraint. But negative liberty may be a mockery and of little worth. This consideration leads some to want government to follow policies designed to give worth to liberty; alternatively, it leads to the adoption of a different definition—that liberty is a positive capacity to pursue ends.

■ Reading

Barry, Norman P. (1987) *On Classical Liberalism and Libertarianism*. New York: St. Martin's.

Galston, William A. (1988) "Liberal Virtues," *American Political Science Review* 82 (December), 1277–89.

Greenleaf, W. H. (1983) *The British Political Tradition*. Vol. 1, *The Rise of Collectivism*. Vol. 2, *The Ideological Heritage*. New York: Routledge.

Hartz, Louis (1962) *The Liberal Tradition in America*. New York: Harcourt Brace Jovanovich.

Manning, D. J. (1976) *Liberalism*. New York: St. Martin's.

Moon, J. Donald, ed. (1988) *Responsibility, Rights, and Welfare. The Theory and Practice of the Welfare State*. Boulder: Westview Press.

Sullivan, William M. (1982) *Reconstructing Public Philosophy*. Berkeley: University of California Press.

Van Dyke, Vernon (1995) *Ideology and Political Choice. The Search for Freedom, Justice, and Virtue*. Chatham, N.J.: Chatham House.

Communism: The Russian Tragedy

*Soviet communism inspired a book entitled **The God That Failed**.*

By 1988, Communist Party leader Mikhail Gorbachev's "glasnost" policy was encouraging opponents of Soviet restrictions to speak out. Open discussion of controversial views, agitation among ethnic minorities, and resignations of Soviet "old guards" who had been in power for almost half a century combined to turn Russian Communism on its head.

The British liberals described in the preceding chapter were not the only ones who saw deficiencies and evils in laissez-faire capitalism. The critic who made himself most famous was Karl Marx (d. 1883). *Das Kapital* is his major work. Along with Friedrich Engels he also wrote *The Communist Manifesto*—a clarion call for the revolutionary transformation of the political, economic, and social system and a statement of the allegedly justifying reasons.

Marx and Engels did more than any other writers of modern times to influence the course of history and to shape political struggles over the world. They especially influenced the thought and writing of the founding father of the Communist party of the Soviet Union, V. I. Lenin, producing Marxism-Leninism. This is the ideology that guided the Bolsheviks in seizing power in 1917 and in ruling thereafter, the ideology that the Soviet Union imposed on the countries of eastern and southeastern Europe at the close of World War II, and the ideology that also came to prevail in China, Vietnam, and Cuba.

Although still nominally endorsed in the three countries just named, Marxism-Leninism has lost its appeal. The Soviet Union has broken up, and in Russia, its principal successor, the old Communist party, although still significant, is a shadow of its former self. The leaders and people of the countries of eastern and southeastern Europe, released from the Soviet grip, have repudiated communism, although some of them continue to support communist parties that have changed their names. With varying degrees of urgency and thoroughness, the countries of the former Soviet orbit are all seeking to become "normal" rather than totalitarian societies.

The main purpose of this chapter is to characterize Marxism-Leninism and to ask what went wrong. What was the nature of the Soviet system, and why did it fail? How well is "normalization" proceeding? The following chapter will focus on China and will ask about the meaning of socialism.

■ Revolution in Marxist-Leninist Theory

Marxism-Leninism once captured the minds and hearts of millions of people, inspiring fanatical and intolerant faith. Its adherents were True Believers, confident beyond question that they knew how to build a better society and lead people to a better life. They appointed themselves representatives of the people and went on to claim that all who opposed them were enemies of the people.

In these respects, communists were not unique. All political parties and leaders claim to know what policies should be followed and may have unshakable faith that they are right. But most noncommunists recognize that they might be wrong; and even if they are convinced that they are right, most believe that certain rules and procedures must be maintained, even if this leads to their defeat. Not so the communists. To them the emancipation of the world from evil was an end that justified the use of any means. Enemies of the people were not to be respected or given a chance to win elections but instead were to be eliminated from political life, perhaps by being killed.

The source of the fanaticism and intolerance of the communists was a belief that in Marxism-Leninism they commanded a science that made them comparable to medical doctors, uniquely qualified to diagnose the ills of society and prescribe remedies. In contrast, those not tutored in the science were like quacks who should be barred from medical (political) practice.

According to the science of Marxism-Leninism, capitalism, although contributing to historical development at one stage, had become predominantly a source of evil, for it rested on the private ownership of property, private enterprise, and the profit motive. It thus brought about the division of society into classes and gave dominance to the property-owning class, the *bourgeoisie*, in both economic and political life. Bourgeois owners employed workers and paid them as little as possible, exploiting their labor. The members of the *proletariat* were ground down as wage slaves.

In addition, according to Marxist-Leninist theory, the bourgeoisie controlled the state and used it to keep the workers down, adding oppression to exploitation. Political power, as *The Communist Manifesto* said, was "the organized power of one class for oppressing another."

Further, capitalists became imperialists, using the state to get control over foreign markets and foreign sources of supply and thus extending their system of exploitation and oppression. And they engaged in competitive struggles with other imperialists for power and profit, bringing on war.

Communists held that these evils could not be eliminated without eliminating capitalism itself, and they believed that capitalists would never permit it to be eliminated through elections. They therefore held that violent revolution was necessary. Given this view, communist parties had to be parties of a different sort. Their object was not to win elections but to win armed revolutionary struggle. This meant that the party needed to be limited in membership, consisting of selected persons willing to dedicate (and perhaps sacrifice) their lives to the cause.

In hindsight, Lenin should have described the communists as the pied pipers of the proletariat, but actually he described them as its "vanguard." In his view, the goal of the vanguard was to raise the proletariat to full class consciousness and rally it to revolutionary action whenever circumstances became favorable. World revolution was the goal.

According to Lenin, ultimate success was assured. The capitalist/imperialist system was so beset by "contradictions" that it could not survive. The "contradictions" were between the capitalists and the workers, for example, and between capitalists of different countries. But though capitalism was doomed, communists were to employ all their energy and skill to hasten its inevitable collapse. They were the agents of history, giving effect to its ineluctable laws. They had to be willing to use any means that would promote their triumph, for the end justified the means. Anything would be moral "which serves to destroy the old exploiting society and to unite all the toilers around the proletariat"— that is, around the communists.

■ Democracy in Marxist-Leninist Theory

Given the changes in the former Soviet sphere, communists and ex-communists now generally give the word *democracy* its long-standing meaning, but faithful Marxist-Leninists historically gave the word their own special meaning. In fact, they denied that there was any such thing as democracy pure and simple. To them, the state was a class instrument, and the principles on the basis of which the state was governed were class principles. Where democracy existed under capitalism, it was therefore *bourgeois democracy*. And *bourgeois democracy*, Lenin declared:

> is always bound by the narrow framework of capitalist exploitation, and consequently always remains in reality a democracy for the minority, only for the possessing classes, only for the rich. Freedom in a capitalist society always remains just about the same as it was in the ancient Greek republics: freedom for the slave owners (Lenin 1932, 217).

The bourgeoisie, according to Lenin, may organize itself in two or even more political parties and permit the voters to choose the one to govern them, but it responds to any challenge to its dominance by declaring martial law and using violence as necessary. In short, Lenin held, "the most democratic bourgeois republic was never, nor could it be, anything else than a dictatorship of the bourgeoisie" (Lenin 1935, 35).

Communists demanded the transfer of power to the proletariat, proposing to replace the dictatorship of the bourgeoisie with a dictatorship of the proletariat. And of course the dictatorship of the proletariat turned out to be the dictatorship of its vanguard, the communists.

Nevertheless, the dictatorship of the proletariat was ostensibly democratic—"a million times more democratic," Lenin claimed, "than the most democratic bourgeois republic." It was democratic not because the communists had electoral support and won in competition with other parties. Rather, it was democratic because it served the *true interests* of the people, these *true interests* being determined not by the people themselves but by those schooled in the science of Marxism-Leninism.

> The democratic or anti-democratic nature of public life of a state, of a government's policy, is determined not by the number of parties but by the substance of the policy of this state, of these parties—by whether this or that

policy is carried out in the interests of the people, in the interests of its over-whelming majority, or in the interests of its minority (Aleksandrov 1948, 23).

As the statement indicates, communists concerned themselves prima-rily with what they regarded as the *interests* of the people. They also spoke of *rights*. Successive versions of the constitution of the USSR set forth lists of rights that people ostensibly have. But respect for those rights, especially the civil and political rights, never had high priority. The Soviet constitution reflected the communist view in specifying that no one may exercise his rights "to the detriment of the interests of so-ciety or the state." Of course, it was the communists, not the people, who decided what the interests of society and the state were. And not surprisingly, their view was that the supreme interest of society lay in the continuation of their own dictatorship. Or at least this was the view until 1990.

Nevertheless, the communists held elections for governmental of-fices. Voters had no choice but to elect communists or nonparty persons acceptable to the communists. On election day they voted for or against the official slate, the usual announcement being that about 99 percent voted for. An ostensibly democratic facade was thus maintained.

So far as the internal operations of the party were concerned, Lenin made a bow in the direction of democracy by proclaiming the principle of "democratic centralism." The theory was that the party adhered to democratic rules in selecting its leaders and in determining party policy and then insisted on centralized control and disciplined obedience in implementing the policies, once adopted. But the tendency was to for-get about the democratic and to put the emphasis on centralism. The communist leadership in the Soviet Union became a self-perpetuating elite. As leaders died or were killed, the survivors co-opted replace-ments, getting endorsements of their choices later in unanimous votes in the appropriate electoral body.

■ The Party and the State

Soviet communists exercised their dictatorship through the party, which in turn controlled the government. Until 1990 they insisted that their party be the only one, describing it in the constitution as "the leading and guiding force in Soviet society." They based their monopoly of power on either or both of two alleged justifications. One was that given knowledge of the Truth provided by the science of Marxism-Leninism, any competing party would necessarily be upholding Error, which should not be permitted. The other was that a political party is to be re-garded as the instrument of a class. Societies divided into classes might therefore need more than one party, but since the Soviet Union had only one class, and was determined to be a one-class (or classless) society, it needed only one party.

As indicated earlier, the party was in principle selective, the rule being that it would grant membership only to persons whose loyalty and commitment were unwavering. Like all parties, it organized itself hierarchically, with a Congress, a Central Committee, and (at the top of the hierarchy) a Politburo. The Politburo was generally accepted as the center of power within the party. It met more or less continuously and made decisions on party and governmental matters without needing any special authorization from the Central Committee or the Congress; further, it made recommendations to the Central Committee concerning the selection of party leaders, including the general secretary—the topmost leader.

Nominally, and sometimes actually, the Politburo acted on a collegial basis, power being shared among its members. But (as is frequently the case with political parties) the tendency was for one person to emerge as the boss, and he then was able to control elections throughout the system and thus control the composition of the ruling bodies. Accountability to the membership of the party turned out to be an illusion, for the person (or the few) at the top dominated and controlled the rest.

Alongside the party was the government, with the party giving the government whatever directives it saw fit. Many of the highest-ranking leaders of the party were also among the highest-ranking leaders of the government, making it especially easy for the party to exercise its control.

■ Stalin

Dictatorship in the Soviet Union took somewhat different forms at different times. Under Stalin, the most notorious of the Soviet leaders, a savage, terroristic despotism developed. Stalin consolidated his control over the party and the government in the four or five years following the death of Lenin in 1924 and remained in control until his own death in 1953.

Under Lenin the government had already "expropriated the expropriators," that is, it had nationalized various kinds of property, without compensating the owners. It claimed that this was a step away from the exploitation of man by man. At first the government engaged in central economic planning and attempted to establish central economic controls, but several kinds of difficulties forced an abandonment of that policy through most of the 1920s, when what was called a "New Economic Policy" (NEP) provided for a mixed economy in which free enterprise and the open market played significant roles.

Stalin reverted to centralization and made it extreme. He adopted the first of the five-year plans (1928–33) calling for the rapid industrialization of the country and the transformation of the agricultural system from one based on privately owned farms to one based on collective and state farms. Opposition to this program and skepticism about it existed within the party itself, and large elements of the population resented the hardships imposed upon them. The peasants especially resisted or refused to cooperate, but Stalin was ruthless—determined to push his program through regardless of costs. And the costs turned out to be appalling.

To work his will, Stalin forced peasants to deliver grain and other produce to the state even if it meant that they would starve. And they did. Famine became widespread. Further, Stalin expanded forced labor camps—the Gulag Archipelago—throwing people into them by the millions. From 8 to 15 million persons languished in them every year for many years. Death rates were high.

Following the struggle over the first five-year plan and collectivization, Stalin ordered the Great Purge, aimed mainly at leaders and members of the Communist party itself. Among those executed were many of the most prominent leaders—old Bolsheviks like Stalin himself. A number of them figured in show trials in which they were somehow induced to confess to a variety of uncommunist errors and sins. Stalin extended his purge into the military, executing most of its highest commanding officers and hundreds of lesser officers not long before becoming involved in World War II. He let up on terrorism during the war but never abandoned it. Robert Conquest's estimate is that the Great Terror took some 20 million people to their deaths, with another 20 million "repressed" (Conquest 1990, 486).

To a large extent, Stalin and his secret police seemed to pick their victims in a haphazard way, but there was method even in arbitrariness, for it cowed the entire party and population. And there were other explanations for the terror. It is common for True Believers to detect heresy in others. The party had experienced splits while Lenin was alive, and it is not surprising that differences continued to show up under Stalin. Moreover, given a science that pointed to the correct line of action, it was easy to assume that those who made mistakes were traitors.

It is one of the paradoxes of history that a movement inspired by noble aims should have brought such general catastrophe. The belief is that in Stalin's last years he was planning to intensify the purge again, but his death intervened. The belief also is that in his last years he was mentally deranged, but his power was so absolute and those around him were living in such abject fear that he continued in office nevertheless.

After Stalin's death some 12 million people were released from the camps, many of them former communist leaders. They pressed for the condemnation of the whole Stalinist system and got the support of many others. In 1956 the leader of the party, Khrushchev, made the condemnation public and official, and subsequently hundreds of thousands of Stalin's victims were rehabilitated, implying an official admission that under Stalin the party and government had committed heinous wrongs.

But to admit that the man who had led the party for so many years had committed such wrongs was to jeopardize the claim that the party had a moral right to rule. Further, Stalin had not acted alone, and to denounce him was also to denounce his accomplices, who numbered in the tens of thousands. Moreover, many had gained from the ruin and death of others. The result was that, though some continued to emphasize Stalin's sins and crimes, others glossed over them and looked for achievements with which to credit him. Forty percent of the respondents in a public opinion poll in the summer of 1992 rated him as a "great leader."

■ Public Ownership and Central Planning

Among the disastrous features of Marxism-Leninism is that it said little about problems of government and about the organization of economic life once the revolution was achieved. It called for the "expropriation of the expropriators," and it advanced the slogan "From each according to his ability, to each according to his need." It looked forward to the establishment of an egalitarian, classless society in which the state, a class instrument, would wither away and in which the exploitation and oppression of people would give way to the administration of things. But aside from vague formulas like these, Marxism-Leninism gave little heed to questions about specific policies to follow after the revolution. Communists assumed the responsibility of governing with only grand and vague ideas about what to do.

As noted above, the basic change that the communists brought about after their revolution was public ownership of the means of production and distribution. Factories, systems of transportation and communication, natural resources (including land), and virtually all enterprises dependent on hired labor came to be collectively owned.

Except for the period of the NEP, centralized planning went with public ownership, with government making decisions that in a free enterprise system are dispersed among thousands and millions of persons. The bureaucrat replaced the entrepreneur. Government decided how much to invest in new or expanded productive facilities and how much to invest in the production of consumer goods. It decided just what to produce and how much of it to produce. It decided what prices to charge and what wages and salaries to pay. It decided on the arrangements for selling or transferring products to the persons or firms who would use or consume them. And it decided what to sell and buy abroad.

The decisions the government made were interrelated in myriad ways, so planning was a complex process. Suppose, for example, the decision was to build new facilities to produce automobiles. Hundreds of other decisions were thereby made necessary. The production of new cars called for the production of every component of the cars: steel and other kinds of metal, tires and the materials from which tires are made, carburetors, spark plugs, springs, paint, robots, and so on and on. How many additional cars should be produced? Precisely where should they be assembled, and where should all the component parts be produced? Did the production of steel and the other materials that go into the manufacturing of cars need to be increased? How about the production of coal and oil? How about the transportation facilities that would be used in getting the components where they belonged and getting the eventual cars to the market? How about attracting the necessary labor to the new plant sites? How about housing for the workers? If new housing was necessary, how about all the materials needed to build it? And how about water, sewage, and electric lines, new roads, new stop lights, and so on? How about garages where cars would be repaired and filling stations where they would be fueled? How about provisions for health care?

In a free-enterprise system, entrepreneurs and consumers combine, in a sense, to regulate production. Enterpreneurs decide what and how much to produce and what price to charge. They must aim at profit, but that may leave them with considerable leeway, depending on how competitive the situation is. Should they make the price relatively low, aiming at a mass market, or relatively high, aiming at a higher profit per unit sold? Price rationing occurs, the product being effectively available only to those who are able to pay the price and choose to do so. Production is encouraged or discouraged by the decisions of those who might theoretically buy. "Consumer sovereignty" is said to exist—in the sense that the willingness of the consumer to buy dictates what should be produced. Producers who make many wrong decisions go broke. Managers and workers shift from unprofitable to profitable enterprises.

Soviet planners did not like consumer sovereignty. They preferred the visible to the invisible hand, provided that the visible hand was their own. They decided what to produce and, within limits, what the demand would be. Their conception of social needs was controlling. Stalin imposed sacrifice on workers and consumers in order to build up heavy industry, which suggests the possibilities of the system—possibilities having to do with the allocation of material resources and the manipulation of human resources.

The planners decided not only what to produce but at what price to sell. They could fix prices high enough to add to the revenue of the government or low enough to imply governmental subsidies. Especially when the prices were low, demand might be greater than the supply, and then rationing of a sort occurred—the rationing implicit in queues or in special stores to which only people of a certain status had access or in some other priority arrangement. Of course, if products were shoddy or unattractive, people might fail to buy; to that extent the market was free.

Agricultural production was a special problem. The collective and state farms that Stalin set up were in general under strict governmental control—meaning that farmers were told what to plant and when and were required to turn quotas of their products over to state agencies, which paid prices so low that even good Marxists would have to call them exploitative.

After Stalin's death in 1953 a greater effort was made to provide financial inducements to those on the farms—inducements in the form of higher prices, higher wages, and bonuses. Moreover, farmers were permitted to have the use of private plots on which to grow food that they could either consume themselves or sell as any free enterpriser would. Something like a quarter of the agricultural production of the Soviet Union occurred on these plots in the late 1970s (Nove 1980, 125– 27).

Even so, agriculture remained a problem. In a book published in 1980, Alec Nove declared that "nowhere is the Soviet Union further behind the developed West than in agriculture" (Nove 1980, 135). Some of the difficulties are imposed by nature—a short growing season, for example. Some can be attributed to the fact that the younger and more imaginative persons tended to leave the farms for the cities. But some stem from inadequacies associated with central planning and control: the failure to provide certain kinds of machinery, or enough of it, or machinery of suitable quality; the failure to provide adequately for spare parts, repair, and upkeep; the failure to provide good transportation links (hard surface roads, for example) between farm and market; the failure to provide adequate storage facilities; and so on.

One of the problems with the socialist system was that it did not have unprofitability as a built-in corrective. Enterprises that would otherwise have had to close down because they were unprofitable were kept going by government subsidies. And public criticism of the sort that might threaten the system was forbidden. The paradox developed that communists ostensibly dedicated to service to the people were freer to neglect and violate the interests of the people than capitalists inspired by the profit motive.

■ What Made the Soviet Regime Totalitarian? _____

Just as the communist ideology was comprehensive, so were the accompanying controls pervasive. This is what made the regime *totalitarian*. The word *totalitarian* refers to coverage, to the extent of domination and control. Communist practice was to control all activities of any moment in the lives of the people. With a limited exception concerning churches, they either controlled or outlawed all organizations of any economic, political, or social significance. They controlled the mass media, deciding what the people should be permitted to read, see, and hear. They could not tolerate independent trade unions or an independent bar association or an independent organization of medical doctors or independent universities or an independent youth organization. Just as they controlled the government, so they insisted that only party members or persons acceptable to the party should have positions of leadership in nongovernmental activities and associations of any significance. Aside from the plots allowed to farmers, they kept private economic activity at a minimum, insisting that the governmental bureaucracy make decisions about everything from production and marketing to publishing books and providing entertainment.

Totalitarian control by communists did not mean the absence of criticism. The communists decided that, within limits, criticism might be helpful. But they did not permit challenge to the basic principles of the system. As noted above, the position was that Marxism-Leninism (as interpreted by successive leaders) revealed the Truth. The leading and guiding role of the party had to be preserved. Criticism that served the party's purposes was invited, but criticism that undermined the party was not tolerated. It turned out, however, that even though the party permitted some criticism, it was too repressive for its own good.

◼ The Soviet Communists and the Outer World

After the seizure of power in 1917, some of the Bolsheviks thought that their revolution could not succeed unless it spread to other countries, and they wanted to promote it abroad even if their effort brought their own downfall. The *Communist Manifesto* had called on the workers of the world to unite, telling them that they had nothing to lose but their chains. The general communist assumption was that nationalism was like religion—the opium of the people, an instrument of the ruling classes in advancing their class interests. The proletariat, led by its vanguard, should rise above the divisiveness of national patriotism and unite the world.

But Lenin faced up to the very practical fact that the Bolsheviks had seized power in Russia and that they might lose it if they placed great emphasis on promoting revolution abroad. So he took the view that the paramount duty of the Bolsheviks was to preserve the revolution in the country where it had first succeeded.

Nevertheless, in Lenin's time the party led in establishing the Third International—an international organization of communist parties. Through the Third International the Soviet communists came to dominate foreign communist parties, giving them various forms of assistance and obtaining their loyalty. The idea was to use these parties either as agents of revolution in their own countries or as instruments in defending and promoting the interests of the USSR. The second of these functions was perhaps dominant from the beginning. Certainly it became dominant when the threat of Hitler's Germany developed in the 1930s.

Stalin was so concerned about preserving the USSR that in 1939 he made a pact of neutrality and nonaggression with Hitler. This was a shattering blow to communist parties in Europe and elsewhere, for Stalin thus seemed to renounce any duty to the world proletariat and to do it in the most cynical way.

In 1941 Hitler invaded the Soviet Union despite the pact, giving Stalin no choice but to put prime emphasis on defense. Moreover, in World War II Stalin found himself an ally of Britain and the United States. In these circumstances he seemed to abandon any thought of extending the revolution. In fact, he dissolved the Third International.

Events at the end of the war went in the opposite direction. The Red Army then dominated Poland, Rumania, Bulgaria, Czechoslovakia, Hungary, and Eastern Germany; and a friendly communist party controlled Yugoslavia. In these circumstances the Soviet interest in extending revolution coincided with its interest in trying to guarantee itself against any future invasion of the sort that Hitler had mounted.

Whatever the relative influence of these concerns, the Soviet Union saw to it that all of the countries dominated by the Red Army got governments friendly to it. The communist parties of those countries were so small and weak when the Soviet Union placed them in power that they needed the help of noncommunists in staffing governmental offices; and relationships with the wartime allies were such that the Soviet communists thought it politic to make a gesture, however limited, in the direction of democracy as understood in Washington and London. Throughout eastern and southeastern Europe, the Soviet Union therefore allowed noncommunist parties to be represented in coalition governments; but that phase lasted only a few years, and then the transparent mask over communist control was removed. Whatever the motive, Moscow brought about an extension of communism and thereby launched the cold war.

The Yugoslav communists came to power without direct help from the Red Army, and Yugoslavia avoided occupation by the Red Army. For a few years the Yugoslav communists continued in their loyalty to Stalin, but then a split occurred. The communists remained in power, but in defiance of Moscow.

Determined to prevent anything like this from happening in other countries of the area, the Soviet Union stood poised with the Red Army. It intervened militarily in East Germany (1953), Hungary (1956), and Czechoslovakia (1968); and in Poland it shifted from the Polish Communist party to the Polish army as its instrument of control. Brezhnev, the Soviet leader from 1965 to 1982, formalized such policies in a doctrine that bears his name: that every triumph of communism is irreversible—that once a country has come under the control of communists loyal to Moscow, it must remain under their control.

In 1979 the Soviet Union intervened militarily in Afghanistan, likewise on a revolutionary mission. And the Soviet Union gave varying degrees of support to communist or leftist parties and governments in different parts of the world—for example, in Cuba, Ethiopia, Nicaragua, and Vietnam.

■ Perestroika and Glasnost

Fundamental change has come to what was the Soviet Union and the communist world. Historians will be sorting out the reasons and putting them into different orders of importance for decades to come.

The most obvious relevant fact is that Gorbachev was elected general secretary of the Communist party in 1985 and began calling for *perestroika* (restructuring) and *glasnost* (openness; public disclosure and discussion). A faithful Marxist-Leninist would not put much emphasis on Gorbachev's rise to power, for he would have to say that material conditions and changes in them control the course of history, bringing to the fore whatever kind of personality the circumstances require. But Gorbachev played a central role in the course of events, and so have a number of others. It is difficult to believe that the world would be the same if he—and Marx and Lenin and Stalin—had never been born. But why would Gorbachev and the others want change? Their main problems were of three sorts: economic, moral, and political.

Economic Problems

Information about the Soviet economy is unreliable and incomplete. You get different accounts depending on the sources on which you draw, and it is uncertain where the truth lies. If some of the statistics are to be believed, no reason would seem to exist for the Soviet breakdown, yet the breakdown occurred.

The communists transformed the economy that they managed. When they seized power in 1917 Russia was backward even by the standards of the time; and on top of that the two world wars brought untold devastation. In addition to the 20 million persons killed by Stalin, another 20 million or so lost their lives in World War II. Nevertheless, the years of communist control (at least down to the late 1970s and early 1980s) were years of great economic progress. The official claim is that "Soviet national income increased 149 times between 1917 and 1987, and over 18 times between 1940 and 1987." And "Soviet industrial production, about 3 percent of the global total in 1917, had increased to about 20 percent by 1987" (White 1993, 102–103). Whether or not these figures are accurate, no doubt exists that levels of production went up markedly. And quantitative increases reflected substantial technological progress, too, as indicated both by Soviet success in developing nuclear weapons and by *Sputnik*, which the Soviet Union put into orbit in 1957, before the United States had a comparable capacity. For a time the boast seemed plausible that, in terms of standards of living, the Soviet Union would catch up with and surpass the countries of the West.

But despite the above, the Soviet economy and the whole communist system collapsed, raising the question what went wrong. The most fundamental part of the explanation is that comprehensive central economic planning is simply impractical, and it is impractical for two kinds of reasons. On the one hand, modern economies are too complex to be run from one office. Too many activities have to be decided upon and coordinated. On the other hand, a problem of motivation arises both among the leaders and among the followers. Even in the Soviet system something akin to a profit motive operated, as those rising to certain positions got the accompanying perquisites. And the Soviet system dispensed honors to those who achieved in outstanding ways. But nevertheless it is clear in hindsight that something was lacking in the motivation provided. Too many people failed to order their lives in accordance with the values on which significant progress depends—values such as ordinary honesty, zeal for work, and a desire for personal achievement. Instead of public ownership and centralized planning, the West relies on the private ownership of property and the profit motive, which obviously work better.

Some of what is said above can be put in other terms: that what a governmental bureaucracy can do successfully has its limits. The record of capitalist countries, including some governed along social-democratic lines, indicates that activist governments may give the economic system a boost, but they do it in limited and carefully selected ways. No one knows exactly what the limits are, but they relate both to the problem of amassing and coordinating the necessary knowledge and to the problem of motivating people appropriately. The more complex the system, the more difficult central planning and control become, and the more responsibility government assumes, the more irresponsible people tend to become. More on this below.

I note above that in the realm of technological progress the Soviet system did well in some respects, as in its programs relating to outer space and nuclear weapons, but it did not do well across the board. You do not hear, for example, of Soviet contributions to the development of the computer or of Soviet discoveries relating to medicine or pharmacology. And of course their "contributions" in the social sciences were mainly on the negative side. Nobel prizes in the sciences and social sciences have gone in far greater number to citizens of the United States than to citizens of the Soviet Union. The summary point is perhaps that bureaucrats are not to be relied upon as innovators and risk takers. They are too likely to take the safe and comfortable "steady-as-you-go" course.

On the more obvious and mundane side, it is clear that in a multitude of instances the bureaucrats made mistakes. They emphasized production more than distribution, with the result that considerable proportions of what was produced (most notably in agriculture) never reached the market. Even the emphasis on production did not always work out well, for too much of one item was often produced and too little of another. The Soviet market was notorious for its random shortages and for its queues.

Further, the Soviet planners generally fixed goals in quantitative terms, stressing the numbers or the amount to be produced regardless of quality, with the result that an unusually high proportion of the products were shoddy or badly designed. Production might be high, but without a proportionate contribution to human happiness or well-being. Similarly, in choosing between guns and butter, the Soviet Union put an unusual degree of emphasis on guns, which count in the GNP but contribute little toward higher living standards. Given the emphasis on guns, statistics on gross production are misleading as indicators of the extent to which human needs were met.

As intimated above, other features of the Soviet system surely help explain its failure: the assumption of responsibility by the government and, as a counterpart, the reduction in the opportunities for individual initiative and competitive effort; and the virtual elimination of the profit motive. Individual persons were left with inadequate incentive to do their best, and commercial enterprises that went into the red could count on the government to bail them out.

In addition, and helping to explain at least the slowdown of the Soviet economy, factors operated like those affecting the more advanced countries of the West. As the years went by, fewer and fewer young people could be recruited from the farms to operate the factories of the cities, and more and more people came to be in the upper age groups, consuming more than they produced. And as the years went by, the raw materials tended to get more and more expensive as producers had to shift from the more to the less accessible sources of supply. Oil is the outstanding illustration. To get it, producers had increasingly to drill deeper and to go to oil fields where the costs of production were higher.

The result is that, contrary to the party's prediction that Soviet living standards would be the highest in the world by the 1980s, they apparently reached no more than about a third of the US level, which was all the worse because of rising expectations stimulated by people's rising educational level and increased knowledge of the outside world. Levels of consumption that aroused little protest in earlier times came to seem intolerable. The situation is suggested by the fact that, as of 1992, 40 percent of the hospitals had no hot water and 18 percent were not connected to a sewerage system. Half of the population were drinking unhygienic water. Life expectancy was declining.

The system of comprehensive economic planning might have been abandoned on the basis of the above considerations alone, but in fact additional considerations contributed to the result.

■ The Moral Problem

A number of analysts of Soviet affairs describe the collapse of the system as not only economic but also ideological and moral. For example, Ludwikowski speaks of an "irreversible deterioration of public morality, a breakdown of confidence in the communist leadership, and a growing distrust of the basic tenets of communist ideology." He describes the *nomenklatura* (those in the upper reaches of the bureaucracy) as "a self-serving bunch" whose main interest lay in protecting their own status and privileges (Ludwikowski 1986, 6, 17, 59).

Ludwikowski goes on to say that communist management of the economy "stifled the initiative of workers and their incentive to be truly productive." He speaks of "the lack of any true incentive to achieve more efficient production" and of "low labor discipline, hooliganism, drunkenness, bribe-taking, a dual standard of morality between Soviet workers and the technical intelligentsia, neglect of equipment, absenteeism, and a destructive trend called 'steal-and-let-others-steal'" (Ludwikowski 1986, 8).

Shmelev and Popov (1989) offer similar interpretations. They say that, given the "command-administered economy,"

> the public became apathetic and indifferent, acquired a parasitic belief in guaranteed jobs and social security, and considered that it was useless and even humiliating to put their shoulders to the wheel and work unsparingly ("we pretend to work and you pretend to pay us"). A significant part of the nation degenerated physically and spiritually as a result of drink and idleness; ethics and morality declined; massive theft of public property and disregard for honest labor was accompanied by bitter envy of others who were able to increase their incomes (75).

Mandel (1989) reports similarly. He points to alcoholism as "a terrible scourge in the Soviet Union," saying that it is undoubtedly the main cause of the drop in life expectancy. He speaks of demoralization, boredom, and the absence of hope or ideals (107). Others speak of the passivity bred by many decades when initiative was discouraged, when dependency was accepted, and when people learned that they could not trust their neighbors or even other members of the family.

After the "velvet revolution" that overthrew the communists in Czechoslovakia, Václav Havel spoke of the distress that had come from living a lie. The people of the Soviet Union had abundant reason for the same kind of distress. While Stalin lived and despite his horrible record, people felt obliged to attribute genius to him, pretending that he made the sun to rise and the rain to fall. After his death, despite the evil associated with his rule, his embalmed body was put on reverential display in a national shrine. Through the whole period of the Soviet regime, people participated in elections knowing that they were frauds. The constitution itself declared that "the advantages of the socialist way of life are becoming increasingly evident," when everyone knew that this was not true. People were "showered with propaganda about socialist well-being" while living in inadequate housing, getting inadequate medical care, and suffering shortages of both the necessities and the luxuries of life.

In 1988, by which time the Soviet Union was about to dissolve, school authorities in the Soviet Union made an implicit comment on the moral crisis to which communism had led when they canceled end-of-term history tests on the ground that so much of what had been taught was untrue or misleading (Laqueur 1989, 48).

It is difficult to be sure how much influence moral considerations had on the course of events. Rulers well endowed with cynicism can go on imposing their rule after their moral right to do so is gone, and many others can serve their private purposes by continuing to support a government that has become illegitimate. But not all persons are in these categories. Rulers generally need the sense that they have a right to rule, and people need to believe in the legitimacy of government if they are to give it their support. When a government becomes illegitimate in the minds of both the rulers and the ruled, it is in trouble.

■ The Political Problem

The economic and moral problems of the Soviet Union inevitably generated a political problem. Communists differed among themselves on the proper course of action, and so did noncommunists. Some communists, disillusioned, sought reform, whereas others wanted to continue down the established path. Perhaps the latter—the "hard-line" communists—could not accept the view that they had devoted their lives to a ghastly mistake, or perhaps they responded to overwhelming considerations of self-interest. The reformers divided between those who thought they could do best by working within the party and those who went into more or less open opposition.

Communists seeking reform from within the party won out with the election of Gorbachev as general secretary in 1985. He led in bringing about fundamental changes. Under him the party and government endorsed freedom of speech and press and, in general, pledged respect for human rights, permitting people for the first time in their lives to say and print what they pleased without fear. Further, in 1990 the party gave up its claim to a legally protected "leading role," meaning that it accepted the right of people to organize competing parties and nominate candidates for election. It adopted a program entitled "Toward a Humane, Democratic Socialism," and the next year it elaborated on this commitment, calling for the separation of powers, the rule of law, and the amendment of existing laws to make them conform to international norms concerning human rights (Salvetz and Jones 1994, 15). The implicit admission was that the party had not been serving these values.

Gorbachev and the reformers brought fundamental change in foreign as well as in domestic affairs. As already indicated in chapter 11, they abandoned the Brezhnev doctrine in favor of the Sinatra doctrine and committed themselves to a withdrawal of Soviet forces from the countries of eastern and southeastern Europe. Moreover, the reformers called for greater emphasis on the United Nations, on arms control, and on international cooperation in general. These policies terminated the cold war and have led to the transformation of NATO. The sixteen parties to NATO are now associated with some twenty-two other countries, including Russia, in a Partnership for Peace.

Although reformists obviously controlled the executive branch of the government in Moscow, others opposed the changes, and in 1991 they attempted a coup. Although they failed miserably, they got enough support within the party that the government froze the party's funds and prohibited any further activity on its part, only to see these actions declared unconstitutional later on. The party resumed its legal existence and activities in 1993.

Meantime the USSR dissolved. Beginning with the Baltic countries, the various republics of the Soviet Union all declared their independence, and the central government made no attempt to keep them in the Union. Without a unified country to govern, Gorbachev resigned; and in the largest and most important of the republics, Russia, Boris Yeltsin became the leading figure.

In Russia a struggle developed between Yeltsin and the Russian Congress of People's Deputies, which had been elected in 1990 under rules that assured the communists of control and which resisted reform. One interpretation is that a parliamentary rebellion initiated the struggle, and another is that Yeltsin unlawfully overthrew an elected parliament and the constitutional order.

In any event, Yeltsin emerged strengthened from both these tests, but the very fact that he rules more through presidential decree than on the basis of parliamentary support suggests that democracy in Russia is fragile. Elections at the end of 1993 failed to provide full reassurance. The voters approved a constitution that Yeltsin supported, providing for a strong president and a weaker parliament, but they also gave more votes to an ultranationalist right-wing party than to any other—23 percent of the total. A coalition supporting Yeltsin got 15.4 percent, and the Communist party got 12.4 percent.

Economic and moral problems remain fundamental. The economy was doing badly even in the stable times of centralized planning, and it got worse. Industrial production declined each year from 1990 at least through the first quarter of 1994, when it was 25 percent below the 1993 level, which itself was below the level of 1992. Official statistics for the summer of 1992 indicate that about half the population of Russia was living below the subsistence level (White 1993, 273). Inflation became extreme. But privatization went on apace: by 1994 approximately 60 percent of Russia's income was produced in the private sector. And signs of economic recovery began to show: car ownership in Moscow rose by 40 percent from 1992 to 1994. Household incomes rose by 18 percent from 1993 to 1994.

Observers offer different explanations of the economic troubles. William Overholt points to the better economic record of the Chinese communists, who have insisted on maintaining their political control and who have introduced economic reforms on a gradualist basis. He considers this strategy superior to the strategy employed in the Soviet Union, where political and economic reform have been sought more or less simultaneously and where the economic reform has been on a "big bang" basis. And he generalizes beyond China: "The pattern of the successful Pacific Asian countries . . . has been for an authoritarian government to build the institutions, liberalize the economies, and create the educated middle class, and then to experience the emergence of freedom and democracy whether the leaders encourage these political changes or not" (Overholt 1993, 123).

In contrast, others put less stress on grand strategy and more on distinctively Russian circumstances. Russian culture is "deeply anticapitalist." The people have a "visceral hostility" to foreign investment. Experience with communism has left them unfit for a market economy, for they are averse to risk-taking, inclined to depend on government, disinclined to take initiatives, and distrustful of others. They are accustomed to "group responsibility [and] personal irresponsibility."

The moral problem is suggested by the sharp increase in crime. One observer declares that "organized crime touches at least half of all economic transactions." Asked in a 1992 poll who ruled Russia, 22 percent named the Mafia and 10 percent said no one did. Less than 4 percent named Yeltsin's government (White 1993, 270).

One of the paradoxes associated with the collapse of communism, not only in the former USSR but also in the countries of eastern and southeastern Europe, is the continued support that communists get in elections and in public opinion polls. To be sure, most of the parties led by former communists are operating under a different name, and most of them abjure centralized economic planning and totalitarian controls. But their continued support is both striking and puzzling. Terrible as Stalin's crimes were, more Russians said in 1992 that they would rather live in a communist society than in a society like that of the United States. And in Albania, Bulgaria, Lithuania, Rumania, and Slovakia, to say nothing of a number of the former republics of the USSR, communists (under whatever name) have obtained enough electoral support to return to power or to command a place in a coalition government. This does not necessarily mean that the voters want a return of communism, for many of the communists who get electoral support are themselves champions of reform. But it raises questions. Perhaps a major part of the answer lies in the simple fact that communists and ex-communists are the ones with political ambition and with political experience and tested organizational capacities. Another part of the answer may well be that many people want, if not a socialist society, then a highly developed welfare state. In the poll of 1993 in which more respondents favored a communist society than a society like that of the United States, still more (23 percent) wanted a social democracy like that in Sweden.

It was perhaps not to be expected that the influence of communism would disappear overnight. The system provided what Erich Fromm called an "escape from freedom"—an escape from the hazards associated with self-reliance and free enterprise; and many are uncertain about how much they want a new order in which those hazards are revived. Further, many remain faithful to some version of the idea of egalitarianism and cast their votes accordingly.

◼ Review

Communism has been a powerful influence, and experience with it will no doubt affect political life for decades to come. But communists are in about the same position as members of a religious cult whose prophecies have failed.

Soviet communism was based on Marxism-Leninism, which has inspired millions to an intolerant and fanatical faith. True Believers claimed that Marxism-Leninism was a science and that those tutored in it were uniquely qualified to diagnose social ills and prescribe remedies. Thus, they should rule. They should socialize the means of production and distribution and engage in central economic planning. They should brook no opposition, for an opposition would necessarily be championing error. Their dictatorship, however, would be a true democracy, for democracy exists when the interests of the people are served.

Marxist-Leninist hopes have been dashed. In the Soviet Union, Stalin set up a savage, terror-ridden despotism, killing or ruining the lives of millions. The Soviet GNP grew for several decades, but then decline set in, to the point that communists themselves saw that reform was imperative. This involved an admission of their own failure and led to the conclusion that they had no moral right to rule.

The result is drastic change. Once reform started, it had no clear stopping point. The former satellite states were freed from Moscow's control, and after an attempted coup against Gorbachev, the various republics of the USSR became independent, which means that the USSR dissolved. The cold war ended. Within Russia, the principal republic of the old USSR, Yeltsin became the dominant leader, and after a crisis in 1993 he secured the adoption of a new constitution strengthening his office and weakening the parliament. The various democratic freedoms now prevail, including the freedom to organize political parties and compete in elections, but former communists (both hard-line and reformist) have influence in most of the states in what was the Soviet orbit.

The effort to switch from a centralized, command economy to a free-market system has involved grave disruption in Russia, with production declining, inflation becoming extreme, and crime becoming rampant. The standard of living in Russia is low and the future of the country is uncertain.

■ Reading

Cohen, Carl (1982) *Four Systems. Individualist Democracy, Socialist Democracy, Fascism, Communism.* New York: Random House.

Ludwikowski, Rett R. (1986) *The Crisis of Communism: Its Meaning, Origins, and Phases.* Washington, D.C.: Pergamon-Brassey's.

Roeder, Philip G. (1993) *Red Sunset: The Failure of Soviet Politics.* Princeton: Princeton University Press.

Salvetz, Carol R., and Anthony Jones, eds. (1994) *In Search of Pluralism. Soviet and Post-Soviet Politics.* Boulder: Westview Press.

Vaksberg, Arkady (1992) *The Soviet Mafia.* New York: St. Martin's Press.

White, Stephen (1993) *After Gorbachev.* New York: Cambridge University Press.

Communism and Socialism: China

China is flourishing economically, but not because of communism.

This is Brian Duffy's comment on the response of the communist government to a mass, student-led demonstration for democracy in Tiananmen Square in Beijing in 1989.

Communists completed their conquest of the mainland of China in 1949 and have ruled there ever since. In 1949 and for many years thereafter they were obviously devoted to Marxism-Leninism, supplementing it with the thought of Mao Zedong, who dominated the party and the government until his death in 1976. This means that they established a totalitarian system similar to that of the Soviet Union, nationalizing the means of production and distribution and engaging in central economic planning. Since Mao's death, although denying any abandonment of the faith and maintaining their political hegemony, the communists have gone far toward establishing what they call a socialist market economy. The object here is to describe and appraise these developments and their ideological implications.

■ Ideological Extremism

When the Chinese communists seized power they were inspired by a revolutionary élan comparable to that of the Bolsheviks in 1917. In Marxism-Leninism-Mao Zedong Thought they had what they regarded as a science that would guide them in remaking society. The existing order would give way to a socialist order in which class divisions and the class struggle would disappear, superseded by a collective effort to promote the general good. The nobility of the end justified the use of any means. Those standing in the way would have to be eliminated as enemies of the people.

And so the communist regime set about collectivizing agriculture and nationalizing industry and most of the rest of the economy. Collectivization involved attacks on landlords, "some millions" of them being killed. Within a decade, peasants, comprising more than three-quarters of the population of the country, were organized into communes in which they worked for wages, planting what they were told to plant and selling their "surplus" to the state at a price it fixed (Fairbank 1992, 350–52). Industry, too, came under control of the state, and a five-year plan for industrial progress was adopted.

Relatively quickly, the program led to one of the greatest catastrophes in history. In the late 1950s what might have been a second five-year plan became a Great Leap Forward—a frenzied effort at economic development in which the whole population was caught up. The feature of the program that got the most foreign publicity at the time was the construction of a million or so backyard iron smelters that turned out to be inefficient, producing little that was usable. Of more lasting benefit were new roads, dikes, dams, lakes, afforestation, factories, and even cities built by a people "mobilized in nationwide efforts of unparalleled intensity and magnitude" (Fairbank 1992, 371).

But 20 to 30 million rural people died. Crucial among the causes was the tendency of local authorities to fix overambitious agricultural goals and then to report overachievement, with the government then taking the "surplus." And since in fact the "surplus" was fictitious, the rural people were left to die, whether because of malnutrition or outright starvation. In a free society this could not have happened, at least not on the same scale; but with the party-government in control of the means of communication, the tragedy went unreported at the time, and pressures to avert or alleviate it never developed.

The disaster of the Great Leap Forward was implicitly a criticism of Mao Zedong. He was forewarned about attitudes toward him by the outcome of the Hundred Flowers campaign of 1956–57, so-called because of his brief support for open discussion: "Let a hundred flowers bloom together, let the hundred schools of thought contend." But when open discussion revealed serious discontent with his leadership, he clamped the lid on again and inaugurated an anti-Rightist campaign that included the branding of somewhere between 300,000 and 700,000 people as enemies of the people.

Now in 1966, given the manifest and gargantuan errors of the Great Leap Forward and fearing what he considered "revisionism," Mao lashed out, this time launching a Cultural Revolution, analogous to Stalin's purges of the 1930s. Mao's instruments were teenagers ("Red Guards") on whom he called to attack the Four Olds—old ideas, old culture, old customs, old habits. In effect, his call was for attacks on the educated elite, including members of the Communist party itself. Goaded on by Mao, the teenagers mounted "a brutal reign of terror, breaking into homes of the better off and the intellectuals and officials, destroying books and manuscripts, humiliating, beating and even killing the occupants." They roamed the streets, dealing out their conception of revolutionary justice. There was "an unprecedented wave of state-instigated persecution, torture, gang warfare, and mindless violence" based on the assumption that those attacked were enemies of the people. Three million intellectuals, scientists, officials, and skilled workers suffered some kind of persecution, 400,000 of them being done to death. About 60 percent of the officials of the party were purged (Fairbank 1992, 386–402; Goldman 1994, 28).

Nominally Mao Zedong called off the Cultural Revolution in 1968, disbanding the Red Guards, but it continued to a degree until his death in 1976. Among other things, it spread in the 1970s into the countryside, with peasants required to abandon all productive activities aimed at their direct benefit, like raising their own chickens and pigs. Uncertainties persisted even after Mao's death, for the so-called Gang of Four (including Mao's wife) were influential and radical; and even two years later the man who became premier called for slavish conformity with Mao Zedong Thought. But Deng Xiaoping, a victim of the Cultural Revolution, was rehabilitated in 1977, and within a year or so he and his associates were in firm control (Chi 1991, 3–4).

■ A Socialist Market Economy

Whether Deng Xiaoping had in mind a coherent plan for comprehensive reform when he rose to power is uncertain. Not daring and perhaps not wanting to repudiate Mao completely, he pled for flexibility. Pragmatism rather than dogmatism should prevail, and four modernizations should be the goal: in industry, in agriculture, in science and technology, and in national defense. What he wanted was economic development.

Deng began with agriculture, abolishing the commune system in favor of a "household responsibility system" that was akin to private ownership; households made contracts with the state to provide grain or some other product at a price fixed by the state, gaining freedom to sell on the open market whatever they produced over and above the contract amount. The change produced spectacular results, the farmers tripling their real income in eight years. Troubles have developed more recently as the prices of goods that the farmers must buy, like fertilizer, have gone up more than the prices of what they have to sell, but this is one of the possible implications of capitalism.

Other reforms followed in coming years: the legalization of nonstate enterprises, whether controlled by units of local government (township and village enterprises), by collectives, or by private owners; the creation of special economic zones where foreign-owned businesses can operate, perhaps in joint ventures with Chinese entrepreneurs; arrangements giving the managers of state-owned enterprises more incentive to operate efficiently and to give more attention to the quality of their products; the establishment of a capital market, with stocks and bonds bought and sold (Ding 1994, 166). Not that state enterprises were eliminated; they continue to operate and to provide a so-called "iron rice bowl" to many millions of workers and their families—welfare from the cradle to the grave. Most of them still depend on state subsidies.

But, although the state enterprises remain important, they are being engulfed by nonstate enterprises that have sprung up and flourished on the basis of Deng's reforms. By 1992 the prices of most sorts of goods in China, whether agricultural or industrial, had been decontrolled (Overholt 1993, 46). According to Doak Barnett, writing in 1993, "roughly two-thirds of the economy is no longer subject to centralized state planning, and roughly one-half of the output of even the industrial sector of the Chinese economy now comes not from state-owned enterprises but from urban collectives, township and village enterprises, private enterprises, and joint Chinese-foreign ventures" (Leng 1994, 8).

As in agriculture, so in the economy generally the results of the reforms are spectacular. Even during the horrifying years of the Great Leap Forward and the Cultural Revolution, China's GDP grew by something like 5 percent a year, and once the reforms took effect it grew by something like 9 to 10 percent a year, this in a period when economies in the West were thought to be doing well if they achieved a 3 percent growth rate. According to one calculation, per capita income in China quadrupled from 1978 to 1991 (Leng 1994, 172). Development is especially rapid in Guangdong province, adjacent to Hong Kong. From 1978 to 1990 the average annual growth rate there was just over 12 percent; in 1992 it was almost 20 percent. At the meeting of the National People's Congress in March 1995, the leadership claimed that the growth rate for all of China in 1994 was 11.8 percent.

Of course, China's economic development having started from a low base, a quadrupled standard of living is still a low standard of living. About 120 million rural Chinese live without electricity in their homes or villages. Between 50 and 100 million Chinese have left their homes in search of work and are not settled. In some regions unemployment rates are high. Nevertheless, extraordinary changes led one observer to say that "no other country has progressed more rapidly in improving people's lives over the past decade" (Overholt 1993, 143). At the rate the Chinese economy has been growing, it will be the biggest in the world (in aggregate but not per capita terms) early in the next century. China will be a superpower (Overholt 1993, 183).

The problem of state enterprises remains. Despite greater freedom and responsibility for their managers, they are generally inefficient; and they are burdened by the need to provide not only jobs but also, in most cases, housing, health care, pensions, and education. Thus, it is no wonder that they require governmental subsidies. But their share in the economy is declining relatively as the nonstate enterprises grow.

Contrasts between Russia and China are sharp, and, as indicated in the preceding chapter, the reasons are in dispute. Russia, along with some other states of the old Soviet sphere, attempted to shift to a market economy on a "big bang" basis, accepting "shock therapy," and the result everywhere is economic disorganization and sharp drops in output; standards of living have declined. In contrast, China is flourishing, with production and standards of living going up at a rapid pace. Overholt is confident that the differing strategies account for the differing results—that if Russia and the states of the Soviet sphere had reformed their economies on a gradualist rather than a "big bang" basis, they too would be flourishing (Overholt 1993, 37–44). Perhaps. Analysts will be probing the question for years to come. The peoples of the Soviet Union lived in a collectivist system far longer than the people of China—for seventy years rather than for about thirty—and this may have affected their inclination and capacity to adapt to a competitive market.

Although the economy of China is flourishing, its future is questionable. The fiscal and monetary policies of the government have led to a high rate of inflation; the consumer price inflation rate in 1994 is said to have been over 24 percent. One result is that, although foreign investment in China occurs, so does capital flight from China. Whether economic growth can be maintained is uncertain.

Further, widespread corruption accompanies economic development. Entrepreneurs sometimes get their results by bribery. Party members and government officials take advantage of opportunities to enrich themselves or to make riches available to relatives and friends, ignoring the law. Nepotism is widespread, the children of party members and government officials taking advantage of their connections to enrich themselves, becoming known as "princelings." On some occasions the government has cracked down, even executing persons whose offenses have been especially egregious, but it has not made equal treatment under law a reliable expectation. To a degree, corruption may help facilitate economic development in a transition period before laws and institutions are adequately adjusted to the new order, but surely it is corrosive and debilitating in the longer run.

■ The Ideological Stance

Although going far in the direction of a free market, the leaders of China talk in terms of socialism, not of capitalism, and they insist on keeping the Communist party in the leading role. Democratization is not on the horizon.

Along with the call for the four modernizations, Deng proclaims four cardinal principles: the socialist road, the dictatorship of the proletariat, the leadership of the Communist party, and Marxism-Leninism-Mao Zedong Thought (Goldman 1994, 50). Especially since the road he is actually taking looks more like capitalism than socialism, the question is why he insists on these principles and how likely it is that they will continue to get support.

Possibly Deng believes in the principles. Possibly he sees, either intuitively or in full self-consciousness, that Marxism-Leninism-Mao Zedong Thought is the only justification for a communist dictatorship, so he must claim to be upholding the ideology even while abandoning it. Possibly he thinks that continued rule by communists is the only way to assure stability and that stability is essential to economic development. In any event, developments in China are occurring in the name of "socialism."

The first formula that the communists used to reconcile their capitalist practices with their socialist theory, announced in 1987, was that China is in the primary or beginning stage of socialism, the implication being that practices were acceptable that would be superseded when subsequent stages were reached; but the intimations were that the primary stage might last 100 years (Ding 1994, 172). Later Deng advanced another formula: that what China seeks is "socialism with Chinese characteristics." Both formulas have the advantage of vagueness: they permit the adoption of virtually any policy the party or its leaders want and the rejection of almost anything they do not want. What they desire, they can justify either as socialist or as giving socialism a distinctive Chinese characteristic; and what they oppose they can condemn either as nonsocialist or as alien to China.

The shift toward a market economy encouraged many to hope for and to demand some kind or degree of democratization. Deng himself gave mixed signals. He declared in 1978 that "democracy has to be institutionalized and written into law . . . . These laws should be discussed and adopted through democratic procedures." Later, although decrying "spiritual pollution," he intimated a relaxed attitude about ideological purity in declaring that "it does not matter whether a cat is black or white, as long as it catches mice." In stressing economic development, Deng in effect called off the class struggle, which means that he at least suspended one of the major requirements of Marxism-Leninism.

Further, Deng supported policies and practices that allowed hope for democracy to develop. The National People's Congress of 1979, wanting to oust Maoist officials, endorsed competitive elections for local people's congresses, and at least on some occasions multiple candidates competed for election to the Central Committee of the party itself (Goldman 1994, 13, 47, 60). Two successive general secretaries of the Communist party, who surely did not think of themselves as going against Deng, encouraged democratic hopes, looking benignly on a "democratic elite [that] increasingly emphasized the need to introduce democratic institutions as a means of curbing the party's power" (Goldman 1994, 2, 25). They permitted substantial freedom of speech and even, in some degree, freedom of the press, and they opened China to greater influence from abroad (Leng 1994, 13). In the spring of 1989 the government tolerated a huge forum at People's University with free and open debate about the relative merits of democracy and "neo-authoritarianism," both sides agreeing that the goal should be a market economy, a strong middle class, ideological and interest pluralism, and democracy (Goldman 1994, 282). Many of those agitating for reform were members of the Communist party itself (Chi 1991, 269).

But toleration of pro-democratic activities had limits. Already in 1979 Deng closed down the "Democracy Wall" in Beijing, on which people had displayed posters that he regarded as antiparty and counterrevolutionary. Another crackdown occurred in 1986–87, including the expulsion of dissidents from the party and the removal of the general secretary, who was judged to be too indulgent (Goldman 1994, 203–207, 214–15).

Then, in 1989, came the demonstration on behalf of democracy in Tiananmen Square in Beijing, continuing for several weeks. On some days a million persons were involved. Two thousand or more students went on a hunger strike, demanding concessions. But Deng decided to crack down. He concluded that this Democracy Movement was a challenge to the Communist party, threatening the country with chaos, and he called in the military, killing hundreds of demonstrators (over a thousand?), wounding many more, and later imprisoning the surviving leaders or forcing them to flee abroad.

Surprisingly enough, however, the party-government reverted to a quasi-tolerant policy after Tiananmen. William Overholt's interpretation is that the party so desperately needs the help of intellectuals that it must permit them to express critical thoughts in public debate. In any event, speech and press are more or less free. Communication with the outside world is open. Elections at the local level continue to be competitive, with party candidates "losing . . . in droves." "Organized dissidence and published criticism of the leadership of the Communist party brings immediate repression, [but] . . . the party says as long as you don't curse us, and as long as you don't demand that we step down, you can say anything you want" (Overholt 1993, 138–41). But Asia Watch reports that in 1994 500 of the Tiananmen protesters, including the principal leader of the democracy movement, remained in prison.

What the Chinese communists seem to be saying is that, although they will permit voters to reject some local candidates and will permit a measure of free speech, they will not permit direct challenge to the party's control over the country. They will not permit a competing party to operate, except in local elections where they themselves decide whether to tolerate competition and, if so, how much. They have control and intend to keep it.

■ Is Democracy Coming?

Several scenarios are plausible. One is that the party will succeed in maintaining its control for the indefinite future, resorting to repression and massacres as necessary. This assumes that the leadership of the party remains substantially united and confident of its right to rule. Moreover, it assumes that the party continues to have the loyal support of the military. The record of the communists in the Soviet Union and eastern and southeastern Europe suggests that the first of these assumptions is fragile, but the fact that the Chinese communists have been doing so much better economically may reinforce their belief in their right to rule. Further, they can appeal to nationalism, whereas the communists of the Soviet Union and Europe could not. And the Confucian tradition does more to support authoritarian rule than to call for democracy.

A second scenario has China breaking up. Deng's reforms involve extensive decentralization, which means a relative weakening of the government in Beijing. Some provinces are developing economically at a much faster pace than others. Some have already resorted to economic protectionism, restricting imports. China's record, notably in the first half of this century, is one of provincial war-lordism. All this makes it thinkable that decentralization might go so far as to leave the central government with little power. The extreme would be the breakup of the country.

A third scenario has China developing into a democracy. The argument is that economic development has ineluctable political consequences. A managerial class tends to come to the fore, concerned with the practical problems of growth more than with the achievement of some messianic goal. Educated administrators gain increasing importance. A middle class gets larger and larger, and more and more people get more and more education, including more and more knowledge of the outer world. The practical, educated people, having little faith in ideologues, seek a share in decision making for themselves, above all when it is so clear that the ideologues have made egregious mistakes and have themselves abandoned the part of their ideology that relates to economic life. Fewer people of ability become ideologues, for an ideology that leads to disaster is unattractive, and the remaining ideologues come to hold fewer and fewer offices and have to share decision making with more and more others. More and more of those who join and lead the party do it for careerist reasons, not out of idealism, and thus are motivated more by self-interest than by dedication to a cause. They and others tend increasingly to switch the emphasis to nationalism. Perhaps gradually, perhaps in a crisis of major proportions, the ideologues lose out and the democrats come to the fore.

The statement should perhaps be that "democrats" come to the fore, thus acknowledging a question about the meaning and appropriateness of the word. It is uncertain how many of those in China who call for "democracy" want democracy in the Western sense or even have a clear understanding of the word. In *Sowing the Seeds of Democracy in China*, Merle Goldman keeps referring to "the democratic elite" without saying just what makes this elite democratic. The debate on which she dwells is between those calling for rule by "the democratic elite" (or perhaps the "educated elite") and those espousing "neo-authoritarianism," none of these terms being given a clear meaning. Ding, dealing with the same subject, speaks of an intellectual elite and a political elite sharing power in an "elite democracy" that would pave the way for a "popular democracy" (Ding 1994, 44). Overholt says that some of those calling for "democracy" are really calling for a right to oppose certain evils, like inflation, corruption, and nepotism. "Most are infinitely more concerned about enlarging the scope of personal freedom than about electoral democracy. . . . These groups are terribly serious about reform, but not necessarily . . . about democracy in its Western form." Overholt's own view is that "economic reform precedes freedom, and freedom precedes democracy." He thinks that the West has it wrong in calling for democracy first (Overholt 1993, 99–100, 126). Others speak of "a distinctive 'Asian' path to reform, in which economic reform and growth come first, major changes in society follow, and political pluralization leading to ultimate democracy comes later, with a lag of perhaps 20 to 30 years" (Leng 1994, 12).

In any event, the argument is that regardless of the intentions of those who bring about economic development, the more they succeed the more likely it is that democracy will some day develop. Those making the argument point especially to South Korea and Taiwan, where authoritarian governments presided over economic development and where authoritarianism has given way to democratic systems. For that matter, as indicated in chapter 10, the history of many democratic countries shows a sequence from authoritarianism to democracy, with economic development playing a role in the transition; and the history of many democratic countries shows a sequence from a restricted to a universal suffrage.

■ Socialism

The word *socialism* has appeared frequently in this chapter and in the preceding one. A word concerning it is thus in order.

The word has many meanings. Here I will start with the meaning assigned to it by the Fabian Society of Britain and the British Labour party in the first half of this century. They were critical of capitalism, wanting to replace it with socialism. They criticized capitalism because of its emphasis on the private ownership of property and the profit motive and thus its emphasis on selfishness and greed. They assumed that the hiring of workers meant the exploitation of workers and therefore injustice. They were appalled by poverty and squalor in the midst of relative plenty and dismayed by the thought that under capitalism the highest human qualities of so many people are never fully developed. And they assumed that the owners and managers derived unfair and unearned advantage from the system.

The Fabians and the British Labour party sought a cure for these evils. Their basic concern was with *equality*—equality of opportunity, to be sure, but, even more, a greater degree of equality of economic condition. And like the French revolutionaries who called for liberty, equality, and fraternity, they concerned themselves with brotherhood. "One gets at the heart of [their] ethical message with the concept of fellowship" (Beer 1982, 128).

The Fabians and the Labour party called for an emphasis on serving, not on selfishness—on the "obligation to create conditions which will enhance the ability of all to live and live well." They wanted to replace the private ownership of the means of production with public ownership and wanted production to be for use and not for profit. They wanted to replace private enterprise with collective enterprise, partly to reduce the role of greed. They wanted to reduce competition for private advantage and replace it with cooperation aimed at the common good. Thus, they hoped to eliminate the exploitation of man by man, to improve the lot of the masses, and to stimulate a flowering of the personalities and talents of a much higher proportion of the population.

In the above respects, the Fabians and the Labour party did not differ sharply from the Marxist-Leninists. The big difference is that the Fabians and the Labour party did not take the view that the end justifies the means. They accepted both moral and legal rules concerning the treatment of people and concerning the methods that are acceptable in political struggle. Their socialism had a human face from the beginning, with a commitment to evolutionary, persuasive, and democratic methods. They sought power through elections and were prepared to give it up if they lost a subsequent election. They abjured violence.

The differences between the Fabian socialists and Marxist-Leninists relate more to means than to ends. Marxist-Leninists see no need to restrict themselves to democratic means. In fact, as the discussion of Lenin in the preceding chapter indicates, they view this as a prescription for defeat. They call for revolution and, more broadly, for the use of any means necessary to victory: the end justifies the means. And the result in both the Soviet Union and China is that those guided by Marxism-Leninism—supplemented in China by Mao Zedong Thought—have killed or caused the death of people by the tens of millions. And after all that, they found that publicly owned and planned economies do not provide for human needs as well as market economies. In the Soviet Union the discovery led to the abdication of the communists, and in China it led them to switch toward support for a market system.

The discrediting of the public ownership of the means of production and of economic planning leaves communists in a quandary. In Europe the tendency has been for communist parties to change their names, to pledge themselves to democratic methods, and to endorse the market system. In China the communists go on ruling even after abandoning a central feature of their program.

Noncommunist socialists are in a quandary, too. The British Labour party illustrates the fact in that until 1995 Clause Four of its constitution called for the "common ownership of the means of production, distribution, and exchange." This idea having been discredited, the chance that the Labour Party would ever implement it has long been remote. But in 1994, when the new party leader, Tony Blair, asked the party conference to endorse the repeal of Clause Four, it refused. Later he had his way, but the struggle illustrates the difficulty parties have in giving up what has long been a central feature of their programs.

Their best course is perhaps to seek fellowship or brotherhood in a different way. Sweden, which has been governed by its Social Democratic party most of the time for more than half a century, provides a possible example. It has not engaged in nationalization to any extent, but it intervenes in the economy in other ways. Providing for the usual social security and social welfare services, its claim to distinction lies in the lengths to which it goes to minimize unemployment. It operates an employment service, helping to place workers in jobs and helping with moving costs if relocation is involved. Moreover, it trains and if necessary re-trains those seeking employment. The program costs, the government taking approximately half of the GDP in taxes and requiring those with the highest incomes to pay more than three-fourths of what they earn. But social solidarity is maintained, and the Swedish standard of living is well above the average in the countries of western Europe. Success is made easier because the workers of Sweden are highly organized and because the unions and management have come to an accommodation concerning wage policies.

As Swedish tax policies suggest, socialists are concerned about gross disparities in income but they do not seek to equalize conditions of life. Levels of equality and inequality correlate much more with the level of economic development in a country than with the ideology of those who control the government. Inequality tends to go down as the level of economic development goes up (Dye and Zeigler 1988).

■ Review

Marxism-Leninism, supplemented by Mao Zedong Thought, inspired the Chinese communists when they seized power in 1949, just as it inspired the Bolsheviks, and it led even more quickly to disaster. After killing several million of the richer farmers in connection with collectivization, the Beijing regime went on to kill 20 to 30 million more through malnutrition and starvation in connection with the Great Leap Forward of the late 1950s. Then in 1966 it launched the Cultural Revolution, which was mainly an attack on the more educated Chinese, including a substantial portion of the members of the Communist party itself. The horrors lasted until Mao's death in 1976.

Deng Xioaping and his associates rose to the top in China after the death of Mao. Although insisting on "cardinal principles" that call for dictatorship, Deng champions "four modernizations"; and to achieve them he has gradually reduced economic controls, shifting toward an endorsement of a free market. Even during the period of Mao's horrors, China's GNP grew remarkably, and since Deng's reforms it has been growing phenomenally. The contrast with economic developments in Russia and the former communist countries of Europe is sharp. If the growth continues, China will be a superpower in the visible future.

Believing itself threatened by a movement for democracy that led to mass demonstrations in Tiananmen Square in Beijing in 1989, the Deng regime called in the army, obviously determined to maintain authoritarian communist control no matter how many it needed to kill. But it allows freedom of speech and press up to the point where it considers its hold on power threatened.

The Chinese communists say they seek "socialism with Chinese characteristics." Here and elsewhere, the word *socialism* lacks clear meaning. It is historically identified with a search for fellowship or brotherhood and a belief that fellowship or brotherhood can be achieved through public ownership and management of the means of production and distribution—a belief that is now discredited.

■ Reading

Baum, Richard (1994) *Burying Mao. Chinese Politics in the Age of Deng Xiaoping.* Princeton: Princeton University Press.

Chi, Hsi-Sheng (1991) *Politics of Disillusionment. The Chinese Communist Party Under Deng Xiaoping 1978–1989.* Armonk, N.Y.: M.E. Sharpe.

Ding, X. L. (1994) *The Decline of Communism in China. Legitimacy Crisis, 1977–89.* New York: Cambridge University Press.

Kristof, Nicholas D., and Sheryl Wudunn (1994) *China Wakes. The Struggle for the Soul of a Rising Power.* New York: Times Books.

Leng, Shao-chuan, ed. (1994) *Reform and Development in Deng's China.* Lanham, Md.: University Press of America.

MacFarquhar, Roderick, ed. (1993) *The Politics of China 1949–1989.* New York: Cambridge University Press.

Overholt, William H. (1993) *The Rise of China. How Economic Reform is Creating a New Superpower.* New York: Norton.

Schell, Orville (1994) *Mandate of Heaven. A New Generation of Entrepreneurs, Dissidents, Bohemians, and Technocrats Lays Claim to China's Future.* New York: Simon and Schuster.

Tu Wei-ming, ed. (1994) *China in Transformation.* Cambridge: Harvard University Press.

What do these contrasting views of FDR suggest about his relationship to progressive liberalism?

Progressive Liberalism

Roosevelt championed "a changed concept of the duty and responsibility of Government toward economic life."

Free enterprise and laissez-faire lead to problems, as noted in chapter 18. They do not provide for national defense, for protecting people from harm, for constructing public works and developing public institutions, or for concerted efforts to stimulate economic growth and to keep the economy going in high gear. They do not call for action to meet a variety of needs, such as those relating to public order, education, roads and bridges, poverty, unemployment, health and safety, and so on. Adam Smith himself did not recommend laissez faire pure and simple. He specifically approved governmental action in a number of the areas named above; and the new liberals of Britain went beyond him in seeking an activist government, one that attempted to solve social problems or ameliorate social conditions.

In the United States the problems associated with free enterprise and laissez-faire got increasing attention throughout the nineteenth century. A number of the state governments became catalysts of economic development, granting exclusive franchises and charters, providing venture capital, and setting limits on competition through the regulation of private undertakings (Lipset 1963: 48–54). They began to establish and maintain schools at all levels, and they adopted legislation designed to give various kinds of protection to consumers.

And the federal government involved itself in development efforts, too. It made land grants to promote education and to assist in the building of railway lines. It established the Interstate Commerce Commission, adopted antitrust laws, set aside forest preserves and national parks, and developed a national banking system. During World War I it intervened massively in economic life to mobilize military power. And then came the Great Depression, bringing the question of laissez-faire versus governmental intervention to the top of the political agenda.

President Hoover acknowledged the problems that the Great Depression created but responded in such meager fashion that the voters refused to re-elect him in 1932. Franklin D. Roosevelt took his place, championing a New Deal and later describing himself as a "liberal." I am calling his ideology *progressive liberalism*, and my object in this chapter is to analyze its characteristics and some of the pro and con arguments relating to it. It remained the dominant ideology in US political life until the election of Ronald Reagan as president in 1980.

■ The Great Depression _____

The 1920s were years of optimism and growth in the United States, except in agriculture, which faced chronic problems; but unemployment began to increase and output to decrease in the summer of 1929, and a stock market crash occurred in October. Unemployment rose sharply thereafter—from 3.2 percent of the labor force in 1929 to almost 25 percent in 1933—and the number of workers holding only part-time jobs rose proportionately. The GNP declined even more than the number employed, dropping by 1933 to 70 percent of the 1929 level. Corporations that enjoyed net profits of $10 billion in 1929 suffered net losses of $2 billion in 1932. Millions of business firms, farmers, and households were unable to pay their taxes or their debts. By the end of 1932 more than one out of every five banks had failed, and most of the others were closed when Roosevelt took office (Chandler 1970, 1–9). A great many local governments and even a number of state governments were unable to meet their financial obligations (Patterson 1969, 31).

The psychological impact of the Depression was also severe. Unemployment was of short duration for some, to be sure, but many others who sought work were rebuffed over so long a period of time that they lost hope. Even those who were employed were likely to be living in straitened circumstances and to find it oppressive to witness the distress of so many others. The general climate was one of fear and despair (Allswang 1978, 6–7).

■ The Responses of Hoover and Roosevelt

President Hoover, in office from 1929 until 1933, could not ignore the Depression, and he championed some legislation designed to alleviate it. His most notable measure was the establishment of the Reconstruction Finance Corporation (RFC), which, by making money available through loans, mainly to banks, mitigated the severity of the Depression; and it was in his administration that the Agricultural Marketing Act was adopted, giving the federal government a role in the attempt to alleviate the distress of the farmers.

But although these measures were important, they were meager in light of the needs. Necessarily acknowledging that many people were in dire want, Hoover stressed the virtues and the obligation of private charity. He quoted a statement by Grover Cleveland that " 'though people support the Government, the Government should not support the people. . . . Federal aid . . . encourages the expectation of paternal care on the part of the Government and weakens the sturdiness of our national character.' " People should "fight their own battles in their own communities." Action by the federal government would threaten the foundations of local government—the very basis of self-government.

Hoover favored unemployment insurance, but only if offered by private firms; governmental unemployment insurance would turn into a dole, and the net result would be to "endow the slacker." The objective, he said, should be "the least possible Government entry into the economic field, and then only in temporary and emergency form. . . . Economic wounds must be healed by action of the cells of the economic body" (Myers 1934, I, 429–30, 496–97, 502, 579).

Hoover is reported to have made a campaign statement likening life to a race:

> We, through free and universal education, provide the training of the runners; we give them an equal start; we provide in government the umpire of fairness in the race. The winner is he who shows the most conscientious training, the greatest ability, and the greatest character (Hofstadter 1948, 294).

Note the claim that people have an equal start, that government is a neutral umpire, that the personal qualities and efforts of the competitors alone determine their fate, nothing beyond their control having an effect, and that government has no moral obligation relating to the outcome. Hoover's view was that those thrown out of work by the Depression were losers in a system of fair competition. Let their failure test their mettle! Or, if they had to have help, let it come from neighbors or, at worst, from local governments. As I will note in the next chapter, Friedrich Hayek, whose writings inspire the libertarians, takes a similar view.

Roosevelt held views that were different though vague. He lacked a clear and coherent ideology or philosophy, and he was inconsistent in what he said and did, but strands of thought that showed up at an early point later became dominant. Most outstanding was his championship of activism on the part of government—his belief that government, and most notably the federal government, had an obligation to try to revive the economy and stimulate growth. And he held that government should also take direct measures to alleviate distress. Government was an appropriate instrument to use in attacking problems and promoting progress.

Roosevelt gave intimations of his outlook while he was still governor of New York. "What is the State?" he asked; and he answered that it is the instrument of an organized society of human beings, "created by them for their mutual protection and well-being." Government is the machinery through which "mutual aid and protection" are achieved (*Public Papers*, Roosevelt, I:457– 58). As president, Roosevelt took the view that government "owes the definite obligation to prevent the starvation or the dire want of any of its fellow men and women who try to maintain themselves but cannot." Moreover, he found it unacceptable to leave the burden to local governments, for in many cases they were the least able to bear it; state governments and the federal government itself must play a role.

Roosevelt contrasted the "old philosophy" of laissez-faire with a new philosophy aimed at "social justice through social action." He saw "one-third of a nation ill-housed, ill-clad, ill-nourished," and he declared poverty "largely preventable." He thought of government as the appropriate agency for meeting these challenges. If governmental action meant paternalism, he was willing to be paternalistic (*Public Papers*, Roosevelt, I:772, 776; VI:5).

In line with the above, Roosevelt called for a New Deal—"a changed concept of the duty and responsibility of Government toward economic life" (*Public Papers*, Roosevelt, I:782). With the support of Congress, he championed various measures relating to economic recovery and the regulation of business, old age and unemployment insurance, the creation of job opportunities, and welfare.

■ New Deal Measures

The measures aimed at economic recovery and the regulation of business were varied. The most flamboyant was the NRA (the National Recovery Administration), which repudiated laissez-faire in wholesale fashion. It sought to stimulate recovery mainly through what amounted to cartels—agreements among potential competitors concerning the rules of fair competition, wages and hours, and labor-management relations (Romasco 1983, 188–89). Whether it did more to stimulate than to impede recovery is in dispute, but it marked the exercise by the federal government of a major economic role. The Supreme Court declared it unconstitutional in 1935.

The New Deal also included both the continuation of the RFC and an extension of the program to help farmers—the extension taking form in the Agricultural Adjustment Administration (AAA). The AAA was based on the view that overproduction was the source of the farmer's difficulties and that, with respect to selected crops, the government should seek to solve the problem by paying the farmers to reduce the acreage devoted to them.

A number of other measures also provided either for direct governmental participation in economic life or for the regulation of private enterprises. Prominent among them was the National Labor Relations Act, protecting trade-union rights and requiring collective bargaining. There were also the Housing Act, the Railroad Retirement Act, the Banking Act, the Public Utility Holding Company Act, and the Homeowner's Loan Act, and acts setting up a series of operational or regulatory agencies: the Federal Deposit Insurance Corporation, the Securities and Exchange Commission, the Federal Communications Commission, the Rural Electrification Administration, and the Tennessee Valley Authority.

Of special significance, too, was the Social Security Act of 1935, providing for old-age and unemployment insurance. Both depended on a payroll tax, with the worker and employer each paying a share. The revenue went into a general fund that was drawn upon to provide benefits to the unemployed and the retired. Although there was no separate piggy bank for each person, the arrangement encouraged the view that those who paid into the system during their working years established an entitlement to benefits when they themselves became unemployed or reached retirement age. They were regarded not as recipients of charity but as persons who had paid for what they later got.

The principal agencies providing jobs for people who presumably would otherwise have been unemployed were the Civilian Conservation Corps (CCC), the Public Works Administration (PWA), and the Works Progress Administration (WPA)—all temporary and all terminated before the end of the 1930s.

Finally, various measures provided for "welfare." I put the word in quotation marks because it has come to have at least two meanings. When it is used alone, it has come to refer to governmental assistance to the poor in cash or in kind, and it is based on a means test. In contrast, when the word is used in the expression "the welfare state," it includes not only means-tested assistance to the poor but also benefits that go to people regardless of their income level, such as social security. For that matter, public support for an educational system is sometimes included as an aspect of "the welfare state."

The New Deal included provisions for "welfare," extended mainly through grants-in-aid to the states to help them provide relief for the poor among the elderly, dependent children, and the blind and to help them promote maternal and child welfare and vocational rehabilitation.

All these measures indicate that Roosevelt's outlook differed sharply from Hoover's. And Roosevelt gave further evidence of the fact in his state-of-the-union message in 1944 when he proclaimed that the country had accepted a second bill of rights: the right to a job—a job that pays enough to provide adequate food, clothing, and recreation; the right of the farmer to a decent living; the right of the businessman to be free from unfair competition; the right to a decent home, to an education, and to adequate medical care; and the right to protection from the economic fears of old age, accident, and unemployment (*Public Papers*, Roosevelt, XIII:41). In describing these as *rights* he was in effect saying that government is obliged to take action giving effect to them.

The claim that the country had accepted the second bill of rights was at best questionable. Votes in favor of measures designed to create jobs, for example, did not necessarily reflect a recognition of a right to work. You can support a policy without thinking that in so doing you are responding to a claim of right.

■ Roosevelt's Ideology

Roosevelt had a problem in naming his ideology. He might have called himself a progressive, but that term was suggestive of Republicans like Theodore Roosevelt and Robert LaFollette (Rotunda 1968, 390). He might have called himself a social democrat, but that term had European connotations suggestive of socialism. What he did was to call himself a *lib-*

eral, a term that had so far been little used in US political debate (Beer 1965, 144; Beer 1978, 14), and he came to insist that his principal opponents, mainly Republicans, be called *conservative* (*Public Papers*, Roosevelt, VII,1938: xxix). Opponents were slow in accepting the label, but eventually they did.

Had Roosevelt wished to do so, he could have identified his program with the new liberalism of Britain, but in fact he did nothing to invoke the British tradition. It was Hoover who did, insisting for a time that he, not Roosevelt, was the true liberal. Hoover obviously had classical liberalism in mind.

A summary statement of the principal characteristics of Roosevelt's progressive liberalism may be helpful. The underlying assumption was that a national community existed with problems that were national in scope. Equally important was an activist outlook on government, an assumption that government—notably the federal government—should take a leading role in trying to solve economic and social problems and advance the public good. The problems with which he was primarily concerned were the ones brought to the fore by the Depression and by World War II, but the principles apply to the problems of any time. Government, Roosevelt assumed, should promote higher levels of prosperity, finance public works, regulate business activities, sponsor insurance programs to protect people against some of the hazards of life, provide jobs in times of high unemployment, and help the needy. In war government should mobilize economic power as necessary.

In addition to defining problems as national and emphasizing the role of government, especially the federal government, Roosevelt's liberalism included a welcoming attitude toward change—a search for progress through reform. Not that Roosevelt or his advisers had a well-thought-out and coherent plan of attack on the Depression when he took office, but he was determined to act and to be optimistic about the probable consequences. If things were going badly under one dispensation, he would seek another. After all, something might work, and it was better to act, even if on a trial-and-error basis, than to do nothing.

Roosevelt did not explicitly emphasize either liberty or equality. Implicitly, his policies suggest that he valued liberty (individual freedom), but they suggest even more that he was not satisfied when conditions deprived liberty of its worth. This means that he was not satisfied with the negative view that a person is free in the absence of restraint or coercion. He said implicitly that such negative freedom is not enough and that, if need be, government should act to give worth to freedom, perhaps by seeing to it that jobs become available. The effort to give worth to freedom for one person might require that some kind of cost be imposed on another, probably in the form of a tax, and Roosevelt was willing for this to happen. He took it for granted that the income tax should be progressive.

As to equality, the main questions related to the blacks and to the poor, and in both connections Roosevelt's record was mixed. To get the legislation that he wanted from Congress, he usually needed the votes of conservatives, including southern senators who supported white supremacy, so a sharp attack on Jim Crow practices would have been costly. The upshot was that he did not issue a clear and sweeping challenge to racial discrimination.

But he—and his wife—offered limited challenges. The rule in some PWA projects was that blacks must be employed on a proportional basis, and toward the end of World War II Roosevelt issued an executive order prohibiting racial discrimination in defense industries. Moreover, when the Daughters of the American Revolution refused to allow a black, Marian Anderson, to sing in Constitution Hall, Eleanor Roosevelt arranged for her to do it at the Lincoln Memorial.

The result was that blacks tended to shift their support from the Republican to the Democratic party, but the fact that they would do this on the basis of such meager action to uphold their rights is mainly evidence of the grossness of the discrimination that they had been suffering. Roosevelt's support for the rule of equal treatment was limited.

The same is true of his attitude toward the poor. He wanted to improve the lot of the "forgotten man," and thus to reduce the gap between the rich and the poor; he favored equality of opportunity (for white men) and denounced the "money changers" and the "economic royalists," but he was obviously not a leveler. It would give a false impression to speak of him as an egalitarian.

The appeal of Roosevelt's program and thus of progressive liberalism was made all the stronger in the 1930s by the lack of an attractive alternative. The Great Depression was so severe that it was difficult for anyone to argue on behalf of maintaining or restoring the system that had brought it on. The rule of laissez-faire in a free market seemed to have failed. The argument developed later that government shared the blame for the failure—the claim being that the Federal Reserve Board responded to the stock market crash in precisely the wrong way and therefore accentuated the Depression. But this was not the belief at the time. The New Deal had its opponents, of course, but they were disorganized and were not in agreement on an alternative ideology or public philosophy.

Participation in World War II added to the strength of progressive liberalism. The war was obviously a national problem, and the waging of it strengthened inclinations to think in national terms and to look to the federal government for action. If the government could champion a collective purpose in foreign affairs and intervene in economic life to achieve it, then why should it not do the same in the domestic realm?

■ The Growth of Government

Roosevelt's "changed concept of the duty and responsibility of Government toward economic life" came to be widely accepted. Through the years after World War II, Democrats tended to support it more fully than Republicans, but for long it was not much of a partisan issue. Both parties accepted the view that it is the business of government to avert or minimize recessions and to stimulate economic growth. Republican administrations were about as likely as Democratic administrations to expand regulatory and welfare programs, to sponsor public works, to rely on a progressive income tax, and to use the government as a means of promoting national goals, including economic goals. Running as the Republican candidate for president in 1964, Goldwater rejected the consensus that had developed concerning the role of government, but he was roundly defeated.

Given such attitudes, government played a more and more important role in national life and grew accordingly. The land grant universities and the county agents helped bring about a revolution in agriculture, vastly expanding agricultural production. The National Institutes of Health, operating in part through research grants to universities, brought striking progress in the field of medicine. The Department of Defense and NASA, operating in part through contracts with universities and private concerns and grants to them, stimulated a technological revolution, notably in the development of computer chips and aircraft.

The federal government took the lead in the development of the interstate highway system and played a major role in developing airports and regulating the airlines. After *Sputnik*, it adopted not only the space program but also a National Defense Education Act. It took on major roles in other fields, establishing such agencies as the National Science Foundation, the National Endowment for the Humanities, and the National Endowment for the Arts. And it adopted measures to protect the environment, to protect consumers, to promote occupational safety, and so on.

Further, the programs identified with a welfare state expanded in terms of both the number of people covered and the costs. The Old Age Insurance program of 1935 continues as OASDI (Old Age, Survivors, and Disability Insurance). At the end of 1950, it was paying out $1 billion in benefits to 3.5 million persons, and at the end of 1992, $286 billion to 41.5 million persons (*Statistical Abstract* 1994, Table 582).

Similarly, the Aid to Dependent Children (ADC) program of 1935 continues as Aid to Families with Dependent Children (AFDC), and it has also expanded phenomenally. In 1950 it was providing aid to fewer than a million persons, but by 1992 the number had risen to 13.7 million. Costs have grown accordingly, rising in 1992 to a total for the federal and state governments of almost $25 billion (*Statistical Abstract* 1994, Table 577). In addition, beneficiaries are automatically eligible for Medicaid and food stamps.

AFDC is not popular. Designed to give aid to children in poverty, it has come to be thought of as giving aid to mothers, frequently to unmarried mothers, who are disproportionately black. These mothers go on "welfare," and it is easy for critics to charge that "welfare" encourages both imprudence and indolence on their part. The evidence indicates that factors other than the welfare payments account for the trend toward single-parent families and for the unemployment of women, but the thought that the availability of welfare plays a role is plausible enough to be widely believed (Ellwood 1988, 57–61, 68). The fact that about two-thirds of those aided are children tends to be forgotten.

Roosevelt tried but failed to get congressional support for a health insurance program. In 1950, however, Congress offered matching funds to states providing medical care for those on welfare, and ten years later it extended its offer to include support for state-run programs of medical care for the elderly poor. The major decision, however, came in 1965, when Congress amended the Social Security Act of 1935 to provide for Medicare and Medicaid.

Medicare is a health insurance program administered by the federal government. It covers all those on social security (mainly the elderly and people with disabilities) and end-state renal dialysis patients. Medicaid, in contrast, depends on taxes, not on insurance premiums, and provides for the poor.

In 1960 the federal, state, and local governments spent $6.4 billion for health and medical care. Then with the adoption of Medicare and Medicaid the costs began rising, reaching a total for the federal and state governments of about $275 billion by 1993 (*Green Book* 1994, pp. 125, 796).

Congress provided for Medicare and Medicaid during the presidency of Lyndon B. Johnson. Johnson calls for a special mention in connection with welfare legislation, for in his first state-of-the-union message he followed the example set by Lloyd George of Britain in 1909, calling for a "war on poverty."

What legislative and other measures ought to be counted as shots fired in the war on poverty is a question. Johnson launched the war by sponsoring several measures, especially the Economic Opportunity Act of 1964 and the Elementary and Secondary Education Act of 1965. They provided for the expansion of a few existing programs and the inauguration of a few new ones: programs to provide training and work experience to teenagers and to retrain unemployed workers; a program to provide legal services to the poor; a program to give poor children a better educational start in life (Head Start) and to help them make the jump from high school into college (Upward Bound); and support for public school systems. The Office of Economic Opportunity (OEO) was set up to administer or coordinate most of the programs.

The OEO programs were badly funded. Patterson comments that if all the OEO money had gone directly to the poor as income—and most of it did not—each poor person in the United States would have received around $50 to $70 per year. "Most poor people have had no contact with it, except perhaps to hear the promises of a better life to come. . . ." Perhaps no government program in modern US history promised so much more than it delivered (Patterson 1986, 151). If the OEO programs are the only ones counted in the war on poverty, it is not far off the mark to say that the war was never fought (Matusow 1984, 270). If you want to count social security and Medicare as parts of the war on poverty, then the amount spent goes up as indicated above, and the conclusion must be that this part of the war has been a signal success: poverty among the elderly has been sharply reduced.

■ Equal Treatment

In discussing Roosevelt and the New Deal above, I noted that Roosevelt did little to promote equal treatment. Nevertheless, a concern for human well-being was at the heart of the New Deal and set the stage for action on behalf of the equal enjoyment of civil and political rights.

The civil rights campaign of the 1960s triggered the action that the federal government took. Blacks in Montgomery, Alabama, got national attention in boycotting the municipal bus system, and blacks elsewhere got national attention through sit-ins at lunch counters and by staging marches and other demonstrations—all in protest against racial discrimination. And blacks insisted that schools be integrated in accordance with the judgment of the Supreme Court that segregation was unconstitutional. Lyndon Johnson responded to the challenge, inducing Congress to enact the Civil Rights Act of 1964 and later the Voting Rights Act of 1965. Like the classical liberals and the libertarians, he accepted freedom for the individual as a fundamental value, but he rejected the negative conception of freedom associated with classical liberalism, aligning himself instead with those concerned with positive liberty or with the worth of liberty.

"It is not enough," he said, "just to open the gates of opportunity. All our citizens must have the ability to walk through those gates." With the blacks in mind, he went on:

> You do not take a person who, for years, has been hobbled by chains and liberate him, bring him up to the starting line of a race and then say, "You are free to compete with all the others," and still believe that you have been completely fair. . . . We seek not just legal equity but human ability, not just equality as a right and a theory but equality as a fact and equality as a result (*Public Papers*, Johnson 1965, II: 636).

The words lend themselves to differing interpretations. They clearly reject a purely negative conception of freedom. They seem to call for some kind of remedial action to reduce the extent to which disadvantages created by past discrimination are carried into the future. They at least call for action to assure equality of opportunity.

Why Johnson spoke of equality of result is a puzzle, for he made it clear that he was not aiming to eliminate differences of income or status. Rather, he wanted "to give 20 million Negroes the same chance as every other American . . . ."

The Civil Rights Act and the Voting Rights Act were the most tangible expressions of Johnson's new deal for blacks—and for other minorities and women. Along with decisions of the Supreme Court based on the equal protection clause of the Fourteenth Amendment, these measures provided the legal basis for the equal treatment aspect of Johnson's Great Society program. Both acts followed the New Deal precedent in regarding equal treatment as a problem that called for governmental action, and it was the federal government that should take the action. This was vitally important, for in some states white supremacists and conservatives were powerful enough to prevent local or state action on behalf of change.

The Civil Rights Act concerned discrimination based on race, sex, language, religion, or handicap. With a few variations and exceptions that in the main have been removed by subsequent legislation, it prohibited such discrimination in places of public accommodation, in employment, and in programs or activities receiving federal financial assistance. Places of public accommodation include stores, restaurants, hotels, sports arenas, theaters, and so on.

The Voting Rights Act prohibited electoral requirements and practices whose purpose or effect is to deny or abridge the right to vote because of race or language.

Together with judicial decisions and supplementary legislation the acts have been profoundly important. They have opened up economic, educational, and political opportunities to blacks—and also to other minorities and to women—in an unprecedented way.

Economic conservatives, especially those influenced by libertarianism, face a problem with respect to discrimination. They are likely to be against it, but at the same time they want to maximize individual liberty (negatively defined) and to minimize the role of government, especially the role of the federal government. This means that their inclination is to apply the rule of laissez-faire: respect the liberty of everyone—that is, keep governmental restraint and coercion at a minimum—and let the forces of the free market operate. The assumption is that discrimination is unprofitable and that it will therefore end.

In contrast, progressive liberals, impressed by the decades and centuries of slavery and discrimination, are not willing to wait, for they have no confidence that forces operating in the market offer a solution to the problem.

Conservatives, libertarians, and even some centrist liberals have an even greater problem with remedial action—that is, with measures designed to reduce the extent to which disadvantages resulting from past discrimination are carried into the future. In a broad sense, the problem is what to do about great historical wrongs. Is there any way by which they can be made right without being unfair to those now living who did not commit the wrongs?

Remedial action is affirmative action, and it is likely to include preferential treatment. Think, for example, of the state trooper force in Alabama, which was lily-white into the 1970s. A federal court then considering the matter found Alabama guilty of "a blatant and continuous pattern and practice of discrimination." What should the court have then done? The judge obviously had no confidence that an admonition would be enough to assure fairness. What he did was to order those recruiting troopers to give every other new appointment to a black until blacks comprised 25 percent of the trooper force. This implied a possibility that, on occasion, a better qualified white would be passed over so that a black could be employed. The court called this "ratio hiring." If you wish, you can say that the court imposed quota hiring.

The issue of "quotas" comes up in other kinds of circumstances, too. In *Bakke* the Supreme Court outlawed their use in admissions to a college of medicine, although it permitted race to be taken into account in the name of achieving diversity in the student body. In another case the Supreme Court struck down a requirement in Richmond, Virginia, that prime contractors with the city subcontract at least 30 percent of the dollar amount of the contracts to minority business enterprises. Many other cases of these sorts might be cited.

In considering such cases, it is worth noting that the history of discrimination against blacks is a history of preferential treatment of whites. Discrimination and preferential treatment are opposite sides of the same coin. It is also worth noting that the preferential treatment of whites has normally involved quotas—100 percent quotas. So preferential treatment and quotas are not new. What is new about them is that they are now used for the benefit of blacks and women rather than for the benefit of white men. You can say, of course, that wrong done to blacks in times past does not justify wrong to whites today. But you are likely also to be uncomfortable in the thought that so many are now defending equality of opportunity in order to safeguard the gains that whites have made by denying it in the past.

President Reagan, a self-styled conservative influenced by libertarianism, showed his attitudes by appointing persons to enforce civil rights legislation who insisted on equality of opportunity without qualification; that is, they opposed affirmative action when it took the form of preferential treatment. And Reagan was publicly reluctant about signing a bill renewing the Voting Rights Act. In 1990 President Bush vetoed a bill designed to clarify and extend the meaning of the Civil Rights Act—declaring, however, that he agreed with many parts of it. Bush's claim was that the bill would make employers believe it prudent to hire by quota. A year later he signed a bill of a similar sort.

Efforts to eliminate discrimination have effects going in opposite directions. On the one hand, the elimination of a given kind of discrimination is sometimes a challenge to the ingenious to find a different way of accomplishing approximately the same result. Thus, white supremacists who can no longer deny the vote to blacks engage in gerrymandering and choose electoral systems so as to minimize black political power. On the other hand, attacks on discrimination have increased sensitivity to it and have widened and intensified the challenges. Thus, discrimination based on sex, sexual orientation, language, and age gets far more attention than ever before (Van Dyke 1990).

■ The Essence of Progressive Liberalism _____

The description of Roosevelt's ideology given above is suggestive of the nature of modern progressive liberalism, but a fuller and more coherent statement is in order. It is clear already that progressive liberals favor activist government; that is, they favor the kind of government that seeks both to protect people from harm and to promote the public good. In contrast, libertarians seek minimal government, and most conservatives want at least to reduce the role of government.

The potential harms from which government can give protection are of various sorts. In chapter 18, I spoke of externalities—the effects of an action on persons not party to it (side effects, neighborhood effects). Some externalities are benign, and some impose costs that are relatively insignificant and can thus be ignored. But some impose intolerable costs on individuals and on society as a whole. One relatively new area of major concern relates to the environment, where the practices of private parties lead to problems that can be handled only by governmental action.

Harm may also come from sources other than externalities—for example from fraud and deception, and from discrimination. And again the argument is that government should be a major source of protection. Conscience and free-market competition have not sufficed as safeguards.

Progressive liberals do not stop with the argument that government should protect people from harm. They also want government to promote the good, with liberty (freedom) as one of the central goods. But what is liberty? When are people free? Some progressive liberals join conservatives in defining liberty as what exists in the absence of governmental restraint or coercion, but then they part company with conservatives, wanting government to go on with positive measures designed to give liberty worth. Others reject the negative definition entirely and think of liberty instead as a power or a capacity. Only when people have the power or capacity to pursue their ends are they free.

The idea that government should seek to give worth to liberty or try to empower people is broad, relevant to a long list of potential activities. When government maintains public order, it is contributing to the worth of liberty. So is it contributing to the worth of liberty, or empowering, when it provides for education, for health, for the development and maintenance of means of transportation and communication, for technological development, for the advancement of knowledge, and so on. The liberal perspective makes the potential role of government open-ended.

The problem with the perspective is that governmental activity costs money, and costs lead to taxes. Moreover, when government collects taxes, it reduces the worth of liberty to those taxed, or reduces their capacity to pursue their ends, and this raises questions. It is not to be expected that people will gain from government in direct proportion to the taxes that they pay. Taxes are ordinarily redistributive, some taxpayers losing and others gaining. Extreme libertarians (anarcho-capitalists) object to this in principle, as the next chapter indicates, claiming that government has no moral right to take from some for the benefit of others; to them, taxation is theft. The more moderate libertarians and the economic conservatives accept the necessity of some government, and therefore accept the inevitability of some redistribution through taxes, but they want to keep the taxes low and the redistribution minimal. Their emphasis is on the view that in the main, money will be used more wisely by the person who earns it than by the government.

Progressive liberals are more inclined to stress the idea of solidarity (whether or not they use this specific term), the idea that we should be concerned with each other's well-being—that we are all together in a social order that we should want to maintain and improve. If the social order is allowed to break down (as it has in recent years in Somalia and Rwanda, for example), almost everyone suffers. Since people benefit from the social order, they can legitimately be expected to contribute to its preservation and improvement, and those who benefit most can be expected to contribute most.

Note that the definition of liberty accepted by libertarians and many conservatives focuses on the absence of *governmental* restraint or coercion. Progressive liberals say that this is too narrow—that threats to liberty, or to the worth of liberty, also come from private parties, most notably from employers. Their power to hire and fire makes others dependent on them and potentially subservient to them. The New Deal included an effort to bring the relationship more nearly into balance by guaranteeing the right of workers to organize into trade unions and by requiring employers to bargain with unions in good faith. Support of this sort for labor continues to be a feature of progressive liberalism.

Equality of opportunity is like liberty in getting general support: everyone favors it. But again the appearance of agreement is deceptive. In chapter 8 I have already described the various meanings given to the idea. Suffice it to say here that progressive liberals are inclined to give equality of opportunity a more extensive meaning than simply what exists in the absence of discrimination. They are also concerned about disadvantages or handicaps imposed by policies of the past and, more generally, by disadvantages and handicaps for which the individual is not responsible. The ideal is stated by John Rawls, that "those who are at the same level of talent and ability, and have the same willingness to use them, should have the same prospects of success regardless of their initial place in the social system, that is, irrespective of the income class into which they are born" (Rawls 1971, 73).

Most of what government does to give worth to liberty also contributes potentially to equality of opportunity. For example, provision for education at public expense, or at least for education subsidized by government, contributes to equality of opportunity, so progressive liberals are likely to favor it. In contrast, most libertarians and many conservatives want to shift to private schools. For example, David Frum's attack on "big government" includes regret that state governments ever began extending aid to higher education. He thinks that "the universities would be more wholesome places from a conservative point of view" if they were private, and he favors making them private even if this means that fewer people will be able to get a higher education. He shows no concern for the worth of liberty or the effectiveness of opportunity (Frum 1994, 28–29). Let people be self-reliant!

Given the fact that progressive liberalism seeks to give worth to liberty and make equality of opportunity effective, is there a more general goal? T. H. Green, whom I cited in chapter 18, had an answer. His concern was with the power of people "to make the most and best of themselves." Liberty should have worth, and opportunity should be effective, so that people can be the best they can be. The development and use of talents is the goal. Many decades later the liberal senator Hubert Humphrey paraphrased Green's thought, and Lyndon Johnson expressed the thought, though in different words, when he urged the adoption of the Civil Liberties Act of 1964. Green's thought shows up in the speeches of President Clinton, who refers again and again to the goal of helping people develop their God-given talents.

Progressive liberalism has additional characteristics that I will mention only briefly. Along with most other ideologies it supports the various civil rights and civil liberties and the rule of law. It puts stress on reason and rationality, not appealing to a transcendental source for its principles of conduct or its conception of the good. Although calling on government to keep the economy in high gear, promote economic development, and regulate economic life in various ways, it nevertheless accepts the free market as the central feature of the economic system. Believing in freedom, progressive liberalism necessarily calls for tolerance of diversity. It is concerned with the general welfare. And it regards democratic government as a useful instrument in promoting its goals.

■ Welfare

Given the above, let me go on to comment on the most difficult problem that progressive liberalism faces: what to do about those who, for whatever reason, are not self-supporting. With respect to them, it is scarcely enough to say that the issue concerns the worth of liberty or the effectiveness of opportunity, for life itself may be at stake.

The problem differs according to circumstances. Some are unable to support themselves because of a disability, and in their cases agreement is widespread that public support must be extended, although questions are raised about the amount of the support and the arrangements for identifying those who qualify.

Public assistance based on the insurance principle also tends to get wide support. I speak of both unemployment insurance and social security, the crucial feature of these systems being that they are supported by special payroll taxes. In effect, when people work they (or their employers) pay for the benefits received later during periods of unemployment or after retirement. Libertarians object, wanting to minimize the role of government and wanting to let people decide for themselves how to spend their money. Many economic conservatives object for about the same reason, and some want to restrict social security to those in need; or they may propose that eligibility for social security should begin at a later age. But nevertheless these programs are not major sources of controversy.

The main controversy about aid to those who are not self-supporting concerns families with dependent children. If children could be supported without also supporting able-bodied parents, few questions of principle would be raised, but that consideration points to the heart of the problem: the AFDC program provides support not only for children but also for the caretakers of the children, usually the mothers. Insofar as this helps women extricate themselves from bad marriages, it is perhaps all to the good; but more publicity is given to the argument that when you make governmental aid available you make it more likely that single women, including teenage girls, will bear children whom they cannot support. This possibility leads Charles Murray, a libertarian, to recommend the complete elimination of all aid for the mothers. Let them support themselves, giving up their children for adoption or placing them in governmentally supported orphanages. Progressive liberals are troubled by the problem but do not agree on a solution—other than keeping aid so low as to leave those who depend upon it in poverty.

A curious problem arises when a breadwinner works full time the year around but is not paid enough to bring his family above the poverty level. One answer, generally supported by progressive liberals, is minimum wage legislation. Another is the earned-income tax credit. This credit goes only to those who work, and the more they earn, up to a point, the greater the tax credit. If the credit is greater than the tax due, the individual gets a "refund," which can be paid month by month. Thus, the earned-income tax credit is in effect a wage subsidy, and it can be adjusted to lift an employed person's total income up to whatever level is chosen. A major consideration in its favor is that it encourages work, not idleness. The weakness is that it is relevant only to those who are on a payroll (Ellwood 1988, 114–21).

Problems relating to welfare lead to a question about the characteristics of the poor. Are they pretty much like everyone else, making approximately the same kinds of choices when facing the same kinds of incentives? Or are they different, comprising an underclass and doomed to remain an underclass unless and until they can somehow be made over?

Approximately the same issue can be posed in a different way: If A can make it from rags to riches, why can't B? If one person can be a Horatio Alger, why can't another? Given the success of some, shouldn't we regard the failure of others as their own fault?

Progressive liberals generally assume that the poor are pretty much like everyone else, responding to economic incentives in more or less the usual way and aspiring to a better life. And although progressive liberals join others in applauding the Horatio Algers, they are also impressed by the fact that in many cases circumstances beyond people's control affect their fate, advantaging some and disadvantaging others. The "natural lottery" confers advantages and disadvantages unequally. Some are born with more talent than others, enjoy better health, have more helpful parents, and live in communities that offer greater opportunities. Progressive liberals take note of the fact that the fetus has no opportunity to take out insurance against being born into poverty.

Further, the ups and downs of the economic system and of individual businesses affect people differently, and some of the differences are arbitrary. Those who begin their careers at a time of economic upswing may well get a better start in life than those who begin when few jobs are to be had. If an employer's business does badly for any reason, or if a recession or depression occurs, some lose their jobs through no fault of their own. Large numbers of the poor can justifiably say that their poverty is due to forces beyond their control. And the counterpart is that many of those with advantages got them and keep them, at least in some degree, not as a reward for personal merit but as a matter of luck.

Given this situation, progressive liberals favor the acceptance of obligations toward the poor and the weak. They do it partly as a matter of moral judgment and partly on the basis of guesses about long-term costs and benefits.

The above discussion of welfare risks giving the impression that governmental aid goes only or mainly to the elderly and the needy. In fact, however, the federal government follows policies aimed at promoting the well-being of people in a number of different categories. Sometimes the aid is at least half hidden, as with tax expenditures.

By a tax expenditure I mean a special concession that excuses people from paying a tax that would normally be collected. The result is the same as if the government collected the tax and then gave the money back, but when the tax is not collected in the first place, people are less inclined to think that aid has been given or a transfer payment made.

One of the many illustrations concerns people with mortgages on their homes: they pay no federal income tax on the portion of their income that goes for interest on the first million dollars of the mortgage. That interest is deductible. The odd implication is that, up to the million dollar point, the more expensive the home, the greater the benefit. The people who are aided are people with incomes high enough to enable them to buy. Thus, it is a question of aid for the rich rather than for the poor. The total cost of the mortgage interest exemption to the federal treasury is more than $30 billion per year—far more than the cost of the AFDC program and far more than the cost of the housing assistance that goes to the poor (Dreier and Atlas 1990, 18; Schwartz 1984, 162). The numerous kinds of tax expenditures make up more than a fifth of what the federal government spends, and almost all states have comparable policies (Surrey and McDaniel 1985, 77–78).

Quite apart from tax expenditures, the US government spends vast sums for certain enterprises that mainly benefit the middle- and upper-income groups. The outstanding illustration is the federal guarantee of deposits in savings and loan associations, leading to astronomical costs to the federal treasury. A more mundane illustration relates to aid to agriculture—mainly to well-to-do owners of large farms. As a result of government subsidies, farmers in California pay about $10 per acre-foot for water that costs ten times that much simply to pump to them. Every time you travel by air, you benefit from federal safety regulations and from the work of the federal civil servants in the control towers. The middle and upper classes—those who are politically organized—get far more aid from the federal government than the poor.

■ Human Rights

Human rights are in the first instance moral rights. They are rights to which human beings are said to be entitled simply by virtue of the fact that they are human. At the international level these rights are divided into two main categories: civil and political rights on the one hand and economic, social, and cultural rights on the other. Progressive liberals join many others in endorsing rights in the first of these categories— rights to freedom of speech and press, to freedom of religion, to vote and be elected to public office, to personal security and due process of law, and so on. Alleged rights in the second category are more controversial, some holding that they are not rights at all but should be classified as ideals. Nevertheless, progressive liberals can in principle endorse these rights, whether or not they in fact do. Libertarians perforce reject them, as do most conservatives.

The rights in question are enumerated in the international Covenant on Economic, Social, and Cultural Rights and in the European Social Charter, to which the states of western Europe subscribe.

The Covenant asserts that everyone has certain rights: to work, to fair wages and equal remuneration for work of equal value, to social security, to safe and healthy working conditions, to an adequate standard of living, to "the enjoyment of the highest attainable standard of physical and mental health," and to education. Further, the Covenant binds governments: to recognize the right of workers to form and join trade unions and to strike; to accord the "widest possible protection and assistance . . . to the family," including special protection for mothers before and after childbirth; and to adopt special measures for the protection and assistance of children and young persons.

■ Review _____

Progressive liberalism took shape in the United States in Roosevelt's responses to the Great Depression. In contrast to Hoover and to classical liberals, Roosevelt favored using government as an instrument for promoting both general prosperity and individual well-being. He championed a New Deal, calling himself a liberal, and his administration was notable for its interventions in the working of the economic system. He sought "social justice through social action."

With the laissez-faire system discredited by the Great Depression, a widely shared consensus developed on policies of intervention. Through both Republican and Democratic administrations, New Deal regulatory agencies continued to function, and policies for promoting prosperity and welfare were maintained and extended. Progressive liberals took the lead in securing the adoption of federal laws concerning equal and nondiscriminatory treatment.

Progressive liberals are like classical liberals in focusing on the individual and stressing liberty. But they are not satisfied with a negative conception of liberty—with liberty defined as an absence of governmental restraint or coercion. Either they want government to act so as to give worth to liberty or they define liberty positively—as a power or capacity to pursue ends. They thus call for activist government—government that seeks to improve conditions of life and to solve social and economic problems.

One of the biggest problems for liberals, and for others, is what to do about able-bodied people who are not self-supporting, most especially mothers with young children. They cannot be left to starve, yet to give them support is in many cases to encourage irresponsibility.

Human rights are generally divided into two categories. Progressive liberals join almost everyone else in endorsing civil and political rights and are more likely than others to go on to endorse economic, social, and cultural rights. The ideal of progressive liberals is that individuals should be enabled to be the best they can be, with the market contributing to the realization of this goal and with government acting to promote its realization where the market falters or fails.

■ Reading

Cottingham, Phoebe H., and David T. Ellwood, eds. (1989) *Welfare Policy for the 1990s*. Cambridge: Harvard University Press.

Ellwood, David T. (1988) *Poor Support. Poverty in the American Family*. New York: Basic Books.

Ford Foundation (1989) Project on Social Welfare and the American Future. *The Common Good*.

Johnson, David (1994) *The Idea of a Liberal Theory. A Critique and Reconstruction*. Princeton: Princeton University Press.

Lockhart, Charles (1989) *Gaining Ground. Tailoring Social Programs to American Values*. Berkeley: University of California Press.

Marmor, Theodore R., Jerry L. Mashaw, and Philip L. Harvey (1990) *America's Misunderstood Welfare State: Persistent Myths, Enduring Realities*. New York: Basic Books.

Moon, J. Donald, ed. (1988) *Responsibility, Rights, and Welfare. The Theory of the Welfare State*. Boulder: Westview Press.

Rawls, John (1993) *Political Liberalism*. New York: Columbia University Press.

Libertarianism

Conceiving liberty as what exists in the absence of governmental restraint, libertarians want to reduce the role of government, especially the federal government.

Libertarians resent government, above all the federal government, and want to keep it out of the lives of people insofar as possible. The call is for extreme laissez faire—for a "let 'em alone policy." In this cartoon, tyrannical rule is being plowed under.

Chapters 19 and 20 describe communism by focusing on Russia and China, and chapter 21 describes progressive liberalism by focusing on the United States. This chapter on libertarianism cannot use any one country as an illustration. Although libertarianism influenced governmental policies in the United States under Reagan, it was not the sole or even the dominant influence; Reagan described himself as a conservative. The situation in Great Britain under Thatcher was similar. Thus, instead of focusing on a country in describing libertarianism, we can do best by focusing on the writings of theorists.

No one writer stands out as the champion of libertarianism, but a series of them offer challenging analyses and prescriptions. I aim to characterize the positions that their writing suggests, focusing first on the writings of Friedrich Hayek and Milton Friedman—both distinguished economists who emphasize interrelationships between economic policy and political life. I also describe the similar yet differing views of a number of others, including Robert Nozick, George Gilder, Murray Rothbard, James Buchanan, Gordon Tullock, and Mancur Olson.

In the United States the libertarians hold some views in common with various kinds of conservatives. I deal with conservatives in the next two chapters.

■ Liberty for Individuals!

Libertarianism is the modern version of classical liberalism. Its overwhelming emphasis is on liberty (freedom) for the individual, negatively defined as the absence of restraint or coercion, especially governmental restraint or coercion. Thus, libertarians want to reduce the role of government, many of them seeking minimal government and a few wanting to eliminate government entirely. In these respects libertarians contrast with progressive liberals, who champion an affirmative conception of freedom and who want governmental activism.

Libertarians pay no heed to the possibility that conditions surrounding liberty, negatively defined, may make it worthless. Even if a person has no money with which to buy a meal, they hold that he is nevertheless free to buy, and that is what matters. They want people to be self-reliant—to assume responsibility for their own fates. No paternalism! No coddling! To permit people to be dependent on government is to reduce their incentive to provide for themselves. And libertarians argue that in any case individuals know their own interests better than any bureaucrat and will be more zealous in pursuing them.

Libertarians give little attention to the question of whether it is reasonable to expect everyone to be self-reliant—children, for example. Their overwhelming preoccupation is with able-bodied adults, and they tend to forget about the rest.

The counterpart of the libertarians' individualism is a warning against the pursuit of collective ends. The pursuit of such ends, they argue, means that individuals must be coerced—compelled to give up ends of their own so as to contribute to the collective ends. Thus, their liberty is restricted, they become tools of others, and when they become tools they are diminished as thinking and valuing persons.

Hayek puts special emphasis on this point (Barry 1979, chap. 4). It is one of the central features of his thought that the ends to be pursued should be those of the individual, not those of society. Individuals may well be able to identify their own interests and to adopt an effective strategy for pursuing them, but they cannot do the same for society as a whole. The social system is so big and complex that it is impossible for anyone to know what its interests are or how to promote their achievement, and those who take a contrary view are deluding themselves. They are guilty of "constructivist rationalism," that is, they entertain the false belief that reason can be a reliable guide in efforts to shape the future. This is dangerous. Deliberate efforts to shape the future, being based inevitably on inadequate knowledge, are likely to be wrong-headed and to do more harm than good. Instead of making such efforts, we should be grateful to history for having given us a system that works—the market system. Even this system is not the result of rational planning but developed naturally as individuals sought to promote their interests. And just as it was not deliberately created, so it cannot be deliberately improved. Above all, there is no place for central planning, which is "the road to serfdom." Further, the focus on the individual confers a bonus in that the different choices of individuals produce what amounts to experimentation, those who make wise and imaginative choices setting an example for others and contributing to general progress.

Hayek was correct, of course, in thinking that the market system developed independently of any advance blueprint, but this does not mean that human decisions played no role. Neither does it mean that the market system has necessarily reached its final and definitive form, no further improvement being possible. And if human decisions played a role in developing the system, surely they may in principle play a role in improving it. The communists clearly went wrong, as Hayek said, in switching to centralized economic planning, but it is not clear that the same can be said of the ameliorative planning for welfare that is associated with progressive liberalism. Sweden is the epitome of the activist welfare state, but its people are among the freest in the world, and their standard of living is among the highest. Sweden does not appear to be on the road to serfdom.

Nozick joins Hayek in wanting to restrict the functions of government (Nozick 1974). Like John Locke, he imagines a state of nature. In his state of nature the basic units are adult persons: "men." Individual men are the original possessors of rights and liberties. No association—no government or state—has any rights or ever gets any rights except those that individual men delegate to it, and they can delegate rights only by unanimous consent.

Given a state of nature in which individual liberty is unlimited and given the requirement of unanimous consent before any liberty is delegated, it follows that the liberties retained by individuals are extensive. And it also follows that a large proportion of the restrictions imposed by the modern state are illegitimate. This is the conclusion that Nozick reaches.

The question is whether Nozick's case does not depend on the assumptions with which he starts. Neither he nor anyone else has concrete, reliable information about an alleged state of nature. Its characteristics are a product of imagination, not of historical research. You and I are free, if we choose, to imagine a state of nature that differs from Nozick's. Our state of nature can be one in which children depend on parents and in which members of the family work together in a desperate struggle to provide for common needs. As time goes by, the family develops into a clan and the clan into a tribe, with the individual succored by the community and expected to observe its customs and help meet its needs. Uncooperative individuals are coerced, restrained, or expelled.

If Nozick had imagined a state of nature along these lines, he might still be a libertarian but he would have to have a different basis for his choice.

■ Government as a Source of Coercion

Hayek thinks that government, including democratic government, has become the major source of coercion and thus the major threat to freedom. He points out that government once had few powers and that democracy related only to the exercise of those few powers. But, he says, governments have extended their powers, and democracy has come to mean that the majority may do whatever it wishes. He ignores the limitations imposed by constitutions and by international commitments to human rights. "The root of all evil," he says, "is . . . the unlimited power of the legislature in modern democracies" (Hayek 1978, 108).

Hayek's argument goes as follows. Given their great power, legislatures can confer benefits. Moreover, they can do it differentially, helping some more than others. This creates a situation in which political parties are irresistibly tempted to buy the support of particular groups by promising benefits. In effect, parties become the tools of coalitions of special interests that seek to use government for their own advantage. Thus government takes from some and gives to others, interfering increasingly in the lives of people. It adopts collective ends that can be pursued only in a coercive way. And coercion is the antithesis of freedom.

In a few passages Hayek acknowledges the possibility that coercion may come from sources other than the government. He says that "life in society necessarily means that we are dependent for the satisfaction of most of our needs on the services of some of our fellows," and he acknowledges that "our fellows" may make their services available only if we meet conditions that they fix (Hayek 1960, 136). He is especially fearful of the coercions that trade unions can bring to bear. Through strikes and collective bargaining, unions may compel employers to pay wages above the market rate and may prevent them from cutting wages and dismissing workers when market conditions become unfavorable. Moreover, by establishing closed shops or union shops, and by picketing, unions may coerce workers. All such coercion, according to Hayek, is incompatible with the freedom of individuals and with the requirements of a free market.

In contrast, Hayek plays down the coercions that managers and employers may bring to bear. He assumes that people have free choices. "So long as the services of a particular person are not crucial to my existence or the preservation of what I most value, the conditions he exacts for rendering these services cannot properly be called 'coercion'" (Hayek 1960, 136).

Actually, in the eyes of most other people, coercions of a nongovernmental sort may play a major role in life. Not only trade unions but also those who own or manage property may control services or opportunities crucial to the existence of others or to the preservation of what they most value—to use Hayek's words. They control jobs. They control opportunities for advancement. They control knowledge—medical knowledge, for example. They control the means of production and the products on which the well-being of others depends.

In most eyes, the accompanying coercions are as significant as any for which government is responsible. And it is plausible for a person who believes in liberty to conclude that one of the major functions of government should be to protect the weak from the coercions that private persons and business concerns can bring to bear.

Here we get back to a point made earlier: conditions affecting the exercise of freedom may be about as important as freedom itself. Most democratic states have adopted legislation, for example, protecting the freedom of workers to organize into trade unions, to bargain collectively, and to strike. And, to the chagrin of the libertarians, they have adopted many other kinds of legislation aimed at reducing or eliminating private coercion or at alleviating conditions that impair the enjoyment of freedom. Libertarians condemn such measures. They assume that, as a rule, individuals can somehow escape private coercions—perhaps by taking a different job or moving to a different community.

A longtime speaker of the US House of Representatives, Tip O'Neill, quotes a "beautiful statement" by Hubert Humphrey: "The moral test of a government is how it treats those who are in the dawn of life, the children; those who are in the twilight of life, the aged; and those who are in the shadows of life—the sick, the needy, and the handicapped." O'Neill says that this spells out his own philosophy and values. Both he and Humphrey classify as progressive liberals (O'Neill 1987, 203).

Neither a libertarian nor an economic conservative would regard Humphrey's statement as beautiful. On the contrary, they might refer to O'Neill and Humphrey as "bleeding-heart liberals." Their solution to the problems of those in the dawn, the twilight, and the shadows is to encourage self-reliance insofar as possible and to leave remaining problems to private charity. As a last resort they might endorse relief measures by local government, but they would prefer that government not become involved at all.

■ Social Justice as a Mirage and a Disreputable Concept ___

In the preceding chapter I note that Roosevelt sought "social justice through social action." Hayek leads the way in denouncing the very idea of social justice. He assumes and extols what he calls a *catallaxy*, which is the same as a market economy. Hayek objects to the term *economy* because to him it connotes the coordination of activities in the pursuit of agreed upon ends, and he wants to get away from that connotation.

In a catallaxy millions of transactions occur. Those involved in each transaction seek advantage for themselves. They follow certain rules just as those who participate in a basketball game follow rules, but in neither situation is there agreement on what the outcome ought to be. So long as the game is played according to the rules, no question of justice arises. One should not speak of distributive justice, Hayek says, where no one distributes it (Hayek 1978, 57–58). The whole concept is "intellectually disreputable."

Hayek's view is obviously not the only possible view. His position that the market system developed naturally rather than on the basis of human choices is obviously questionable. If choices helped shape it in the past, then choices may improve it in the future. Rules that persistently favor the interests of some and fail to serve the interests of others can be changed. Further, government, operating outside the market, has much to do with the question of the extent to which the interests of different portions of the population are served. Think of its support for slavery and of its role in connection with segregation and Jim Crow. Think of the way it imposes taxes and confers tax breaks. And think of the many other kinds of decisions that allocate burdens and benefits.

■ Libertarian Recommendations _____

As already indicated, libertarians differ in the lengths they want to go to in limiting the role of government. Minimalists place themselves near the extreme. Those at the extreme want to eliminate government entirely.

Milton Friedman and his wife, Rose Friedman, are minimalists. According to them the strong presumption should be against utilizing government at all. This is a rebuttable presumption, but according to the Friedmans, those who attempt a rebuttal need a strong case. Moreover, governmental power should be decentralized, with as much of it as possible assigned to the local level. Thus, individuals have a better chance to control it; and if they don't like what goes on in one locality, they have the choice of moving to another.

Nevertheless, the Friedmans grant that government is needed. It is "essential both as a forum for determining the 'rules of the game' and as an umpire to interpret and enforce the rules decided on." It is essential also to administer a monetary system and to provide for national defense.

The Friedmans debate other possible governmental functions, endorsing some and rejecting others. They are among the few libertarians who consider the question of the treatment of those who are inevitably dependent (their reference being to children and madmen), and they reluctantly grant the need for some governmental paternalism. They also accept a need for government where "neighborhood effects" (side effects, externalities) occur, including those having to do with pollution. They speak of the possibility that persons might abuse their freedom by combining to reduce or eliminate competition, and again governmental action may be necessary. They grant that some roads and some public parks should be the responsibility of government, although they believe that any roads and parks that might be operated by collecting tolls and fees should be privatized.

The Friedmans devote special attention to the problem of education. For a variety of reasons that vary in importance according to circumstances, they accept the need for governmental involvement, but they would limit that involvement as much as possible. In the United States, they accept the need for public schools at the elementary and secondary levels, but they want to create more competition. To foster competition, they would estimate the per-pupil cost of public schooling and then have government (through a voucher) turn an equivalent sum of money over to any parents who prefer to send their children to a private school. The system is referred to as a voucher system. It also gets support from economic and social conservatives, especially from the religious right.

Like David Frum, to whom I referred in the preceding chapter, the Friedmans see no justification for the system prevailing in the United States at the college and university level—a system in which state schools are subsidized. Their recommendation is that any subsidies should be granted to the parents or the students, not to state schools that thereby gain an automatic competitive advantage over private schools.

To the Friedmans, vocational and professional schooling presents a special problem. They accept the need to make such schooling possible for those who have the necessary talent and motivation but who lack the necessary funds. It should be made possible, however, not through free tuition or scholarships but by arrangements that enable students to borrow. If student borrowers lack collateral, the Friedman solution is to have them pledge a certain fraction of their future earnings to the lenders, making the fraction large enough to induce the lenders to accept the unusual risk (Friedman 1982, 100).

The Friedmans decide against the government more decisively with respect to old age and survivors insurance. Such programs, they claim, unduly interfere with the freedom of people to choose what to do with their own money. Let private persons buy retirement annuities if they wish, and let employers make arrangements for retirement a part of their contract with employees if they please; but bring governmental coercion to an end! Let those who have already paid into a public social security program be properly reimbursed, and then let government wash its hands of the problem!

Even with respect to what the Friedmans call "technical monopolies"—for example, a local telephone system—they reject government involvement. They speak of a choice between evils; private monopolies, public monopolies, and governmental regulation are all evil. Facing such evils, the Friedman rule is to chose the private monopoly, buoyed by the hope that new technical developments will make it short-lived, as when railway monopolies were ended by the development of automobiles, trucks, and airplanes.

The Friedmans list a number of other governmental activities that they think cannot be justified: price-support programs for agriculture; restrictions on foreign trade; rent control; controls on production, prices, and wages; the regulation of banking; control of radio and TV; public housing; licensing those who want to enter a profession or set up a business; and peacetime conscription. And they say that their list is far from comprehensive (Friedman 1962, 36).

As noted above, one of the functions the Friedmans are willing to leave in the hands of government is the administration of a monetary system, and they recommend *monetarism*. The central claim of monetarists is simple: that, other things remaining the same, government can maintain a stable and growing economy and a desired price level simply by regulating the supply of money. The theory is that if more money is put into circulation, prices will rise, and that if the amount in circulation is allowed to fall, prices will decline. The Friedman contention is that government, by regulating the quantity of money, can safeguard a country against recession or depression. Spending to maintain demand is unnecessary, and the need for special governmental programs to create jobs or provide relief is averted.

Along with monetarism, the term "supply-side economics" has come to the fore. Ronald Reagan championed supply-side economics in the United States, and Margaret Thatcher did so in Britain. The meaning of the term is vague. A contrast with Keynesian economics is intended, Keynes having emphasized the importance of maintaining demand. He was a "demand-sider." He thought that people should be encouraged to spend when a recession threatens and that, if they do not spend enough, government should step in with a spending program of its own. The assumption was that as long as demand is maintained, the economy will flourish. Keynesianism encouraged activism in government and the development of the welfare state.

In contrast, supply-siders emphasize the supply of capital for investment and thus the incentives that lure investors into the market. In other words, they look to entrepreneurs, to people who launch new enterprises, taking risks in hope of profit. According to the Friedmans,

> In every country a tiny minority sets the pace, determines the course of events. In the countries that have developed most rapidly and successfully, a minority of enterprising and risk-taking individuals have forged ahead, created opportunities for imitators to follow, have enabled the majority to increase their productivity (Friedman and Friedman 1980, 60–61).

George Gilder joins Friedman in glorifying entrepreneurs. Gilder holds that the activity of entrepreneurs, based on their willingness to risk their capital, is the central activity of capitalism. Without entrepreneurs the economy becomes sluggish and everyone suffers. With them, economic development and ever-increasing wealth for all are assured. That is the claim.

It follows that, according to Gilder, the central problem is to establish and maintain conditions favorable to entrepreneurs. And the principal favorable condition is the possibility of profit, including at least the faint possibility of fabulous profit.

> A successful economy depends on the proliferation of the rich, on creating a large class of risk-taking men who are willing to shun the easy channels of a comfortable life in order to create new enterprise, win huge profits, and invest them again (Gilder 1981, 288).

The proper role for government thus comes into question, for the prospect of profit and the willingness to risk capital may depend in some degree on the taxes that government imposes. Gilder's complaint is that activist governments collect so much in taxes that they discourage enterprise. Sometimes the complaint is more specific and is directed at the marginal tax rate—the rate applying to the last dollar earned. The greater the proportion of the national income collected in taxes and the higher the marginal tax rate, the less the incentive to supply the capital necessary for the launching of new enterprises. The people who might have been entrepreneurs withdraw their money from productive uses. They seek tax shelters or seek otherwise to evade taxes. They hoard gold or invest in art. "The rich discover that it is easier and more gratifying to spend money than to earn it for the government, and they get a yen to travel and invest abroad" (Gilder 1981, 288).

Gilder concerns himself not so much with total tax burdens as with taxes on the rich—that is, on those capable of financing new enterprises. "The key to growth," he says, "is quite simple: creative men with money. The cause of stagnation is similarly clear: depriving creative individuals of financial power" (Gilder 1984, 144). Cutting the taxes of the rich, according to Gilder, is the key to economic growth.

Coupled with this outlook is the judgment that many governmental welfare measures (which contribute in a major way to high tax rates) are undesirable anyway. "Excessive welfare," Gilder says, "hurts its recipients, demoralizing them or reducing them to an addictive dependency that can ruin their lives" (Gilder 1981, 33). Further, when the income that a household receives through welfare approaches or exceeds what can be earned by working, the incentive to work is undermined. "The poor choose leisure . . . because they are paid to do so." Better to cut the taxes of the rich! They can then launch enterprises that give jobs to everyone else! And as a bonus those hitherto on welfare can be cured of their "addictive dependency"!

The further claim is that even if taxes are cut, enough will be collected to meet reasonable governmental needs. Gilder credits Arthur Laffer with showing "that lower tax rates can so stimulate business and so shift income from shelters to taxable activity that lower rates bring in higher revenues. The private sector can be relieved of its onerous tax rates without requiring cuts in public-sector services" (Gilder 1981, 214). The best of all possible worlds is thus assured.

Perhaps it is needless to say that not all economists agree with Friedman and Gilder. Lester C. Thurow is among those who are unimpressed (Thurow 1983, 50–103, 124–41). The Reagan administration cut taxes more or less according to Gilder's prescription, ended up with huge deficits, and left the country saddled with a monstrous debt.

Libertarian recommendations extend to other subjects, too. For example, both Milton Friedman and Richard A. Epstein oppose governmental efforts on behalf of equal employment opportunity. Both uphold the idea of freedom of contract and want to leave it to individuals to work out acceptable relationships. To Friedman racial discrimination is not a moral issue but rather a matter of taste in which government should not interfere. And Epstein looks to the market rather than to government for a solution to the problem: racial discrimination goes counter to the profit motive and so will eventually disappear. Discrimination is to be blamed in large part on government anyway, for it adopted laws requiring it. The general rule is that government should keep its hands off. The same goes for zoning regulations, which prevent the market from having its beneficent effects on economic development.

■ Libertarians and Democracy

A distrust of democracy—and even more broadly a distrust of politics—is implicit in the libertarian attitudes described above. The general theme is that the free market operates for the general good and that governmental interference is ordinarily bad. The further theme is that democracy makes interference virtually unavoidable. Political parties must necessarily cater to those who have the vote, promising benefits to buy support. Various kinds of official coercion follow. Above all, taxes are imposed on the rich to help the poor—against the real interests of both.

Among the libertarians mentioned so far, Hayek is most nearly explicit in attacking democracy. Recall the statement quoted above that "the root of all evil is . . . the unlimited power of the legislature in modern democracies." It is not surprising, therefore, that Hayek proposes institutional change. He wants to drastically curtail the power of legislatures. Further, he suggests that members of legislatures be at least forty years old, be elected for fifteen-year terms, and be ineligible for reelection. This he hopes will make them less susceptible to the pressures of special interests.

The other authors cited are not so explicit about attacking democracy and politics, but their position is reasonably clear nevertheless. From their point of view, as Bosanquet says, a struggle is going on

> between the forces of light working in the longer term through the economy and the forces of darkness working through the political process. Choices freely made in the economic sphere will nearly always be in society's interest . . . . But politics presents extreme dangers: attempts to bring about improvements through conscious design however well intentioned will almost always go wrong (Bosanquet 1983, 11, 13).

■ Anarchocapitalism

The libertarians whom I have described so far want to limit government and may count as *minimalists*. Others, more extreme, classify as *anarchocapitalists*, seeking to abolish the state while preserving capitalism.

Murray Rothbard is the leading theorist of anarchocapitalism. He insists that "whatever services the government actually performs could be supplied far more efficiently and far more morally by private and cooperative enterprise" (Rothbard 1978, 25).

Where Hayek dwells on the evils of coercion, Rothbard stresses the evils of aggression. According to him, "the libertarian creed rests upon one central axiom: that no man or group of men may aggress against the person or property of anyone else. This may be called the 'nonaggression axiom' " (Rothbard 1978, 23).

Rothbard gives the "nonaggression axiom" an extreme interpretation. In his eyes, the right to person and property is absolute and unqualified. Taxation, which involves the taking of property, is "legalized and organized theft on a grand scale" (26). Everything, according to Rothbard, should be left to voluntary private action, perhaps cooperative. Law itself is to grow naturally out of customary practice and out of the decisions of courts and arbitral tribunals voluntarily established. People should arrange through voluntary action for any police protection they believe they need. They should "return to a commodity money (e.g., gold or silver) so that the money-unit would once again be a unit of weight of a market-produced commodity rather than the name of a piece of paper printed by the State's counterfeiting apparatus" (193). Roads should be constructed and maintained by private enterprise. And so on and on. The state is to give up all its functions and cease to exist. It is not necessary even for national defense, for an anarchic society could not be a threat to anyone and therefore would be unlikely to be the target of attack (238).

By claiming that anarchy is the path to safety against attack, Rothbard theoretically solves a major problem that plagues the minimalists: how to reconcile the desire for minimal government with national security. In the face of this dilemma, minimalists tend to be isolationists, trying desperately to play down the need for national defense. But it takes a peculiar reading of history to conclude that those who do not threaten others are not likely to be attacked. The American Indians did not find this true in relation to those who followed Columbus. And in more recent times neither did Afghanistan or Kuwait.

Rothbard's antipathy for the state is unqualified. "What is the state," he asks, ". . . but organized banditry? What is taxation but theft on a gigantic scale? What is war but mass murder on a scale impossible by private police forces? What is conscription but mass enslavement? . . . In trying freedom, in abolishing the State, we have nothing to lose and everything to gain" (236–37).

■ Social Rigidities

Mancur Olson advances a theory that suggests libertarianism but that nevertheless differs. His concern is with economic growth, and his assumption is that "in these days it takes an enormous amount of stupid policies or bad or unstable institutions to *prevent* economic development. . . . An economy with free markets and no government or cartel intervention is like a teenage youth; it makes a lot of mistakes but nonetheless grows rapidly without special effort or encouragement" (Olson 1982, 175, 177).

For present purposes the point to notice here is that in addition to being suspicious of governmental intervention in economic life Olson speaks of "cartel intervention." That is, he recognizes the possibility that private collusion as well as governmental action may prevent the market from bestowing its benefits. He does not go along with what he calls "monodiabolism," that is, with the assumption that the government is the only devil. Entrepreneurs in search of their selfish advantage may establish monopolies or divide up the market or limit or eliminate competition in any number of ways. They form "distributional coalitions" to maximize their own profits regardless of the interests of consumers and regardless of the public good. The longer a country enjoys stability the greater the number of coalitions and the more of a role they play. The coalitions that are "encompassing" may not do much harm, for their good may be indistinguishable from the good of the country, but not many are in this category. Most are better described as special interests that seek their own good at least in part at the expense of others. The longer a country enjoys stability, the more numerous these distributional coalitions become. and, supplementing governmental interventions, they lead to "social rigidities" or "institutional sclerosis," impeding growth and progress.

Olson does not offer a solution to the problem. The main point is that he sees problems as well as benefits in a free market, and his analysis raises the question of whether government may not be needed to reduce the extent to which private collusions limit competition.

■ Public Choice

In recent decades a "public choice perspective" has come to the fore, advanced by the "Virginia school" of economists, most notably by James M. Buchanan and Gordon Tullock. The chief elements of the public choice perspective are the catallactics approach to economics and the *"homo economicus* postulate concerning individual behavior" (Buchanan 1986, 19).

I have already described the catallactics approach, which focuses on the market as a multitude of individual transactions that are not coordinated to serve an agreed-upon public purpose. The *homo economicus* postulate is that the parties in these transactions are simply seeking to further their own self-interest, or, as Buchanan likes to say, to maximize their utilities.

For present purposes the crucial point is that, according to public choice theorists, the concern for self-interest is not confined to economic transactions. It dominates the political realm, too. "Tullock's law" is that those engaged in political and governmental activity are self-interested 95 percent of the time and altruistic 5 percent (Rowley 1987, 3). Voters seek their own advantage regardless of the interests of others. Bureaucrats want to protect their jobs and get higher pay, and in addition they want to protect the office or agency for which they work and expand its functions and its budget. Political leaders serve special interests while posing as the champions of the public good.

The upshot is that government is not an instrument for promoting the general welfare but an arena in which individuals and special interests struggle for private advantage, everyone trying to gain at the expense of everyone else (Barry 1987, 65).

Gordon Tullock uses the illustration of five farmers, three of whom will gain if a road is repaired. Constituting a majority, the three get government to do the job, thus compelling the two who will not benefit to pay part of the costs. The five divide up differently when other issues arise, the three who will gain always able to impose part of the costs on the two who will not. Thus government grows, and taxes increase. Democracy makes big government inevitable, not because it promotes the public good but because of the self-serving activities of all of those involved (Tullock 1988, 8–35).

In the economic realm the tendency is to trust to the invisible hand to take care of the public good. In the political and governmental realm, in contrast, such trust is rare, and the public choice theorists implicitly reject it. They take it for granted that those who manage to use government for their private advantage do it at the expense of others. The allocation of tax burdens figures prominently in the struggle (Kelman 1987, 236). Big government is bad government.

But Buchanan cannot bring himself to advocate the elimination of government, even though he says that anarchy would be ideal (Buchanan 1975, 92). He accepts the state as a means of assuring internal and external order and as an agency that enforces rights and contracts.

And interestingly enough, Buchanan assigns additional functions to the state. In contrast to most libertarians and most public choice theorists, he is concerned about equality of opportunity and fears the results of extreme inequality of condition. He thinks that "libertarians go too far and reduce the force of their own argument when they reject genuinely constitutional . . . arrangements that act to promote some rough equality in pre-market positions and act so as to knock off the edges of post-market extremes." Governmental action on behalf of equality is "vitally important in the generation of personal attitudes toward the 'justice' of any social order." Among other things, this line of thought leads him to endorse governmentally financed education (Buchanan 1986, 134, 139–40).

It goes without saying that, although everyone agrees that people are guided by self-interest, especially when that interest is stark, direct, and of major importance, not everyone agrees with the idea of minimizing the role of concern for the public good. Concern for that good has led to relatively complex decision processes, including checks and balances, so that those whose interests are immediately at stake do not necessarily exercise control. People take stands and influence decisions even when their personal stake in what happens is minimal or nonexistent: on abortion, capital punishment, banning nuclear weapons, support for the United Nations, and so on. They get committed to certain principles and make decisions in accordance with those principles, especially with respect to broad issues of public policy.

Ideology as well as self-interest may influence what people do. And those inclined to dwell on the role of self-interest in public life need to go on and make a distinction: although self-interest can sometimes be pursued only at the expense of others, it is sometimes shared with large numbers of others, in which case action to satisfy the interest may promote the general welfare. And a society is surely better off if those seeking to promote their own interests feel obliged to justify themselves in the name of the public good (Kelman 1987, 239–57).

■ Review

Libertarianism is the modern version of classical liberalism. Although not the dominant ideology in either the United States or Britain, it influences policies in both countries.

Libertarians attach paramount value to the liberty of the individual, defining liberty as what exists in the absence of restraint or coercion. They thus warn against the pursuit of agreed-upon or collective ends, and against centralized planning, because of the coercion entailed. Most libertarians (for example, Hayek and Nozick) seek minimal government, but some (for example, Rothbard) want to eliminate government entirely. In the private realm, Hayek especially deplores the coercion that trade unions can bring to bear.

Hayek speaks of a "catallaxy" rather than of an economy, wanting to avoid any implication that an agreed-upon social goal is pursued; each party in the exchanges simply seeks his or her own advantage. Assuming that all the parties observe the rules, the question of justice does not arise, any more than in a basketball game. "Social justice" is a "disreputable concept."

Friedman spells out the idea of limited government, listing functions that government should and should not exercise. He recommends monetarism, claiming that through its simple principles government can keep the economy in high gear. Gilder recommends reducing the tax burden of entrepreneurs, thus enabling them to invest and provide jobs for others. Keynesian efforts to keep up demand are unnecessary. Minimal government is enough.

The above implies distrust of democracy and of politics. Reluctantly accepting government, Hayek recommends changes to limit the role of legislatures and insulate them from popular demands.

Mancur Olson does not accept the "monodiabolism" of the libertarians. He sees the operations of the free market impeded by social rigidities stemming from private collusions as well as from governmental interventions.

Buchanan and Tullock stress the role of self-interest in politics and government. Voters, special interests, bureaucrats, and political leaders all try to use government to gain at the expense of others, and no invisible hand sees to it that the public good is served.

■ Reading

Bergland, David (1990) *Libertarianism in One Lesson*. 5th ed. Costa Mesa,Calif.: Orpheus.

Boaz, David, and Edward H. Crane, eds. (1993) *Market Liberalism. A Paradigm for the 21st Century*. Washington, D.C.: Cato Institute.

Buchanan, James M. (1986) *Liberty, Market, and State: Political Economy in the 1980s*. New York: New York University Press.

Friedman, Milton (1962, 1982) *Capitalism and Freedom*. Chicago: University of Chicago Press.

Friedman, Milton, and Rose Friedman (1980) *Free to Choose: A Personal Statement*. New York: Harcourt Brace Jovanovich.

Hayek, Friedrich A. (1978) *New Studies in Philosophy, Politics, Economics, and the History of Ideas*. Chicago: University of Chicago Press.

Kelman, Steven (1987) *Making Public Policy. A Hopeful View of American Government*. New York: Basic Books.

Kuttner, Robert (1984) *The Economic Illusion. False Choices Between Prosperity and Social Justice*. Boston: Houghton Mifflin.

Olson, Mancur (1982) *The Rise and Decline of Nations. Economic Growth, Stagflation, and Social Rigidities*. New Haven: Yale University Press.

Page, Benjamin I. (1983) *Who Gets What from Government?* Berkeley: University of California Press.

Raimondo, Justin (1993) *Reclaiming the American Right. The Lost Legacy of the Conservative Movement*. Burlingame, Calif.: Center for Libertarian Studies.

Sowell, Thomas (1987) *A Conflict of Visions*. New York: William Morrow.

Waligorski, Conrad P. (1990) *The Political Theory of Conservative Economists*.Lawrence: University of Kansas Press.

Conservatism: Conservative and Reactionary

Nothing should be done for the first time. Big government is bad government.

" TO LIFE, LIBERTY, AND THE PURSUIT OF AVOIDING TAXES."

Economic conservatism has a streak of libertarianism in it. Wanting to restrict the role of government, especially the federal government, economic conservatives also want taxes to be as low as possible. Although tax money, properly spent, may serve the public interest, individuals may gain by not paying them. Here the *National Review*, a conservative journal, lampoons a conservative attitude.

389

Like liberals, conservatives differ among themselves—so much so that it is difficult to find a common core of attitudes and beliefs, except that all conservatives deplore "liberalism." Moreover, conservatives and students of conservatism differ in the classification schemes they employ. I will put the attitudes and beliefs into four categories, speaking of conservative, reactionary, progressive, and new (neo-) conservatism. This chapter deals with conservative and reactionary conservatism, and the next chapter with progressive and neo-.

■ Conservative Conservatism

For obvious reasons I hesitate about the use of the label *conservative conservatism*. But if one kind of conservatism can be progressive (Canada has a Progressive Conservative party), then it is plausible to think that another kind can be conservative.

The word *conservative* suggests that *conserving* is the purpose. The conservatives who focus on this purpose accept what exists as better than any alternative that could be deliberately created. They are distrustful of rationalism, that is, distrustful of theoretical (utopian?) schemes for making the world better. Marxism-Leninism is the epitome of the kind of rationalism they distrust, and they denounce it along with many lesser schemes as "social engineering." Their fear is that, given the complexities of the world, deliberate efforts to make it better will only make it worse. People are too limited in both their intellectual and their moral development—too limited in their abilities, too ignorant, and too venal—to be trusted to plan social, economic, and political arrangements. Liberty itself is dangerous, for it releases inclinations toward disorder, depravity, violence, and sin. The knowledge that we can bring to mind and articulate is only a small part of the knowledge distilled in customs and traditions, and in addition those customs and traditions are surer guides to a moral order than our own free choices are likely to be. Better to think of tending to the arrangements that history has produced, better to maintain customs and traditions, than to plunge into the unknown.

Russell Kirk, who exemplifies conservative conservatism, makes the point in saying that "we have no right to imperil the happiness of posterity by impudently tinkering with the heritage of humanity" (Kirk 1953, 50). History reveals God's purposes better and more reliably than our own thoughts could, so the customs and traditions embedded in history should be our guide.

A caricature of the conservative conservative position says that nothing should be done for the first time. Or, to quote Russell Kirk again, conservatives are people "who prefer the devil they know to the devil they don't." Which leads G. K. Chesterton to comment that the best we can do is to maintain a "democracy of the dead."

The above does not mean that conservative conservatives want to freeze the status quo, but they are resistant to change, skeptical about it, slow to accept it. If it comes, it should be incremental and not sweeping—a further application or perhaps an elaboration of principles that have already stood the test of time. Anything new that is acceptable should somehow be intimated in the old and be a natural next step. The burden of proof is on those who favor change, and the sharper the change, the heavier the burden. One of the tests of the statesman is "to distinguish healthy change from the processes of dissolution" (Kirk 1953, 276).

Conservative conservatives do not choose the direction in which to go. They have no grand goals. If they accept movement at all, it is to be in a direction already set. They do not as a rule try to undo what has been done, even if they opposed it when it was done. Whatever the nature of the existing order, it is to be maintained. Thus, conservatives at different times and in different countries may stand for different principles. Those who fought the New Deal in the 1930s would later defend any of its innovations that became a part of the established order. Soviet communists who were radical extremists in introducing a centrally planned economy became conservative later when they sought to maintain it: it is not necessarily a contradiction in terms to speak of a conservative communist. The odd implication is that a defender of an extreme right-wing regime in one country and a defender of an extreme left-wing regime in another may both be conservative. Conservatism becomes "a series of trenches dug in defense of last year's revolution," regardless of the nature of that revolution (Gottfried and Fleming 1988, xv).

Russell Kirk denies some of the above, and in conservative conservative circles his views have great weight. In his eyes, religious belief, or at least belief in an enduring moral order derived from a transcendental source, is an essential feature of conservatism. Godless communists cannot be accepted as conservative even if they are trying to conserve. Kirk insists on deference to the divine intent that "rules society as well as conscience, forging an eternal chain of right and duty which links great and obscure, living and dead." In a book that he published in 1953 he said that during the remainder of the century one of the principal problems for conservatives to address was "the problem of spiritual and moral regeneration; the restoration of the ethical system and the religious sanction upon which any life worth living is founded" (1953, 414).

■ Reactionary Conservatism

Reactionary conservatives want to roll back developments that they regard as objectionable and revert to an earlier time. They believe that a wrong turn was taken in the past, or a series of wrong turns—that history is a record of decline from a better, if not a golden, age. And they want to get back on the right track. They may call themselves paleoconservatives.

Reactionary conservatives divide into several categories, depending on what they identify as the wrong turn in the past. Economic conservatives, in the first category, share some of the beliefs of the libertarians, described in the preceding chapter; as the name indicates, they focus on wrong turns relating to government and economic life. Social conservatives, in the second category, pick out wrong turns relating to social and moral issues having to do mainly with family, religion, and neighborhood. Classical or traditional conservatives, in the third category, idealize a culture of the past and want to defend not the most recent revolution but an earlier one and to restore the traditions of an earlier time; they are like the conservative conservatives except that they want to restore rather than to conserve.

Since these categories are not mutually exclusive, it is possible for the same person to belong in some degree in all three of them, or at least for a candidate to appeal to all three groups for political support.

Economic Conservatism

Economic conservatives are similar enough to libertarians that much of what is said in the preceding chapter applies here again. Economic conservatives stress individual liberty and the importance of a free market. They are hostile to government, especially to "big government," and above all to the federal government, and want to reduce its role. To them, as Reagan said, government is part of the problem, not part of the solution. Or, as Senator Phil Gramm puts it, they want to cut government back "not because it doesn't do anything right but because it *can't* do anything right." This means that economic conservatives are hostile to "bureaucrats" and to the regulatory activities of bureaucrats. They denounce "the welfare state," and they want to be tough on crime, abandoning their hostility to government in this connection. They treat self-interest as virtually the only incentive that counts, save perhaps patriotism.

Hostility toward government and the bureaucracy translates into hostility toward taxes, above all taxes that might reduce the rewards of entrepreneurs. The regular assumption is that taxes are too high, regardless of their level. The inclination, illustrated by Reagan, is to regard taxation as theft. Reagan used that word, and he spoke to the voters of getting the government "our of your pockets." He made the income tax less progressive, thus benefiting the well-to-do. (At the same time he increased the social security tax, thus adding to the burdens of the working poor.) Further, he accentuated the already-existing tendency of the federal government to make tax expenditures. *Tax expenditures* occur when government excuses people from paying a tax that they would otherwise owe; it is as if government collected the tax and then gave the money back.

The mortgage-interest exemption provides the easiest illustration of a tax expenditure, although this is an exemption for which liberals share responsibility. It makes interest on mortgages tax deductible and thus subsidizes those already rich enough to buy a home; the bigger the mortgage the greater the subsidy. Those who buy a second home get a second subsidy if a mortgage is involved. Tax expenditures of the federal government increased tenfold from 1967 to 1985.

The insistence of economic conservatives on lower taxes is associated with supply-side theory and Laffer's curve, which suggest that lower taxes spur investment, leading to increased economic activity that produces enough additional taxable income to maintain or increase governmental revenue. You can have your cake and eat it, too.

Critics of this view point out that there is no guarantee that money left in private hands will be invested in job-producing enterprises. People do all sorts of things with extra money, including purchasing government bonds. And if the government gets the money by borrowing rather than taxing, the economy is not stimulated. In any event, the tax cuts of the Reagan years had no discernible effect on rates of investment.

Nor is it clear that tax policies in other countries have especially significant consequences for economic activity. *The Asian Miracle*, a 1993 study by the World Bank of the reasons for the phenomenal economic growth of a number of Asian-rim countries, gives no special emphasis to tax policies. Instead, to the discomfiture of libertarians and economic conservatives, the World Bank study emphasizes the extent to which the governments of the Asian rim countries played active roles in promoting economic development; they did not simply get out of the way. Among the activities of government, the development of human capital through education and measures relating to health gets special emphasis.

Similarly, a study by the Organization for Economic Cooperation and Development (OECD) gives no support to the view that low taxes are the key to economic growth. Other countries that have higher taxes than the United States do as well or better economically. In 1989 total tax revenue was almost 50 percent of the GNP in Denmark, 38 percent in Germany, and only 30 percent in the United States. In 1990 the United States was almost at the bottom of the list of the twenty-four OECD countries in terms of the proportion of the GNP taken in taxes. I assume that these figures are typical of earlier years as well, yet from 1972 to 1988 the standard of living in the United States went up only about a fourth as much as in the other six major industrial countries of the OECD (OECD 1992, Table 3).

Hostility to taxes fits, of course, with the desire for limited government. But no one has yet found a way to build roads or bridges, or to provide for public education and the expansion of knowledge, to say nothing of national defense, simply by reducing taxes or providing tax breaks.

Hostility to "big government" translates not only into a demand for lower taxes but also into a demand for fewer governmental regulations. Economic conservatives do not want to hamper the entrepreneur who brings about economic growth. They tend to be hostile to trade unions, and they oppose minimum wage legislation. They champion freedom of contract, the idea being that employers should not be limited in decisions about hiring and firing. More specifically, they should not be required to engage in affirmative action. Forgetting the many decades during which white men got preferential treatment, they claim to be champions of equality of opportunity and thus oppose anything they can call "quotas" in connection with the hiring of blacks and women. They deplore the Americans with Disabilities Act (a "horrendous piece of regulatory nonsense") and are generally hostile to regulations to protect the environment, for these regulations add to the cost of doing business. In principle, at least, they are hostile to regulations that limit competition, as was once the case with the trucking industry and the airlines.

Economic conservatives are generally hostile to "welfare" and "the welfare state." They stress self-reliance, assuming that we should all assume responsibility for our own fate. Horatio Alger is the model. They further assume that, at least as a general rule, the distribution of income and wealth reflects the fruit of industry and indolence, with all persons absolutely entitled to what they legally acquire, owing nothing to the government that maintains the legal order within which they operate or to society as a whole. They therefore become indignant at the thought of taxing some for the benefit of others—indignant about redistributive policies. Redistribution, they hold, is morally unjustified and is made all the worse because the property is taken from those who have proved that they are industrious and productive and given to those who are lacking in either industry or talent or both; and redistribution through welfare programs is made all the worse because it encourages people to accept dependency and undermines their motivation to work. Nevertheless, economic conservatives qualify this attitude by the acceptance of a duty to help the "truly" needy.

I mention Ronald Reagan and Phil Gramm above as economic conservatives. I might also mention Barry Goldwater and his book *Conscience of a Conservative* (1960). Goldwater represented Arizona in the Senate for many years and in 1964 was the Republican candidate for president. Focusing on the federal government in Washington and on "the natural tendency of government to expand in the direction of absolutism," he wanted to "reverse the trend" (18, 22). He thought that "the first duty [of] public officials is to divest themselves of the power they have been given" (23). He wanted not to pass laws but to repeal them, to reduce the size of government. He cited a number of areas in which the federal government has taken on functions that, in his view, the Founding Fathers never intended it to have—functions that were intended for the states and should now be returned to the states.

The attitude of libertarians and economic conservatives toward government is in a sense a reflection of their view of human nature. Liberals take what is sometimes called an optimistic view, expecting people to have the various qualities necessary to make government an instrument of the good. They expect people to be honest, efficient, knowledgeable, and concerned for the general welfare. In contrast, libertarians and economic conservatives are more pessimistic, more impressed by human ignorance and by tendencies toward selfishness and sin. And they thus look on government as something to be distrusted and feared, lest the ignorant, the selfish, and the sinful use it for antisocial purposes.

Social Conservatism

The second group of reactionary conservatives are the social conservatives. They are sometimes described as the New or Moralistic Right, and they include the Religious Right. Paul M. Weyrich, one of its more prominent leaders, distinguishes it from what he calls the "Old Right" in several ways. One difference pertains to social class. The Old, he says, tends to be intellectual and upper-class, while the New tends to be middle-class, blue-collar, and ethnic (Whitaker 1982, 52). On this basis, the New tends to be populist, anti-elitist, suspicious of "the Establishment," that is, suspicious of "bankers, big business, publishers, the academy, [and] most prominent East Coast figures" (Moulton 1990, 23). The Old, and especially the libertarian right, gives a ringing endorsement to laissez-faire, whereas the New is more ambiguous about it. The New believes in free enterprise and individual initiative and opposes the expansion of governmental interference in individual lives, but according to Weyrich it also

> believes that the individual [has] personal responsibility to society. . . . The Old Right's "live and let live" idea is not reflective of Christian moral teachings. A common assumption of New Right activists is that government should support certain moral truths. . . . Christian social doctrine teaches that, just as individuals have a certain responsibility to individuals, so does government. We reject the total indifference advocated by libertarians, just as we reject the extremes advocated by liberals. I would, for instance, want to see government—through churches and private institutions—ensure care for the helpless. I want to see government by law protect the helpless, be they unborn or senile, against the self-interest of others (Whitaker 1982, 53).

Note the reference to "certain moral truths." It is characteristic of social conservatives, especially of those on the Religious Right, to believe that these moral truths come from God, or at least from a transcendental source. Thomas Jefferson assumed this when he spoke of the laws of Nature and of Nature's God and said that all men are endowed by their Creator with certain rights. More recent commentators hold that "objective standards of right and wrong exist independently of human preference" and that "moral absolutes [exist] that human beings do not create but discover." Jerry Falwell claims on occasion that God tells him what to do. Declaring himself "a Fundamentalist—big F," he goes on to say that "a Fundamentalist believes the Bible to be verbally inspired by the Holy Spirit and therefore inerrant and absolutely infallible" (Neuhaus and Cromartie 1987, 19). And Pat Buchanan, who has twice sought the Republican nomination for the presidency holds that "the Old and New Testaments are not only infallible guides to personal salvation; they contain the prescriptions for just laws and the good society."

The other side of the coin, at least for the Fundamentalists among the social conservatives, is a denunciation of "secular humanism," conceived as "a man-centered philosophy that attempts to solve the problems of man and the world independently of God." The unacceptable feature of secular humanism is that it denies the existence of absolute values, denies the existence of fixed and objective standards of right and wrong. This is so unacceptable that one of the leading social conservatives, a Fundamentalist, declares that "no humanist is qualified to hold any governmental office in America." He endorses "the triumphalist idea" that authority should be exercised by the righteous (LaHaye 1980, 36, 93; Atwood 1990, 48-49). And Pat Buchanan speaks of "a religious war . . . for the soul of America," a war in which those on the Religious Right are confident that they fight on the side of the Lord.

Secular humanists respond with alarm, for those who believe they know the will of God have no reason to consult the will of the people. "Why bother to pay attention to anyone else's ideas if we've already heard from God?" The logical implication of the belief that you know God's will is theocratic dictatorship, not democracy. And a potential implication is even more extreme, illustrated by the view of a "mainstream Muslim cleric" in Egypt that secularists are such a danger to society that it is the duty of government to kill them.

Apart from alarm, secularists respond with skepticism, suspicion, and mistrust. After all, the record shows that the messages that people claim to get from God differ, and different people who look to the Bible for guidance pick different passages and give them different interpretations. The possible inference is that those who claim to know God's will are in fact projecting their own thoughts onto Him, seeking authority to which they are not entitled. The excesses that have occurred in history in the name of religion, and the current excesses in Iran a few other Islamic countries, are not reassuring about the consequences if Fundamentalists come to exercise political power. It is interesting to note that Singapore (not a model democracy, to be sure) authorizes the appropriate cabinet minister to prohibit religious leaders from promoting a political cause while propagating or practicing a religious belief.

As noted above, the moral values with which the social conservatives are concerned have to do mainly with family, religion, and neighborhood. More particularly, social conservatives want government to prohibit abortion—in contrast to many others who believe that the right to liberty extends to freedom of choice about abortion. Social conservatives want even the most seriously defective newborn infants to be treated as persons with disabilities and kept alive as long as possible, even with taxpayers' money. They want to maintain or restore the traditional role of women, which means that they opposed the Equal Rights Amendment when it was so heatedly debated; they oppose no-fault divorce; and they tend to oppose any governmental involvement in arrangements for child care on the ground that this encourages mothers to work outside the home and thus neglect their children. Social conservatives oppose racial hiring quotas, which Weyrich describes as "culturally destructive." They are aroused, as are many others, about crime and the abuse of drugs, upholding capital punishment and demanding in general that government be "tough on crime." A concern for ethnic interests, if not a degree of racism, surely lies behind some of these attitudes.

Many of the social conservatives want to lower the wall between church and state. The most prominent specific demand is that prayer be permitted in the public schools, and many also want the biblical story of creation taught along with, if not instead of, evolution (Watt 1985, 109). They oppose sex education in the schools, denounce pornography, and are appalled when the taxpayers' money is used to support artists whose work they consider pornographic, obscene, or sacrilegious. They oppose any action by public officials, any teaching in the schools, and any public measure that might tend to make homosexuality seem acceptable. They are likely to oppose busing as a means of integrating the schools, preferring the more traditional neighborhood school. They want government to give vouchers to parents who prefer to send their children to private schools, including church schools—the vouchers to be used in paying tuition; the long-run objective is to get rid of public schools entirely in the expectation that church schools will then flourish.

Classical Conservatism

Classical conservatives might arguably be included with the conservative conservatives, but they are less inclined to conserve than to restore. They may also have a vision of the future, provided it is not utopian.

Burke's statement is to the point—that society is "a partnership not only between those who are living but between those who are living, those who are dead, and those who are to be born." Concern for the future, however, should add to the appreciation of the past, for the past is a more reliable guide than any blueprint, no matter how attractive that blueprint may appear.

Classical conservatives tend to look back to the nineteenth century and earlier and to emphasize the value of associations intermediate between the individual and the state—family, church, social class, and local community. Individuals find their station in life through these intermediate associations and faithfully perform the duties implied, serving their fellows as befits their status. Rugged individualism is unknown, as is the idea of a self-made person. Authority and order are of great importance, and respect for authority and order impose caution on the exercise of liberty. The state and the traditional intermediate associations all have their proper spheres and each respects the proper spheres of the others (Nisbet 1986, 34-39).

Russell Kirk elaborates on this point in expressing the conviction that "civilized society requires orders and classes" (1953, 8). And he cites the supporting views of Burke: Men are equal in the sight of God, but not in other ways. They differ naturally, and the natural distinctions are to be accepted. Political equality is unnatural.

> Nature has furnished society with the materials for an aristocracy which the wisely-conducted state will recognize and honor—always reserving, however, a counterpoise to aristocratic ambition. Just as it is a fact of nature that the mass of men are ill qualified for the exercise of political power, so it is written in the eternal constitution of things that a few men, from various causes, are mentally and spiritually suited for social leadership. The state which rejects their services is doomed to stagnation or destruction (Kirk 1953, 54).

Reactionary conservatives in all three groups tend, when they look abroad, to be nationalistic and patriotic. They are sensitive to the importance of sovereignty and national security. Along with nationalism and patriotism goes suspicion of deliberate efforts to create and shape international institutions. If anything, conservatives are more distrustful of social engineering at the international than at the domestic level, for it is necessarily influenced by alien attitudes; and international institutions might be difficult to control.

Those in all three groups tend to be distrustful of generalizations about the rights of man or human rights. To them, pronouncements concerning rights tend to have the character of manifestos calling for change. The idea of economic, social, and cultural rights is especially suspect, for to endorse these rights would be to ask government to take on the role of social engineer.

Ronald Reagan as president was a reactionary conservative, mainly an economic conservative but also appealing to social conservatives. In Britain the Thatcher government was reactionary, reflecting the libertarian strand of thought in the Conservative party; most notably, it made a point of privatizing—selling off nationalized concerns to private entrepreneurs.

■ Review

Conservative attitudes differ, and scholars differ in classifying them. This chapter deals with conservative and reactionary conservatism.

The principal characteristic of conservative conservatism is a desire to conserve, an inclination to resist change. The assumption is that the wisdom of the ages is distilled in history and tradition and that history and tradition are therefore more reliable as guides than blueprints advanced by social engineers.

The principal characteristic of reactionary conservatism is the desire to roll back developments that are regarded as objectionable and to revert to an earlier time. Reactionary conservatives differ in their emphasis, some focusing on the role of government in economic life, others on social and moral issues, and still others on the problem of recapturing the culture of an earlier time. The three groups are, respectively, economic conservatives, social conservatives, and classical or traditionalist conservatives.

Economic conservatives are similar to libertarians in stressing individual liberty and the market. They are hostile to "big government" and the governmental bureaucracy, which limit the freedom of entrepreneurs by taking money in taxes, imposing regulations, and (through the promotion of welfare) redistributing wealth.

Social conservatives are more concerned with moral issues. They call for the observance of moral rules derived from God, or at least from a transcendental source, and they denounce secular humanism. The rules that they stress relate to such matters as abortion, prayer in the schools, and homosexuality.

■ Reading

Barry, Norman P. (1987) *The New Right*. New York: Croom Helm.

Blumenthal, Sidney (1986) *The Rise of the Counter Establishment: From Conservative Ideology to Political Power*. New York: Times Books.

Evans, M. Stanton (1994) *The Theme Is Freedom. Religion, Politics, and the American Tradition*. Washington, D.C.: Regnery.

Frum, David (1994) *Dead Right. The Fall of the Conservatism of Hope and the Rise of the Conservatism of Fear*. New York: Basic Books, A New Republic Book.

Goldwater, Barry (1960) *The Conscience of a Conservative*. New York: Hillman Books, Paul Gottfried (1993) *The Conservative Movement*. 2d ed. New York: Twayne.

Himmelstein, Jerome L. (1990). *To the Right. The Transformation of American Conservatism*. Berkeley: University of California Press.

Kirk, Russell (1990) *The Conservative Constitution*. Washington, D.C.: Regnery Gateway.

———— (1993) *The Politics of Prudence*. Bryn Mawr, Penna.: Intercollegiate Studies Institute.

Lind, William S., and William H. Marshner, eds. (1991) *Cultural Conservatism. Theory and Practice*. Washington, D.C.: Free Congress Foundation.

Nisbet, Robert (1986) *Conservatism: Dream and Reality*. Minneapolis: University of Minnesota Press.

Conservatism: Progressive and Neo-

CHAPTER
24

"Conservatives must realize that they have no alternative but to declare an assault on poverty."

Richard Nixon, pictured here as Santa Claus, appealed to progressive conservatives in some of the programs he sponsored, but he also adopted a southern strategy designed to appeal to more traditional conservatives. Thus, different parts of his team of reindeer went in different directions.

As is already clear, conservatism comes in different varieties. The preceding chapter focuses on conservative and reactionary conservatism, and the present one on progressive conservatism and neoconservatism.

■ Progressive Conservatism

It would be easy to dismiss *progressive conservatism* as a contradiction in terms, but if you are tempted to do that, you should ask yourself what definition of conservatism you are assuming and whether you are right in thinking that no other definition is acceptable. I am more inclined to say that all those who call themselves conservative should be regarded as such and that definitions of conservatism should be developed accordingly.

The term *progressive conservative* is not my invention. I get it from Jack Kemp, a Republican leader and secretary of the Department of Housing and Urban Development (HUD) in the Bush administration. He calls himself a "a radical, bleeding-heart progressive conservative." If such terms apply to him, then they apply to many others with similar views.

In fact, progressive conservatism has a long history. In *The British Political Tradition* (1983), W. H. Greenleaf speaks of two main strands of thought in the British Conservative party: right-wing radicalism and benevolent paternalism (Greenleaf 1983, 2:193).

The right-wing radicals of the nineteenth century, emphasizing minimal government and laissez-faire, were not clearly distinguishable from the classical liberals; and they would now be classified as libertarians. The benevolent paternalists, in contrast, championed "altruistic Toryism," seeking to use government to promote social welfare and the public good (2:199). They accepted "a doctrine of responsibility towards the underprivileged," a "duty of social amelioration," and they sponsored legislation accordingly. One of the Tory claims was that "we have been in the forefront of the battle to help the people of this country to raise themselves, more than a generation before the word Socialism was coined" (2:202).

Disraeli was one of the progressive conservative leaders. His promise in the middle of the nineteenth century was to "support all those measures, the object of which is to elevate the moral and social condition of the Working Classes, by lessening their hours of toil—by improving their means of health—and by cultivating their intelligence" (2:208).

Later in the century another conservative leader, Joseph Chamberlain, "attacked the Liberal leaders for failing to see that social reform was the question that must dominate contemporary politics." He rejected what he called "the theory of everyone for himself and the devil take the hindmost," and he applauded "the intervention . . . of the State on behalf of the weak against the strong, in the interests of labor against capital, of want and suffering against luxury and ease" (2:227–28). A colleague described him as " 'the destroyer of laissez-faire and the founder . . . of the Welfare State.' "

Similarly, another Conservative leader, Lord Salisbury, said in 1891 that " 'the Conservative Party has always leaned . . . to the use of the State, so far as it could be properly used, for improving the physical, moral, and intellectual condition of our people, and I hope that mission the Conservative Party will never renounce' " (2:228).

As indicated in chapter 18, the classical liberalism of nineteenth-century Britain evolved into new liberalism. Once this happened, the new Liberals and the progressive Conservatives stood on common ground with respect to the principle that government is to be used as an instrument of social amelioration, and the Labor party joined them in this respect when it developed.

The progressives in the Conservative party continued to control it after the end of World War II, as suggested by the statement of Harold Macmillan, Conservative prime minister in the later 1950s, that "true Tories" accepted with growing enthusiasm a conservatism oriented toward planning and the welfare state (2:312).

I suggest above that definitions of conservatism should be made to reflect usage, which may seem to assume that the word lacks a core meaning. Russell Kirk, however, points out that the British Tories made the idea of the nation "the kernel" of their social theories. They rejected atomistic individualism and refused to see men as soldiers in a class struggle. Instead, England was a community in which all had their proper place, and the development of capitalism had tended to depress the working classes below their proper place. "The mass of Englishmen, the peasantry, and the forgotten town laborers [had been] hideously neglected, abandoned to ignorance, vice, monotony, and poverty, [with] less voice in affairs than they had in the Middle Ages." This meant that the nation—the community—was rotting, and it was up to the Crown, the Church, and the aristocracy to rescue it. Disraeli led the way (Kirk 1953, 236–40).

The counterpart in the United States would be for conservatives to take the view that the poor, and particularly the black poor, had been abandoned, denied their proper place in the national community, and that therefore special measures of social amelioration should be taken.

In addition to being guided by a concern for a national community, British conservatives were at least mildly traditionalist in the sense described earlier. This is indicated by a statement in 1875 by a minister in a Disraeli cabinet. Conservative policy, he said, is

> to distrust loud professions and large promises; to place no confidence in theories for the regeneration of mankind, however brilliant and ingenious; to believe only in that improvement which is steady and gradual, and accomplished step by step; to compare our actual condition, not with the ideal world which thinkers may have sketched out, but with the condition of other countries at the present day, and with our country at other times; to

hold fast what we have till we are quite sure that we have got hold of something better instead (Greenleaf 1983, 2:191–92).

As indicated above, a "radical right" existed within the Conservative party along with the progressives. The view of those on the radical right is suggested by the fact that one of them wrote a book under the title *The State as Enemy* and another declared that "government, politics itself, must be reduced to the uttermost minimum, for in no other way will human energy be fully released"—a position suggestive of the anarchocapitalist wing of libertarianism. Margaret Thatcher did not go so far to the right, but she was nevertheless more libertarian than progressive.

As for progressive conservatism in the United States, we start by focusing on *Out of the Poverty Trap. A Conservative Strategy for Welfare Reform* (1987) by Stuart Butler and Anna Kondratas. Butler and Kondratas do not call themselves *progressive* conservatives, but surely the label fits. They start with "the plain fact, confirmed in poll after poll, . . . that the American people care deeply about the poor and the underprivileged— even if they do not know how to solve the problem" (p. 5). They go on to speak of a general acceptance of "the principle that a civilized society is duty-bound to provide sufficient assistance to those who are infirm, disabled, or otherwise unable to support themselves to reach a minimum acceptable standard of living." Further, if the able-bodied fall on hard times, "there is broad agreement that it is in the interest of society, as well as an obligation of society" to give them temporary support . . . . [P]roviding the able-bodied poor with a sufficient degree of education and skills to achieve an acceptable living standard makes for good economics as well as good social philosophy" (p. 51).

In a separate article Butler says that "conservatives must realize that they have no alternative but to declare an assault on poverty. If they don't they will forever be on the moral and intellectual defensive" (Butler 1989, 27). Butler and Kondratas commend the goals of the Great Society program, proposing a different strategy for achieving them.

Where the New Deal and the Great Society emphasized activism on the part of the federal government, Butler and Kondratas put their main emphasis on reducing its role. They would reduce its role partly by putting more emphasis on state and local governments, but even more by relying on the market, the family, and the local community and by insisting more vigorously on individual self-reliance and responsibility.

Butler and Kondratas join many others in regarding teenage mothers as a major problem. They would first of all try in several ways to reduce the magnitude of the problem. They assign a role to the schools, although not including the distribution of condoms in that role. Instead, they take the view that schools have become too indulgent, too unwilling to censure socially undesirable conduct. Teachers, they say, "have a responsibility to uphold the positive values of society." Parents too have been permitted to become irresponsible and must be made to accept responsibility for the sexual behavior of their children; that is, parents of minor children who become fathers and mothers must be obliged to help provide for their grandchildren. And Butler and Kondratas would come down "decisively and heavily" on absent fathers.

Butler and Kondratas do not expect to eliminate the problem of teenage motherhood or of families in poverty, so they accept a continued need for an AFDC program. They would, however, limit the eligibility of any person for aid to a lifetime total of no more than four years, with remaining needs being met by the states and local communities. And they would "add a work component to every welfare program."

With respect to health care, the recommended strategy divides the population into two groups, depending on income level. Those whose incomes are high enough to make it possible (more than twice the poverty level?) must accept self-protection for themselves and their families as a legal obligation and obtain insurance that covers both working years and retirement years, including coverage for catastrophic and long-term health care costs. They are to obtain the insurance either individually or through employers. Premiums are to be tax deductible, and government is to impose regulations that require insurance companies to accept persons who are bad risks. Those with low incomes (less than twice the poverty level?) are to obtain insurance, too, but with state aid— perhaps through "medical assistance vouchers" sold on a sliding scale of charges (Butler and Kondratas 1987, 215–25). Both Medicare and Medicaid would presumably go out of existence.

Butler and Kondratas leave it to others to guess how the insurance premiums would compare to the taxes that might otherwise be paid to support a universal federal health insurance system. And they say little about methods of enforcement (liens on wages?) or about the way people at various income levels are likely to react to their proposal. The relative burden would clearly be highest for those with low incomes.

If the law is to require people to take out health insurance to meet the needs of old age, it would be logical also to require them to take out insurance to provide retirement incomes, thus getting the federal government out of the business of providing for social security. And it would be logical to require them to take out unemployment insurance. But Butler and Kondratas say nothing about these subjects.

I mention medical assistance vouchers above. In general, Butler and Kondratas recommend the use of vouchers wherever possible. Parents are to get vouchers to provide for the education of their children— vouchers permitting them to send their children to private schools if they choose to do so. And those who qualify for help with respect to housing will also receive vouchers to use in lieu of rent. The theory is that vouchers "empower" those who have them—that is, give them choices;

and further that the possibility of choice will engender competition, leading to better prices or to higher quality in the educational and other services obtained.

The strategy would also "empower" the poor in another way, that is, by turning certain service activities over to people at the local level—most notably by providing for tenant management of public housing projects. This is an aspect of a more general but vague goal of restoring emphasis on the idea of community, just as the program against teenage pregnancy is an aspect of a more general goal of restoring emphasis on the family.

The plan sketched above implements the principles stated at the outset. The federal government would have a reduced, although still significant, role. It would maintain AFDC, even if it cuts the number served. It would require the purchase of health insurance, which means that it would assume a power that it has never exercised—a power that it may not even have under the Constitution; and it would regulate the insurance companies. The federal government would presumably share other roles with state and local governments—helping to provide vouchers for various purposes and using the schools to inculcate values. The insurance and voucher schemes would transfer some functions to the market and provide for increased competition. In various respects the strategy, if it worked, would increase self-reliance and the sense of personal responsibility.

Other progressive conservatives express comparable views. Thus, Adam Meyerson, editor of the Heritage Foundation's *Policy Review*, says:

> Voters throughout the world continue to support a large government role in health, education, and social insurance; generous aid to the needy; and strong safety and environmental regulation. Ronald Reagan, for all his popularity, was forced to beat a hasty retreat when he was perceived as undermining Social Security. Thrice elected Margaret Thatcher is trying to inject market competition into Britain's National Health Service, but knows it would be political suicide to take the government out of health care altogether. The spirit of the age seems to favor both some sort of welfare state and greater freedom for economic decisionmakers (Meyerson 1989, 66).

Meyerson goes on to say that Adam Smith would have approved. He entitles his article "Adam Smith's Welfare State."

Richard Nixon can reasonably be described as a progressive conservative. Succeeding Lyndon Johnson in the presidency, he went along with the Great Society program, signing measures into law that did not get enacted while Johnson was still in office. He presided over significant increases in social security benefits, and through a Family Assistance Plan he proposed to guarantee a minimum income for all families with children.

As a progressive conservative, Jack Kemp recommends governmental action to help low- and moderate-income people get on the "ladder of opportunity." He says that "in a democratic society people are going to demand problem-solving by government" (quoted in Kuttner 1990, 24). So he endorses "capitalism with a social conscience"—a phrase reminiscent of the search for "communism with a human face."

Kemp speaks of a "new war on poverty," wanting conservatives to "become the vanguard of a crusade to end the scourge of poverty." In contrast to economic conservatives, who emphasize self-reliance and the assumption of personal responsibility, he wants to extend help. Every person, he says, should have "the opportunity to achieve his or her capacity. . . . All of our nation's people should have the opportunity to share in the blessings of freedom, democracy, and equality of opportunity." Like Butler and Kondratas, Kemp seeks to "empower" the poor. He wants to "build a new national consensus around economic growth and opportunity, greater access to property, jobs, and entrepreneurship." He rejects "social engineering . . . and huge entitlement programs," but he also rejects "the idea of . . . a social Darwinian society in which only the fittest survive [and the idea that] government can do nothing to help alleviate conditions of poverty, despair, and hopelessness."

The goals that Kemp and the progressive conservatives endorse are clearly similar to those of the progressive liberals. The differences lie mainly in the choice of methods. Kemp cites "the four little words: 'Government must do more' " and goes on to reject the thought. "Government doing more simply means more wasteful spending. More taxes. More money thrown at failed government programs. More misguided welfare spending. More meddling in private business. More punishment for people like you and me who work hard, and who save and invest our earnings. And less individual freedom. I don't buy it, and neither should you." Rather than having government do more, Kemp wants to cut it back. He wants to rely largely on tax reductions and tax expenditures: cutting the capital gains tax; raising the income level at which liability for the income tax begins; allowing higher income tax exemptions for dependents and tax credits for child care and health insurance; extending tax concessions and other kinds of aid to help low-and-moderate income people become home owners; providing tuition tax credits; and granting tax concessions for commercial activities that provide jobs in "enterprise zones" in poverty-stricken urban areas.

Tax concessions are ways of "empowering" the poor, and the poor are to be empowered in other ways, too: by transferring the management, if not the ownership, of public housing to the tenants; by greater use of rental vouchers; by greater federal support for community-based programs relating to mental health, drug abuse, job training, and day care; by permitting choice of the school one's children attend; and by assuring the equal enjoyment of all civil and political rights (Kemp 1990; Kuttner 1990; Barnes 1990). The National Affordable Housing Act of 1990 provides for assistance in a number of these categories.

As the above suggests, Kemp is a "supply-sider," finding "the cornerstone of growth" in Laffer's "insight" that government can get as much revenue, or more, from lower taxes. Kemp plays on this theme endlessly. "The primary task of our government," he says, "should be to unlock the capital being held back from the market by misguided taxation, and then step out of the way." Among other things, as suggested above, he would designate areas of concentrated poverty as "enterprise zones" in which those who create jobs get special tax concessions. Unlike the conservatives who treat the poor as belonging to a "culture of poverty," incapable of managing their lives properly, Kemp assumes that the poor are pretty much like everyone else except that they are poor. "Our inner cities are overflowing with human capital, an untapped reservoir of human creativity." "Most Americans—rich and poor alike— share the same values, hopes, and dreams." Kemp would "recognize the dignity and potential of every person in America." He would have government provide them with incentives and increase their opportunities.

Kemp's stress on enterprise zones gets a mixed response. Critics make several points. One is that the many enterprise zones established by state and local governments have had only modest success, and they say that this is not surprising in light of the quality of the local labor force and in light of the fact that taxes constitute so small a proportion of the costs of doing business. Further, tax concessions are significant mainly if they lead to the development of an enterprise that would otherwise not have been established at all; if they lead simply to the choice of one location rather than another, the gain for one community is a loss for another. And, of course, critics raise more fundamental questions of strategy: whether the attack on poverty should not begin with prenatal care and then be supplemented with education, health care, and the inculcation of proper values. Further, the question is raised whether the market can be counted on to create the necessary jobs or whether government must not stand ready to provide community-service jobs to those who otherwise would be unemployed and in need of welfare.

This kind of question, a question of fundamental strategy, is raised implicitly in an article published in 1991 in *Policy Review*, published by the Heritage Foundation. The article, calling for greater investment in "human capital," focuses on Texas, but the message has wider application.

A strong conservative case can be made for increasing the size and scope of Texas's public sector where long-term economic benefits demonstrably exceed short-term costs to the state's taxpayers. Education, public health and safety, malnutrition, mental health, and adult illiteracy would appear to be priority areas for carefully targeted increases in government spending.

In the above I stress Kemp's call for lower taxes. I should acknowledge that in 1994 he came out in favor of switching from "the current system of high [tax] rates and lots of loopholes [to] a flat tax of 17 percent on income and no specific breaks." How well this fits with his proposed war on poverty is not clear.

Gottfried and Fleming, in *The Conservative Movement* (1988, vii) comment that "a distinctive feature of the contemporary American Right is its emphasis on progress: moving beyond the past toward a future of unlimited material opportunity and social improvement." The statement is true of both the economic and the progressive conservatives. The question is whether the means that these conservatives prescribe are appropriate and adequate.

■ Neoconservatism

Neoconservatism came into existence in the late 1960s. The most prominent among the early neoconservatives are former liberal and leftist intellectuals, some of them former communists, perhaps Trotskyites. Their principal identifying characteristic is a concern for Western values and social virtue; and they are not as hostile as most other conservatives to government or as critical of the welfare state. They were long notable for their anticommunism and their denunciations of anti-anticommunism, but these characteristics have lost significance.

Where economic and social conservatism are both notable because of evidence of mass support for them, neoconservatism is notable more for the quality of its intellectual champions. Most widely known are Irving Kristol and Norman Podhoretz. Kristol is author of *Two Cheers for Capitalism* (1978) and *Reflections of a Neoconservative* (1983) and is associated with the *Wall Street Journal*, *The National Interest*, and *The Public Interest*. Podhoretz was for long editor of *Commentary*. Three former presidents of the American Political Science Association are or have been neoconservatives.

For long the neoconservatives manifested their concern for Western values mainly through their anticommunism, but with it went a determination to defend the United States. Podhoretz deplores "the hatred of 'Amerika' that increasingly pervaded the New Left and the counterculture" of the 1960s and says that it led neoconservatives to "a new appreciation of the American political system and of its economic and social underpinnings. . . . Almost every idea espoused by the neoconservatives relates back to this central impulse to defend America against the assaults of the left." Podhoretz thinks that liberals (the liberals that I call progressive) lack a "true sense . . . of the amazing success of the American system." American democracy is worth fighting for.

Capitalism is "a form of freedom in its own right and a necessary (though not sufficient) condition of freedom in the political realm." Traditional moral values, condemned by the counterculture as oppressive, are more conducive to health and happiness than any alternative, providing an indispensable foundation for a prosperous society (Podhoretz 1989, 57).

Antagonism toward the New Left and the counterculture expanded into a negative view of egalitarianism. Kristol decries the "New Class of self-designated intellectuals [who] pursue power in the name of equality," and his reading of John Rawls leads him to accuse Rawls of considering a social order just and legitimate "only to the degree that it is directed to the redress of inequality." Saying that progressive liberalism "can be fairly described as neosocialism," Kristol identifies it with a deplorable concern for equality. This concern is deplorable because it assumes the existence of a consensus about the nature of the common good and leads to a belief that government should promote the good, brushing aside those who stand in the way. According to Kristol, liberals find it "difficult to detest left-wing (i.e., egalitarian) authoritarian or totalitarian regimes" and dislike free societies because of their inevitable inequalities (1978, 171, 183, 192).

Aaron Wildavsky goes farther, writing a whole book denouncing "radical egalitarianism," which, according to Wildavsky, calls for the reduction and elimination of distinctions of all sorts—distinctions of income and wealth, of status and authority, of right and wrong—distinctions that need to be maintained (Wildavsky 1991).

Whether liberals or any other significant group are in fact so devoted to "egalitarianism," radical or otherwise, is a good question. Of course, liberals want people to enjoy the equal protection of the laws, which means that they oppose arbitrary discrimination, and many concern themselves with the widening gap between the rich and the poor, but I see no evidence that they want "egalitarianism" in the sense of the even-Steven leveling of incomes. Kristol himself cites and approves the Aristotelian view that "a just and legitimate society is one in which inequalities—of property, or station, or power—are generally perceived by the citizenry as necessary for the common good." Most liberals would surely join Kristol in approving this view.

In addition to reacting against the left and the counterculture of the 1960s and criticizing egalitarianism, neoconservatives concern themselves with virtue. Kristol, giving two cheers to capitalism, cannot give it three because of its emphasis on selfishness and its neglect of the values essential to a good society. Given the emphasis on property and on liberty, what happens to the good? Of course, the pursuit of private vices sometimes leads to public benefit, as in Mandeville's *Fable of the Bees*, but to emphasize private vices is to neglect "the life of the mind, the psyche, the spirit" and to make no provision for a "community of mutual love" (1978, x–xi).

The problem, in Kristol's eyes, is traceable to liberalism as well as to capitalism, for liberalism insists on secularism, and secularism leads to a diminished role for religion and religious faith. Further, liberalism puts little emphasis on tradition. Without religious faith and without respect for tradition, people lack both a guiding star and an anchor. Anything goes. Even those who benefit from the system seek profit in ways that undermine it, for example, by sponsoring TV shows and distributing movies that celebrate the immoral. Kristol illustrates the neglect of virtue and the emphasis on the material by noting that "the law insists that an 18-year-old girl has the right to public fornication in a pornographic movie—but only if she is paid the minimum wage." And he comments that "the current version of liberalism, which prescribes massive government intervention in the marketplace but an absolute laissez-faire attitude toward manners and morals, strikes neoconservatives as representing a bizarre inversion of priorities" (1978, 66, 76, 138). Family and religion are "indispensable pillars of a decent society"; the goal is "an intellectually and morally reinvigorated liberal capitalism" (1983, 75–77).

> Who wants to live in a society in which selfishness and self-seeking are celebrated as primary virtues? Such a society is unfit for human habitation. . . . It is preposterous to think that the mass of men will ever accept as legitimate a social order formed in accordance with the laws of the jungle. . . . Can men live in a free society if they have no reason to believe that it is also a just society? I do not think so. My reading of history is that, in the same way as men cannot for long tolerate a sense of spiritual meaninglessness in their individual lives, so they cannot for long accept a society in which power, privilege, and property are not distributed according to some morally meaningful criteria. . . . I conclude that man cannot accept the historical accidents of the marketplace—seen as mere accidents—as the basis for an enduring and legitimate entitlement to power, privilege, and property (1978, 85, 262–63).

Blaming capitalism and liberalism for the problem, Kristol does not claim that "conservatives" have a solution. In fact, he berates them for failing "to articulate any coherent set of ideals and to suggest a strategy for achieving them." And Kristol's own suggestions are vague. He clearly looks to government to attack the problem, thus joining social conservatives in favoring governmental activism of a sort; and he speaks of the possibility of censorship as a means of protecting cherished values, but he does not suggest specifics. Writing about "America's Mysterious Malaise," he speaks appreciatively of economic progress and the "successful creation of a Welfare State" but then points to associated evils: increased criminality, more teenage pregnancies, more abortions, more use of drugs, the development of a dependent, self-destructive underclass, and more negative attitudes toward government and political leaders—all suggesting a coming crisis; and he thinks the crisis may be resolved by the development of "some kind of 'post-modern' politics, one that distances itself from the very building blocks of modernity— rationalism, secularism, science, technology, and representative government" (1992b, 5). Meantime he calls for a war on poverty—spiritual poverty—and commends traditional bourgeois values: "a willingness to work hard to improve one's condition, a respect for law, an appreciation of the merits of deferred gratification; a deference toward traditional religion, a concern for family and community, and so on" (1992a, 46). Further, he calls for "civic virtue": "the willingness of the good democratic citizen, on critical occasions, to transcend the habitual pursuit of self-interest and devote himself directly and disinterestedly to the common good" (1983, 53).

Kristol looks for help from the religious conservatives. "Today it is the religious who have a sense that the tide has turned and that the wave of the future is moving in their direction. . . . They are going to be the very core of an emerging American conservatism" (1993).

James Q. Wilson has concerns similar to Kristol's. He deplores increased illegitimacy, increased willingness to be dependent on government, increased willingness to engage in deficit financing and pass the burden on to the next generation, and increased crime. Questions of character are at the bottom of these developments, and this points to the importance of promoting the private virtues on which the public good depends. Both private and public interests will be served by seeking to develop and strengthen "the moral sense," by taking up "the incomplete task of moral development" (Wilson 1992).

William J. Bennett writes along the same line. Our afflictions, he says, are primarily moral, cultural, and spiritual. "The enervation of strong religious belief . . . has demoralized society." Religion

> provides society with a moral anchor—and nothing else has yet been found to substitute for it. Religion tames our basest appetites, passions, and impulses. . . . If we have full employment and greater economic growth—if we have cities of gold and alabaster—but our children have not learned how to walk in goodness, justice, and mercy, then the American experiment, no matter how gilded, will have failed (Bennett 1994a, 1994b).

Bennett is the editor of *The Book of Virtues*. He calls for the return of religion to its proper place, and he thinks that the importance of politics has been greatly exaggerated.

Recall the reference above to Kristol's expression of appreciation (in 1992) for the successful creation of a welfare state. The point now is that he qualifies that appreciation. He wants the emphasis to be on economic growth, saying that "poverty is abolished by economic growth," and he is inclined to rely on cutting taxes as the means of promoting growth. But he implicitly grants that *abolished* is too strong a word, that poverty continues despite economic growth. So what to do?

Kristol's answer is tentative. He is critical of means-tested programs, particularly AFDC, but at the same time he grants that we have a moral obligation to "provide a safety net for those unable to participate fully in the economy" and that "people need governmental action of some kind if they are to cope with many of their problems: old age, illness, unemployment, etc." He calls not for the dismantling of the welfare state but for changes designed to create a "conservative welfare state"—a "social insurance" state. Hesitantly, he mentions "universal" as opposed to means-tested programs, wondering whether the principle of universality ought to be extended beyond public education, social security, and Medicare to, for example, children's allowances and some form of national health insurance.

Kristol's views on the welfare state are obviously similar to Kemp's. In fact, Kemp is quoted as saying, "Irving Kristol shaped my consciousness to recognize the necessity of the welfare system, or the safety net."

Neoconservatives are nationalistic, but though they agree in condemning those who "blame America first," they disagree on other possible implications of nationalism. Some envision a global democratic order with the United States as its champion, it being understood that a predominantly market economy is a necessary condition of democracy. "Americans have a missionary streak, and democracy is our mission" (Gottfried and Fleming 1988, 68). Others call for a greater degree of "realism" and a narrower definition of the national interest (Judis 1990, 35–36). How these differences will be worked out—and, in truth, whether neoconservatism will survive as a distinct ideology—remains to be seen.

■ Review

This chapter concerns progressive conservatism and neoconservatism.

Progressive conservatives pursue goals similar to those of progressive liberals, wanting to wage a war on poverty and to enable people to make the best of themselves, but they recommend different strategies. They want to reduce the role of government, especially the role of the federal government, and to rely mainly on the reduction of taxes (for example, in enterprise zones) to get the results they seek. Rather than have the federal government provide benefits and services of different kinds, they are more inclined to impose legal obligations on individuals (for example, with respect to taking out health insurance) or to have it provide vouchers so as to "empower" the poor.

Neoconservatism began as a reaction against the New Left and the counterculture of the 1960s. It is critical of "egalitarianism." Even more, it is concerned with the problem of promoting virtue—the problem of upholding and promoting moral values. It accepts the need for governmental welfare programs.

■ Reading _____

Butler, Stuart, and Anna Kondratas (1987) *Out of the Poverty Trap: A Conservative Strategy for Welfare Reform*. New York: Free Press.

Dorrien, Gary (1993) *The Neoconservative Mind. Politics, Culture, and the War of Ideology*. Philadelphia: Temple University Press.

Himmelstein, Jerome L. (1990). *To the Right. The Transformation of American Conservatism*. Berkeley: University of California Press.

Kristol, Irving (1983) *Reflections of a Neoconservative. Looking Back, Looking Ahead*. New York: Basic Books.

Rightist
Authoritarianism

Rightist authoritarians usually picture themselves as saving the country from some kind of evil.

POLAND

Next!

The swastika was the symbol of Hitler's Nazism. Daniel R. Fitzpatrick rendered it as "a huge, tumbling engine of destruction" (his words), emphasizing the apparently overwhelming strength of the Nazis and the seeming helplessness of their victims.

Fascism and National Socialism are the outstanding illustrations of rightist authoritarianism. Neither attracts a large following today, but they deserve attention partly because of the profound effect they have had on twentieth-century political life and partly because of the possibility that they—or ideologies of a similar sort—might become important in the future. And a few other forms of rightist authoritarianism deserve a note, too—both those represented by rulers who pay little attention to ideology and those represented by ideologists who have not succeeded in becoming rulers.

■ Fascism and National Socialism

Fascism is identified with Mussolini's rule in Italy (1922–43) and with Hitler's rule in Germany (1933–45). The name *Fascist* derives from the Italian word for a bundle of sticks that gain in strength when aligned and tied together. Mussolini used such a bundle as the party emblem. Hitler called his party the National Socialist German Workers Party. It is commonly referred to more briefly as the *Nazi* party.

Both leaders died when their countries were defeated in World War II; Mussolini was executed by partisan forces and Hitler committed suicide. Fascist or quasi-Fascist regimes survived for several decades in Spain and Portugal, but they were gone before the end of the 1970s. Whether any other recent regimes deserve to be called fascist is a question. Both *fascist* and *communist* tend to be used as epithets, and criteria for deciding whether the label is appropriate are especially vague with respect to *fascist*.

The two ideologies developed in an atmosphere of national humiliation in both countries. To be sure, Italy was on the winning side in World War I, but many Italians thought that they had "lost the peace." Germany was defeated in World War I, suffering the *Diktat* of Versailles—an imposed peace treaty. Moreover, in the years after World War I, both countries (along with many others) floundered in economic difficulties. And both attempted to make a go of democracy, but neither had a firm democratic tradition.

In this situation, the Fascists and Nazis put great emphasis on nationalism and on promises to restore national pride. Where liberals put prime emphasis on freedom and justice for individuals, and where the Russian communists proclaimed their devotion to the workers of the world and to an international proletarian revolution, the fascists put prime emphasis on the nation, or (in Germany) the *Volk*.

In Italy the fascists went on from this point to endow the nation-state with a life of its own, distinct from the lives of the human beings composing it. They regarded the nation not simply as an aggregation of individuals but as a corporate body, a living organism, a Being. The Char-

① What is racism?

② What are some Xamples?

ter of Labor formulated under Mussolini clearly expressed this conception. It asserted that

> the Italian nation is an organism having ends, life, and means of action superior to those of the separate individuals or groups of individuals which compose it. It is a moral, political, and economic unity that is integrally realized in the fascist state (Schneider 1928, 333).

Far from denying the emotional and mystical basis for such a stand, the fascists affirmed it and gloried in it. They were contemptuous of reason, extolling instead instinct, intuition, or drive of will. They deliberately and avowedly created a *myth*, believing that people would be more likely to do great things when inspired by a myth than when guided by reason. Thus Mussolini declared:

> We have created our myth. . . . Our myth is the nation, our myth is the greatness of the nation. . . . The foundation of Fascism is the conception of the State, its character, its duty, and its aim. Fascism conceives of the State as an absolute, in comparison with which all individuals or groups are relative, only to be conceived of in their relation to the state. . . . Everything for the state; nothing against the state; nothing outside the state (Mussolini 1935, 13).

The slogan just quoted expresses the central thought of *totalitarianism*, on which I will comment below.

Mussolini's statement identified his goal: the *greatness of the nation*. Theoretically he might have sought greatness in various ways—by promoting the arts or stimulating scientific and technological developments or contributing in other ways to the well-being of the people of Italy or of the world. But he did not think of such possibilities. To him it was automatic that greatness was achieved by conquering foreign peoples, so he launched a war against Ethiopia and conquered it. He sent some of his armed forces to help Franco win in Spain and set up a fascist dictatorship there. And he entered World War II after Hitler started it.

Hitler had a similar outlook. He sought "a place in the sun" for Germany, which to him required that Germany throw off the shackles of the Treaty of Versailles and take territory from neighboring countries. "That foreign policy will be acknowledged as correct only if, a bare century from now, 250 million Germans are living on this continent, and then not squeezed together" (Hitler 1939, 979).

Implicit in the above is the fact that the fascists and Nazis welcomed and even glorified violence. Of course, communists are willing to use violence, too, and so, for that matter, are all governments; but where others regard violence as an unfortunate necessity, the fascists and Nazis seemed to find it good. And with their glorification of violence went the nurturing of a military ethos. This did not mean an emphasis on the traditional military establishment, for one of their problems was to fully subordinate that establishment to fascist control. Primarily it meant the organization of party militia. Mussolini had his Black Shirts, and Hitler his Brown Shirts and his SS. The militias were made up of swaggering young men proud to assert masculine dominance and pledged to unswerving loyalty to their leaders.

Both Mussolini and Hitler rose to power at the head of a political party, and both made their states one-party states, but they put more emphasis on their personal leadership than on the party. Hitler especially emphasized the *Fuehrerprinzip* (the leadership principle), though Mussolini also styled himself as the *Duce* (leader).

Fascism, according to one of its theorists, insists that government be entrusted to men capable of rising above their own private interests in favor of "the higher demands of society and history." It therefore relied not on majority rule but on "the intuitiveness of rare great minds" (Rocco 1935, 687). According to Hitler, "A majority can never replace the Man. . . . The parliamentary principle of decision by majority . . . sins against the aristocratic basic idea of Nature" (Hitler 1939, 103, 105). The gratuitous presumption was that Mussolini had a "rare great mind" and that Hitler was at the top of Nature's aristocracy.

Though emphasizing leadership by one man, both Mussolini and Hitler sought mass support, reducing the mass media to their control and using them to rally the people to their sides. Hitler was particularly notable for staging party meetings as great pageants and for holding plebiscites in which voters were invited to approve what he did. And the sobering fact is that in the late 1930s and the early part of World War II, Hitler apparently did have the support of a high proportion of the German people, educated and cultured though they were.

Both leaders were *authoritarian*, and the systems that they established are commonly described as *totalitarian*. But their totalitarianism fell considerably short of that of the Soviet communists. Morton Kaplan captures the difference. He speaks on the one hand of "traditionally oriented authoritarian systems that sit loosely upon the societies they exploit and that rarely sink their roots below the surface or break up traditional social institutions"; and on the other hand he speaks of the Soviet system that "fragments and destroys traditional social organizations, prevents the emergence of more modern ones, and extends its control apparatus into every bloc, every factory, and every form of activity" (Kaplan 1978, 22). The fascists and Nazis were more nearly in the first of these categories than in the second, leaving the economic order and the social structure substantially intact. When Hitler and Mussolini were gone, most of the traditional German and Italian social institutions were still in place and could resume playing their historical roles, with the people upholding their traditional values. In contrast, communist totalitarianism included the socialization of the means of production, the destruction of a whole social class, and an assault on values basic to a market system.

Unlike Mussolini, Hitler made racism, and particularly anti-Semitism, a central feature of his program. He said that the "folkish" view

> by no means believes in an equality of the races, but with their differences it also recognizes their superior and inferior values, and by this recognition it feels the obligation in accordance with the Eternal Will that dominates this universe to promote the victory of the better and stronger, and to demand the submission of the worse and the weaker . . . .
>
> Peoples which bastardize themselves, or permit themselves to be bastardized, sin against the will of eternal Providence, and their ruin by the hand of a stronger nation is consequently not an injustice that is done to them, but only the restoration of right (Hitler 1939, 452, 579–80).

Hitler had difficulty identifying the master race, first speaking of Aryans and later mainly of Nordics. Among peoples in Europe, however, he had no difficulty in picking out those who, in his view, were not simply inferior but so dangerous to the higher culture to which he aspired that their very survival was intolerable—mainly the Jews and the gypsies. Most German Jews took warning and fled the country, but during the course of World War II some nine million other Jews came under Nazi control, and about six million of them perished—from a variety of causes, but mainly and most notoriously by being deliberately killed in extermination camps at Dachau and Auschwitz (Parkes 1964, 100–101). This was the Holocaust.

I said at the outset that neither fascism nor Nazism attracts a large following anywhere today, but relatively small groups influenced by them operate in most countries of western Europe as well as in the United States and South Africa. They are usually hate groups, like the skinheads, directing their hate toward blacks, Jews, and homosexual persons; members are macho in their bearing and inclined to violence, especially against persons in the categories just named. And they are extreme nationalists. Such groups become known by their activities more than by their championship of a body of thought, for thought is not prominent among their characteristics.

■ Military-Bureaucratic Authoritarianism

Authoritarian regimes of a military-bureaucratic sort do not stand out as the self-conscious champions of an ideology. Their concern is for the traditional order, which they usually view as the natural order, and which they want to save from the dangers or the evils that their predecessors have brought about or failed to eliminate. In a plural society, their concern may be with the relative power positions of the different ethnic or racial communities. Thus, they are ordinarily conservative in some sense.

Such regimes generally originate in illegal action. Perhaps an elected government sets the constitution aside and rules on the basis of military support instead of popular support. More often an illegal seizure of power occurs—a *coup d'état.*

Scholars differ on the question of whether coups are more or less random events, occurring whenever a military group gets the notion, or whether some kind of a common set of conditions indicates their probability. Focusing solely on the forty-five black African countries in the period from 1960 to 1982, Thomas H. Johnson and two colleagues take the second of these positions (Johnson, Slater, and McGowan 1984, 622–40).

They count fifty-two successful coups, concentrated in twenty-five of the forty-five black African countries. They also count fifty-six attempted coups and 102 reports that coups were plotted. They say that some kind of military intervention occurred in the political life of thirty-eight of the forty-five countries.

They find various sets of conditions that affect the probability of coups. One set concerns the military itself. If the military is ethnically divided, an initial coup is less likely than otherwise, but if one ethnic group within the military seizes power, then subsequent coups become more likely. If the military gets a relatively high proportion of the public expenditures, a coup is more likely—because the military may conclude that it must seize power to avoid losing its favored position. If the military plays an important role in defending the government against domestic opponents, it tends to get involved in politics and to become more inclined to seize power itself. In contrast, a coup is less likely if the military is not called upon to keep the government in power and if instead the government permits some degree of party competition.

Some of the above conditions belong simultaneously to another set—one based on political participation and pluralism. Johnson and his colleagues find that a coup is less likely if a country has a strong mass party together with minority parties that are allowed to compete in elections. The mass party should have nationwide support; it should not be a regional party or a party serving just one ethnic group. "African states that have either maintained or restored some degree of party competition have considerably less military involvement than more authoritarian states."

Another set of relevant conditions is economic. "One does not have to be a vulgar Marxist to recognize that a stagnating economy in conjunction with rising unemployment and underemployment, recurrent balance-of-payments crises, and flagrant corruption create an environment in which military *coups* can become highly probable events." The military may see its own future threatened by worsening economic conditions—for example, through cuts in its budget. It may feel obliged to act in what it regards as the national interest if adverse economic conditions create or accentuate domestic problems. Such economic factors are especially likely to develop in countries whose well-being depends on exporting one or a few commodities. Conversely, of course, *coups* are less likely in countries noted for economic growth and honest and efficient government.

A final set of relevant conditions has to do with "social mobilization"— that is, economic, political, and social change, leading people to shift from one pattern of life to another. Johnson and his coauthors measure social mobilization in terms of the shifting of people from agriculture into industry and in terms of the percentage of the population living in the capital city. They find that "early social mobilization . . . is strongly related to subsequent military *coups* and other interventions" and that "early and rapid population growth in the capital city . . . is equally destabilizing." Conversely, later and slower social mobilization proves more compatible with stable constitutional procedures.

> To summarize, we find that African states with relatively dynamic economies whose societies were not much mobilized before independence and which have maintained or restored some degree of political participation and pluralism while keeping their military forces small and nonpoliticized have been the most stable, whereas countries with the opposite set of characteristics have experienced considerable political instability in the form of military coups and associated forms of military intervention in politics (Johnson, Slater, and McGowan 1984, 635).

Coups have also been common in Latin America and, in truth, through much of the Third World. Systematic recent studies concerning them comparable to the one relating to black Africa are not available. Deteriorating economic circumstances together with a desire to forestall or terminate socialist or leftist programs have clearly stimulated some of the coups in Latin America. And threats to the budget and status of the military have played a role, too (Linz 1975, 306–50).

Frequently the initial steps toward the coup come from civilian quarters. Alarmed civilians—perhaps the leaders of one or more of the political parties that are out of power—persuade one or more military men that some evil or danger makes it their duty to step in. Of course, men in the military sometimes generate such thoughts all by themselves.

The argument or the thought is likely to be that only the military is in a position to save the country. Military people are oriented toward patriotic service and think of themselves as able to maintain order and discipline. They can often count on the tolerance if not the support of substantial portions of the country's elite and of the population in general.

Those who stage coups tend to discount the fact that they have limited experience in politics and limited knowledge of political issues (including issues relating to the economy). They are accustomed to relatively simple situations permitting them to issue orders and to expect results accordingly. They and their supporters apparently assume that almost any set of able, honest, and devoted persons can improve on the government about to be overthrown. Some may be lured on by the heady thought of enjoying and benefiting from the perquisites and trappings of government. (*Perquisites* are the special benefits and rewards of a position, over and above the normal salary.)

The thinking of the military men who seize power may go beyond what is suggested above. They may regard the various civilian leaders and parties as spokespersons not for the country as a whole but for special political or economic interests, and they may think of themselves as above the usual political fray and uniquely able to represent the national interest. They may regard themselves as representative of the country in the sense that the personnel of the armed forces come from the various social classes and from all geographic regions. They may see before them a country so polarized that no effective civilian government is possible.

Further, if they think of themselves as especially responsible for national security, they may go on to see a possible implication: that they should concern themselves with the many features of national life on which military power, and therefore the security of the country, depend—including the satisfactory operation and development of the country's economy (Snow 1979, 61–79; Linz 1975, 285–305).

Those who attempt a coup take a risk that civil war will develop, but it rarely does. The outcome ordinarily depends on the loyalties of that portion of the armed forces located in or near the capital. The ringleaders try to assure themselves that this portion of the armed forces will support them or stay neutral. If they read the situation correctly, they can surround a few key government buildings, announce their takeover via radio and TV, and then exile, imprison, or kill one or more leaders of the ousted government. If they read the situation incorrectly, of course, they may well end up dead or in exile themselves.

An authoritarian regime of a military-bureaucratic sort may or may not be associated with a political party. If so, the party is likely to play a restricted role. The regime can be expected, of course, to outlaw political parties and organizations that stand seriously in its way. It is not there to rally mass support or to urge mass participation in political life but rather to get the country through some kind of crisis. And it is likely to want simply to be left alone to do the job. It can be expected to control the media and to repress dissidence in so far as that seems necessary to the preservation of its power.

A regime of this sort is rarely totalitarian. Seeking to maintain or restore the traditional order, it is likely to permit a degree of pluralism. That is, it is likely to permit a number of kinds of private organizations and associations to go on functioning, seeing no need to bring them under the control of the government or of an associated political party.

The military regimes established now and again in Turkey have some of the more creditable records. Turkish generals have seized power on several occasions when civilian governments seemed unable to function effectively. They have imposed law and order against all challengers, whether from the left or the right. They have pursued nonrevolutionary, moderate policies, co-opting the services of many civilians in the hope of making their rule effective and successful. And they have then returned government to civilian control on certain conditions. The Turkish military has seemed to regard its political mission as limited both in its duration and in the kind of program to be implemented. At the same time, the countries of the European Union, which Turkey wants to join, have been severely critical of Turkish regimes, both military and civilian, for their violations of human rights.

A number of military regimes have made themselves notorious for violating widely accepted international standards having to do with human rights and international law. In the 1970s General Amin of Uganda used government as an instrument of ethnic warfare and was, in addition, ruthless in eliminating persons and groups who seemed to threaten his corrupt rule. Through roughly the same years, Equatorial Guinea was ruled by a despot so brutal that, according to estimates by Amnesty International, nearly half the population of the country fled. And several of the military dictatorships in Central and South America have resorted to dirty war, seeing to it that opponents on the left are killed with attendant publicity or that they simply disappear.

■ "Sultanistic" Authoritarianism

Juan Linz calls an authoritarian regime *sultanistic* when a ruler holds power not on the basis of any tradition or ideology or sense of special mission but rather on the basis of control over carrots and sticks— rewards and punishments (Linz 1975, 259). The sultanistic ruler exercises power with little regard for the well-being of the people whom he rules. His concern is for his own psychological gratification and personal enrichment and perhaps for the status and support of his family or clan. The country is his domain, to be exploited in whatever way he can manage, with no more than a vague distinction, if any, between the revenues of the state and his personal income.

The sultanistic ruler wins support by doling out his carrots—conferring benefits on those who support him. Perhaps this amounts to no more than giving protection to others (landowners, for example) who are operating their own systems of exploitation. And the ruler saves himself from enemies by arresting or otherwise disposing of them. He survives on the basis of the passivity of the masses—whom the sultanistic system is likely to leave illiterate and in squalor.

The Mobutu regime in Zaire is sultanistic in the above sense. So was the Somoza regime that operated for many years in Nicaragua.

■ Corruption

Some degree of corruption is common in government. I have mentioned this in chapter 3 on parties and interest groups and need to mention it again in connection with authoritarianism. Though scholars have not assembled and evaluated evidence on the point, it is plausible to suppose that corruption is, if anything, more widespread in authoritarian than in democratic systems, for authoritarian rulers can shield themselves more fully from public criticism. At the same time, it is possible that corruption is associated more directly with the stage of a country's development than with authoritarianism as such. In any event, the fact of widespread corruption ought to be noted, whatever the reason for it.

In *The African Predicament* (1968) Stanislav Andreski includes a chapter titled "Kleptocracy or Corruption as a System of Government." The theme of the chapter is that "the use of public office for private enrichment is the normal and accepted practice in African states and the exceptions are few and inconclusive" (94). Loyalty to the state is weak, and so is the idea that those on the public payroll should give honest service. On the contrary, the general expectation is that those ostensibly serving the government will use their positions to enrich themselves and to obtain benefits for their family or clan.

"In Africa . . . genuine solidarity is confined to the clan, and there are no restraints on cupidity beyond its confines. . . . In relations between non-kinsmen power normally occasions uninhibited spoliation." The officeholder expects anyone seeking his service to pay for it. If he lets a contract or engages in any kind of commercial transaction on behalf of the government, he extracts his cut. "After only a few years in office the top politicians have amassed fortunes worth a hundred times the sum of salaries received. . . . The police are regarded by the ordinary people as extortioners or even uniformed bandits" (Andreski 1968, 93, 95, 104–105).

Andreski does not suggest that kleptocracy is peculiar to black Africa. It also prevails in many countries outside Africa. Wherever it exists, and to the degree that it exists, respect for government is bound to be low, and government is likely to be inefficient as well. In an authoritarian regime, in which the head of the government may well be the chief kleptomaniac, little opportunity exists to criticize what goes on and to agitate for reform.

As I said at the beginning of the chapter, I have made no attempt to provide categories into which all authoritarian governments fit. They vary greatly among themselves, and some are unique. I might note that special problems arise in plural societies, illustrated by relationships among different sorts of groups in different countries: among the races in the United States and South Africa; among linguistic groups in Canada and Malaysia; among religious groups in Lebanon; and among the ethnonational groups of Cyprus. In divided societies it is not unusual for one element to dominate; within itself, it may operate democratically, as the whites of South Africa did for long, but from the point of view of any subordinate group, the government that they confront is authoritarian.

■ Review

Most of the chapter focuses on rightist authoritarian regimes: Fascist, National Socialist, military bureaucratic, and "sultanistic."

As compared with communist regimes, the ideologies associated with rightist authoritarian regimes have been poorly developed. Mussolini and Hitler both gained power in countries that had suffered the humiliation of defeat in war, and both put great stress on nationalism and the state. They sought to rally the people in a search for greatness or a place in the sun. They also stressed the importance of a "leader." Hitler made racism a central feature of his program, especially anti-Semitism.

Military-bureaucratic and "sultanistic" rulers rarely concern themselves with an ideology and rarely try to rally the masses in support of a cause. As a rule the military-bureaucratic ruler comes to power by a *coup d'état* and pictures himself as saving the country from a previous regime that in his view was intolerable. He is conservative but rarely totalitarian. The "sultanistic" ruler has little or no sense of special mission, ruling for more or less private purposes, such as self-enrichment.

Conditions affecting the probability of coups concern the military itself, the prevailing arrangements for political participation, the ethnic composition of the population, the performance of the economy, and "social mobilization" or social change.

Corruption is widespread in politics but seems to be especially associated with developing countries under authoritarian rule. Some of them are called "kleptocracies."

■ Reading

Altemeyer, Bob (1988) *Enemies of Freedom: Understanding Right-Wing Authoritarianism*. San Francisco: Jossey-Bass.

Cohen, Carl (1982) *Four Systems. Individualist Democracy, Socialist Democracy, Fascism, Communism*. New York: Random House.

Greenstein, Fred I., and Nelson W. Polsby, eds. (1975) *Handbook of Political Science*, Vol. 3, *Macropolitical Theory*. Reading, Mass.: Addison-Wesley.

Lee, Stephen J. (1987) *The European Dictatorships, 1918–1945*. New York: Methuen.

Linz, Juan J. (1975) "Totalitarian and Authoritarian Regimes," in Greenstein and Polsby, 1975.

Parkes, James (1964) *Antisemitism*. Chicago: Quadrangle.

Payne, Stanley G. (1980) *Fascism. Comparison and Definition*. Madison: University of Wisconsin Press.

EPILOGUE

What kind of government should we have? What should we have it do, and what should we keep in private hands? What dreams (that is, what hopes) are appropriate, and what nightmares are possible? These are the questions of the final two chapters.

Government and Its Functions

"Democracy is the worst form of government except for all the others."

© Dallas News

"I'M NOT APATHETIC, I JUST DON'T GIVE A DAMN."

It may never have occurred to this "typical" voter, or nonvoter, to think of democracy as better or worse than other forms of government. But unconsciously he is contributing to one of its weaknesses. Although almost all adults in America are eligible to vote, a great many do not.

429

What kind of government should we have, and what should we expect government to do? These are the basic questions of political life.

In the Western world the answer to the first question is generally taken for granted: we should have democracy and should avoid any kind of authoritarianism. Democracy has shortcomings, but other systems have more.

The second question is the one that arouses controversy, with no agreement in sight.

■ Democracy

In ancient Greece, Plato spoke of putting government in the hands of a philosopher-king, a wise and benign authoritarian ruler. Such persons are rare; at least, they rarely show up in political office. As knowledge increases, it is sensible to refer more and more questions about public policy to experts, but even experts can be wrong. And expertise alone does not give an adequate basis for deciding whose interests should be served and in what degree, or for choosing among values. With many persons and groups disagreeing about ends and means in political life, governing is difficult, and no system of government is likely to win everyone's applause.

The possible choices are between democracy and authoritarianism. The choice of democracy is based on the assumption that human beings (or at least citizens) should be free and equal. Each person should be free to define and pursue her own interests, respecting the right of others to do the same; and the interests of one person should have as much consideration as the interests of another. With these assumptions goes another: that people are more likely to get consideration and respect from government if they have rewards and penalties at their command—if they can reward governmental behavior that they approve and penalize behavior that they oppose.

Thus, the democratic approach is to make government *responsive* and *accountable* to the people. And the central method of accomplishing this is to use elections to determine who will hold a variety of offices. Voters are given a chance to elect the candidates they prefer and to defeat the others. Once elected, those in office are hedged about with various kinds of constitutional and legal requirements and restraints. In many cases two or more offices or agencies must agree before action can be taken, or one agency can block action by another. And if people think that an elected official performs inadequately, they can throw him out at the next election.

Further, the elections themselves are held under conditions designed to make them meaningful. For example, voters have had schooling and have access to relevant knowledge; they are free to organize politically and to sponsor candidates, which means that elections may be competitive; and the arrangements for casting and counting the votes are fair.

The democratic approach is reinforced by several of the ideologies described in the preceding chapters, especially those that stress reason and rationality. To be sure, nothing about reason or rationality prevents leaders from appealing to political passions, and they often do it—especially to passions of a nationalist-patriotic sort. And the passions sometimes prevail. But democratic government is set up so as to require substantial amounts of consensus before action can occur and to maximize the prospect that reason and rationality support whatever is done.

Authoritarian approaches are different. None of them stress the freedom and equality of individuals. This statement should perhaps be qualified with respect to communism, for the theory was that freedom and equality would prevail in the ultimate communist society; but they were never expected to prevail during the transition period, and the transition has been toward collapse rather than toward the ideal.

Authoritarian systems put rulers under few restraints. Such systems give the people only limited opportunity, if any, to put the principles or the actions of the government under critical public scrutiny and do little to enhance the prospect that a bad decision by the ruling person or the ruling body will be checked or vetoed elsewhere. They give the people no legal opportunity to throw officials out and select new ones. It was Hitler's war, and not a decision of the people, that brought his regime and that of Mussolini to an end. More often than not, an authoritarian regime comes to an end when a coup occurs that sets up another regime of the same type.

Democracy has weaknesses, too. Although almost all adults are eligible to participate in the affairs of political parties, relatively few choose to do so; and although almost all are eligible to vote, a great many do not. Those who ostensibly represent the people in public office and who presumably are glad to give effect to the will of the people have difficulty determining what that will is; and in connection with many issues, for a variety of reasons, no public will is ever clearly formed. In truth, especially in the larger and more advanced countries, government has become so huge an enterprise with so many matters to attend to, many of them complex, that even the elected representatives of the people cannot be expected to play a significant role with respect to them. Still less can the individual citizens play the role that ideal democracy assigns to them.

The result is that decisions, big and small, tend to be made by the few: those who organize for political action, those who provide the money for political campaigns, those with the fullest access to the media, those who hire the most persuasive lobbyists, those who hold key positions in legislative bodies and their advisory staffs, those who administer the law and thus interpret it, and so on. And when the few make the decisions, it is to be expected that they will serve their own interests, or a selected set of interests, more fully than any others.

But if the few make decisions that arouse opposition, democracy at least gives the opposition a chance to bring about a reversal or other change. And the very fear of this reduces the likelihood that unwelcome decisions will be made. Moreover, authoritarianism, far from offering a solution to the problem, tends to accentuate it. By definition it *is* government by the few. It excludes almost everyone from the political process and includes no arrangement for holding public officials accountable. In theory a rare philosopher-king might be benign, but the general expectation has to be that authoritarian systems will serve the interests of the few more fully and more surely than is likely in a democracy.

For democracy to prevail, it is vital that the relevant circumstances be such as to make more or less coherent and stable government possible. The relevant circumstances are varied. The basic one is the existence of a constitutional consensus—a widely accepted agreement about the fundamental rules and principles on which political life should proceed. And associated with the consensus should be the absence of deep and irreconcilable divisions—racial, ethnic, religious, or ideological—that preclude trust, tolerance, and mutual respect. Deep divisions between major elements of the population make all kinds of government difficult and may make democracy impossible.

Winston Churchill once described democracy as the worst form of government except for all the others; and it obviously has many weaknesses and failings. The record, and Churchill's comment, suggest how difficult it is to develop and maintain a governmental system that is clearly good.

■ Ideologies

Four kinds of comments suggest themselves, relating severally to (1) the confusion that attends ideologies, (2) the fervor that attends them, (3) the role of facts and values in choosing among them, and (4) their implications for human rights.

The confusion is obvious. The labels *liberal* and *conservative* do little to identify points of view. To be sure, all liberals concern themselves with the liberty of the individual, but otherwise they divide. They divide over the very meaning of liberty—whether a negative conception suffices (that liberty exists in the absence of restraint) or whether a positive conception should be endorsed (that liberty exists only in the presence of the ability to take advantage of it). Those who endorse the negative conception (libertarian or classical liberal in outlook) go on to argue, with a few qualifications, that a governmental policy of laissez-faire is enough and that the great emphasis should be on the self-reliance of individuals and their acceptance of responsibility for their own lives and fate. This attitude calls for a minimal state, but it also calls for national defense, which cannot always be achieved with a minimal state. In contrast, those who endorse the positive conception (progressive in outlook) argue for governmental action here and there designed to give liberty worth. This attitude leads to "big government."

Disagreement among conservatives does not focus on any one issue. Some conservatives simply want to conserve, defending the existing order, whatever its characteristics. Some are reactionary, wanting to restore the conditions and policies of an earlier time—usually an earlier time when government was smaller and taxes were lower, or when conceptions of morality and the role of religion differed. Some are progressive, sharing the goals of progressive liberals but wanting to pursue them by different means. Some, although sharing many of the beliefs of the progressive liberals, call themselves conservative (neoconservative) mainly to distance themselves from certain leftist and progressive liberal attitudes with which they have come to disagree.

These categories may seem neat, but they imply confusion. A standpat conservative may want to preserve an order originally developed by a progressive liberal. A reactionary conservative may be indistinguishable from a classical liberal or a libertarian. Both a progressive conservative and a neoconservative could without too much strain call themselves progressive liberals.

The confusion grows when differences in attitudes toward people are factored in. According to one view, all people in a given country or region are pretty much the same in their values, having similar motivations and aspirations. Of course, they may differ in their talents and in their zeal for work, but differences in their fates and fortunes are to a significant degree held to be traceable to different circumstances: their family and community backgrounds, their education, the opportunities open to them, the good or bad luck that they experience. According to the other view, people differ fundamentally, some belonging in a cultural underclass with distinctive motivations and values that go far to account for the blighted character of their lives. The second of these attitudes is reminiscent of the Salvadoran landowner who spoke contemptuously of "those peasants who have no souls."

The first of these views encourages the thought that deserving people may face difficulties and that action to help them out may have a payoff both for them and for society. The second view suggests despair: as long as those in the underclass retain their distinctive motivations and values, not much can be done to improve the quality of their lives.

Differences among ideologies also relate to classifications of another sort. Those emphasizing self-reliance obviously do not have babies, children, and the disabled in mind. And they usually do not have the elderly in mind, either, for if they did, they would prescribe for those who become elderly without having provided for their own support. With a few exceptions, the advocates of self-reliance simplify their problem by largely ignoring elements of the population to which their prescription does not apply.

In contrast, the progressives (both liberal and conservative) give major attention not only to able-bodied adults but also—in words that Hubert Humphrey admired—to those in the dawn, the twilight, and the shadows of life.

Even the above does not give a full sense of the ideological confusion that prevails, for it suggests that people take clear ideological positions. Of course, some do. But it is more common for people to vaguely mix views from the different categories that I identify above. In fact, although I have sometimes spoken as if these are categories in which persons fit, it would perhaps be better to think that I have provided a classification scheme for attitudes rather than for persons. The same person make take attitudes from different categories, making the person herself difficult to classify.

The second comment, concerning the fervor that attends the different ideologies, can be briefer. Many years ago Eric Hoffer wrote a book entitled *The True Believer*. The True Believer was a person with a fanatical faith, convinced beyond any doubt that he commanded the one and only Truth, that his cause was righteous, that history was on his side, and that his opponents were enemies of the people, not only wrong but evil, deserving to be crushed; and he was able to shut his eyes and ears to evidence and reasoning that, if taken into account, might shake his faith.

When Hoffer wrote, the communists were the True Believers, but they have obviously been disillusioned. It would be too much to say that any contemporary political movement has a faith quite comparable to that of the communists in Hoffer's time, but the libertarians, the conservatives seriously influenced by them, and the public choice scholars all come close. They are the zealots of the day, the ones who know that they are right.

Patrick Buchanan even speaks of rallying True Believers in a campaign for the presidency (Buchanan 1988, 3). Two public-choice scholars acknowledge without protest that they are regarded as "true believers in classical liberalism," and that even if they are not true believers in Rothbard's anarchocapitalist libertarianism, they would nevertheless die in the same ditch with Rothbard "fighting against the same enemies of liberty" (Rowley and Wagner 1990, 43). You do not find that kind of language or that kind of spirit in the writings of progressive liberals. Their faith, perhaps never quite as strong, has been chastened by experience.

The significance of zeal is difficult to assess, but at least in the relatively short run it is surely an advantage. Libertarians are assertive, confident that they know the answer. Progressive liberals are hesitant, perhaps defensive, wondering what would be best.

The most complex of these final comments concerns the role of facts and values in ideological differences. Values clearly play a role. Some are shared, undergirding most or all of the ideologies. I assume that few if any of those engaging in the ideological debate deliberately want some people to be unemployed or to live in poverty or to lack medical care. On the contrary, I assume that virtually all think of themselves as championing policies that will be better than competing policies in providing for the general well-being. Similarly, I assume that few if anyone is a leveler in the sense of wanting everyone to have the same income. On the contrary, I assume that virtually everyone wants people rewarded differentially, presumably in proportion to their contributions or their merit. Further, virtually everyone professes support for equality of opportunity. And almost as many agree on the general strategy for promoting these values; that is, they agree on maintaining a capitalist system based on the private ownership of property and the profit motive.

Agreement on such fundamentals is, of course, of great importance, but it also leaves important questions unanswered. I have stressed these questions already: What to do about those who cannot be expected to make it in a competitive system, most notably babies, children, and many of the handicapped; what to do about adults who through no fault of their own are unemployed or otherwise without adequate means of support; what to do about those who need medical care that they cannot afford; and what to do about those who theoretically might provide for their old age but who are unable, or fail, to do so?

You can of course say that parents should provide for babies and children, including those who are handicapped. But what do you do when parents (sometimes single parents) are unable to do it?

Some say that private charity is the answer, raising questions of both fact and value. What does experience show concerning the adequacy of private charity? And do you want to leave those in need of help dependent on those who might theoretically be charitable?

Some claim that governmental "welfare" does more harm than good, that people become ensnared in a welfare trap, weakening their incentives to be self-reliant and inviting imprudent and irresponsible behavior. This is largely a question of fact, still to be answered by research. The research that has been reported on suggests that the argument has some merit, but not much.

Libertarians in particular reinforce their recommendation of private charity and their opposition to all of the various programs of the welfare state by denouncing governmental coercion, especially the coercion involved in collecting taxes. With respect to insurance-type programs like social security, their argument is that people should be left to decide for themselves how to spend their money, and with respect to welfare programs their argument is that government has no business "stealing" money from some for the benefit of others.

But this raises several kinds of questions: (1) whether taxation should count as theft or whether it should count as dues necessary to the survival and progress of the system in which money can be earned, (2) whether those who want to terminate the programs of the welfare state can do so without destroying democracy itself, and (3) whether a system that left large numbers of people dependent on private charity could long survive.

The final comment concerns human rights. People adhering to various ideologies joined in developing most of the civil and political rights, but the progressive liberals and progressive conservatives played the leading roles. The right to equal treatment is especially identified with progressivism, particularly with socialist, social democratic, and liberal progressivism. To a much greater extent, the enumeration and recognition of economic, social, and cultural rights are the work of socialists, social democrats, and progressive liberals. Libertarians and libertarian conservatives must deny that such rights exist. The requirement of respect for them would do too much to limit the freedom of the entrepreneur.

CHAPTER 27

Dreams and Nightmares

Should government be minimal or activist?

"WHATEVER HAPPENED TO GOOD OLD KING KONG?"

GREENMAIL

MONSTER TAKEOVERS

JUNK BONDS

LEVERAGED BUYOUTS

SUPER-CONGLOMERATES

©1988 HERBLOCK

Herblock pictures a nightmarish scene in which, in the absence of government regulation, big business grows monstrous and begins destroying itself and the country.

437

So far, the concern of this book has been with what is. The focus has been on existing institutions, practices, theories, and ideologies. Analysis, reasoned analysis, has been the method. Now the focus shifts to what the future may hold.

The attempt to analyze what exists has pitfalls, for failures of understanding and downright error are always possible, but the attempt to sketch out possible futures is even more hazardous. Analysis of the present and the recent past shows change and movement in more than one direction; it shows currents and crosscurrents. Further, analysis of the present and recent past makes it clear that many kinds of problems and tensions exist that may lead to crisis or breakdown (or possibly to solutions) at almost any time. In other words, the future may come quickly or it may be long delayed. We can dream that change and movement in the direction that we like will prevail and that problems and tensions will be resolved or managed satisfactorily. But we face possible nightmares, too, for the change that comes may be dreadful, and problems and tensions may be handled disastrously.

The object here is not to predict, but to identify possibilities. The thought is that with a clearer conception of the possibilities, we may be more likely to promote the realization of those that we favor and avert those that we dread. Our dreams and nightmares must concern both domestic and international politics.

■ Domestic Possibilities

The domestic possibilities to be considered relate to role-of-government issues, to racial and ethnic problems, to honesty and corruption, and to order v. violence.

Role-of-Government Issues

Two major possibilities exist with respect to the role of government. I sketch them in extreme terms, leaving it to you to decide which is the dream and which is the nightmare.

One possibility is to minimize the role of government and put maximum stress on individual freedom, the market, self-reliance, and personal responsibility. In this context freedom is what exists in the absence of governmental restraint or coercion. Government enforces criminal law, issues currency, provides for those features of the infrastructure that cannot sensibly be left to private enterprise, and is charged with protecting the country against foreign aggression, but otherwise does little. It leaves entrepreneurs free to pursue their economic interests as they see fit, allowing freedom of contract, doing nothing, for example, to prevent the development of monopolies or to regulate practices relating to hiring and firing. It does not seek to protect consumers from potentially harmful products. It does not regulate banks or other financial institutions or seek to protect people from incompetence, fraud, or dishonesty. It does not try to protect the environment. It does nothing about education. It does not prohibit or regulate the sale or use of drugs. It does not prohibit or regulate immigration but permits free entry into the country. It does not provide help of any sort for those unable to support themselves, leaving those unavoidably dependent to get their support from relatives or private charity. It does not provide unemployment insurance. People are on their own. They are expected to be self-reliant, pursuing their own self-interest.

The dream of those who want such a minimal government is that it will work out to the general advantage. They assume that people, left to their own devices, will have no choice but to assume responsibility for their own fate; and they further assume that people know their own interests and are more zealous in pursuing them than any government. People are thus challenged and rise to the challenge, developing the attitudes and the skills necessary to survival and success. Among other things, they see that it is in their own interest to get an education, and they borrow as need be to do it. They necessarily work, partly because life depends on it, partly because they want comforts and luxuries, and partly because of the satisfaction that work brings. The work ethic is dominant. Entrepreneurs come forward to do whatever is worth doing (that is, whatever is profitable). Moreover, they are sensitive to the common good, for their success depends at least in part on the success and well-being of others; for example, they cannot sell their products unless customers are there who can buy. And the invisible hand adds assurance that the public interest is served, for enterprises that serve it flourish and those that flout it fail. Those who damage others or encroach on the rights of others are sued. Some people do badly, of course, and suffer penalties, but their example spurs others to do better. No one starves or is left in extreme distress, for private charity helps those in real need.

To others, minimal government is more likely to lead to nightmare. Under minimal government a relatively small portion of the people do extremely well, but most lead lives of deprivation. Those already advantaged accentuate their advantage. Them that has, get. They get an education, substantial portions of them getting a higher education. They become the entrepreneurs and the professional people, and in pursuing their interests they give scant consideration to the interests of others except when this is to their direct advantage. They hire with discrimination and fire as they please. They do not tolerate trade unions. They pollute and despoil the environment. They mislead and defraud consumers. Controlling government, they see to it that taxes are imposed mainly on others. Godfathers among them offer protection at a price and muscle in on legitimate enterprises in other ways. Most of those at the lower socioeconomic levels remain substantially uneducated, if not illiterate, and the few who make it through college and graduate school spend half their lives trying to pay off their debts. Those who need professional services, such as the services of a doctor or lawyer, have difficulty deciding who is qualified to provide them and have even more difficulty paying for the services rendered. The use of drugs is widespread. Society is divided between an affluent elite and a depressed mass. Private charity takes care of a few of those who are unable to support themselves, but a large proportion of them live in destitution. Crime is widespread, with the rich concentrating their homes in walled-off and guarded enclaves. Life expectancies decline. Government does not prevent anyone from getting ahead, but neither does it do anything to promote effective and fair equality of opportunity.

Now consider activist government as the alternative prescription. Activist government serves as an instrument for giving worth to the liberty that people enjoy. It respects and depends on the free market, but imposes regulations, mostly designed to protect people from harm, including the harm that might come from despoiling the environment. Through subsidies and otherwise, it promotes the enhancement of knowledge and the development of the arts. It emphasizes education, either providing it free or subsidizing it from preschool through various kinds of post-graduate work. It acts in various ways to promote and protect public health, perhaps providing health care. It administers a pension system for the elderly and for those suffering disabilities. It administers a system of unemployment insurance and provides welfare for the indigent. It regulates the sale and use of drugs, prohibiting the sale and use of dangerous drugs. It regulates immigration. It assumes a considerable measure of responsibility for the functioning of the economy, striving to prevent the development of monopolies and to maximize employment. It relies on self-interest as a major motive and insists that all support themselves if at all possible, but it fosters altruism as well. Once a decent standard of living is achieved, people get as much satisfaction from socially valuable work as from additional income, for their work permits them to develop and use their talents while they are contributing to the public good. A sense of social solidarity exists, people being concerned with each other's well-being and with the progress of the society as a whole.

The dream of those who favor activist government is that it will promote the ideal as stated by John Rawls: "those who are at the same level of talent and ability, and have the same willingness to use them, should have the same prospects of success regardless of their initial place in the social system" (Rawls 1971, 73). To the extent that government can prevent it, people are not handicapped through life by bad luck in the natural lottery, for example by birth in a poverty-stricken home. Everyone has fair equality of opportunity. All can develop and use their talents to the fullest. And those who cannot support themselves are given a minimally decent life at public expense.

As this last statement indicates, the programs of a benign government cost money, and it must tax accordingly. It becomes redistributive, taking money from some for the benefit of others. According to the activist dreamer, this is justifiable on several counts. Although people who earn a lot of money usually deserve it, they do not earn it entirely on their personal merit. They earn it in part because of the social system in which they live; and it is in their interest, as well as in the general interest, that they should support the system on which their affluence depends. Further, in many cases they earn it in part as a matter of luck, making it reasonable to transfer some of what they have to others whose luck was bad. In any event, it is undesirable to allow too great a discrepancy to develop between the social classes in a society. Even the lowliest have rights (moral claims on society) that ought to be respected. And it is dangerous even to the well-off to try to maintain a system in which large bodies of people believe that they are exploited or that life is unfair.

In contrast, those who believe in minimal government fear that activism will lead to nightmare. They hold that an activist government undermines self-reliance, undermines the work ethic. People expect to get something for nothing. Sturdy character should be the goal, not dependence on government. Further, activist government is redistributive, and redistribution is not the business of government. People have a right to the money they earn, and it is theft if government takes it away. In any case, people can always spend their own money more wisely than government can. Given their head, entrepreneurs provide jobs for everyone, whereas when restrained by regulations and deprived of rewards, they have little incentive to develop and use their talents; and then the whole society suffers. People settle into a dull routine, living below the standard of living that they could achieve in an unregulated market system, with no one inspired to do great things.

You can perhaps fill out this sketch of contrasting prescriptions and expectations and decide which to consider the dream and which the nightmare.

Racial and Ethnic Relations

By racial relations I mean relations between African Americans and others, the others being mainly white. By ethnic relations I mean relationships between Hispanics and others.

In the field of race relations, imagine opposite possibilities. One is that government pursues activist policies designed to reduce differences to insignificance, that is, to achieve a nonracial society, and the other is that, apart from requiring the equal protection of the laws, government follows a laissez-faire policy about race, allowing relationships to develop on the basis of private choices.

The achievement of a nonracial society depends on the virtual elimination of socioeconomic and cultural differences between the races. By the elimination of socioeconomic differences I mean mainly that income differentials between African Americans and whites disappear. African Americans in the various quintiles have about the same income as whites in the various quintiles. The major implication is that African Americans are represented in the various lines of work in about the same proportion as others.

By the elimination of cultural differences I mean that differences in education and in values disappear. African Americans in the various quintiles are at about the same educational level as whites. And the values (the conceptions of the desirable) that inspire behavior are distributed in about the same way. More specifically, African Americans and others are indistinguishable in terms of the various kinds of choices that they make—concerning education, work, recreation, religion, place of residence, and so on. African Americans graduate from college and go into the professions and the arts in about the same proportion as whites.

Given the elimination of socioeconomic and cultural differences, intermarriage between the races is commonplace and goes unremarked. Differences of skin color persist but are reduced in a high proportion of the population.

A decision to seek to achieve a nonracial society involves implications. Government continues to enforce the constitutional requirement concerning the equal protection of the laws and it continues to require nondiscrimination in places of public accommodation. If anything, it enforces these requirements more rigorously than in the past. But this is not enough. You do not wipe out the effects of generations of slavery and Jim Crow simply by granting the equal protection of the laws.

During the period of slavery and Jim Crow all of those involved, African Americans and whites, developed attitudes that persist in some degree in virtually everyone alive today, and many of those attitudes stand in the way of the development of a nonracial society. The attitudes in question are of numerous sorts, including those relating to respect across racial lines, self-esteem and self-confidence, the importance of education, the existence of opportunity, and appropriate ambitions. These attitudes have been changing naturally and gradually since slavery was abolished and since Jim Crow was theoretically banished, but they have not been changed enough. Moreover, not enough has been done to make up for the decades and generations when African Americans got little or no education.

Special measures are therefore necessary to improve and enhance the educational opportunities of African Americans, and additional special measures are necessary to see to it that the opportunities that African

Americans have for employment and advancement are commensurate with their merit. The preferential treatment of whites during the period of slavery and Jim Crow needs to be replaced by the preferential treatment of African Americans, justified both as redress and as essential to the achievement of the nonracial society that is posited as the goal. Thus, government mounts a program to improve the upbringing, education, and training of African Americans. Or, if a specific focus on African Americans is ruled out, it mounts a program to improve the education, training, and upbringing of all those at a given socioeconomic level or living in areas of poverty. It begins with prenatal care and carries on with health care. It provides day care for children of working parents. It administers preschools, kindergartens, and elementary and secondary schools. At all of these educational levels it seeks not only to teach the three R's and other such subjects but also to encourage self-esteem, ambition, and respect for others regardless of race, inculcating values important to success. It actively enlists the cooperation of parents in these educational efforts. It makes arrangements with institutions of higher education, both undergraduate and graduate, to give scholarships and grant loans to qualified students. It tapers these programs off as progress toward nonracialism is achieved.

The reasons for regarding the above as the dream are fairly obvious. It eliminates race as a factor influencing success in life. Whatever the problems during the transition period, it also eliminates race as a source of friction or conflict once a nonracial society is achieved. You can, however, regard the effort to achieve such a society as a nightmare rather than a dream. The relevant argument is that any effort to force the pace toward a nonracial society is likely to do more harm than good. The preferential treatment of African Americans is especially objectionable to some, mainly because it imposes costs on whites who have done no wrong and in many cases rewards African Americans who have suffered no personal discrimination. The innocent are thus penalized for the benefit of the undeserving. And no real favor is done to the undeserving if they are given benefits that they have not earned. On top of that, both some African Americans and some whites want to preserve their distinctive cultures: they do not want a nonracial society.

The second possibility considered here is that government satisfies itself with enforcing the equal protection of the laws and requiring nondiscrimination in places of public accommodation but makes no effort to provide redress for historical wrongs or to achieve a nonracial society. In other words, the second possibility is that present policies are continued, except that all kinds of preferential treatment come to an end.

If you regard this as the dream, it is presumably on the basis of the following line of thought: Much that is good is achieved by requiring the equal protection of the laws and nondiscrimination in places of public accommodation. These policies assure equality of opportunity to African Americans, which is all they are entitled to. When identifiable people discriminate against African Americans they should be penalized, but it is wrong to impose penalties or costs on whites who have done no wrong. Whites alive today should not have to redress the wrongs done by their fathers and grandfathers, and the African Americans of today cannot legitimately expect redress for discrimination suffered by their forebears. To treat today's African Americans as if they were victims is to reduce their incentive to get ahead on their own, and it is to jeopardize the respect given to other African-Americans who make it on their own. It reduces the incentive of African Americans to be self-reliant and it alienates whites, souring racial relations. The African Americans themselves will be better off if they earn what they get, and the country will, too.

The possibilities relating to the Hispanics are very different. One of the possibilities is that the Hispanics integrate into US society like other immigrants. This means that, although they retain some of their Hispanic culture, they do not develop separatist attitudes of a political sort. They do not seek status as a protected minority or any kind of political autonomy; still less do those in the Southwest seek secession so as to join Mexico. For public purposes they take up English, whatever the language of the home.

An alternate possibility is that they become a self-conscious minority determined to preserve their distinctive characteristics. Status for the Spanish language becomes their first demand: the recognition of Spanish as an official language, at least in those states in which Hispanics are a sizable minority, most notably in California, New Mexico, Texas, and Florida. Recognition means that in school districts where Spanish-speaking people are numerous, parents have the option of sending their children to schools where Spanish is the language of instruction; and government offices and agencies are prepared to deal with people in Spanish. Demands are made for a change in the electoral system—perhaps proportional representation, perhaps cumulative voting—so that the members of any self-conscious group of significant size can combine their votes to get representation.

Which is the dream and which the nightmare? For whom?

Honesty and Order

As between honesty and corruption, the dream is surely honesty. But the danger of corruption needs to be recognized. In truth, a certain amount of corruption is inevitable, regardless of the vigilance mounted against it, for selfish and self-serving motives are powerful. So as a practical matter the dream is to minimize corruption, to keep it furtive, to catch and punish enough of those who engage in it to deter as many others as possible from taking the risks. The opposite is a situation in which corruption goes on with virtual impunity. I referred in a previous chapter to kleptocracy in some of the countries of Africa, and it is now known that for many years a high proportion of the governmental officials in Italy comprised a kleptocracy. It surely counts as a nightmare if government officials dilute their concern for the public good with a concern for their own private economic advantage at public expense.

Comparable kinds of comments apply to the possibilities of order and violence. Order is surely the dream. The nightmare takes any of several forms. The worst is civil war, but this is a possibility that we will not consider for the moment. Also possible is the deliberate but sporadic use of violence for political purposes on a continuing basis; or chronic violence engaged in for nonpolitical purposes but beyond governmental control.

In speaking of the deliberate use of violence for political purposes, I do not have in mind occasional assassinations, as in the case of John F. and Robert Kennedy or as in the case of Martin Luther King, nor do I have in mind spontaneous racial riots, disturbing as such violence is. That is, I do not have in mind isolated events. The reference is rather to sustained, persistent, calculated violence. The lynchings associated with Jim Crow are the closest illustration in US history; and if we go abroad, the leftist terrorism and dirty wars in a number of the states of Central and South America in the 1970s and 1980s provide an illustration. So does the violence that has plagued Northern Ireland in recent decades.

In speaking of chronic violence engaged in for nonpolitical purposes but beyond governmental control, the best I can do is to cite the shootings that are an aspect of relationships between urban gangs, perhaps drug-related, including the accidental shooting of bystanders and the creation of such fear in law-abiding people that their patterns of life are affected. The generalization is that the first duty of government is to see to the physical safety of the people, and a government that fails in this duty is in jeopardy. It practically invites a coup by someone, presumably a military leader, who promises to restore order.

Since I am assuming here that order is the dream and violence the nightmare, the only question is how to ward off the nightmare. The answer at the front line lies in government. Government officials must not engage in illegal violence themselves or tolerate it on the part of any other official. They must do nothing to encourage violence—as Senator Helms did when he said that President Clinton would need a bodyguard if he came to North Carolina. They must not turn a blind eye to private violence, as so many did in connection with lynchings, or allow those who engage in private violence to go uncaught and unpunished. Rather, they must be relentless and vigorous in tracking down and prosecuting any private parties who resort to violence for whatever reason.

I say above that the answer at the front line lies in government. Behind the front line lie the media and the whole educational system. Freedom of speech includes freedom to speak of murder, but it also includes freedom to respond with a chorus of condemnation. And among the values to be inculcated through the media and through the educational system are those that support order and condemn violence. This of course leads to difficult questions, most notably concerning the tendency to television to make violence seem acceptable as a normal part of life.

■ International Politics

In discussing domestic politics I have assumed that peace will prevail, for the reference is mainly to the United States and other stable countries; and, assuming peace, I have left some doubt about what to count as the dream and what to count as the nightmare.

In the international field, it is reasonable to assume that for the indefinite future peace will prevail among the advanced countries of Europe and North America. But uncertainties still exist about developments relating to Russia and what was Yugoslavia; and for much of the world stable international peace is the dream, with war as the nightmare. And if nightmare comes to any part of the world, the whole world is bound to be affected.

A considerable portion of this book deals with the problem of war and peace, so all that needs to be done now is to offer a few reminders. The peace that seems secure among the more advanced countries rests on a set of attitudes. Although the governments involved would surely fight if need be in self-defense, they all take the view that nothing justifies aggression. The deliberate initiation of war is unthinkable. Issues must be handled by methods short of war. Nothing that could be gained by war is worth the probable cost.

Although the commitment to peace is strong enough to stand on its own, it gains strength because a number of the advanced countries possess nuclear weapons. The odds are that in the interest of avoiding mutual suicide these weapons would not be used even if war broke out, but the possibility that they might be used strengthens the view that, at least for nuclear powers, war is no longer acceptable as an instrument of policy.

Similar attitudes exist among some countries that lack nuclear weapons, but obviously they are not universal. Events around Bosnia testify to this, and in a number of other parts of the world conditions prevail of the same sort that have caused war through history. Prominent among these conditions are ethnic and national rivalries and animosities, for which no quick cure exists.

If attitudes do not assure peace, law and government are the next best bets; and government must be able to change the law. The problem is that nothing exists that can properly be called world government, and substitute means for changing the law are relatively undeveloped. States have wide latitude to enact law (conclude treaties) that they regard as binding on themselves, and treaties or rules accepted by enough states are said to comprise international legislation, but the principle also exists that the rights of a state cannot be changed without its consent.

The United Nations is, of course, the principal international organization charged with the problem of peace, but compared to governments within stable, advanced countries, it is weak. It is weak because governments want it to be weak. They do not want to subject themselves to a powerful international body. They refuse to give the United Nations legislative, police, and taxing powers comparable to the powers they possess themselves.

Whether you should think of a strong United Nations as a dream or a nightmare depends on the ranking that you choose to give to various values. You should consider it a dream if you make world peace the paramount value. But you might want to consider it a nightmare if you attach more importance to preserving national freedom of action than to the preservation or enforcement of peace.

It may be that the problem of developing anything like government at the world level is simply insoluble. National loyalties, cultural and other differences, historical antipathies, and vested interests of various sorts may all be too strong. If true, this means that the world will muddle along much as it has in the past, with the possibility of war always somewhere in the background as the nightmare.

Nuclear war is the ultimate nightmare. I have already described this possibility as remote among the stable, advanced countries, and it may be remote everywhere. But can rationality always be counted on when passions run high, as they have at times; for example, in relations between India and Pakistan? And what if a Saddam Hussein or any rogue government got control of nuclear weapons?

Violence short of war (low-intensity conflict) should also be mentioned as a possible nightmare. A government is unlikely to use such violence openly, at least against a decisively stronger opponent, for to do so would be to invite war. But the possibilities are suggested by the fact that the United States already designates a few foreign governments as guilty of supporting international terrorism. And the possibilities are suggested by the bombing of the World Trade Center in New York in 1993—a bombing arranged by private persons (Muslims) to protest US support for Israel. Israel has confronted low-intensity conflict for many years. If fanatical international terrorists were to get control of nuclear bombs, a real nightmare would be upon us.

In *The Transformation of War*, Martin van Creveld gives credence to this kind of possibility. "Over the long run," he says, "the place of the state will be taken by war-making organizations of a different type. . . . In the future, war will not be waged by armies but by groups whom we today call terrorists, guerrillas, bandits, and robbers, but who will undoubtedly hit on more formal titles to describe themselves. Their organizations are likely to be constructed on charismatic lines rather than institutional ones, and to be motivated less by 'professionalism' than by fanatical, ideologically-based loyalties" (1991, 192, 197).

Samuel P. Huntington cites another possible nightmare in naming seven or eight civilizations and saying that "the fault lines between [them] are replacing the political and ideological boundaries of the Cold War as the flash points for crisis and bloodshed." These fault lines will be "the battle lines of the future." The seven or eight civilizations are "Western, Confucian, Japanese, Islamic, Hindu, Slavic-Orthodox, Latin American and possibly African" (Huntington 1993, 22, 25, 29). Even in Europe, Huntington thinks, "the Velvet Curtain of culture has replaced the Iron Curtain of ideology as the most significant dividing line" (p. 31). He dwells particularly on relationships between Islam and surrounding civilizations, including Western civilization, pointing out that Islamic fundamentalists uniformly supported Iraq in the recent war; and he quotes an Indian Muslim as predicting that the next confrontation that the West will have to face "is definitely going to come from the Muslim world" (p. 32). Surely a confrontation in which each side thinks that its civilization and perhaps its religion is at stake is among the nightmares, and all the more serious if each side controls nuclear weapons.

I note above that worldwide prosperity is a dream and destitution a nightmare. History shows, of course, that the affluent can live side by side with the destitute, but nevertheless there are limits. Within countries, some of the destitute turn to crime and perhaps to riot and rebellion. Among countries they tend to flee, as in the case of the Cubans and Haitians who try to get to Florida by boat and as in the case of Mexicans who slip across the border. A number of the mass international flights have been from war and massacre, but some have been from starvation. And the refugees pose a problem.

The problem may well be exacerbated in the future by explosive growths in population. The earth now provides for about 5.7 billion people. The projection is that it will need to provide for 8.5 billion by 2025 and for 10 billion by 2050. Something like 95 percent of the increase will be in the poor countries, those least able to provide the education, health care, and jobs that are essential to a satisfactory life. Europeans and North Americans, who made up 22 percent of the world's population in 1950, will make up less than 10 percent by 2025. Surely such changes are portentous, but exactly what they portend is difficult to say. The likelihood is that disparities of wealth and poverty will increase over the world. The poorest countries may be helpless in their poverty like the poorest countries in the world now, but more and more people may seek to escape from poverty by fleeing to the more prosperous countries. And governments of some of the poor countries may be more and more demanding. They haven't much to lose. Theoretically, the reduction in trade barriers called for by the General Agreement on Tariffs and Trade should help, but it is scarcely to be expected that it will help enough. Supplementary measures may need to be taken to help build up the economies of countries from which people might otherwise flee.

The dream, of course, is that economic and cultural development will occur all over the world, assuring peace and progress.

GLOSSARY

Accountable. Subject to giving account. A government is accountable to the people if it holds elections in which opposition parties and their candidates are free to compete.

Anti-Semitism. Hostility to Jews simply because they are Jews, manifested in discrimination, persecution, or even genocide.

Apartheid. Policies of racial separateness and discrimination once pursued in South Africa.

Arbitration. The process of settling a dispute through the judgment of an appointed third party, usually a tribunal. Parties must accept the judgment as binding.

Authoritarian. Describes a political regime that is not accountable to the people.

Balance of power. An equilibrium in the power of different sovereign states or a disequilibirum (as in a bank balance); or any distribution of power.

Bicameral. A legislative body is bicameral if it consists of two chambers or houses.

Bill of attainder. A legislative act convicting a specific person of a crime. Considered a denial of due process and generally prohibited.

Bourgeoisie. The capitalist class—owners and managers.

Cartel. A combination in restraint of trade, usually at the international level. An organization designed to maintain monopoly control over some aspect of the world market.

Catallaxy. Hayek's substitute for the term *market economy*. He prefers the substitute because it does not imply that economic transactions are to serve some agreed-upon social end.

Caveat emptor. Let the buyer beware. The view that the buyer should get no help from government in dealing with those who have something to sell.

Collective security. An international arrangement in which participating states provide for each other's security by collective action.

Communal constituency or system. A communal constituency is set apart by race, language, religion, nationality, or culture rather than by territorial boundary lines. A communal system gives representation to communal rather than to territorial constituencies.

Communism. Communist. Communism is a political ideology based on the writings of Marx and Lenin. It emphasizes class conflict and calls for the overthrow of capitalism, the liquidation of the capitalist class (the bourgeoisie), and the establishment of a centrally planned economic system. Democracy is replaced by a dictatorship of the proletariat, which the communists also call "true democracy."

Comparative advantage. The greater relative advantage that a country has in producing one kind of item rather than another. The doctrine of comparative advantage is that each country should produce and export what it can produce most advantageously and import the rest.

Constituency. A body of people grouped together for purposes of elections and representation. The body of people to whom a representative is accountable. More generally, a body of supporters.

Coup d'état. A relatively bloodless seizure of power, usually by military leaders.

Democracy. A political system calling for government that is responsive and accountable to the people.

Dependency theory. Concerns economic relationships between the developed and the less developed countries, the claim being that the relationships are biased against the latter.

Dictatorship. A form of government in which one person or a small clique has absolute power.

Discrimination. Unreasonable or arbitrary differentiation. Differentiation for an illegitimate purpose or based on criteria that are irrelevant to a legitimate purpose. "Active" when specifically directed by one person against another. "Passive" when unchallenged, giving no reason for action. See *equal treatment*.

Distributive justice. The justice of the distribution (allocation) of wealth and income. Does everyone get his or her due?

Dumping. Selling products abroad at prices below those charged at home.

Egalitarianism. A doctrine emphasizing the idea of human equality. Equality of opportunity. Equal (nondiscriminatory) treatment. A closer approach to equality of condition, calling for a narrowing of the income gap between the rich and the poor.

Elite. A minority with special qualities or status giving them leadership or making them models.

Eminent domain. The right of the state to take private property for public use in return for just compensation.

Empirical. Knowledge, or the method of acquiring it, is said to be empirical when it rests on observation as opposed to purely mental processes.

Entrepreneur. A person who launches or operates a business enterprise, taking risks in hope of profit.

Equal-population principle. The principle that electoral districts sending the same number of representatives to a legislative body should be equal in population. Designed to assure that votes in elections have equal weight.

Equal treatment. Treatment of the same kind of cases in the same kind of way. Does not require that different kinds of cases be treated in the same way, but classification and differentiation must be reasonable.

Ex post facto law. A law with retroactive effect, making an act a crime that was not a crime when committed.

Fascism. A right-wing political ideology especially associated with Mussolini's dictatorship in Italy.

Federal. A political system with subdivisions (such as the states of the United States) that have powers that the central government cannot take away.

First-strike capacity. The capacity in nuclear war to knock the other side out with one blow, precluding significant retaliation.

Freedom (or liberty). What exists in the absence of some kind of socially created restriction or constraint, or in the absence of certain kinds of coercion. What exists in the presence of a positive capacity to pursue selected ends.

Genocide. The killing of members of an ethnic group not because of anything they have individually done but simply because they are members of that group. Aimed at the destruction of the ethnic group as such.

Gerrymander. The drawing of the boundary lines of an electoral district in a seemingly capricious way to maximize the political strength of one party or racial group and to minimize the strength of another.

Human rights. Rights that belong to all persons by virtue of the fact that they are human. See *rights*

Imperialism. A process by which empires, or unequal political relationships between peoples, are established, maintained, and perhaps extended. An empire is a political structure in which a dominant people rule over subordinate political entities, usually overseas. Communists describe imperialism simply as the highest stage of capitalism. Also defined as a policy aimed at a reversal of the order of power, or as any relationship between a powerful and a weak state.

Interest. A stake in rules, practices, or conditions relating to a value. A group of people who have such a stake. As distinguished from a right, an interest does not necessarily imply any corresponding obligation on the part of any other person or agency.

Intervention. Dictatorial interference by one state in the affairs of another.

Judicial review. The authority of the courts to refuse to give effect to legislative or executive acts on the ground that they are unconstitutional.

Laissez-faire. A governmental hands-off policy in economic matters. A policy that respects the freedom of individuals in economic matters, allowing them to do more or less as they please. The policy assumes the private ownership of property and the profit motive.

Legitimacy, legitimate. A government is said to be legitimate to the degree that it is worthy of support or to the degree that the people consider it worthy of support.

Liberal, liberalism. Liberals stress the liberty or freedom of the individual. Classical liberals saw the state as the principal threat to freedom and thus favored minimizing the functions of the state. "New" or "progressive" liberals see the state as an instrument for enhancing the worth of liberty by protecting the individual against restraints stemming from private persons or impersonal circumstances. See *freedom, libertarian.*

Libertarian. A person who wants to reduce coercion to a minimum, especially the coercion associated with government, and thus to minimize the role of government in directing or restricting behavior.

Liberty. See *freedom.*

Malapportionment. The assignment of seats in a multimember body disproportionately to the population of the electoral districts involved.

Market socialism. Social ownership of the means of production coupled with decentralized control. Self-management emphasized, with little central planning. Price competition among collectively owned enterprises, with profit as the goal.

Mediation. A process in which a third party seeks to help in the handling or settlement of a dispute by providing a channel for communication.

Mercantilism. A governmental policy of extensively regulating foreign and domestic trade and commerce.

Monetarism. The view that government can maintain a stable and growing economy and a desired price level simply by regulating the supply of money. Spending to maintain demand is unnecessary. The view is associated with supply-side economics.

Monopoly. A market situation in which one party has sufficient control over a product or service to dictate the price at which it becomes available. Competition is absent or inconsequential.

National interest. See *interest.*

Nationalism. The belief that all members of the nation should be politically united, usually within one nation-state, and all members of the nation should be loyal primarily to it. Alternatively, nationalism may be the ideology of a subordinate people seeking freedom from imperial control.

National Socialism, Nazism. A right-wing political ideology especially associated with Hitler's Germany, 1933-45.

New Right. Consists of reactionary conservatives who put special emphasis on certain issues of a moral or religious sort, like abortion and prayer in the schools.

Norm, normative. A norm is a standard of ethical behavior, a principle of right conduct, a basis for judging good and bad. The normative concerns norms.

Oligarchy. Government by the few.

Oligopoly. A market situation in which a limited number of parties share control over a product or service. By explicit or tacit collusion they can dictate the price at which it becomes available.

Parliament. A legislative body analogous to the U.S. Congress. In a parliamentary system, the prime minister and his or her cabinet are members of parliament, enjoying majority support at least in the lower house.

People, peoples. Refers variously to the whole population of a political entity or to a population group comprising a nation or distinguished by language, religion, or culture.

Perquisites. Privileges or benefits, other than salary, attached to an office or status.

Plural society. Made up of distinct national, racial, ethnic, or tribal communities that cherish and want to preserve their distinct identities.

Political party. An association performing a number of functions. Its essential feature is that it provides a label under which candidates seek election to governmental office.

Politics. "The activity (negotiation, arguments, discussion, application of force, persuasion, etc.) by which an issue is agitated or settled" (Meyerson and Banfield 1955, 304-305).

President. Title of the head of a republic. A president, as distinct from a prime minister, is separately elected and is not a member of congress or parliament. A presidential system, in contrast to a parliamentary system, provides for the separation of powers.

Pressure group. A nonparty association that seeks to influence the action of a governmental agency.

Primary. An election within a political party in which members, or at least voters, select the party's candidates for office.

Privatization. The partial or complete transfer of ownership and control over a state enterprise to private hands.

Proletariat. The working class.

Proportional representation (PR). The representation of political parties in legislative bodies in proportion to their electoral strength. The percentage of seats allocated to a party should coincide with the percentage of votes it won.

Racism. A view attributing superiority to one race and inferiority to another.

Recall. A special election on the question of ousting a person from a governmental office.

Redistributive. Governmental measures are redistributive to the degree to which they take from some for the benefit of others.

Referendum. A special election permitting the voters to adopt or reject a proposal, usually proposed legislation.

Right. A right is a justified claim. An entitlement. A moral right is justified by a moral rule and a legal right by a legal rule. A right implies a corresponding obligation, for example, on the part of the government.

Sanctions. Measures imposing costs or penalties on a party (perhaps a state) for violating a legal or moral rule. Designed to induce observance of the rule.

Second-strike capacity. The capacity in nuclear war to absorb the worst blows an enemy can inflict and still have enough nuclear power left to inflict unacceptable damage in retaliation.

Security, national. What exists in the absence of significant military threat to political independence, territorial integrity, or other national values. Or what exists in the presence of a capacity to counteract such a threat comfortably.

Sedition. Refers vaguely to any kind of expression that has a tendency to undermine loyalty to the government or constitutional system, stirring up opposition, contempt, or disaffection.

Self-determination. The right of a people to determine for itself what its relationship to other peoples should be.

Social Darwinist. A person believing that human affairs should proceed on the basis of unrestrained struggle and the survival of the fittest. Government should play a minimal role in protecting people or promoting their welfare.

Socialism, socialist. Socialism has historically been the name for an economic system in which the means of production and distribution are for the most part socially owned and where production occurs for use and not for profit. Emphasis on equality and fraternity. Noncommunist socialists generally uphold democracy.

Social security. In the United States the term has come to refer to the federal program of old-age pensions. More broadly, the term refers to governmental programs to financially assist people in meeting a variety of needs—for example, those connected with unemployment, dependent children, health and childbirth, old age, and disability.

Sovereign, sovereignty. A state is sovereign when it is independent of the control of any other state or any international organization. It is subject to international law but supreme over its own domestic law.

Stagflation. A combination of economic stagnation and inflation.

Subsidiarity. The principle that policy decisions should be made, and administrative authority lodged, at the lowest practicable level.

Suffrage. The right to vote.

Supply-sider. The opposite of a Keynesian demand-sider. The supply-sider thinks the emphasis in economic matters ought to be on incentives to produce and thus on the entrepreneur, with taxes reduced.

Territorial constituency. A constituency delimited by geographical boundary lines. Contrasts with a communal constituency.

Terrorism. "The use or threat of violence . . . in order to intimidate or to create generalized, pervasive fear for the purpose of achieving political goals." Though specific victims may be selected, terrorism may also kill indiscriminately.

Totalitarian. A totalitarian state is one in which the government either destroys or establishes its control over all significant social, economic, and political organizations.

Unicameral. A legislative body is unicameral if it consists of only one chamber or house.

Unitary. A political system is unitary when subdivisions have no powers of their own. They exercise only those powers delegated to them by the central government.

Utilitarian. A philosophic point of view associated with Jeremy Bentham, holding that a society's goal should be the greatest happiness (or the greatest good) of the greatest number.

Value. A conception of the desirable.

Welfare state. A state that seeks to promote welfare by relatively direct means, regulating behavior and providing benefits in a major way.

REFERENCES

Aleksandrov, Georgi (1948) *The Pattern of Soviet Democracy.* Washington, D.C.: Public Affairs Press.

Allswang, John M. (1978) *The New Deal and American Politics: A Study in Political Change.* New York: John Wiley.

Almond, Gabriel A., and Sidney Verba (1963) *The Civic Culture. Political Attitudes and Democracy in Five Nations.* Princeton: Princeton University Press.

Andreski, Stanislav (1968) *The African Predicament: A Study in the Pathology of Modernisation.* New York: Atherton Press.

Atwood, Thomas C. (1990) "Through a Glass Darkly. Is the Christian Right Overconfident It Knows God's Will?" *Policy Review,* No. 54 (Fall): 44–52

Barnes, Fred (1990) "Bush's Big Government Conservatives," *American Spectator* 23 (April): 14–15.

Barry, Norman P. (1979) *Hayek's Social and Economic Philosophy.* London: Macmillan.

———— (1987) *The New Right.* New York: Croom Helm.

Beer, Samuel H. (1965) "Liberalism and the National Idea," in Robert A. Goldwin, ed., *Left, Right, and Center: Essays on Liberalism and Conservatism in the United States.* Chicago: Rand McNally.

———— (1973) "The Modernization of American Federalism," *Publius, The Journal of Federalism* 3 (Fall): 49–95.

————(1978) "In Search of a New Public Philosophy," in Anthony King, ed., *The New American Political System.* Washington, D.C.: American Enterprise Institute.

———— (1982) *Modern British Politics: Parties and Pressure Groups in the Collectivist Age.* New York: Norton.

Bennett, William J. (1994a) "America's Cultural Decline Must Be Reversed," *Human Events,* 50 (January 14): 12–14.

———— (1994b) "Revolt Against God. America's Spiritual Despair," *Policy Review,* No. 67 (Winter): 19–24.

Birch, Anthony H. (1993) *The British System of Government.* 9th ed. London: Allen & Unwin.

Bosanquet, Nick (1983) *Economics: After the New Right.* Boston: Kluwer-Nijhoff.

Buchanan, James M. (1975) *The Limits of Liberty: Between Anarchy and Leviathan.* Chicago: University of Chicago Press.

_____ (1986) *Liberty, Market and State: Political Economy in the 1980s*. New York: New York University Press.

Buchanan, Patrick J. (1988) *Right from the Beginning*. Boston: Little, Brown.

Butler, Stuart (1989) "Razing the Liberal Plantation," *National Review* 41 (November 10): 27–30.

Butler, Stuart, and Anna Kondratas (1987) *Out of the Poverty Trap. A Conservative Strategy for Welfare Reform*. New York: Free Press.

Califano, Joseph A. (1981) *Governing America: An Insider's Report from the White House and Cabinet*. New York: Simon & Schuster.

Caro, Robert A. (1982) *The Years of Lyndon Johnson: The Path to Power*. New York: Knopf.

Chandler, Lester Vernon (1970) *America's Greatest Depression*. New York: Harper & Row.

Chi, Hsi-Sheng (1991) *Politics of Disillusionment. The Chinese Communist Party Under Deng Xiaoping 1978–1989*. Armonk, N.Y.: M. E. Sharpe.

Conquest, Robert (1990) *The Great Terror. A Reassessment*. New York: Oxford University Press.

Cross, Colin (1963) *The Liberals in Power (1905–1914)*. London: Pall Mall.

Dahl, Robert A. (1971) *Polyarchy: Participation and Opposition*. New Haven: Yale University Press.

_____ (1975) "Governments and Oppositions," in Greenstein and Polsby, 1975.

_____ (1989) *Democracy and Its Critics*. New Haven, Conn.: Yale University Press.

Ding, X. L. (1994) *The Decline of Communism in China. Legitimacy Crisis, 1977–89*. New York: Cambridge University Press.

Drier, Peter, and John Atlas (1990) "Deductio Ad Absurdum," *Washington Monthly* 22 (February).

Dye, Thomas R., and Harmon Zeigler (1988) "Socialism and Equality in Cross-National Perspective," *P.S.* 21 (Winter): 45–56.

Eban, Abba (1983) *The New Diplomacy: International Affairs in the Modern Age*. New York: Knopf.

Eckstein, Harry (1968) "Parties, Political Party Systems," *International Encyclopedia of the Social Sciences*, Vol. 11, pp. 436–53.

Eldersveld, Samuel J. (1982) *Political Parties in American Society*. New York: Basic Books.

Ellwood, David T. (1988) *Poor Support: Poverty in the American Family*. New York: Basic Books.

Emerson, Rupert (1960) *From Empire to Nation*. Cambridge: Harvard University Press.

Enayat, Hamid (1982) *Modern Islamic Political Thought*. Austin: University of Texas Press.

Epstein, Leon D. (1975) "Political Parties," in Fred I. Greenstein and Nelson W. Polsby, eds., *The Handbook of Political Science*. Vol. 4, *Nongovernmental Politics*. Reading, Mass.: Addison-Wesley.

Fairbank, John King (1992) *China, A New History.* Cambridge: Belknap Press of Harvard University Press.

Freeden, Michael (1986) *Liberalism Divided: A Study in British Political Thought 1914–1939.* Oxford: Clarendon.

Friedman, Milton (1962, 1982) *Capitalism and Freedom.* Chicago: University of Chicago Press.

Friedman, Milton, and Rose Friedman (1980) *Free to Choose: A Personal Statement.* New York: Harcourt Brace Jovanovich.

Frum, David (1994) "It's Big Government, Stupid!" *Commentary* 97 (June), 27–31.

Fukuyama, Francis (1992) *The End of History and the Last Man.* New York: Free Press.

Galston, William A. (1988) "Liberal Virtues," *American Political Science Review* 82 (December): 1277–89.

Gilder, George (1981) *Wealth and Poverty.* New York: Bantam.

———— (1984) *The Spirit of Enterprise.* New York: Simon & Schuster.

Ginsberg, Morris (1965) *On Justice in Society.* Ithaca, N.Y.: Cornell University Press.

Goldman, Alan H. (1979) *Justice and Reverse Discrimination.* Princeton: Princeton University Press.

Goldman, Merle (1994) *Sowing the Seeds of Democracy in China: Political Reform in the Deng Xiaoping Era.* Cambridge: Harvard University Press.

Goldwater, Barry (1990) *The Conscience of a Conservative.* Washington, D.C.: Regnery Gateway.

Gottfried, Paul, and Thomas Fleming (1988) *The Conservative Movement.* Boston: Twayne.

Green Book. U. S. Congress. House. Committee on Ways and Means. *Overview of Entitlement Programs.* 1994 Green Book. 103d Cong., 2d Sess.

Greenleaf, W. H. (1983) *The British Political Tradition.* Vol. 1, *The Rise of Collectivism.* Vol. 2, *The Ideological Heritage.* New York: Routledge.

Greenstein, Fred I., and Nelson W. Polsby, eds. (1975) *The Handbook of Political Science.* Vol. 3, *Macropolitical Theory.* Reading, Mass.: Addison-Wesley.

Grubel, Herbert G. (1981) *International Economics.* Homewood, Ill.: Irwin.

Haq, Mahbub Ul (1976) *The Poverty Curtain: Choices for the Third World.* New York: Columbia University Press.

Hayek, Friedrich A. (1960) *The Constitution of Liberty.* Chicago: University of Chicago Press.

————(1978) *New Studies in Philosophy, Politics, Economics, and the History of Ideas.* Chicago: University of Chicago Press.

Hitler, Adolf (1939) *Mein Kampf.* New York: Reynal & Hitchcock.

Hoffer, Eric (1963) *The True Believer: Thoughts on the Nature of Mass Movements.* New York: Time.

Hofstadter, Richard (1948) *The American Political Tradition. And the Men Who Made It.* New York: Knopf.

Huntington, Samuel P. (1968) *Political Order in Changing Societies.* New Haven: Yale University Press.

_____(1991) *The Third Wave. Democratization in the Late Twentieth Century*. Norman: University of Oklahoma Press.

_____ (1993) "The Clash of Civilizations?" *Foreign Affairs*, 72 (Summer): 22–49.

India, Office of the Registrar General—Language Division (1971). *Language Handbook on Mother Tongues in Census*. Census Centenary Monograph No. 10. Census of India 1971.

Johnson, Thomas H., Robert O. Slater, and Pat McGowan (1984) "Explaining African Military Coups d'Etat," *American Political Science Review* 78 (September): 622–40.

Judis, John B. (1990) "The Conservative Crackup," *American Prospect* (Fall): 30–42.

Kaplan, Morton A., ed. (1978) *The Many Faces of Communism*. New York: Free Press.

Kelman, Steven (1987) *Making Public Policy: A Hopeful View of American Government*. New York: Basic Books.

Kemp, Jack (1990) "Tackling Poverty: Market-Based Policies to Empower the Poor," *Policy Review* 51 (Winter): 2–5.

Kirk, Russell (1953) *The Conservative Mind: From Burke to Santayana*. Chicago: Regnery.

Kristol, Irving (1978) *Two Cheers for Capitalism*. New York: Basic Books.

_____ (1983) *Reflections of a Neoconservative: Looking Back, Looking Ahead*. New York: Basic Books.

_____ (1992a) "The Cultural Revolution and the Capitalist Future," *American Enterprise*, 3 (March/April): 42–51.

_____ (1992b) "America's Mysterious Malaise," *The Times Literary Supplement*, No. 4651 (May 22): 5.

_____ (1993) "The Coming 'Conservative Century,' " *Wall Street Journal*, (February 1): A10.

Kuper, Leo (1981) *Genocide: Its Political Use in the Twentieth Century*. New Haven: Yale University Press.

Kuttner, Robert (1990) "Bleeding Heart Conservative," *New Republic* 202 (June 11): 22–25.

LaHaye, Tim (1980) *The Battle for the Mind*. Old Tappan, N.J.: Fleming H.Revell.

Laqueur, Walter (1989) *The Long Road to Freedom: Russia and Glasnost*. New York: Scribner's.

Leng, Shao-chuan, ed. (1994) *Reform and Development in Deng's China*. Lanham, Md.: University Press of America.

Lenin, V. I. (1932) *Collected Works*. Vol. 21, Bk. 2. New York: International Publishers.

_____ (1935) *Selected Works*. Vol. 10. New York: International Publishers.

Levi, Werner (1981) *The Coming End of War*. Beverly Hills, Calif.: Sage.

Levy, Jack S. (1983) *War in the Modern Great Power System, 1495–1975*. Lexington: University Press of Kentucky.

Lijphart, Arend (1984) *Democracies: Patterns of Majoritarian and Consensus Government in Twenty-One Countries*. New Haven: Yale University Press.

Lijphart, Arend, and Bernard Grofman, eds. (1984) *Choosing an Electoral System: Issues and Alternatives*. New York: Praeger.

Linz, Juan J. (1975) "Totalitarian and Authoritarian Regimes," in Greenstein and Polsby, 1975.

Lipset, Seymour Martin (1963) *The First New Nation: The United States in Historical and Comparative Perspective*. New York: Basic Books.

Locke, John ([1690] 1956) *A Second Treatise of Government (An Essay Concerning the True Original Extent and End of Civil Government)*. Oxford: Basil Blackwell.

Ludwikowski, Rett R. (1986) *The Crisis of Communism: Its Meaning, Origins, and Phases*. Washington, D.C.: Pergamon-Brassey's.

Lupsha, Peter (1971) "Explanation of Political Violence: Some Psychological Theories Versus Indignation," *Politics and Society* 2 (Fall): 89–104.

Mandel, Ernest (1989) *Beyond Perestroika: The Future of Gorbachev's USSR*. New York: Verso.

Matusow, Allen J. (1984) *The Unraveling of America: A History of Liberalism in the 1960s*. New York: Harper & Row.

Meyerson, Adam (1989). "Adam Smith's Welfare State: Generous Government Is Consistent with a Market Economy," *Policy Review*, No. 50 (Fall): 66–67.

Meyerson, Martin, and Edward C. Banfield (1955) *Politics, Planning, and the Public Interest*. Glencoe, Ill.: Free Press.

Mill, John Stuart ([1859] 1956) *On Liberty*. Indianapolis: Bobbs-Merrill.

——— (1965) *Collected Works*. Vol. 3, *Principles of Political Economy*. Toronto: University of Toronto Press.

Miller, David (1976) *Social Justice*. Oxford: Oxford University Press.

Moon, J. Donald, ed. (1988) *Responsibility, Rights, and Welfare: The Theory and Practice of the Welfare State*. Boulder: Westview Press.

Moulton, William P. (1990) "Naught's Had, All's Spent. Conservatism in Its Latter Days," *Liberty* 3 (May): 17–26.

Mussolini, Benito (1935) "The Political and Social Doctrine of Fascism," *International Conciliation* 306 (January).

Myers, William Starr, ed. (1934) *The State Papers and Other Public Writings of Herbert Hoover*. Garden City, N.Y.: Doubleday.

Neuhaus, Richard John, and Michael Cromartie, eds. (1987) *Piety and Politics. Evangelicals and Fundamentalists Confront the World*. Washington, D.C.: Ethics and Public Policy Center.

Nisbet, Robert (1986) *Conservatism: Dream and Reality*. Minneapolis: University of Minnesota Press.

Nordlinger, Eric A. (1968) "Political Development: Time Sequences and Rates of Change," *World Politics* 20 (April): 494–520.

Norton, David L. (1991) *Democracy and Moral Development*. Berkeley: University of California Press.

Nove, Alec (1980) *The Soviet Economic System*. London: Allen & Unwin.

Nozick, Robert (1974) *Anarchy, State, and Utopia*. New York: Basic Books.

OECD (1992) *Revenue Statistics of OECD Member Countries, 1965–1991.*
Olson, Mancur (1982) *The Rise and Decline of Nations. Economic Growth, Stagflation, and Social Rigidities.* New Haven: Yale University Press.
O'Neill, Thomas, with Robert Novak (1987) *Man of the House: The Life and Memoirs of Speaker Tip O'Neill.* New York: Random House.
Overholt, William H. (1993) *The Rise of China. How Economic Reform Is Creating a New Superpower.* New York: Norton.

Parkes, James (1964) *Antisemitism.* Chicago: Quadrangle.
Patterson, James T. (1969) *The New Deal and the States: Federalism in Transition.* Princeton, N.J.: Princeton University Press.
———— (1986) *America's Struggle against Poverty 1900–1985.* Cambridge: Harvard University Press.
Plamenatz, J. P. (1938) *Consent, Freedom, and Political Obligation.* London: Oxford University Press.
Podhoretz, Norman (1989) "New Vistas for Neoconservatives," *Conservative Digest* 56 (January/February) 2: 56.
Powell, G. Bingham (1982) *Contemporary Democracies. Participation, Stability, and Violence.* Cambridge: Harvard University Press.
Public Papers and Addresses (1938–50). Franklin D. Roosevelt. Compiled by Samuel I. Rosenman. New York: Random House.
Public Papers of the Presidents of the United States. Lyndon B. Johnson. Washington, D.C.: Government Printing Office, 1965–70.

Rawls, John (1971) *A Theory of Justice.* Cambridge, Mass.: Belknap Press of Harvard University Press.
Riker, William H. (1964) *Federalism: Origin, Operation, Significance.* Boston: Little, Brown.
Ritchie, David G. (1916) *Natural Rights: A Criticism of Some Political and Ethical Conceptions.* London: Allen & Unwin.
Rocco, Alfredo (1935) "The Political Doctrine of Fascism," in Spahr, 1935.
Romasco, Albert U. (1983) *The Politics of Recovery.* New York: Oxford University Press.
Rondinelli, Dennis A., John R. Nellis, and G. Shabbir Cheema (1983) *Decentralization in Developing Countries: A Review of Recent Experience.* World Bank Staff. Working Papers, No. 581. Washington, D.C.: World Bank.
Rose, Richard (1989) *Politics in England.* 5th ed. Boston: Little, Brown.
Rosenberg, Nathan (1979) "Adam Smith and Laissez-Faire Revisited," in Gerald P. O'Driscoll, Jr., ed., *Adam Smith and Modern Political Economy.* Ames: Iowa State University Press.
Rothbard, Murray (1978) *For a New Liberty: The Libertarian Manifesto.* New York: Libertarian Review Foundation, 1985 reprint.
Rotunda, Ronald D. (1968) "The 'Liberal' Label: Roosevelt's Capture of the Symbol," *Public Policy* 17:377–408.
Rowley, Charles K, ed. (1987) *Democracy and Public Choice: Essays in Honor of Gordon Tullock.* New York: Basil Blackwell.
Rowley, Charles K., and Richard E. Wagner (1990) "Choosing Freedom: Public Choice and the Libertarian Idea," *Liberty* 3 (January): 43–45.

Rustow, Dankwart A. (1967) *A World of Nations: Problems of Political Modernization.* Washington, D.C.: Brookings.

Sabato, Larry J. (1989) *Paying for Elections: The Campaign Finance Thicket.* New York: Priority Press.

Salvatore, Dominick. (1993) *International Economics.* 4th ed. New York: Macmillan.

———— ed. (1993) *Protectionism and World Welfare.* New York: Cambridge University Press.

Salvetz, Carol R. and Anthony Jones, eds. (1994) *In Search of Pluralism. Soviet and Post-Soviet Politics.* Boulder: Westview.

Sartori, Giovanni (1965) *Democratic Theory.* New York: Praeger.

Schneider, Herbert W. (1928) *Making the Fascist State.* New York: Oxford University Press.

Schwartz, Nathan. H. (1984) "Reagan's Housing Policies," in Anthony Champagne and Edward J. Harpham, eds., *The Attack on the Welfare State.* Prospect Heights, Ill.: Waveland Press.

Schwarz, John E. (1980) "Exploring a New Role in Policy Making: The British House of Commons in the 1970s," *American Political Science Review* 74 (March): 23–37.

Seligson, Mitchell A. (1984) *The Gap Between Rich and Poor: Contending Perspectives on the Political Economy of Development.* Boulder: Westview Press.

Shmelev, Nikolai, and Vladimir Popov (1989) *The Turning Point: Revitalizing the Soviet Economy.* New York: Doubleday.

Smiley, Donald V. (1972) *Canada in Question: Federalism in the Seventies.* Toronto: McGraw-Hill Ryerson.

Smith, Adam ([1776] 1976) *An Inquiry into the Nature and Causes of the Wealth of Nations.* Oxford: Clarendon.

Snow, Peter G. (1979) *Political Forces in Argentina.* New York: Praeger.

Sorauf, Frank J. (1988) *Money in American Elections.* Glenview, Ill: Scott, Foresman.

Spahr, Margaret, ed. (1935) *Readings in Recent Political Philosophy.* New York: Macmillan.

Spencer, Herbert (1898) *The Principles of Ethics.* New York: Appleton.

Statistical Abstract of the United States (1990) Washington, D.C . U.S.: Treasury-Department, Bureau of Statistics.

Stern, Philip M. (1988) *The Best Congress Money Can Buy.* New York: Pantheon.

Stohl, Michael, and George A. Lopez, eds. (1984) *The State as Terrorist: The Dynamics of Governmental Violence and Repression.* Westport, Conn.: Greenwood.

Surrey, Stanley S., and Paul R. McDaniel (1985) *Tax Expenditures.* Cambridge: Harvard University Press.

Thurow, Lester C. (1983) *Dangerous Currents: The State of Economics.* New York: Random House.

Tullock, Gordon (1970) *Private Wants, Public Means.* New York: Basic Books.

———— (1988) *Wealth, Poverty, and Politics.* New York: Basil Blackwell.

van Creveld, Martin (1991) *The Transformation of War*. New York: Free Press.

Van Dyke, Vernon (1964) *Pride and Power. The Rationale of the Space Program*. Urbana: University of Illinois Press.

———— (1990) *Equality and Public Policy*. Chicago: Nelson-Hall.

Viner, Jacob (1928) "Adam Smith and Laissez Faire," in John Maurice Clark et al., eds., *Adam Smith, 1776–1926*. Chicago: University of Chicago Press.

Walzer, Michael (1977) *Just and Unjust Wars: A Moral Argument with Historical Illustrations*. New York: Basic Books.

Watt, James G. (1985) *The Courage of a Conservative*. New York: Simon & Schuster.

Whitaker, Robert W., ed. (1982) *The New Right Papers*. New York: St. Martin's.

White, Stephen (1993) *After Gorbachev*. New York: Cambridge University Press.

Wildavsky, Aaron (1991) *The Rise of Radical Egalitarianism*. Washington, D.C.: The American University Press.

Wilson, James Q. (1992) "The Moral Sense," *American Political Science Review*, 87 (March), 1–11

■ Cases

Abrams v. *U.S.* 1919. 250 U.S. 616.

Brown v. *Board of Education of Topeka, Kansas*. 1954. 347 U.S. 483.

Plessy v. *Ferguson*. 1896. 163 U.S. 537.

INDEX